SCOTTISH CASE
PARTNERSHIPS AND COMPANIES

SCOTTISH CASES
ON
PARTNERSHIPS
AND
COMPANIES
(EXCLUDING WINDING UP
AND RECONSTRUCTION)

BY

ENID A. MARSHALL
M.A., LL.B., PH.D., Solicitor,

Reader in Business Law
at the University of Stirling

EDINBURGH

W. GREEN & SON LTD.

ST. GILES STREET

1980

First published in 1980

©
1980. Enid A. Marshall

ISBN 0 414 00658 5

PRINTED IN GREAT BRITAIN BY
THE EASTERN PRESS LTD.
LONDON AND READING

PREFACE

THIS collection of Scottish cases has developed out of a type-script collection with the same title produced for the use of students on a business law course at the University of Stirling. The increasing emphasis now being placed in Scotland on the law of business organisations, and in particular of registered companies, as a subject in its own right suggests that the time is ripe for this collection to be offered to a wider readership—to business studies students as a study-tool and substitute for consultation of law reports themselves, and to law students as an *aide-mémoire* and incentive to consult such original sources when and where they can.

The exclusion from Part II of winding up and reconstruction (on which topics there is no dearth of Scottish cases) was decided on in order to keep the publication within acceptable limits of size and price, and to enable a selection of partnership cases to be included as part of the same volume. In view of the obvious affinity between partnerships and companies on the business scene and of the tendency for topics naturally falling at the end of a company law course to be scantily " covered " by lecturers and to feature in no great detail in examination papers, the usefulness of including the material on partnerships seemed to outweigh the deficiency resulting from the exclusion of winding up and reconstruction.

The Notes attached to the cases which comprise the main entries are not intended primarily for comparative purposes: there are several English casebooks in which comparable English cases may be readily traced without access to the law reports. Although several of the leading English cases necessarily receive incidental attention, the Notes have been mainly devoted to shorter treatment of additional Scottish cases and to the giving of a brief indication, where this was called for, of the present source and substance of the statutory provision in question.

A glossary of Latin words and phrases used in the book is supplied in the Appendix.

I am grateful to Julian S. Danskin, lecturer in business law at the University of Stirling, for giving generously of his time to assist with the correction of proofs.

ENID A. MARSHALL

November 1979

TABLE OF CONTENTS

vii

PART II: COMPANIES

(EXCLUDING WINDING UP AND RECONSTRUCTION)

CHAPTER 2—COMPANIES—INTRODUCTORY

CHAPTER 3—MEMORANDUM OF ASSOCIATION

CHAPTER 9: MEMBERSHIP—*continued*

CHAPTER 10—CONTRACTS

CHAPTER 11—SHARE CAPITAL

TABLE OF CASES

(Page numbers in bold type indicate a main entry)

PAGE

PART I

PARTNERSHIPS

CHAPTER 1

PARTNERSHIPS

Constitution of partnership: agreement that parties not to be considered partners

Stewart v. Buchanan

(1903) 6 F. 15

B. let his premises Nos. 16 and 20 Springfield Court, Queen Street, Glasgow, with their fittings, fixtures and furniture to Saunders who was about to carry on business there under the name of the City Stock Rooms Company. B. also advanced sums of money to Saunders for the purposes of the business.

A memorandum of agreement between B. and Saunders provided that B. was not to be or be held to be a partner in the business or liable for its debts or obligations.

Stewart, a wine merchant who had supplied goods to the City Stock Rooms Company, brought an action for the price of the goods against the firm, and Saunders and B. as partners of the firm.

Held that B. was a partner in the business, and liable for its debts.

LORD TRAYNER (at p. 21): "It is enough for the decision of the case in the pursuer's favour if we hold that Buchanan was interested in this business as a partner, and of this I have no doubt.... If any question arises between Saunders and Buchanan as to their relative rights and liabilities under the agreement, it may be that Saunders may be able to shew that as between them he is not a partner or liable as such. But, meantime, it is enough to hold that Buchanan is a partner, and on that ground to give the pursuers decree."

LORD MONCREIFF (at p. 22): "I do not think that anyone can read the documents which formed the contract between the defenders without seeing that the true trader, with the largest interest in the concern, was Buchanan, and not Saunders. In other words, that, truly construed, the documents disclose a contract of partnership between Buchanan and Saunders....

"... A person who is truly a partner will not escape responsibility, however emphatically he may declare in the contract that he is not a partner and is not to be considered a partner.

"In each case the whole circumstances must be considered."

1

Constitution of partnership: part ownership

Sharpe v. Carswell
1910 S.C. 391

S. owned 10 sixty-fourth shares of the schooner *Dolphin,* which carried cargoes between Dalbeattie and Liverpool. S. performed the duties of master, and received a fixed remuneration for his services as master.

S. died in Liverpool as the result of injuries sustained by him on board the *Dolphin* while he was acting in the course of his employment as master.

S.'s widow claimed compensation under the Workmen's Compensation Act 1906 from C., the managing owner of the *Dolphin.*

Held that S. had been a "workman" employed by C., and not a partner or joint adventurer in the trading of the vessel.

LORD ARDWALL (at p. 393): "It appears that the late Mr. Sharpe was master and part owner to the extent of 10 sixty-fourth shares of a small vessel called the *Dolphin.* So far as I can see, these two characters have nothing to do with each other. He was a part owner, and held and could dispose of his shares independently of his co-owners. But besides being the owner of ten shares, he was employed by the appellant to act as master of the vessel.... I cannot doubt that he was a ' workman ' within the meaning of the Act....

" ... In attempting to argue that there was a partnership or joint adventure in this matter, the appellant is forced to rely solely on the fact that Mr. Sharpe was an owner of shares in the ship along with the appellant and Captain Tait. Now, it is quite settled that the fact of persons being co-owners of shares in a ship does not make them partners. They have little power as regards each other, and the majority cannot pledge the credit of the minority against their will, and if they disagree as to the management of the vessel, any of them may bring an action of sett and sale for disposal of their shares or of the whole vessel—in short, joint owners are not partners, but are separate individuals holding definite shares in a common subject, and where there are several of them, the subject in which they are all interested is in the ordinary case managed by a manager or managing owner, who within certain limits is empowered to act for them in the management of the ship, but this does not render them either partners or joint adventurers."

Constitution of partnership: sharing of gross returns

Clark v. G. R. & W. Jamieson
1909 S.C. 132

C. was employed to work a small boat in Shetland. His remuneration took the form of a share of the gross earnings of the boat.

C. was drowned by an accident arising out of and in the course of his employment, and his mother and sister, who were both wholly dependent on his earnings, claimed compensation under the Workmen's Compensation Act 1906 from the firm which had employed him.

Held that C. had been a " workman " employed by the firm, and not a partner in a joint adventure.

LORD MCLAREN (at p. 138): " Each of these two men, Robertson and Clark, was to receive a share of the gross earnings of the boat—not a share of the profits, for that would have implied deductions for expenses of management, repairs, stores, and perhaps bad debts. . . . Now, the Partnership Act 1890, which to a large extent is an embodiment of principles of the common law familiar to lawyers, says, sec. 2: — ' In determining whether a partnership does or does not exist, regard shall be had to the following rules: —(2) The sharing of gross returns does not of itself create a partnership, whether the persons sharing such returns have or have not a joint or common right or interest in any property from which or from the use of which the returns are derived.' The provision is different in the case of sharing profits. . . . We have nothing to do with sharing of profits; and as regards sharing of gross returns, with which we have to do, this under the statute is not even *prima facie* evidence of the existence of a partnership. I think the framers of the Act were well advised in so providing, because it is known that managers of departments of houses of business are often remunerated by a share of the gross returns of their departments. As sharing in the gross returns of the boat does not constitute a partnership between the persons who share the gross returns, I think this is not a case of joint adventure.

" The result is, what is sufficiently obvious even to one who is not a lawyer, that this is just a contract of service. That being so, the Workmen's Compensation Act applies."

NOTE

Lord McLaren defines " joint adventure " as follows (at p. 138): " Joint adventure is just a partnership limited to a particular season or a particular enterprise, in which there is either no power in the partners to bind one another, or such power is limited to the particular adventure."

Separate persona *of firm*

Forsyth v. Hare and Co.
(1834) 13 S. 42

F., an upholsterer in Aberdeen, alleged that he had given an order for certain goods to a traveller of John Hare and Co., floor-cloth manufacturers in Bristol, and that that firm had accepted the order but failed to implement it.

F., using arrestments to found jurisdiction, brought an action against the firm by its social name without specifying the individual partners.

Held that the action was competent.

LORDS PRESIDENT (HOPE), BALGRAY, GILLIES, COREHOUSE, FULLERTON, and MONCREIFF (at p. 43): " As a mercantile company is understood in the law of Scotland to be a separate person, capable of maintaining the relations of debtor and creditor, distinct from those held by the individual partners, and as the firm or company name forms the designation of that separate person, and of the whole individuals in their social character, under which name obligations are effectually contracted by and to the company, there does not appear to us to be any legal inconsistency or incongruity in allowing action or diligence either at the instance of, or directed against, a partnership by its firm."

LORD MEDWYN (at p. 46): " In the commercial states of Europe, the history of commerce shows, that while the traffic with the more distant quarters of the globe was carried on by regulated and joint stock companies, associations consisting of two or more individuals were formed for carrying on home trade and manufactures under a company firm. Scotland, following this example, adopted a similar plan, having both public and private associations of this kind in the seventeenth century. The first were encouraged by various acts of Parliament. . . . As to the latter, Erskine says, ' According to our present practice, the partners in private companies generally assume to themselves a firm or name proper to their own company, by which they may be distinguished in their transactions; and in all deeds, subscribed by this name of distinction, every partner is, by the nature of the copartnery, understood to be intrusted with a power from the company of binding them.'

" A copartnery for trade using a social firm, under which contracts are made with the public, is a separate person (Bell's *Principles*, 357,) from any, or the whole individuals of which it consists, and is capable of maintaining the relation of debtor and creditor separate and distinct from the obligations of the partners as individuals (*Bell on Bankruptcy*, Vol. ii. p. 619). It is a quasi corporation, possessing many, but not all the privileges which law confers upon a duly constituted corporation. A mercantile company can hold moveable property; it has even been adjudged that it can hold a lease of an heritable subject. . . . A company binds itself by subscribing a personal bond or bill by its firm, and, in like manner, a bond or bill granted in its favour, is an available document of debt. ' If a partner acquires a right in name of the company, the property is vested directly in the company ' (Ersk. iii. 3, § 20). One company may become a member or individual partner of another company (Bell, Vol. ii. p. 627) . . .

" It arises from thus viewing the company as a separate person from the individual partners, that it is incompetent to arrest a company debt for a debt of one of the copartners; that the company funds are, in the first instance, liable for company debts; . . . that a company creditor, after ranking on the company funds, may then rank on the individual estates of the partners; . . . and that the share of the company's funds due to a partner may be arrested in the hands of the company (Ersk. iii. t. 3, § 24). . . .

" By indorsing a bill granted to a company with the company firm, the property is transferred; the property of a moveable bond, or other moveables, will also be transferred by assignation subscribed by the company; . . . and the only effectual discharge of the one or the other, is in like manner by this company firm. When a company is creditor of a bankrupt, and concurs in his discharge, the discharge is subscribed by the firm (Bell, Vol. ii. p. 472).

" Finally, a company may be rendered bankrupt under the act 1696; . . . and may be sequestrated under the bankrupt act, § 20, which farther provides, that ' it shall be sufficient to cite the partnership, by leaving a copy at the home or shop where their business is or was carried on, or where any of their acting partners reside.'

" The only limitation on the rights of a private company seem to be, that they cannot hold heritable property, as they cannot maintain the character of superior or vassal; and that a penal action cannot be directed against them; . . . neither can they be pursuers of such. . . .

" When a charge is given to a company for payment of a bill on which they are obligants, if they have any defence to state against the claim, a bill of suspension is presented in their name, as being the party charged to pay. . . . If a company has thus a *persona standi* to obtain a suspension, can there be any reason why a company should not also pursue an ordinary action *socio nomine*?

" When the proceedings against a company commence by an ordinary action, it has been held that the company must be called; and it is not competent to pursue one or more of the individual partners without calling the company. . . .

" If, then, a company may and must be defenders in a claim against them; if diligence may issue in their name, at their instance, or against them; if they may suspend *socio nomine*, it would be a singular anomaly if they could not also, when they can hold property, and sustain the relation of a creditor, raise action except in the name of their individual partners. Accordingly, it does not appear that any such doubt had ever occurred till recently, when we have become more acquainted with the doctrines of the English law, which ' on this point is peculiar.' We cannot turn up a page in our reports without finding innumerable instances of companies, both pursuing and defending *socio nomine*; and, so far as I can see, without a doubt of the correctness of such a procedure, either in our courts or in the House of Lords. . . .

" When this question was first stirred, in the year 1828, I set myself to examine it carefully for my own satisfaction; and besides looking into the authorities in our own law, I examined the works of foreign jurists, and even obtained opinions from lawyers of Germany, Italy, Holland, and France. I found, as I expected, that the law relative to mercantile societies in the continental states, was the same as that which was recognised among ourselves, that although a corporation (*universitas*) had alone the privilege of suing and being sued in its corporate character, and that an ordinary private society (*societas*) had not, yet that mercantile usage had sanctioned the use of mercantile firms, that they had acquired this privilege of a corporation, and that they sue and are sued as persons by their firm, which had grown up from and was sanctioned rather by the practice of the Courts than by any express enactments. . . .

" The law of England seems to be the only law which has not allowed usage to confer this privilege upon a mercantile company. . . .

" . . . I have no difficulty in holding that an ordinary mercantile firm such as that under which the defenders trade and deal with the public, can be properly brought into Court by a summons against them, *socio nomine*."

NOTES

1. In *Gordon* v. *British and Foreign Metaline Co.* &c. (1886) 14 R. 75, the court held that a partnership could be sued for damages for judicial slander, notwithstanding that malice had to be proved against the defender.

Lord Justice-Clerk (Moncreiff) (at p. 83): " It may be quite true in one sense that the company cannot be guilty of moral wrong. It is said that a company has no *animus*. Nor has it. It has no will, it has no memory, it has no conscience. But notwithstanding all that, the supposed or imaginary *persona* which constitutes a company may contract obligations although it has no will, or memory, or conscience, and may be compelled to fulfil the obligations so undertaken. It is mere metaphysical subtlety to say that a company cannot be guilty of malice where the very nature of the proceeding in which the plea is taken necessarily implies that the *persona* has a power of action and a power of judgment. I therefore think that it is no answer to an action of damages for wrongous use of arrestments, or for judicial slander, that it is directed against a company."

2. In *Mair* v. *Wood*, 1948 S.C. 83, a partnership was held not vicariously liable to one partner for injury suffered by him at the hands of a co-partner who was acting in the course of the partnership business.

Lord President (Cooper) (at p. 86): " It is fundamental to the Scots law of partnership that the firm is a legal *persona* distinct from the individuals who compose it. This rule, which dates from the seventeenth century, has been expressly preserved by the Partnership Act, section 4 (2), and it is the source of most of our distinctive rules both of substantive law and of procedure. . . . One of the leading consequences of the doctrine of the separate *persona* is the principle that a firm may stand in the relation of debtor or creditor to any of its partners, and the rule of process that a partner cannot be sued for a company debt until that debt has first been constituted against the firm. . . . Partners are of course liable jointly and severally in a question with a firm creditor for the obligations of the firm, but the theory of Scots law views them as being so liable only *subsidiarie*, the partners being in substance guarantors or cautioners for the firm's obligations, and each being entitled on payment of a firm debt to relief *pro rata* from the others. . . .

" Both in Scotland and in England a firm has long been recognised as liable for wrongs committed by its partners in relation to the firm's business. . . . But all the examples of this rule are cases in which the party damnified by the wrong has been a third party, and I know of no formulation of the rule which would admit of a like liability where the party damnified was himself a partner of the delinquent. I regard this distinction as critical and of the essence of the rule. When in section 10 of the Partnership Act the liability of a firm for the wrongful acts or omissions of a partner was formulated, the rule was in terms limited to the case where loss or injury had been caused to any person *not being a partner of the firm*. . . . Section 10 of the Act is simply declaratory of the common law of Scotland."

Relations of partners to persons dealing with them: authority of partner to bind the firm

Bryan v. Butters Brothers & Co.
(1892) 19 R. 490

Bryan was a partner of the firm Butters Brothers & Co., contractors, engineers, and machinery merchants, Glasgow. He borrowed £100 from his wife for the firm, and she received a receipt which, on Bryan's instructions, was written by a clerk and signed by the firm's cashier "*pp.* Butters Bros. John Gibson." The money was paid to the cashier, and put to the credit of Bryan in the firm's books.

Bryan deserted his wife, and left the country. She raised an action against the firm for repayment of the loan.

Held that (1) Bryan, as a partner of a mercantile firm, had power to borrow money and bind the firm for its repayment; (2) the receipt, though neither holograph nor tested, could be used to prove the loan; and (3) the receipt, having been signed on the instructions of a partner, was a writ of the firm.

LORD TRAYNER (at p. 499): " I think it is a proposition good in law, and one which is now long past the region of controversy, that the partner of a trading or mercantile firm (and the defenders' firm was of that class) has an implied mandate to borrow money in the name and on the credit of his firm, and to bind his firm as obligants therefor by granting an acknowledgment or voucher in his firm's name for the money so borrowed. This being so, the defenders' liability for the sum sued for (undoubtedly borrowed from the pursuer by her husband for his firm) cannot be disputed, if the alleged loan is established *habili modo*. Such a loan can only be proved, according to our law, by the writ or oath of the borrower.

" Accordingly the real question—indeed the only question—in the case is, whether the document produced by the pursuer is the writ of the defenders proving the loan. On this question the defenders maintain first, that the document produced by the pursuer cannot be looked at as their writ, or receive any effect, because it is not probative or holograph. . . .

" Whatever the law may have required in regard to deeds constituting obligation or title, it does not require the same, as matter of solemnity, in documents used only *in modum probationis*. . . .

" The defenders maintain, in the second place, that the writ . . . is not their writ, but the writ of their cashier, Gibson, who had no authority to borrow money for the firm. . . .

" . . . Nobody suggests that Gibson borrowed the £100 now sued for. It was borrowed by Mr. Bryan, one of the partners of the firm. . . . I take it for granted that Mr. Bryan, having power to borrow money on the credit of his firm, had also the power to grant an acknowledgment in the firm's name that he had done so, and if he had adhibited the firm's signature to the document in question, it would have been the writ of the firm. But it seems to me to be quite as much the writ of the firm although signed by the cashier for the firm, because the cashier so signed it on the authority and by the direct instructions of one of the partners, who himself had power to grant such a writ. In signing that document Mr. Gibson says,—' I was always acting under his,' *i.e.*, Mr. Bryan's, ' instructions in connection with the firm, and did exactly what I was told.' Mr. Gibson therefore signed the document in question on the direct authority of that partner, who could have validly signed it himself, and the signature of an authorised agent is equal to the signature of the principal, and binding on him. . . . I come therefore to the conclusion that the writ produced is the writ of the defenders, and that it establishes the loan to them of the sum sued for.

" The plain justice of the case points also to the pursuer being entitled to decree. Her £100 was not retained by her husband. It was actually delivered by him to the cashier of the firm, and went into the firm's bank account, and should now be accounted for by them. That their cashier subsequently allowed one of the partners to deal with that money as his own, by putting it to his private account, and afterwards withdrawing it, is a matter with which the pursuer has no concern. The pursuer can scarcely be called on to suffer for what she could in no way control."

NOTES

1. *Cf. Ciceri* v. *Hunter & Co.* (1904) 12 S.L.T. 293 (O.H.): Saunders and Hunter had entered into a copartnery to carry on a business of hotelkeepers in Edinburgh under the name of " H. & Co.," Hunter having the sole control of the business and Saunders not being bound to give personal attention, though he had the right to be consulted on all matters of importance.

Hunter instructed C. to make a revaluation of the furnishings for the purposes of the firm's balance-sheet. Before C.'s fee had been paid, Hunter and H. & Co. became bankrupt.

Held that C. was entitled to recover his fee from Saunders, the solvent partner, because in instructing the revaluation Hunter had acted within the scope of his mandate as managing partner and so the firm, and not merely Hunter, was bound.

2. In *Nisbet* v. *Neil's Trustee* (1869) 7 M. 1097, a letter written and signed by one partner in the firm name was held to be holograph of the firm.

Lord President (Inglis) (at p. 1100): " It was argued . . . that the letter acknowledging the debt is not entitled to the privileges of a holograph document, because it bears to be a letter of the firm of J. and J. Neil, and not of the individual partners, and it was contended that no writing by one of the partners in the firm name could be holograph of the firm. That argument struck me both as new and as unsound. . . . On principle . . . I have no doubt that this letter is entitled to the privileges of a holograph writing. I think it is a mere subtlety to say that it is not holograph of the firm. It is holograph of the writer, who was one of the partners, and that is enough, for he was entitled to bind the firm."

Relations of partners to persons dealing with them: agreed restrictions on partner's authority

Paterson Brothers v. Gladstone
(1891) 18 R. 403

The firm of Paterson Brothers, builders and joiners in Edinburgh, had three partners, Robert, William, and John. The contract of copartnery provided that William alone should take full charge of the financial transactions of the firm.

Robert signed the firm's name on certain promissory notes in favour of G., a moneylender, discounted them with G. at the rate of 40 per cent., and fraudulently applied the proceeds to his own use.

Held that the firm was not liable to pay the promissory notes to G. since G. had discounted them in suspicious circumstances without inquiry.

LORD PRESIDENT (INGLIS) (at p. 406): "Robert Paterson, one of the partners of the firm, was expressly excluded from signing the firm's name for pecuniary obligations, and accordingly when he signed the name of the firm to these bills he committed a fraud upon his partners, because he did not use the proceeds for the purposes of their trade, but for his own private purposes. Mr. Gladstone's position is that he met Robert Paterson in the ordinary course of business, and without any inquiry as to Paterson's position, or the authority he had to append the firm's name to the bills, he advanced money upon them, retaining discount at the rate of 40 per cent. per annum. The circumstances were such as to create a suspicion against the conduct of Robert Paterson. . . . He must have had suspicions aroused that things were not all right when a firm of builders in good repute required to borrow at 40 per cent. He must have known that the strain would be such as very shortly to bring any ordinary business to an end, and that it was not a likely thing that a firm in good repute would find it necessary to resort to him for such a purpose. It was quite in Mr. Gladstone's power to ascertain whether Robert Paterson was dealing fairly by him and with his copartners, and whether his action was authorised by the firm. But he abstains from inquiry of any kind, and is satisfied to take his 40 per cent and incur all risks.

". . . Paterson Brothers were perfectly faultless in the circumstances, and I do not see by what precautions they could have saved themselves. When their position is contrasted with that of Mr. Gladstone, the case seems a very clear one. He had the means of finding out the true nature of the transaction, and if he had moved even his finger, no harm would have been done. Accordingly, upon him alone the loss must fall, because if one of two innocent parties is not in fault, and the other is grossly negligent, the latter must suffer as being the party who made the fraud possible."

Relations of partners to persons dealing with them: liability of the firm for wrongs

Kirkintilloch Equitable Co-operative Society Ltd. v. Livingstone
1972 S.C. 111

Jackson, a partner in a firm of chartered accountants, had for several years prior to 1967 acted as the official auditor of a registered industrial and provident society. The annual audit fee was paid to the firm, and Jackson was assisted in his audit by the employees of the firm.

The firm was dissolved in 1967, and the society, alleging that as a result of Jackson's negligence certain accounting errors had remained undetected between 1963 and 1966 and had involved the society in loss, brought an action of damages against all the partners of the former firm.

Jackson's former copartners contended that, as directed against them, the action was irrelevant since the firm could not lawfully have been an official auditor of the society and that Jackson had therefore been acting as an individual and not within the ordinary course of the firm's business in carrying out the audit.

Held that the auditing of the society's accounts was within the ordinary business of the firm and that there was no reason why the official auditor could not have had the authority of his copartners to act as such; and the plea to relevancy *repelled*.

LORD PRESIDENT (CLYDE) (at p. 117) "The main question in the reclaiming motion is whether relevant averments have been made against the reclaimers which, if proved, did make them liable jointly and severally along with the third defender in respect of the negligence connected with the preparation and auditing of the society's accounts. Under section 10 of the Partnership Act 1890 it is provided, *inter alia*, that 'where, by any wrongful act or omission of any partner acting in the ordinary course of the business of the firm, or with the authority of his co-partners, loss or injury is caused to any person not being a partner in the firm, ... the firm is liable therefor to the same extent as the partner so acting or omitting to act.' The reclaimers maintained before us that this section did not involve them in any liability, since the third defender in preparing and auditing the society's accounts was not acting in the ordinary course of the business of the firm but in his special capacity as an official auditor under the Industrial and Provident Societies Acts. In other words, he was acting as an individual and not as a partner of his firm.

"But the pursuers deny this in fact. They make a twofold case, based on both the branches of section 10 of the 1890 Act. In the first place they found on the words 'in the ordinary course of the business of the firm,' and in the second place they found on the words in the section 'with the authority of his co-partners.' If either of these two branches is established, that would enable them to invoke section 10 of the Act. So far as the first ground is concerned, there is, in my view, no special mystique in preparing the accounts or auditing the accounts of a co-operative society and the criterion in this part of section 10 of the Partnership Act is whether the preparation or auditing of the accounts was one of the kinds of activities which were in contemplation of the partners when they combined together in partnership. In my view it clearly was. There is nothing whatever in the case to justify us in assuming that the third defender was not acting in the ordinary course of the business of his firm, which was the preparation and auditing of accounts. On the contrary, he clearly was so doing. But . . . even if for any reason it could be argued that the third defender was not acting in the ordinary course of the business of the firm, the pursuers expressly found on the alternative branch of section 10 of the Act, when they aver that with the knowledge, consent and authority of the reclaimers he was auditing the accounts in question. The pursuers reinforce this averment by the assertion that in preparing and completing the accounts the staff of the partnership were employed and the remuneration for this work was paid not to the third defender as an individual but to the partnership itself. These averments appear to me clearly to support the general averment already referred to and consequently to warrant an inference of joint and several liability on the partners in respect of the matters in issue in this case."

NOTES

1. In *Thomson & Co.* v. *Pattison, Elder, & Co.* (1895) 22 R. 432, the court held that it was incompetent to sue a firm for damages on the ground of fraud, unless the names of the partners alleged to have committed the fraud were specified, since fraud was necessarily personal to an individual.

Lord Kinnear (at p. 437): " In many cases it is convenient, and not inaccurate, to ascribe to a firm the actions of commission or omission of one of the partners acting within the scope of his authority, but . . . actions based on fraud fall within a different category. Fraud is always personal, and though a firm may be responsible for the individual fraud of one of its partners acting within the scope of his authority, it is incompetent to charge the firm generally with the fraud. Here we do not know how many partners there are in the firm sued, and it would be contrary to justice and procedure to allow a charge of fraud against an indefinite number of persons, without specification of any particular person who had committed the fraud, to go to trial. If the pursuers have a good case they must know who the individual member of the firm of Pattison, Elder, & Company was who committed the fraud in combination with the commercial traveller, and if they cannot make a statement to that effect it is out of the question to allow the case to go to trial."

2. It is no objection to an action against a firm for a wrong that malice must be proved: *Gordon* v. *British and Foreign Metaline Co. &c.* (1886) 14 R. 75 (Note 1 to *Forsyth* v. *Hare and Co.*, p. 7, above).

3. If the person wronged by a partner acting in the course of the firm's business is himself a partner in the firm, he cannot hold the firm liable: *Mair* v. *Wood*, 1948 S.C. 83 (Note 2 to *Forsyth* v. *Hare and Co.*, p. 7, above).

Relations of partners to persons dealing with them: liability of incoming partner for existing debts of the firm

Heddle's Executrix v. Marwick & Hourston's Trustee
(1888) 15 R. 698

In 1878, Mrs. Marwick, the owner of an ironmongery and general merchant's business in Kirkwall, took into partnership with her Hourston, who had been its manager for more than a year previously. There was no written contract of copartnery, and Hourston contributed no capital. The new firm, under the name of Marwick & Hourston, continued the old business and took over its stock-in-trade.

In 1886 the estates of the firm and of its individual partners were sequestrated.

Heddle's executrix lodged two claims in the firm's sequestration, one being for advances of £214 made to the firm between 1878 and 1886 and the other being for advances of over £5,000 made to Mrs. Marwick before 1878. The trustee in the sequestration admitted the claim for £214 only.

Held that Heddle's executrix was entitled to rank also for the other advances.

LORD ADAM (at p. 706): " I do not suppose that anyone will contend that when a new firm is constituted by a person becoming a partner in an existing business, whether carried on by an individual or a firm, the new firm becomes liable for the debt of the old business. Neither do I think that the mere fact of the new firm taking over the whole assets of the old business will *per se* render the new firm liable for the debts of the old business. I think in all cases it is a question of circumstances, and that it must be established by presumption, or by proof of facts and circumstances, that the new firm agreed to adopt the old debts and to become liable for them. . . .

" . . . I think . . . that there are facts and circumstances proved which clearly shew that the new firm took over the whole liabilities of the old business. . . .

" ... On the whole matter I am of opinion that Mrs. Heddle is entitled to rank for the amount of the debt now ascertained to have been due by Mrs. Marwick at the date of the partnership on the ground that the new firm assumed, adopted, and dealt with the debt as a debt of the firm."

LORD SHAND (at p. 709): "It must always be a question of circumstances whether a new firm becomes responsible for the obligations of the old. On the one hand, if an old-established firm, consisting of one or two partners, arranges to take in a clerk and give him a future share of the profits, or if one of the partners has a son who has just come of age and is taken into the business, and they arrange to give him a share of the profits of the new firm thereby constituted, it appears to me that, if the new firm takes over the stock in trade and the book debts and whole business of the old firm and the goodwill of that business, equity requires that they shall take over its obligations .... It appears to me that ... where you have practically a new copartnery, with the transfer of the whole assets of the business and goodwill of the old firm, the creditors must continue to have their hold upon these assets in the new firm. To hold otherwise would be to open a door to fraud. The assumption of a new partner it may be to-day, of another six months afterwards, and of a third six months after that, thereby cutting off the rights of creditors to share in the assets of each separate firm, would produce not only confusion but great injustice to the creditors. On the other hand, if a partner comes into a business, paying in a large sum of capital, and the other partners merely put in their shares of a going business as their shares of the capital, a different question might arise. In such a case as that, probably some special circumstance would require to be proved in order to impose liability on the new partner for transactions entered into prior to the date when he became a partner. Then, again, intermediate cases will occur between these two classes. In all of them it must be a question of circumstances, to be determined by the Court upon the facts, whether there has been liability undertaken, or adoption of the debt of the old firm. In this case ... Mr. Hourston is clearly liable for the debt due to Mr. Heddle's executrix."

NOTES

1. Lord Adam referred to two earlier cases in particular. The first of these was *McKeand* v. *Laird* (1860) 23 D. 846, which was decided by a majority of seven judges:

For several years prior to 1850, L. carried on a draper's business on his own account in Paisley. By January 1850 L. owed £4,981 to McK. In April 1850 L. entered into a contract of copartnery with two of his shopmen, Thomson and Smith. The capital of the firm consisted of £600, contributed by L. alone. The contract of co-partnery did not provide for the taking over of L.'s liabilities. The firm was sequestrated in 1857.

Held that McK. was entitled to rank in the sequestration for the debt incurred to him by L., since that debt had been dealt with as a debt due by the firm.

Lord Justice-Clerk (Inglis) (at p. 851): " I should be very slow indeed to affirm the proposition that any individual trader, by taking in his two shopmen as partners, and giving them a small interest in his business, and executing with them a latent contract of copartnery, can, by the terms of that latent contract, affect the interests of his own prior creditors. That would be a most dangerous doctrine, and, therefore, in the absence of any evidence to show the knowledge of the appellants of the contents of this written con-tract of copartnery, I think it cannot affect them. . . .

" . . . Was it ever heard before, that when a transaction was entered into, the beginning, and end, and whole meaning and dis-tinctive character of which amounted to this, that the two shopmen were to have each one-eighth share in the business as part of their remuneration for their services, that that constitutes a new company to the effect of handing over to the new firm the whole stock of the individual trader, and depriving the prior trade creditors of that individual trader of all recourse against his stock and property? Did any man ever hear of such a result flowing from such a transaction? The doctrine is perfectly new to my mind, and it is the most startling thing I have heard."

2. The second case referred to was *Miller v. Thorburn* (1861) 23 D. 359:

Samuel Dickson commenced business as a jeweller in Dumfries in 1844. To enable him to pay for his stock-in-trade and to carry on the business, he procured a cash credit from a bank. This was guaranteed by a cautioner, T.

In 1858, Samuel Dickson, having fallen into bad health, took his son, John Dickson, into partnership. Samuel provided the whole capital.

Samuel died in 1859, and the firm was sequestrated.

T., having paid to the bank the £225 due on the cash account, claimed to be ranked for that amount on the firm's estate.

Held that T. was entitled to be so ranked, because the firm had taken over the father's trade liabilities along with his assets.

Lord Cowan (at p. 362): " In the general case where the whole estate of a company is given over to and taken possession of by a new concern or partnership, the business being continued on the same footing, the estate goes to the new company *suo onere*—that is, the liabilities go along with the effects. To sustain any other principle might result in the greatest injustice. This is the general presumption, although there may be special circumstances in particular cases not admitting of its application. In this case there are no such specialties. Of course private debts are not in the same position as trade debts. But we assume this to be a trade debt. It is distinctly admitted to be so. It is admitted to have been contracted for the purposes of the business by Samuel Dickson, and formed his outstanding bank account when he assumed his son into partnership.

"I would also remark that the son brought no capital into this concern. The stock consisted only of what had been the stock of his father's business. In these circumstances, and with a debt of that character, I have no difficulty."

3. Contrast *Thomson & Balfour* v. *Boag & Son*, 1934 S.C. 2:

Boag carried on a business as joiner in Bathgate, and while doing so was supplied with timber by Thomson & Balfour.

In 1933 Boag entered into an agreement for partnership with Bruce, who had been his foreman. The firm name was Thomas Boag & Son as before. Bruce contributed capital of £340, and the agreement provided that Boag should realise the debts due to him and also pay the debts due by him in connection with his own business, freeing and relieving Bruce of all liability for them. In the books and accounts no distinction was made between work done by Boag and work done by the new firm.

Held that since Bruce had made a substantial contribution to capital, the presumption was that the firm had not assumed the liabilities of Boag's business, and that Thomson & Balfour were therefore not entitled to hold the firm or Bruce liable for a debt incurred before 1933.

Referring to the three cases mentioned above, Lord President Normand said (at p. 10): "The principle is that it would be inequitable to allow a trader to injure his trade creditors by assuming a partner and handing over his whole trading assets to the new partnership without liability to pay the trade debts. But this presumption must not be extended beyond the circumstances to which it properly applies. In *Heddle's Executrix* Lord Shand pointed out (at p. 710) that, if a partner comes into a business, paying in a large sum of capital, and the other partners merely put in their shares of a going business as their share of the capital, special circumstances might have to be proved in order to impose liability on the new partner for transactions entered into before he became a partner. If, again, the new partnership is carried on on the basis that there shall be no liability for the prior debts and no right to collect sums due to the individual partners or the old partnership in respect of prior transactions, the presumption is, I think, displaced."

Relations of partners to persons dealing with them: liability by " holding out "

Hosie v. Waddell
(1886) 3 S.L.R. 16

H., when suing W. for a debt, was met by the defence that W. had paid the debt to Cameron, whom he believed to be H.'s partner.

H. maintained that Cameron had never been his partner, but was only the manager of his business.

Held that, in the circumstances of the case, Cameron had been held out by H. as a partner, that W. had made payment of the debt to Cameron in the *bona fide* belief that Cameron was a partner, and that therefore payment to Cameron had been good payment.

LORD ARDMILLAN (delivering the judgment of the court) (at p. 17): " The defender had previously transacted with Cameron as the representative of the company. It can, therefore, hardly be doubted that the defender was entitled to deal with Cameron as a partner. It was once intended that he should be one, and there was no intimation of any change that could possibly have reached the defender."

Relations of partners to one another: partnership property

Munro v. Stein
1961 S.C. 362 (O.H.)

S., the owner of a dance hall known as " Stein's Dancing Academy," Musselburgh, was in need of immediate cash, and arranged with M., a builder, that M. would pay him £100 and go into the dance-hall business in equal partnership with him. The dance hall was to form part of the assets of the partnership.

Before a formal deed of copartnery had been executed, S. died, and his heir-at-law claimed the dance hall, contending that the dance hall could not have become the property of a partnership without a probative deed of conveyance and that it was incompetent to prove transfer of heritable property to a partnership by parole evidence.

Held that it was competent to prove that the dance hall was the property of the partnership by parole evidence; and that, on the evidence, the dance hall had been proved to be partnership property.

LORD WHEATLEY (Ordinary) (at p. 368): " I regard the submission by defender's counsel as ill-founded. In my opinion, in deciding the constitution of the partnership and what it comprehended, it is competent to prove by parole evidence what each party was bringing into the partnership estate. A different situation might have arisen if the situation had been that the deceased was alleged to have brought the heritable property into the partnership agreement after the partnership had been constituted. . . . The pursuer is entitled . . . to prove *prout de iure* that the deceased brought the property into the assets of the firm when it was formed, and, on that basis, I find both on the oral evidence of the witnesses and the contents of the receipt . . . that this has been established. I find, accordingly, that the pursuer has proved by requisite evidence facts and circumstances which entitle him to the declarator sought."

NOTE

The declarator referred to was that the dance hall formed part of the assets of the partnership as at the date of S.'s death.

Relations of partners to one another: partnership at will

Neilson v. Mossend Iron Co. &c.
(1886) 13 R.(H.L.) 50

A contract of copartnery for a period of seven years contained a clause stipulating that any partner was to have the option of being bought out by his copartners on condition that he gave notice of his desire to exercise that option " three months before the termination of this contract."

After the seven years had expired, the partnership was continued as before without any new agreement.

Held that the clause did not apply to the partnership at will, since in such a partnership there was no date of termination from which the three months could be calculated.

LORD WATSON (at p. 54): " When the members of a mercantile firm continue to trade as partners after the expiry of their original contract, without making any new agreement, that contract is held in law to be prolonged or renewed, by tacit consent, or, as it is termed in the law of Scotland, by ' tacit relocation.' The rule obtains in the case of many contracts besides that of partnership; and its legal effect is that all the stipulations and conditions of the original contract remain in force, in so far as these are not inconsistent with any implied term of the renewed contract. The main distinction between the old contract and the new in the present case consists in this, that the latter is a contract determinable at will. It is an implied term of such a contract that each partner has the right instantly to dissolve the partnership whenever he thinks proper. . . .

" . . . The condition and the rights and obligations arising out of it are totally inapplicable to a contract-at-will. They have plain reference to a fixed *punctum temporis,* the termination of the original contract; but how are they to be applied to a contract which has no definite currency? Time is of the essence of the condition, but a contract-at-will affords no terminus from which it can be measured or computed."

NOTES

1. The House of Lords reversed the judgment of the Court of Session.

2. Contrast *McGown* v. *Henderson,* 1914 S.C. 839:

Henderson, McGown and Cameron were partners in a wine and spirit merchants' business. The contract of copartnery provided that the partnership was to last for five years from 1905, and that, if it were not renewed at the expiry of the five years, the licence was to be valued and Henderson was to have the option of paying out to the two other partners the amount due to them or of having the licence sold and its price divided among the three partners.

The partnership was continued from 1910 to 1913 as a partnership at will. Henderson then dissolved the partnership by notice and claimed the right of pre-emption under the clause in the original contract of copartnery. McGown and Cameron maintained that the clause did not apply to the partnership at will.

Held that the clause had been carried forward into the partnership at will, and that Henderson was therefore entitled to exercise his right of pre-emption.

Lord Cullen (at p. 843): " If the parties by the original contract do no more than simply agree that, on a winding-up of the affairs of the partnership taking place at its expiry, the partner shall have the right of pre-emption as an alternative to open sale, I can see nothing to prevent the right being carried forward."

Relations of partners to one another: fiduciary duties

McNiven v. Peffers
(1868) 7 M. 181

McN. and P. were partners in a wine and spirit business which was carried on in leased premises. P. was sole manager of the business, and the lease was in his name.

Shortly before the lease was due to expire, P., without informing McN., entered into negotiations with the landlord which
resulted in P.'s obtaining a renewal of the lease for himself. The
business was continued after the renewal of the lease without any
apparent change. *Held* that P. was bound to share with McN. the profits of the
business carried on under the new lease.

LORD JUSTICE-CLERK (PATTON) (at p. 186): "It appears to me
perfectly plain that a partner, and especially a managing partner,
who goes to the landlord, and, behind the back of his partner,
obtains from the landlord a new lease of the partnership premises,
is not entitled to retain the profits of that lease for himself. The
landlord naturally dealt with the defender as lessee, for his name
alone appeared on the face of the lease.

"It does not appear to me in such a case to be necessary to
refer to authority. It follows, as the natural result of the plainest
principles of equity applied to such a case, that a partner so acting
must communicate the benefit of the lease so obtained to the copartnery, the interests of which he was bound to have attended to.
The effect of refusing the remedy would be that a valuable
interest in the copartnery, that of goodwill, would be destroyed,
and a private benefit secured by an act grossly wrong in itself."

NOTES

1. *Cf. Pillans Brothers and Others* v. *Pillans* (1908) 16 S.L.T. 611
(O.H.), in which a similar question arose in relation to a purchase of
a business by one partner for himself:
  In 1905, three brothers, Alexander, John and Richard, arranged to
become partners in carrying on business as rivet, bolt and nut manufacturers in Motherwell and elsewhere.
  The following year Richard purchased for himself such a manufacturing business at Greenfield, about four miles from Motherwell.
  The firm and his brothers brought an action against him to have it
declared that the business belonged to the firm and for an account of
the profits from the date when he acquired the business.
  Held that (1) there had been a subsisting partnership when the
Greenfield works had been acquired; (2) that business had to be
regarded as having been acquired for the firm; and (3) Richard was
therefore bound to account to the firm and his brothers for the profits
made at Greenfield.
  Lord Mackenzie (Ordinary) (at p. 614): "There is no dispute in
regard to the law. One partner cannot be permitted to acquire a
benefit for himself to the exclusion of his partners, in relation to any
matter connected with the business of the partnership in which they
are interested as well as himself. The Greenfield business was a rivet,

bolt, and nut manufacturing business. It was of the same nature as that contemplated in the deed of copartnery. The purchase of these works had been discussed by all three partners and by their father. It was a business which would compete with the works which it was contemplated should be started by the partners. The defender founds on the terms of Article 3 of the contract, which provides that the business of the copartnership should be carried on at Motherwell or such other place or places as might be agreed on. He says the partners never agreed to carry on business at Greenfield. They were, however, in my opinion, at least entitled to have an opportunity of saying whether they desired to carry on business there or not. Before the defender could acquire the works for himself it was necessary, in my opinion, that he should have a direct refusal from his partners, and this he has failed to prove. . . .

" The defender's contention is that the law above referred to only applies where a partnership is actually carrying on business; that the partners must be bound in fact and not merely on paper. I do not think that the fact of carrying on business is essential. One can imagine a case of a partnership formed to work minerals where the partners were endeavouring for a considerable period, before commencing operations, to obtain a suitable lease. During this period none of the partners would be entitled to obtain a lease for his individual benefit within the area contemplated by the partnership. . . . It was said that the defender had found the money to buy and finance the business without taking advantage of the firm's credit; but the fact that he got advances on his own credit is not sufficient to make the business his.

" On the whole matter, I am of opinion that when the Greenfield Works were acquired by the defender there was a subsisting partnership. Notice to dissolve this partnership was only given in September 1908. I am of opinion that the business must be held to have been acquired for the firm. Accordingly, there will be a finding that the business at Greenfield was acquired for the firm of Pillans Brothers, and that the defender is bound to account for the profits."

2. A partner is not entitled to retain for himself a profit which he has secretly made for himself at the expense of the firm: *Pender, &c.* v. *Henderson and Co.* (1864) 2 M. 1428:

Certain mercantile firms entered into a joint adventure for the acquisition of steamers to be sold or used in trade for their common profit. One of the firms, Henderson and Co., shipbrokers, was to superintend the acquisition of the steamers. For these services that firm was to receive from the joint adventure a commission of 1 per cent.

Henderson and Co. made contracts with shipbuilders for the building of steamers, and under these contracts Henderson and Co. received a commission from the shipbuilders.

Held that since this additional commission increased the cost of the steamers to the joint adventure, Henderson and Co. was bound to account to the other joint adventurers for the amount so obtained.

Lord Justice-Clerk (Inglis) (at p. 1440): " Now the first question is, whether, having regard to the relation in which Patrick Henderson and Company stood to their co-adventurers, Dunbar, Heatley and Co. and John Pender and Co., they were entitled to make such an arrangement without their knowledge, to the effect of putting a large sum of money into their own pockets at the expense of their co-adventurers. . . . It is enough as between the defenders and their copartners . . . to say that this proceeding in regard to the making of the contracts for both these vessels, and securing these large sums of commission for themselves, as brokers, was a complete breach of contract and breach of faith with their copartners, and that having obtained these sums of money at the expense of their copartners, they are bound to account to them for them."

Lord Neaves (at p. 1442): " I look upon these commissions as virtually, in this case, additions made to the price, and then taken off. . . . I think it was the duty of these defenders, as copartners of the pursuers, to communicate to the shipbuilders the position in which they stood, and to have made that position a ground for obtaining the vessels at the lowest possible price; but instead of doing that, which was their duty, they raised up, in themselves, an adverse interest to the performance of that duty."

3. A partner may become liable to account to the firm and his copartners where he has used partnership property to obtain a profit for himself: *Stewart* v. *North* (1893) 20 R. 260:

In 1876, North obtained from a municipal council in Peru a concession of the exclusive right to supply the town with piped drinking water, and in 1877 he entered into a contract of joint adventure with Speedie and Cockburn for the purpose of carrying out the work.

In 1878, after the work had begun, North, partly by means of the concession, obtained for himself a lease of property belonging to the Tarapaca Water Company, which was then supplying stored fresh water to the town. North then stopped the work of the joint adventure, and, in partnership with Speedie, continued the business of the Tarapaca Water Company. Cockburn knew of these proceedings, but took no action.

In 1885, Cockburn became bankrupt, and in 1887 his interest in the joint adventure was assigned by his trustee to Stewart.

Stewart brought an action of accounting against North, claiming that the profits derived from the lease of the Tarapaca Water Company's property belonged to the joint adventure.

Held that (1) Cockburn would have been entitled to a share of these profits because (a) the business being carried on covered the same ground as that of the joint adventure and (b) North had used the joint adventure's property (the concession) to obtain the lease; but (2) the claim was barred by delay.

Lord President (J. P. B. Robertson) (at p. 268): " Upon the whole I hold that had the defender been in good time called to account for his management of the concerns of the joint adventure he must have accounted to Cockburn for what he drew under the Tarapaca contract. . . .

" Now, there is authority and also reason for holding that claims for profits in joint adventure, particularly of a speculative character, must not be allowed to slumber; and this has a special application to a claim for profits made by some use of the property of the joint adventure which was not in contemplation of the contract. The principle of the law of partnership gives to the absent joint adventurer a right to claim an account of the profits so made in the extraneous enterprise if he chooses to do so; but it is necessary that he should assert his right in reasonable time and should not lie by.

" Well now, in the present case we have a very long lapse of time to begin with, as the trading for which the defender made himself liable to account began in 1878 and terminated in 1879. . . . Cockburn made no claim of any kind whatever. . . . The present claim is made by someone who after Cockburn had become bankrupt got an assignation from the trustee in his sequestration. . . . In this state of things it seems to me that the necessary inference from the undisputed facts of the case is adverse to the subsistence of the present claim.

" My opinion is therefore that the claim comes too late."

Lord Adam (at p. 269): " With reference . . . to the location of the Tarapaca Water Company I am of opinion that that contract was entered into by North on his own account alone, and not on behalf of the joint adventure. He had in fact no power to bind his co-adventurers by any such contract. . . . I think, assuming that the pursuer is not barred from now insisting in the claim, that North would nevertheless have been bound to account for the benefit, if any, derived by him from this transaction. . . . The business of the location was, *inter alia*, to do the very thing which it was the object or business of the joint adventure to do, *viz.*, to supply the town of Pisagua with water. The means to be employed no doubt were different, but that does not appear to me to be material. I think also that the fact that North held the concession of September 1876, which was the property of the joint adventurers, materially contributed to his obtaining the contract, and was made use of by him for that purpose. . . .

" . . . While . . . I think that the pipe scheme had not been abandoned when the location contract was entered into, I nevertheless think that the present claim comes too late.

" I think that where a partner is not bound by a contract entered into by a copartner, but is entitled and desires to have the benefit of it, he must make his claim without delay. He is not entitled to lie by in order to see whether the contract turns out a profitable one or not. If he is to have the benefit he must be prepared to run the risk of loss. North made no secret of his having entered into the contract. . . .

" The contract came to an end in September 1879, but no claim was made under it until the present action was raised in May 1887. In my opinion, that claim comes too late."

Termination of partnership: rescission for innocent misrepresentation

Ferguson v. Wilson
(1904) 6 F. 779

W., an engineer in Aberdeen, advertised for a partner. F. replied to the advertisement, and negotiations took place in the course of which W., without fraudulent intent, misrepresented the trading results of his business.

W. and F. agreed to enter into partnership.

Held that F. was entitled to rescind the agreement on the ground that he had entered into it under an essential error induced by W.'s innocent misrepresentation.

LORD JUSTICE-CLERK (J. H. A. MACDONALD) (at p. 783): " I do not think . . . there is ground for supposing that the defender in making the statements he did was guilty of misrepresentation with fraudulent intent. I think it probable that the defender took a sanguine view, based perhaps on the busy condition in which the works had been, and the increase in the number of employees, that the business was going ahead, and expressed himself in eagerness and not in bad faith. Being anxious to obtain the aid of capital, he may be held to have taken up and expressed a sanguine view without testing it, and I think may have done so without fraud. But it was undoubtedly a misrepresentation—he not knowing the true state of the facts—and representing a view of the facts which was intended by him to be accepted as true, in his knowlege, by those he was dealing with.

" There having been misrepresentation, will it save the defender from a judgment rescinding the contract that no fraud has been proved? I do not think so. The pursuer asks nothing but that it be rescinded, and to that I consider him to be entitled."

LORD MONCREIFF (at p. 783): " The pursuer concludes only for reduction—rescission of the contract; he makes no claim for damages. . . . Proof of fraud is not required in this case.

" Therefore if the pursuer has succeeded in proving that he was induced to agree to enter into partnership with the defender by misrepresentations made by the latter on matters material to the contract and facts which were, or should have been, known to the defender, it is immaterial whether the misrepresentations were made innocently or not."

Termination of partnership: dissolution by death: agreement to the contrary

Hill v. Wylie
(1865) 3 M. 541

H. and W. were in partnership as coalmasters. The contract of copartnery, which was for a term of 19 years, provided that " in the event of the death of either of the parties during the currency of this contract, the copartnership shall not come to an end, but the surviving partner shall continue to carry on the business along with the representatives of the deceasing partner."
W. died during the 19-year period.
Held that the partnership had not been dissolved by W.'s death.

LORD JUSTICE-CLERK (INGLIS) (at p. 543): " I think the clause renders the contract of copartnership binding not only on the partners, but also on their representatives, in this sense and to this effect, that on the decease of a partner his representatives are bound to become partners, and to take the place of the deceasing partner. It is quite different from cases in which the representatives of deceasing partners are entitled to become partners if they choose. If that had been intended, these clauses would have been expressed in the usual way. This is an unusual clause, but it is quite clear what the partners meant. . . . I am of opinion, that if the widow and children represent the deceased partner, they are bound to come in and take his position in the partnership. . . .
" . . . The case of *Warner* v. *Cunninghame* ((1798) M. 14,603) shews that such a clause is not unknown to the law of Scotland. There the contract was for 124 years, and embraced leases of coal, in which the partners bound themselves and their heirs, and that contract was found to be binding on the heirs of the deceasing partner."

NOTES

1. The Partnership Act 1890, s. 33 (1), now provides: " Subject to any agreement between the partners, every partnership is dissolved as regards all the partners by the death . . . of any partner."
2. In *Hoey* v. *MacEwan and Auld* (1867) 5 M. 814, a clerk's contract of service was held to have been terminated on the dissolution, by the death of one partner, of the partnership which was his employer.

Lord President (Inglis) (at p. 817): " The only contracting party with Hoey was the firm, and when it was dissolved by the death of MacEwan the contracting party ceased to exist. The case was the same as if the contract had been with MacEwan as an individual, and his death had put an end to it. There is undoubtedly a great deal of delicacy in the principle of law applicable to the case, and there are cases of hiring not far removed from this one, to which probably a different rule might be applicable. . . .

" Here the only subject-matter of contract is personal service, and the duties Hoey undertook could be rendered only to the persons with whom he contracted. He contracted to serve personally MacEwan and Auld, and to promote, so far as he could, the prosperity of that firm, exactly in the same way as if he had contracted with MacEwan as an individual. He was to receive a salary in return, and a percentage on the profits of the firm during the period of his service. What he was to receive was not an estimated percentage of what at the date of the contract may have been the profits, but a percentage on the profits actually to be made. This seems a purely personal contract, and one that cannot exist after the death of the employer; or, what is the same thing, the dissolution of the partnership by the death of one of the partners."

As dissolution of the partnership by the death of a partner was not a breach of contract, Hoey was not entitled to damages for breach of contract.

3. A bequest of a deceased partner's share in a partnership does not make the legatee a partner: *Thomson* v. *Thomson*, 1962 S.C.(H.L.) 28; 1961 S.C. 255:

Two brothers, Hector and Andrew, carried on a bakery business in partnership under a deed of copartnery which provided that " either partner may by will or otherwise nominate his widow to his share in the partnership."

Hector died leaving a will in which he bequeathed all his estate to his widow. He did not expressly nominate her to his share in the partnership.

Held that the widow was entitled to Hector's share in the partnership assets, but was not a partner in the business.

Lord Denning (at p. 33): " The dominant word in the contract of partnership is ' nominate.' It connotes distinctly that the widow must be nominated to the position of a partner. When coupled with ' share of the partnership ' it means that, not only must the widow be nominated as a partner, but also that she must be so nominated that the deceased's share of the partnership assets is also transferred to her.

" The will of the deceased here was quite ineffective to effect such a nomination. There was no doubt transferred to her the deceased's share of the partnership, but there was no nomination of her to the position of a partner."

Termination of partnership: dissolution by court

Eadie, &c. v. MacBean's Curator Bonis
(1885) 12 R. 660

MacB., the owner of a long-established manufacturing business in Glasgow, assumed three younger men as partners in the business. The contract of copartnery provided that only MacB. was to be entitled to sign cheques and indorse bills of exchange and promissory notes, except that in the event of his indisposition or of his being unable to attend to business from other causes, any of the other partners should be entitled to do so.

MacB., by a stroke of paralysis, became permanently incapable of taking any further active part in the business, and the other partners petitioned the court to appoint a judicial factor to wind up the partnership affairs.

Petition *refused*, on the ground that it was not an essential part of the contract of copartnery that MacB. should give his personal services, and that therefore the other partners were not entitled to dissolve the partnership.

LORD PRESIDENT (INGLIS) (at p. 665): "There can be no doubt that under ordinary circumstances where two or more persons are engaged in business together as partners, and all of them are expected or by contract of copartnery bound to take an active management of the business, the permanent insanity or incapacity of one of the partners necessarily operates a dissolution of the partnership. . . .

"But it is equally clear, I think, that there may be contracts of partnership in which the duties devolved upon the several partners are so defined that even the permanent insanity of one of the partners would not operate a dissolution of the partnership. Nothing is more common than that two persons should enter into partnership, one of whom is an active man of business, of skill and experience in the particular trade, and the other person has no qualification for being a partner except that he has plenty of money. In those circumstances the contract would probably provide that the one man should supply the capital and the other should do all the work. Now, it is very plain, I think, that in a case of that kind the mere incapacity or insanity of the moneyed man would not dissolve the partnership, because his insanity does not render it at all impossible that he should perform his part of the contract."

[After considering the provisions of the contract of copartnery, Lord President Inglis concluded that the case was very much in the " position of a case where to provide the money is the only duty imposed upon one partner, and the active management of the business is left entirely to the other or others."]

LORD SHAND (at p. 669): " Taking the case as one in which I think the petitioners have failed to show that they are entitled to have services to the end of the contract from Mr. MacBean, I am of opinion . . . that they have failed to shew any right to bring this partnership to an end."

NOTES

1. Insanity is now a ground on which an application may be made to court for a dissolution under section 35 (a) of the Partnership Act 1890. The court has a discretion as to whether it will decree a dissolution.

2. One of the other grounds set out in section 35 of the Act of 1890 is:

" (d) when a partner, other than the partner suing, wilfully or persistently commits a breach of the partnership agreement, or otherwise so conducts himself in matters relating to the partnership business that it is not reasonably practicable for the other partner or partners to carry on the business in partnership with him."

The court granted an order for dissolution on this ground in *Thomson, Petitioner* (1893) 1 S.L.T. 59:

A partner, after drawing a cheque in the firm's name, disappeared, taking the money with him. The other partners petitioned the court on the ground that this was a breach of the express terms of the contract of copartnery.

Termination of partnership: winding-up: appointment of judicial factor

Dickie v. Mitchell
(1874) 1 R. 1030

D. and his son-in-law, M., were partners in a joint farming adventure. Both became incapable of managing the farm.

D. presented a petition for the appointment of a judicial factor with special power to wind up the partnership affairs.

Held that in the special circumstances of the case the appointment of a judicial factor was necessary.

LORD PRESIDENT (INGLIS) (at p. 1033): " I have come to be of opinion that the prayer of the petition ought to be granted,—that is to say, that a factor ought to be appointed with the usual powers, but without any special power of renouncing the lease and winding up the estate. If that is a measure which must be resorted to, it will be for the factor to come here and apply in his own person for special powers, after having made himself master of the affairs which he is called on to manage, and having satisfied himself of the necessity of the application. . . .

" None of the cases referred to are exactly in point, for this is not properly the case of a partnership. The petitioner and respondent here are simply joint tenants, and therefore merely joint adventurers without any formal partnership. Still the cases of the appointment of factors on partnership estates are not without important bearing in the present question.

" Two or three general principles may be deduced from them, which are, I think, important: —

" First, when all the partners in a copartnery are dead this Court has the power, and will exercise it, of appointing a factor to wind up the partnership estate. . . .

" Second, if there are surviving partners, then, if there is no fault or incapacity on the part of them or any of them, preventing them carrying on their business, this Court will not interfere, but will leave the surviving partners to extricate their affairs in their own way. . . .

" It may therefore be confidently stated that, in the first case, this Court can and will appoint a factor when neccessary, and that in the second case it will not.

" But, third, where there is a surviving partner or partners, but these partners are unfitted either for carrying on or winding up the affairs of the partnership, whether from failure of duty or incapacity of any one or more of them, then the Court can, and, if satisfied of the necessity, will appoint a factor. All such cases are, in their nature, cases of circumstances; but if the circumstances are strong enough, it is within the competency of the Court to make the appointment.

" Now, the present case, though it is not a case of partnership, very much resembles one. In a popular sense the father-in-law and son-in-law are partners, or at least joint adventurers. The old man is undoubtedly incapable of managing the farm. That is not only stated by himself, but is strongly stated by the respondent in his answers to the petition. That being so, is the respondent a person who should be left in the sole and uncontrolled management of the concern? . . . He . . . says—' I am at times unfit for the conduct and management thereof (that is, of the farm), and have entailed on myself and on said joint tenant serious losses through the facility with which I have been induced to sign accommodation bills for worthless parties, and to conclude rash bargains, from which serious losses have resulted in the management of the said farm and otherwise.' Now, can any one say that a man, who can properly be described in such terms, and who so describes himself, is fit to be left in the management of a farm, and more especially a farm in which another than himself has a joint interest? It is quite impossible to maintain such a thing for a moment. Yet the respondent's management must of necessity continue unless we appoint a judicial factor, for his co-adventurer in the farm is now admittedly incapable of carrying it on."

NOTES

1. The common law is preserved by section 39 of the Partnership Act 1890 which provides that any partner or his representatives may, on the termination of a partnership, apply to the court to wind up the business and affairs of the firm.

2. The appointment of a judicial factor to wind up a partnership business was held to be justified in *Allan* v. *Gronmeyer* (1891) 18 R. 784:

G. was a partner of Thomas and Albert Allan in a wine and spirit business. The capital of about £22,000 had been contributed entirely by the Allans. An article in the contract of copartnery provided that at the termination of the partnership the duty of winding up its affairs was to lie with G.

In 1888, the partners agreed that the partnership should be dissolved and that G. should wind up its affairs in accordance with that article.

G. took no steps towards winding-up but carried on the business as a going concern, with its capital undiminished.

In 1890, the Allans presented a petition for the appointment of a judicial factor, and the court *appointed* an accountant to that office.

Lord Adam (at p. 786): " It is obvious that the petitioners, the Messrs Allan, have a very overwhelming interest in the matter, because they have a capital in the firm of between £20,000 and £30,000, and the respondent has no capital at all. The petitioners therefore have a very clear interest to see that that capital is safe. . . . The late firm . . . came to an end in the spring of 1888. It then became the duty of Mr Gronmeyer to wind up the concern and realise the business, and he has had from 1888 till 1891 to carry out that duty, with the result that the business is as far from being wound up as ever. . . . It has been urged that the business has been successfully carried on, but that is not the question. The question is whether the Messrs Allan wish it to be carried on or not, and they say they do not. It was suggested that the appointment of a judicial factor is not an advantageous way of winding up a business like this. It may be so, but that again is a matter for the Messrs Allan to consider."

3. A case brought under section 39 of the Act of 1890 was *Carabine* v. *Carabine*, 1949 S.C. 521:

A husband and wife were partners in a hotel business, to which both had contributed capital. There was no written contract of copartnery.

The partnership terminated when the wife left her husband. All efforts on the wife's part to have the business realised failed, the husband carrying it on against her wishes. There was an imminent risk that a building society to which interest was due would force a sale of the premises in circumstances disadvantageous to both partners.

The court *appointed* a judicial factor in order that the wife might obtain her rights under section 39 of the Act.

Lord Justice-Clerk (Thomson) (at p. 527): " It is perfectly true that under the Partnership Act one partner is entitled to wind up the affairs of the partnership and to pay out the other partners or the other partners' representatives, and the Court for obvious reasons, particularly from the point of view of expense, prefers and encourages such a course. But such a course is only desirable if there is harmony, or at any rate agreement as to the propriety of such a course being adopted, between the partner who is carrying on the business and the other interested parties, and if the winding-up partner is making a proper effort to get things settled. Here there is no harmony, and the impression I take from what I have been told is that the respondent has just been staying on running the hotel and that he has not the slightest intention of settling up the partnership affairs unless he is subjected to pressure, and this puts the petitioner in a very awkward position and prevents her from enjoying her rights under the Act. That is just the sort of situation which seems to me to make it necessary or expedient that we should intervene. This is not just a dispute between the winding-up partner and the late partner on some matter of detail or accounting arising out of the winding up; it is something much more fundamental which attacks the propriety of the course adopted altogether. What is more, what we were told today about the payments of the building society loan indicates to me that there is also an element of urgency in the matter, and for those reasons I suggest to your Lordships that we . . . appoint a judicial factor."

Lord Jamieson (at p. 530): " The Court will be slow to appoint a judicial factor on a dissolved partnership and will not do so if the partners or the remaining partners are in a position to and can conduct the winding-up. In this case, nothing appears to have been done except that certain offers were made by one partner which were not acceptable to the other. We have today been told that the property which belonged to the partnership is really in the hands of a building society and that certain instalments due to the society have not been paid. In these circumstances, it appears to me that there is danger that the building society may step in and force a sale at a time, or in circumstances which might be disadvantageous to both parties.

" Accordingly I agree with your Lordships that a judicial factor should be appointed, and, if it proves that such appointment causes expense which might have beeen avoided, the parties have only themselves to blame."

4. On the other hand, in *Thomson, Petitioner* (1893) 1 S.L.T. 59 (Note 2 to *Eadie, &c.* v. *MacBean's Curator Bonis*, p. 23, above) the court, while granting the order for dissolution, refused to authorise winding up by the petitioner or to appoint a judicial factor, on the ground that at common law a partner had on dissolution full power to wind up.

Termination of partnership: winding-up: continuing authority of partners

Dickson v. The National Bank of Scotland Ltd.
1917 S.C. (H.L.) 50; 1916 S.C.. 589

A sum of money forming part of a trust-estate was deposited with a bank. The deposit-receipt stated that the sum was to be repayable on signature of a legal firm, A, B & C, the law-agents to the trust.

The firm A, B & C was subsequently dissolved, and eight years after the dissolution B, one of the former partners, by signing the firm-name on the deposit receipt, uplifted the money and embezzled it.

The beneficiaries in the trust brought an action against the bank for payment of the sum deposited.

Held that as the uplifting of the deposit was necessary for one or other of the purposes mentioned in section 38 of the Partnership Act 1890 (winding up the affairs of the partnership and completing transactions begun but unfinished at the time of the dissolution), B had had authority to sign the firm-name, and the bank had been justified in paying over the money to him; and action *dismissed* as irrelevant.

Lord Chancellor (Finlay) (at p. 52): "The Inner House decided the case altogether upon the applicability of . . . section 38. Section 38 of the Partnership Act 1890 really embodied the old law relating to partnership derived orginally from the Roman law, and it is this—that for certain purposes a partnership continues notwithstanding dissolution. There is an interesting passage quoted from Paulus in the Digest by Sir Frederick Pollock in his edition of the Partnership Act, where it is pointed out that, although when one of a firm dies the survivors cannot undertake new transactions on behalf of the firm, they can complete what is left unfinished, and that distinction is really what animates this section 38 and the law of which section 38 is the embodiment.

" . . . In my opinion the Inner House was right in holding that section 38 applied, and therefore that the Bank were discharged by that payment."

Goodwill: use of firm name by seller of goodwill

Smith v. McBride & Smith
(1888) 16 R. 36

James Smith and Joseph McBride had carried on business in partnership as aerated water manufacturers in Greenock under the name of Smith & McBride. In 1884 their partnership terminated, and the parties agreed that Smith should pay £300 to McBride for the latter's " share and interest in the business," and that Smith should acquire the business " with goodwill, machinery, and stock-in-trade," and carry it on in his own name.

About a month after dissolution, McBride entered into partnership with William Smith, a brother of James Smith, and with a third partner, McKelvie. This firm's business, which was also that of aerated water manufacturers in Greenock, traded under the name of McBride, Smith & McKelvie.

After McKelvie's retirement in 1887, McBride and William Smith traded in partnership under the name " Smith & McBride."

James Smith raised an action for interdict.

Held that he was entitled to interdict.

Lord Young (at p. 39): " This is an application by a person who purchased a going business as an aerated water manufacturer, with its stock and goodwill, in August 1884, to have the person from whom he purchased it, and the firm which that person has now formed, interdicted from trading under the firm's name, the right to which he purchased along with the goodwill. . . . It takes a strong case of right in another and consequent danger of injury to him to justify a Court in restraining any man from conducting his business in his own name. But I think this case is of such a character. Smith & McBride is the firm name under which the business was formerly conducted, and, as the advertisement issued when the business was formerly sold bears, ' extensively and successfully ' conducted. The pursuer Smith, one of the partners, purchased it with the right to use the firm name."

Lord Lee (at p. 40): " I think that a man who sells his business with its goodwill cannot derogate from his own grant."

Registration of business names: failure to register: relief granted by court

Clydesdale Motor Transport Co., Petitioners
1922 S.C. 18

In 1920, three individuals formed a partnership to carry on a motor transport business under the name "Clydesdale Motor Transport Company." This name was not registered under the Registration of Business Names Act 1916 because none of the three partners was aware of the existence of that Act and they did not consult any law-agent.

The firm purchased a motor lorry for its business from McCosh & Devine, engineers. The lorry proved defective, and the firm raised an action against McCosh & Devine for rescission of the contract and repetition of the price.

McCosh & Devine put forward the defence that the action was barred by section 8 (1) of the Registration of Business Names Act 1916.

The firm, being thus made aware of the Act for the first time, immediately registered the business name, and petitioned the court for relief under section 8 (1), proviso (a), on the ground that the default had been due entirely to inadvertence and ignorance of the provisions of the Act.

Without inquiry, the court *granted* relief.

LORD PRESIDENT (CLYDE) (at p. 20): "The remedy asked for in this petition is one which we have power to give only on being satisfied that the petitioners' failure to comply with the Act was accidental or due to inadvertence or to some other sufficient cause, or that on other grounds it is just and equitable to grant it. Accordingly, it must not be assumed, in relation to petitions of this kind, that the Court will grant relief merely in reliance upon the statements made in the petition and on the explanations with regard to them given by counsel. But in the present case I do not think there is anything in the petition to suggest the slightest doubt as to the good faith of the petitioners; and, having regard to the explanations which Mr. Gilchrist has given, I think it is one in which we may hold it to be just and equitable in the circumstances to grant the relief prayed for."

NOTE

Under proviso (a) of section 8 (1) of the Act the court must be satisfied as to at least one (but not necessarily more than one) of the following—that the default was "accidental" or "due to inadvertence" or due to "some other sufficient cause" or that "on other grounds it is just and equitable to grant relief." In *Thomas Montgomery & Sons* v. *W. B. Anderson & Sons Ltd.*, 1979 S.L.T. 101 (O.H.), the Lord Ordinary (Ross) was satisfied both that the default had been " due to inadvertence " and that in any event it was " just and equitable to grant relief."

M. & Sons, a firm of potato merchants, in the course of its business supplied potatoes to Gallacher. In December 1975, when Gallacher owed M. & Sons over £5,000, Galacher granted a standard security over his property in Kilmarnock to A. Ltd., a company registered in England and carrying on business as potato merchants. In March 1976 Gallacher was sequestrated.

M. & Sons raised an action in the Court of Session against Gallacher and A. Ltd. for reduction of the standard security. A. Ltd. pleaded that the action was incompetent since the firm was in default of its obligations under the Act of 1916.

M. & Sons then registered in terms of the Act and petitioned for relief under section 8 (1), proviso (*a*). A. Ltd. lodged answers.

Lord Ross (at p. 102): " It was not disputed that it is for the petitioners to satisfy the court that they are entitled to relief . . . , and that the court has a discretion as to whether or not to grant relief in any appropriate case. . . .

" . . . Thomas Montgomery died in or about 1972. . . . His two sons James and Charles . . . were practical men who both drove lorries uplifting and delivering potatoes. . . .

" . . . Inadvertence in this context must mean heedlessness, carelessness or some want of attention. . . .

" . . . The proviso to section 8 (1) of the Act does not specify the persons whose inadvertence will excuse the default in registration, and, in my opinion, inadvertence of any person is sufficient if it was the cause of the failure to register. In the present case, although one cannot determine precisely why no registration was effected, I am satisfied that . . . the default can properly be regarded as ' due to inadvertence.' There must in the circumstances have been negligence or carelessness on the part of some person; there was certainly no deliberate intention to be in default, and I am quite satisfied that there was no bad faith. The Montgomery family were described . . . as being simple and unsophisticated people who placed great faith in their professional advisers. I believe Mr. Charles Montgomery when he states that he did not know about the provisions of the Act of 1916, and I can readily believe that the other members of the family were equally ignorant. There is authority for the view that ignorance by the partners of the obligations imposed by the Act may warrant the granting of relief (*Clydesdale Motor Transport Co.*). In that case too, the aspect of good faith was stressed (see Lord President, 1922 2 S.L.T. at p. 246). . . . Even if there had not been inadvertence, I would have thought it just and equitable to grant relief. . . .

" . . . The object of the legislation must have been to provide for public disclosure of the names of the persons carrying on a business so that those transacting with the business could know with whom they were really doing business and who controlled the business. Here the business was called 'Thomas Montgomery & Sons,' and it was Thomas Montgomery, his wife and his sons who carried on business until 1972, and Thomas Montgomery's sons who carried on business after 1973. There was no question of anyone having tried to conceal who ran the business, and in all the circumstances, had it been necessary to do so, I would have held that it was just and equitable to grant relief. . . .

"In the circumstances, being satisfied that the default of the petitioners as regards registration was due to inadvertence, *et separatim* that it is just and equitable to grant relief, I am clearly of opinion that I ought to exercise my discretion so as to grant relief. . . . The relief granted will operate retrospectively."

PART II

COMPANIES
(EXCLUDING WINDING UP AND RECONSTRUCTION)

CHAPTER 2

COMPANIES—INTRODUCTORY

Common law company: limited liability

Stevenson & Co. v. Macnair and ors.
(1757) Mor. 14, 560 and 14, 667

The Arran Fishing Company had been constituted by a contract of copartnery. Its members had each subscribed £50, which gave the company a capital of £2,000. Its trade was to be carried on by directors, whose powers could be altered by a general meeting.

A clause of the contract of copartnery provided that " nothing herein contained shall be understood to import a power to the directors, or any general meeting, to compel any partner or subscriber to pay or contribute any more money to the stock than the sum by him subscribed."

S. & Co., of the rope-work of Port Glasgow, furnished the company with ropes to the value of £72, and brought an action against M. and others who were members of the company.

The defence was that " the directors could not, by contracting debt, subject any of their partners beyond the sums severally subscribed by them; and that the defenders having paid into the Company the whole sums subscribed by them, they are no farther liable. The pursuers, furnishing to the Company, followed the faith of the Company, and must betake themselves to the Company's stock, for their payment."

This defence was sustained.

" There is an obvious difference betwixt the present case, and a Company trading without relation to a stock. In the latter case, each partner must be liable *in solidum* to the Company's debts; for there is nothing here to limit the credit. . . . The very meaning of confining the trade to a joint stock, is, that each should be liable for what he subscribes, and no farther. . . . Grotius justly observes . . . that it is not expedient to make partners farther liable, because it would deter every one from entering into a trading Company."

NOTE

This early case indicates how Scots company law might have developed under continental influence. English influence, however, proved stronger, and the case does not represent the law which would now apply to any common law company still in existence.

Common law company: legality

Macandrew v. Robertson
(1828) 6 S. 950

The Edinburgh Portable Gas Company was a joint stock company constituted under a contract of copartnery in 1825. Its capital was £50,000 in shares of £10 each, and its affairs were managed by directors. Members were to be free to dispose of their shares provided they first made an offer of the shares to the directors for behoof of the company.

M., one of the many original subscribers, was in the course of selling his shares to R. but had not yet offered them to the directors, when the company demanded payment from him of the amount called up on the shares.

In an action brought against M. by the company, M. pleaded that the company fell under the " Bubble " Act of 1720 and therefore had no title to sue.

At the same time M. raised an action of relief against R. on the footing that he had sold the shares to R. In defence to this action R. contended (i) that the company fell under the " Bubble " Act, and therefore the transaction was illegal; and (ii) that there had been no completed sale because M. had not offered the shares to the directors.

Held (i) that the company did not fall under the " Bubble " Act; and (ii) that the sale of the shares was effectual as between M. and R., although no offer of the shares had previously been made to the directors in terms of the contract of copartnery.

Lord Balgray (at p. 955): " If we were to hold that this company fell under the Bubble Act, we would overturn all the extensive mercantile associations in Scotland. The criterion is, whether it be of a nature prejudicial to the public; but it is absurd to say, that because the shares are transferable, ergo the association is mischievous."

Lord Gillies (at p. 955): " I have no doubt, except on the statute. But, even as to it, I think that the restriction on the power of transferring is sufficient to take the case out of the statute. It is an Act which, so far from having been beneficial, has, I think, been mischievous; and therefore we ought not to extend it to cases which do not fall within the letter of it."

Lord President (Hope) (at p. 955): " By our law such an association is not illegal."

NOTES

1. The " Bubble " Act (6 Geo. 1, c. 18) did extend to Scotland, but the scant notice which it received in reported cases suggests that it was regarded as having little or no legal effect in Scotland.

In England the Act was for almost a century in " entire oblivion " (Bell, *Commentaries*, Vol. II, p. 519), but was resuscitated in the early years of the nineteenth century, on the eve of its repeal by 6 Geo. 4, c. 91, passed in 1825 to restore the common law. The events out of which this case arose took place in 1825 before the passing of the last-mentioned Act.

2. An Act of 1825 (6 Geo. 4, c. 131) mentioned with approval the practice which had prevailed in Scotland of forming joint-stock companies with transferable shares.

3. In later cases there are several *dicta* as to the legality of the common law company in Scotland, *e.g.*:

" In Scotland a joint-stock company was perfectly lawful " (*per* Lord Curriehill in *Graham* v. *Western Bank* (1864) 2 M. 559 at p. 578).

" In Scotland it has always been held that joint-stock companies were lawful, though not incorporated in any way " (*per* Lord Curriehill in *Drew* v. *Lumsden* (1865) 3 M. 384 at p. 392).

" It is necessary to keep in view that by the common law of Scotland joint-stock companies unincorporated, with transferable shares, were legal associations, and that the Bubble Act of 6 Geo. 1, c. 18, was never enforced in Scotland " (*per* Lord President Inglis in *Muir, et al.* v. *City of Glasgow Bank* (1878) 6 R. 392 at p. 399).

Registered company: separate personality

Grierson, Oldham, & Co. Ltd. v. Forbes, Maxwell, & Co. Ltd.
(1895) 22 R. 812

F. Ltd., which had on the market a certain non-alcoholic wine called " Mersano," in 1894 entered into an agreement with G. & Co., wine-merchants, for a space in G. & Co.'s advertising wine-list for a period of three years at £200 per annum.

Eight months after that agreement, G. & Co.'s business was transferred to a newly formed registered company, G. & Co. Ltd.

F. Ltd. declined to pay the rent due for the second half-year of the contract, and G. & Co. Ltd. brought an action against F. Ltd. for declarator that F. Ltd. was bound to implement the agreement or alternatively for damages for breach of contract. *Held* that G. & Co. Ltd. had no title to sue.

LORD JUSTICE-CLERK (J. H. A. MACDONALD) (at p. 817): " I am of opinion that the new limited company cannot be held to be the same contracting party as the old firm, and that Messrs

Forbes, Maxwell, & Company are not under their contract with Messrs Grierson, Oldham, & Company bound to pay for an advertisement in the wine-list of the limited company, with which company they have no contract."

NOTES

1. Another case of the same year also demonstrating the separate personality of a registered company is *John Wilson & Son Ltd.* v. *Inland Revenue* (1895) 23 R. 18.

A partnership, W. & Son, was converted into a registered company, W. & Son Ltd. There was no change in membership, and each partner received shares in the new company equal to the value of his holding in the former partnership.

The question arose of whether the conveyance of the assets of the partnership to the new company was a conveyance on sale within the meaning of the Stamp Act 1891.

Held that it was such a conveyance.

Lord McLaren (at p. 24): " When a number of persons are constituted a company under the Companies Act, the new company is by statute a corporation, having an identity distinct from that of its constituent members or those to whom shares may be allotted."

2. The principle is now generally associated with the English case *Salomon* v. *Salomon & Co. Ltd.* [1897] A.C. 22, *e.g.* in *Woolfson* v. *Strathclyde Regional Council*, 1977 S.L.T. 60.

That case arose out of a compulsory purchase order and raised the question whether W. was, by a lifting of the corporate veil, to be entitled to compensation for disturbance which was otherwise denied to him under the legislation in force at the relevant time.

W. submitted that he and two limited companies should be treated as a single entity or unit, namely W. himself, who as the owner-occupier of the premises would then have been entitled to compensation for disturbance.

Held that the circumstances did not justify a departure from " the general rule as laid down in *Salomon* to the effect of ignoring and not being bound by the *ex facie* legal position " (*per* Lord Justice-Clerk Wheatley at p. 64).

3. The personality of a registered company necessarily differs from the personality of an individual in certain respects, *e.g.* a registered company cannot attend personally and argue its case before the House of Lords as an individual would be entitled to do.

Equity and Law Life Assurance Society v. *Tritonia Ltd.*, 1943 S.C.(H.L.) 88: In a case which came before the House of Lords there were three appellants—Tritonia Ltd., Greig & Millar Ltd. and Blair who was a Glasgow solicitor and a director of the two companies. Blair indicated his intention to argue not only on his own behalf in person but also on behalf of the two other appellants on the ground that he had been appointed by resolutions of the boards of the two companies as their agent for that purpose.

Held that Blair was entitled to argue solely on his own behalf, the rule and practice of the House of Lords being that no one had right of audience except counsel or (if the litigant were a natural person) the party himself.

Lord Chancellor (Viscount Simon) (at p. 89): "In the case of a corporation, inasmuch as the artificial entity cannot attend and argue personally, the right of audience is necessarily limited to counsel instructed on the corporation's behalf."

Classification of registered companies: guarantee company

Robertson v. British Linen Co.
(1890) 18 R. 1225 (O.H.)

The memorandum of a company limited by guarantee purported to confer power "to hypothecate or assign to any corporation or person who shall lend money to the association, the guarantee obligations, letters, and relative documents from ... members of the association."

The executive council (corresponding to the board of directors) hypothecated the letters of guarantee to a bank in security of money advanced to the company by the bank.

The company went into voluntary liquidation, and the liquidator challenged the validity of the bank's security.

Held that (1) it was *ultra vires* of the executive council to create a security over the guarantee fund in favour of a particular creditor, and (2) in any case the hypothecation or pledge of the letters was ineffectual to constitute a preference over the fund in competition with the liquidator, who was entitled to possession of the letters as accessories of the fund.

LORD STORMONTH DARLING (ORDINARY) (at p. 1231): "I do not see any reason for treating a guarantee fund as capital until the commencement of the winding-up.

"If this be so, there is a manifest repugnancy in article 30 (6) which first authorises the executive council to assign and hypothecate 'all or any part of the property and effects of the association,' and then goes on to specify in particular 'the guarantee obligations' which *ex hypothesi* are not part of such property or effects so long as it is a going concern. At all events, it seems to me that whether they be regarded as the property of the association prior to liquidation or not, they are appropriated by the statute for the satisfaction of the company's liabilities *pari passu,* and are therefore not capable of being used for the purpose of giving preference to any particular creditor."

NOTE

This case was commented on and distinguished by the First Division in *Lloyds Bank Ltd.* v. *Morrison & Son*, 1927 S.C. 571.

A company limited by guarantee obtained an undertaking from M., who was not a member of the company, to pay a proportion of any loss arising in connection with the holding of an exhibition.

The company assigned M.'s undertaking to a bank which had given credit to the company, and the bank sued M. upon the guarantee.

Held that the assignation had been valid, since this guarantee fund was an independent fund of credit distinct from the company's statutory guarantee fund.

Classification of registered companies: unlimited company

Nelson Mitchell v. The City of Glasgow Bank
(1879) 6 R.(H.L.) 66; (1878) 6 R. 420

M. sold his £2,500 stock of an unlimited registered banking company on the Glasgow Stock Exchange in the usual way. The purchaser was the bank itself.

Before settlement day the bank stopped payment, and the directors called a meeting to consider voluntary winding up.

The bank declined to transfer the stock out of M.'s name, and M. presented a petition for removal of his name from the register.

Held that, because of the stoppage of the bank and the subsequent actings of the directors, M. was not entitled to have his name removed.

Observations as to the legality of a purchase by an unlimited company of its own shares.

LORD CHANCELLOR (EARL CAIRNS) (at p. 67): " The brokers who bought, bought for the bank, and there is no doubt that the bank, who had authority to buy their own stock under their deed of copartnery, were the purchasers."

LORD PRESIDENT (INGLIS) (at p. 429): " The directors of the company were, under ordinary circumstances, undoubtedly, quite entitled to purchase the stock of their own bank, and they had been in the course of doing so apparently for some time to a large extent."

CHAPTER 3

MEMORANDUM OF ASSOCIATION

Name: whether similarity of name would be misleading

Dunlop Pneumatic Tyre Co. Ltd. v. Dunlop Motor Co. Ltd.
1907 S.C.(H.L.) 15; (1906) 8 F. 1146

Two brothers, R. and J. F. Dunlop, had been in partnership in a cycle and motor repairing business in Kilmarnock.

In 1904 they transferred the motor branch of their business to the Dunlop Motor Co. Ltd., which had a capital of £500 held by the two brothers and some of their friends. Under its memorandum the company had power, *inter alia*, to make motoring " accessories."

An English company, the Dunlop Pneumatic Tyre Co. Ltd., makers of a well-known tyre and manufacturers of motoring " accessories," presented a note of suspension and interdict against the Dunlop Motor Co. Ltd. to have it interdicted from carrying on business under any name containing the name " Dunlop."

Interdict was *refused* since the Dunlop Motor Co. Ltd. had not adopted its name for the purpose of passing off its goods as the goods of the English company and since the name " Dunlop Motor Co. Ltd." was not calculated to deceive the public into purchasing the goods of the Scottish company in the belief that they were goods of the English company.

LORD CHANCELLOR (LOREBURN) (at p. 16): " The real complaint in this case was as to the use of the name ' Dunlop.' That name is the true name of the two brothers who got up the respondent Company. I can see very little proof that anyone was misled by its use, and I can see no proof that any article was bought by anyone from the respondents in the belief that they were a branch of the appellant Company. The two Companies do not, to any considerable extent, in fact deal in the same articles, and I see no ground for thinking that the little repairing business in Kilmarnock does or can do any unlawful harm to the appellant Company."

LORD JAMES OF HEREFORD (at p. 17): " Under the circumstances of the case before your Lordships I do not think that the average citizen of Kilmarnock would be deceived."

NOTE

Cf. The Scottish Union and National Insurance Co. v. *The Scottish National Insurance Co. Ltd.*, 1909 S.C. 318: The Scottish Union and National Insurance Co., which had been formed under a special Act of Parliament in 1878, carried on general insurance business but not marine insurance.

In 1907 the Scottish National Insurance Co. Ltd. was incorporated under the Companies Acts. Its memorandum of association empowered it to carry on most classes of insurance, but in fact the company's business was confined to marine insurance.

The Scottish Union and National Insurance Co. brought a note of suspension and interdict against the Scottish National Insurance Co. Ltd. to prevent the registered company from carrying on insurance business in that name.

Held that as the businesses of general insurance and marine insurance were very different, the similarity of the names was not likely to deceive the public, and interdict *refused.*

Lord Kinnear (at p. 325): "There is no competition between the two companies. I think this is the vital point in the case."

Name: publication of name: personal liability of signatories of bill of exchange

Scottish and Newcastle Breweries Ltd. v. Blair and Others
1967 S.L.T. 72 (O.H.)

S. Ltd. drew a bill of exchange for £7,500 on Anderson & Blair (Property Development) Ltd., but misnamed the drawee as "Messrs. Anderson & Blair, Windmill Hotel, Arbroath."

The bill was accepted on behalf of the company by two directors and the firm of solicitors who were the company secretaries.

On presentation for payment the bill was dishonoured, and subsequently the company went into liquidation.

S. Ltd. brought an action under section 108 (4) (*b*) of the Companies Act 1948 claiming payment from the signatories.

Held that, as section 108 required to be strictly complied with, the signatories were liable, even although the drawer had not been misled or deceived.

LORD ORDINARY (HUNTER) (at p. 73): " It is apparent from the provisions of the said section 108 that the section was intended by the legislature to be both strict and penal in its effect. . . .

"It was submitted by counsel for the compearing defenders that it was necessary to the operation of the statutory provisions in the present case that the pursuers should have been deceived or misled by the failure to mention the correct name of the Company in the said bill. . . . I can find nothing in the language of the statutory provisions which lends any support to such an argument. . . . It is no doubt true that in the present case the pursuers did not name the Company correctly in the address, but it was for those who undertook the responsibility of accepting the bill to see that the name of the Company was mentioned in it in legible characters as required by the statute."

Registered office: change of situation

Ross v. The Invergordon Distillers Ltd.
1961 S.C. 286

The directors of I. Ltd. resolved that R., the secretary of the company, at whose office in Edinburgh the company's registered office was situated, be removed from office, and that the situation of the registered office be changed to Ross-shire.

Before notice of the change had been given to the Registrar of Companies under section 107 of the Companies Act 1948, R. served on the company at the Edinburgh office an initial writ in an action for outlays and expenses brought in the Edinburgh sheriff court.

Held that (1) for an office to be the registered office of a company, notice of its situation had to have been given to the Registrar of Companies, and accordingly the Edinburgh office was still the registered office; and (2) the presence of the registered office within the sheriffdom was sufficient to create jurisdiction, whether the company then carried on business there or not.

LORD PRESIDENT (CLYDE) (at p. 289): "The crucial date at which the matter must be decided is, of course, the date of the service of the writ—17th January. Although the directors had at that date resolved to change the registered office, they had not effectively done so. For, in my view, the new office cannot be the registered office until the statutory machinery of intimation to the Registrar has been carried out, and admittedly this had not been done by 17th January.

" . . . Until intimation of a change, the creditors and others dealing with the company are entitled to assume that the registered office remains where it originally was, and it is only when the necessary steps have been taken to inform the Registrar of the change so that he may record the same in terms of section 107, that the original registered office ceases to be the registered office of the company.

" ... It was contended that the business had been taken away from Edinburgh and transferred to Ross-shire by that date. But ... in my opinion, under the common law jurisdiction of the Sheriff, it is sufficient if the registered office of the company is within the sheriffdom, for that is the domicile of the company."

Objects: distinction between objects and powers

John Walker & Sons Ltd., Petitioners
1914 S.C. 280

W. Ltd. presented a petition for confirmation of a special resolution altering its objects by addition of powers to acquire similar businesses, to sell the undertaking of the company, and to amalgamate with any other firm, person or company.

The court, while confirming the power to acquire similar businesses, *refused* to confirm the other alterations on the ground that they were not within section 9 (1) of the Companies (Consolidation) Act 1908.

LORD SKERRINGTON (at p. 289): " On referring to the so-called ' objects ' which the petitioners desire to add to their memorandum, it will be found that these are not objects in the proper sense of the word, but are merely powers which the petitioners consider might be useful to them in the course of their business. This abuse of the word ' objects ' in connection with registered companies has often been judicially referred to, but I think that it has received judicial approval in a series of applications under the Companies (Memorandum of Association) Act 1890."

NOTES

1. The Act of 1890 and section 9 of the Act of 1908 were precursors of section 5 of the Companies Act 1948, under which confirmation by the court is no longer necessary unless there is objection from a specified minority. Addition of powers to sell the undertaking and to amalgamate would now be permissible under section 5 of the Act of 1948.

2. *Cf. The North of Scotland and Orkney and Shetland Steam Navigation Co. Ltd., Petitioners*, 1920 S.C. 633: N. Ltd. presented a petition for confirmation of a memorandum and articles of association in place of its existing contract of copartnership. The objects clause in the memorandum consisted of 23 paragraphs many of which related, not to objects, but to powers in relation to objects.

The court *granted* the prayer of the petition, subject to modification.

See also *Thompson* v. *J. Barke & Co. (Caterers) Ltd.* in Note 2 to *Life Association of Scotland* v. *Caledonian Heritable Security Co. Ltd. in Liquidation*, p. 54, below.

Objects: " independent objects " clause

The London and Edinburgh Shipping Co. Ltd., Petitioners
1909 S.C. 1

A shipping company presented a petition under the Companies (Memorandum of Association) Act 1890 for the substitution of a memorandum and articles for its contract of copartnery. In addition to the leading object, which was to purchase, hire or build ships and employ them in carrying passengers and goods between Leith and London, 20 other objects were specified in the proposed memorandum and it was provided that " the various businesses or objects specified shall be regarded as independent objects, and in nowise restricted . . . by reference to the name of the Company, or to the businesses or objects contained in any other paragraph."

The reporter was of opinion that the clause quoted should not be approved of because the words used were " such as to render it impossible to place any definite limit to the objects of the Company."

The company restricted a power to lend money specified in one of the clauses to lending to customers and others having dealings with the company.

The court then approved of the proposed memorandum of association including the " independent objects " clause.

NOTES

1. The petitioners had argued that in England it had been established that the true rule for construing a memorandum was to seek for the paragraph embodying the main object and treat all the other paragraphs as ancillary, and that the words objected to by the reporter had been inserted for the purpose of obviating this strict rule of interpretation.

2. Contrast *The Union Bank of Scotland Ltd., Petitioners*, 1918 S.C. 21: U. Ltd. presented a petition for confirmation of a memorandum and articles of association in place of its existing contract of copartnership. The memorandum included powers of carrying on banking business without restriction to any locality, of amalgamating with similar companies and of selling the undertaking or assets of the company.

The court *granted* the prayer of the petition, but modified the proposed power of amalgamation and deleted the power to sell the undertaking or assets.

Before the memorandum was approved by the court, an "independent objects" clause was deleted.

3. In *The North of Scotland and Orkney and Shetland Steam Navigation Co. Ltd., Petitioners*, 1920 S.C. 633 (see Note 2 to *John Walker & Sons Ltd., Petitioners*, p. 50, above) the court refused to sanction an "independent objects" clause.

Ultra vires *doctrine*

Life Association of Scotland v. Caledonian Heritable Security Co. Ltd. in Liquidation
(1896) 13 R. 750

C. Ltd., which had power by its memorandum to lend money on heritable security and to do all things incidental or conducive to the attainment of that object, lent £10,500 on a postponed heritable bond over ground occupied by John Wilson & Co.'s bleaching and finishing works. The prior bond was £14,000.

Owing to John Wilson & Co.'s sequestration the premises became vacant, and in order to prevent an immediate sale by the prior bondholder, C. Ltd. entered into an agreement with the prior bondholder by which C. Ltd. became bound to pay interest on the prior bond and became entitled to enter into possession and grant a lease of the premises for five years to a company (John Wilson & Co. Ltd.) to be formed to carry on the works. C. Ltd. also agreed to pay to the prior bondholder the surplus rents after payment of the interest and insurance premiums, and the prior bondholder agreed not to exercise the powers of sale during the lease.

C. Ltd. went into liquidation, and the liquidator rejected the prior bondholder's claim.

Held that the agreement was *ultra vires* of C. Ltd. and could not receive effect, on the ground that the memorandum did not confer power to enter into such an agreement and that it could not be regarded as "incidental or conducive to the attainment" of C. Ltd.'s objects.

The decision followed *Shiell's Trustees* v. *The Scottish Property Investment Building Society in Liquidation* (1884) 12 R.(H.L.) 14, which related to a building society incorporated under the Building Societies Act 1874.

LORD PRESIDENT (INGLIS) (at p. 757): "It was in realising a bond which the building society had obtained over heritable subjects that the directors were said to have done an act that was *ultra vires*. That seems to me to make that case exactly the same as the present. The essence of the judgment of the House of Lords in *Shiell's* case is perhaps better brought out in the opinion of Lord Watson than in that of any of the other Judges who sat in that case. He says (p. 24), - ' The real test is to consider whether the act is authorised by the statutory rules of the society, which here perform a twofold function; in the first place, they define the power of the directors, and in the second place, they ensure that all who deal with the directors shall have notice of the precise limits of their authority. We cannot assume that the directors have power to do everything which may be usually done by unfettered directors or by individuals. We must consider whether the rules confer, either expressly or by any fair implication, authority upon the directors to grant a bond of corroboration binding upon the society. ... It humbly appears to me that the purchase of time by granting an obligation of guarantee is a transaction altogether independent of, and quite separate from, the realisation of a security.' Now, that expresses so entirely my opinion here that I forbear to say more than that I think it is impossible to distinguish the present case from that of *Shiell's Trustees*, and I need only say further that in the principle of *Shiell's* case, as decided in the House of Lords, I entirely concur."

NOTES

1. An issue of preference shares was held to be *ultra vires* and therefore of no effect in *The Waverley Hydropathic Co. Ltd.* v. *Barrowman* (1895) 23 R. 136.

W. Ltd., which by its memorandum and original articles of association had no power to create preference shares, purported to pass a special resolution that the remaining unissued shares of the nominal capital should be preference shares.

Preference shares were applied for and allotted.

In a special case presented by the company and B., an allottee, the company contended that, although the preference given to the shares was invalid, B. was to be regarded as a holder of ordinary shares.

Held that, as B. had not applied for or agreed to take ordinary shares, he was not to be regarded as an ordinary shareholder, but as a creditor of the company, and that he was entitled to repayment of the price with interest, less any dividend which he had received.

Lord Young (at p. 141): " It was *ultra vires* the company to issue these shares, and that being so the issue must be held to be of no effect at all."

2. Regard must be had to the nature of a transaction and not to the means of its execution: *Thompson* v. *J. Barke & Co. (Caterers) Ltd.*, 1975 S.L.T. 67 (O.H.).

Carter, a director of B. Ltd., borrowed £4,000 from T. in June 1968. Some six months later T. received as repayment three cheques for a total of £4,000. Two of these cheques, each for £1,500, were drawn on B. Ltd.'s account. Both were signed by Carter and Stewart, the sole directors and shareholders of B. Ltd. Payment of both cheques was refused by the bank, and T. sued B. Ltd. for £3,000.

B. Ltd. maintained that the issue of the cheques was *ultra vires*, having been for purposes prohibited by section 190 (1) of the Companies Act 1948.

Held that in the question whether an act was *intra* or *ultra vires* of a company regard had to be had to the nature of the transaction and not to the means of execution, that there was nothing in B. Ltd.'s memorandum which entitled T. to assume that the payment had been made for B. Ltd.'s purposes, that the issue of the cheques was *ultra vires* of B. Ltd., and that T. was barred from founding upon them as the circumstances of their issue to him were such as to impose upon him the duty of inquiry. B. Ltd. was therefore assoilzied.

Lord Dunpark (at p. 69): " I frankly admit that I have had difficulty in deciding whether the drawing of these two cheques in favour of the pursuer was *intra vires* or *ultra vires* of the defenders. . . .

" Counsel for the pursuers submitted that as . . . the defenders' memorandum of association gives them express power to draw bills of exchange and other negotiable instruments, these cheques were validly issued by the defenders; but this is a very superficial approach. There is, in my opinion, a clear distinction between the types of business which companies are authorised to conduct (*i.e.* the objects proper) and acts which are expressly or impliedly authorised for the purpose of conducting the authorised businesses (*i.e.* powers). . . . If the memorandum empowers a company to perform administrative acts, such as borrowing money, granting security, drawing bills of exchange, *etc.*, all such powers must be read by any person dealing with the company as if they were qualified by the words ' for the purposes of the company.'. . .

" . . . I am of opinion that, in order to ascertain whether a particular act of a company is *intra* or *ultra vires*, it is necessary to have regard to the nature of the transaction; for it is this, and not the means of execution, which governs its validity. . . . But what was the nature of *this* transaction—was it merely the issue of two cheques? . . . I do not consider that this was the nature of the transaction. It was the repayment by the defenders of a loan made by the pursuer to their director, Carter, and there is nothing in the defenders' memorandum which entitles the pursuers to assume that this payment was made for the defenders' purposes. The issue of the cheques was only the means of making this repayment. . . .

" The issue in this case, simply stated but not easy to answer, is whether the express power to draw bills of exchange precludes me from examining the true nature of the transaction. I have come to the conclusion that it does not and that the issue of these two cheques to the pursuer was *ultra vires* of the company. . . .

" I find for the defenders on the ground that the issue of these two cheques to the pursuer was *ultra vires* of the defenders—alternatively, that the pursuer is barred from founding upon them in respect that the circumstances of their issue to him were such as to impose upon him the duty of inquiry, which he did not make."

Objects: alteration of objects: " to carry on its business more economically or more efficiently "

J. & P. Coats Ltd., Petitioners
(1900) 2 F. 829

C. Ltd., carrying on the business of thread manufacturers and merchants, craved the court to confirm a resolution altering its memorandum of association by adding to it a clause enabling the company to invest its reserve funds and other moneys not immediately required in such stocks and securities as the company or the directors might think proper, on the ground that it was necessary for the company to have large sums of money at its command and that it was more economical to have these invested in marketable securities than deposited in bank.

Petition *granted.*

LORD PRESIDENT (J. B. BALFOUR) (at p. 831): " The first point ... is whether the proposed alteration ... falls under any of the heads specified in the Companies (Memorandum of Association) Act 1890. The only one under which it is said to fall is subsection (5) of section 1, which authorises the court to confirm any alteration, if required to enable the company ' to carry on its business more economically or more efficiently.' That is a very wide expression, and it appears to me that the alteration proposed might conduce to the more economical and more efficient conduct of the company's business."

NOTE

See now Companies Act 1948, s. 5 (1) (*a*).

Objects: alteration of objects: "to attain its main purpose by new or improved means"

The Kirkcaldy Café Co. Ltd., Petitioners
1921 S.C. 681

K. Ltd. had been promoted for the purpose of managing licensed premises mainly with a view to minimising the evils of the drink traffic. Its memorandum of association provided that surplus profits, after payment of a dividend of not more than 4 per cent., should be applied to purposes of public utility.

A proposed alteration of the memorandum consisted of deleting the clause dealing with the application of the profits.

The court *doubted* the competency of this alteration, but *confirmed* an amended alteration increasing the maximum dividend to 6 per cent., as being, in view of the changed financial situation, an " improved means " of attaining the " main purpose " within the meaning of section 9 (1) (*b*) of the Companies (Consolidation) Act 1908.

LORD MACKENZIE (at p. 685): " Nothing that is done to-day will give any encouragement to companies promoted for philanthropic purposes in seeking to get the sanction of this Court to the deletion of a clause which plays so important a part as clause (18) in the present case. It is, however, quite a different question whether, as a matter of practical business, it is not desirable to bring the 4 per cent., which appears in the original clause (18), more into relation with the value of money at the present time; and so far as we are asked to do that, it appears to me that, if the Company passes a resolution with that in view, it would be in the power of this Court to sanction such a course."

NOTE

See now Companies Act 1948, s. 5 (1) (*b*).

Objects: alteration of objects: "to enlarge or change the local area of its operations"

The Scottish Veterans' Garden City Association (Incorporated), Petitioners
1946 S.C. 415

The memorandum of association of a housing association incorporated in 1919 to provide housing accommodation for disabled ex-servicemen included among its objects the acquisition and management of "lands . . . or other heritable property . . . in Scotland."

The association resolved by special resolution to alter its memorandum by insertion of " or real " after " heritable " and " England, Wales or Northern Ireland " after " Scotland."

A reporter, to whom the petition was remitted, expressed some doubt whether the funds belonging to the association might not have been subscribed on the assumption that the association would continue to operate entirely in Scotland.

The court *refused* to confirm the alteration because no reason had been given to justify such an extension of the sphere of operations.

LORD JUSTICE-CLERK (COOPER) (at p. 419): " We have heard nothing to justify the proposed extension; and, if it were granted, it seems to me that considerable consequential amendments would be required in the articles of association. The change, if it is to be a real change and not merely a paper change, would unquestionably involve a material alteration, not only in the area, but in the scope and nature of the association's activities."

NOTES

1. See now Companies Act 1948, s. 5 (1) (c).

2. A condition which may be attached is a change in the company's name. The practice is referred to by the reporter in *The Kirkcaldy Steam Laundry Co. Ltd., Petitioners* (1904) 6 F. 778.

K. Ltd. had been incorporated for the purpose of carrying on a laundry in " Kirkcaldy or its neighbourhood."

It sought confirmation, under the Companies (Memorandum of Association) Act 1890, of a special resolution altering its memorandum so as to enable it to carry on a laundry or laundries in " Kirkcaldy and Leven and elsewhere in the county of Fife."

The court *granted* the petition without requiring any change in the company's name.

The reporter had stated: " In the circumstances, and as it does not appear to me that anyone dealing with this Company would be misled by the present name, your Lordships may perhaps take the view that no change is necessary."

Objects: alteration of objects: " to carry on some business which under existing circumstances may conveniently or advantageously be combined with the business of the company "

Hugh Baird & Sons Ltd., Petitioners
1932 S.C. 455

B. Ltd. had been incorporated to carry on the business of maltsters and hop merchants. It sought confirmation, under section 5 (1) of the Companies Act 192 9, of a special resolution empowering the company to add to its existing business the business of fruit merchants and canners and preserve manufacturers.

Held that the proposed business might conveniently be combined with the existing business.

LORD PRESIDENT (CLYDE) (at p. 457): "The tendency of the Courts is to be generous in relation to proposals of this kind."

LORD SHAND (at p. 458): "The only doubt, as it seems to me, is with regard to jam making, but I can quite see how it may be ancillary to the fruit industry. Fruit is perishable, and it might be hazardous to deal with fruit on a large scale without the means of putting it to a profitable use if there were no immediate market."

NOTES

1. A few days later the Second Division, without delivering opinions, confirmed an alteration under the same provision of the Act of 1929 in *The Dundee Aerated Water Manufacturing Co. Ltd., Petitioners*, 1932 S.C. 473.

The objects of D. Ltd. were "to manufacture, sell, and trade in ginger beer, lemonade, soda water and other aerated waters and drinks." The proposed alteration was to insert after "drinks" the words "and also to bottle, sell, and trade in all alcoholic beers."

2. In *The King Line Ltd., Petitioners* (1902) 4 F. 504, the court, under the Companies (Memorandum of Association) Act 1890, confirmed additions which the reporter had described as "very considerable and wide-reaching in their effects."

K. Ltd.'s business had by its memorandum of association been limited to that of shipowners. By special resolution clauses were added enabling the company (1) to carry on the business of shipbrokers, insurance brokers, &c., (2) to purchase heritable property for the purposes of the company, (3) to erect buildings, warehouses, wharves, factories and machinery on the property of the company, and (4) to amalgamate with other companies having similar objects.

3. The court has in some cases required a change in the company's name:

(a) *The Scottish Accident Insurance Co. Ltd., Petitioners* (1896) 23 R. 586: The company had carried on the business of insurance against accident. It proposed to extend its business to life, sickness, employers' liability and fidelity insurance.

The court *granted* the petition on condition that the name of the company was changed to "The Scottish Accident, Life, and Fidelity Insurance Co. Ltd.," or such other name as might be resolved upon by the company and approved of by the Board of Trade as well as satisfying the court.

(b) *The Scottish Employers' Liability and Accident Assurance Co. Ltd., Petitioners* (1898) 23 R. 1016: The company had been formed for the purpose of carrying on the business of employers' liability and accident insurance. The proposed extension was to make the objects include sickness and guarantee insurance.

Held that, before the petition could be granted, the company's name required to be altered so as to indicate the proposed extension of its business.

(c) *The Mutual Property Insurance Co. Ltd., Petitioners*, 1934 S.C. 61: The company's objects were to carry on every kind of insurance business except life insurance. The proposed alteration was to enable the company to carry on life insurance.

The alteration was confirmed on condition that the company's name was changed to a name such as " The Mutual Property and Life Insurance Co. Ltd."

4. In *The Edinburgh Southern Cemetery Co. Ltd., Petitioners*, 1923 S.C. 867, the court restricted the scope of the additional proposed objects because of lack of evidence that they could " conveniently or advantageously " be combined with the company's existing business.

The company's object was to carry on business as cemetery owners. The proposed additions were to enable it to act as " stone and marble cutters, masons, quarriers and sculptors, florists, gardeners, and undertakers."

The court *granted* the prayer of the petition, but *restricted* the scope of the additional objects to those which were connected with and incidental to the main business of cemetery owners.

5. An instance of the court's refusal to confirm an alteration in the face of opposition to the additional business from a dissenting minority of shareholders is *The Western Ranches Ltd.* v. *Nelson's Trustees* (1899) 1 F. 812.

W. Ltd. had been formed to acquire a cattle ranch in the United States of America. The proposed alteration was to add to the existing business the separate business of lending money on the security of moveable property including livestock or on the personal obligation of persons engaged in the business of dealing in livestock.

A large shareholder objected, and the court *refused* to confirm the alteration, on the ground that the new business, being totally distinct from the company's existing business, could not be forced on dissentient shareholders.

6. See now Companies Act 1948, s. 5 (1) (*d*).

Objects: alteration of objects: " to restrict or abandon any of the objects specified in the memorandum "

The Strathspey Public Assembly and Agricultural Hall Co. Ltd.
v. Anderson's Trustees
1934 S.C. 385

The objects of S. Ltd. were to acquire land in Grantown and

to erect on it a public hall with shops and cellars, to let the hall for public purposes and to let the shops and cellars to tenants.

Some 50 years after erection, the hall with shops and cellars was destroyed by fire, and the company's only asset was the sum recovered under an insurance policy.

The company proposed to alter its memorandum by deleting all reference to erection and letting of a public hall with shops and cellars and substituting provisions for erection and letting of shops and dwelling-houses and warehouses.

Certain shareholders objected on the ground that the proposed alteration would completely alter the nature of the company's undertaking.

Held that, as the proposed alteration involved a fundamental change in the character of the company, it was not one which could be forced on dissentient shareholders; and petition *refused.*

LORD JUSTICE-CLERK (AITCHISON) (at p. 389): " I do not doubt that that is a very material alteration in the objects of the Company as originally conceived. I think the result of such an alteration is that the substratum of the Company has gone. It appears to me to be so material an alteration in the objects of the Company that it should not be forced on dissentient shareholders, who did not invest their money for any commercial purpose or for the revenue-producing purposes proposed by the alterations in the memorandum, but who, indeed, invested their money for public and social purposes. . . .

" Now, if the shareholders of the Company had been unanimous in presenting this petition, it may be that we should have been entitled to authorise it, notwithstanding that the alterations involved some departure from the fundamental object of the Company."

NOTES

1. See now Companies Act 1948, s. 5 (1) (*e*).
2. If shareholders are unanimous, no confirmation by the court is now necessary.

Objects: alteration of objects: " to sell or dispose of the whole or any part of the undertaking of the company "

The Tayside Floorcloth Co. Ltd., Petitioners
1923 S.C. 590

T. Ltd. presented a petition for confirmation of the addition of new objects including (1) power " to procure the company to be incorporated, registered, or recognised in any foreign country," and (2) power "to sell, let on rent, or lease the undertaking of the company, or any branch or part thereof."

The court, while sanctioning the power to procure the registration or recognition of the company in a foreign country, *refused* to confirm the power to procure its incorporation there; and *restricted* the power to sell, rent, or lease the company's undertaking to "any branch or part of the undertaking ... being an adjunct to the main undertaking."

LORD PRESIDENT (CLYDE) (at p. 592): "The difficulty arises on the word 'incorporated.' ... A proposal to authorise the Company to be 'incorporated' elsewhere than in its own domicile may involve risk of change of status, and may expose it, however unintentionally, to alterations in its constitution which might be inconsistent with its establishment as a British limited liability company. ...

"The other matter arises on paragraph (*r*), where a power is asked 'to sell, or let on rent, or lease the undertaking of the Company, or any branch or part thereof.' That, again, is a power which, as the authorities show, the Court does not consider itself entitled to grant. If it were given to a company, the effect would be to authorise the company to commit suicide so far as its own undertaking was concerned—in other words, to do something which is inconsistent with the purpose of its incorporation. There is no harm, of course, in the Company having power to sell such of its assets as it does not need, or in the Company having power to sell part of its concern, so long as its main undertaking remains unimpaired."

NOTES

1. An alteration to enable a company "to sell or dispose of the whole or any part of the undertaking of the company" is now permissible under section 5 (1) (*f*) of the Companies Act 1948. This provision was added by the company legislation of 1929.

2. Cases prior to 1929 which were authority for the decision in this case include the following:

The Glasgow Tramway and Omnibus Co. Ltd. v. *Magistrates of Glasgow* (1891) 18 R. 675: A company formed mainly for the purpose of working certain tramways in Glasgow under a lease from the Corporation proposed to alter its objects by adding *inter alia* the object of promoting and disposing of tramways.

Held that this was an object foreign to the purposes of the memorandum and could not be sanctioned. The other proposed alterations were confirmed.

Young's Paraffin Light and Mineral Oil Co. Ltd., Petitioners (1894) 21 R. 384: The additional powers sought were to acquire the business of any other company carrying on any business which the company might legally carry on, to sell or dispose of the business, property and undertaking of the company, and to amalgamate with any other company in the United Kingdom established for objects similar to its own.

The court *refused* the petition, expressing opinions that the Act of 1890 did not contemplate that such general powers should be conferred before the necessity for using them arose, but that the court would consider any special transaction which the company might wish to carry out under such powers.

John Walker & Sons Ltd., Petitioners, 1914 S.C. 280: The three additional powers sought were similar to those in the last-mentioned case. It was alleged that English practice was to grant such powers.

The court, while confirming the power to acquire similar businesses, *refused* to confirm the other alterations, on the ground that they were not within the alterations authorised by section 9 (1) of the Companies (Consolidation) Act 1908.

The Union Bank of Scotland Ltd., Petitioners, 1918 S.C. 21: The court modified a proposed power of amalgamation and deleted a proposed power to sell the company's undertaking or assets.

The Aberdeen Steam Navigation Co. Ltd., Petitioners, 1919 S.C. 464: The court *confirmed* a power to sell " any part of " the property, rights and business of the company, but *refused* to confirm a power to sell the undertaking.

The North of Scotland and Orkney and Shetland Steam Navigation Co. Ltd., Petitioners, 1920 S.C. 633: The court *granted* the prayer of the petition, subject to abandonment of the proposed power to sell the undertaking of the company, and *refused* to confirm the proposed power to amalgamate.

3. As is seen in *The Aberdeen Steam Navigation Co. Ltd., Petitioners* (above), a distinction is made between sale of assets of the company and sale of the undertaking of the company.

This point is also made by Lord President Clyde in his opinion in *The Tayside Floorcloth Co. Ltd., Petitioners.*

A further illustration is *Metropolitan Reversions Ltd., Petitioners*, 1928 S.C. 480:

M. Ltd. proposed to alter its memorandum by adding powers to carry on, along with its existing business, that of trust investment, and to sell or otherwise dispose of the whole or any part of its property and assets for such consideration as it might think fit, and, in particular, for shares, stock, debentures, debenture stock, or securities of any company purchasing the property or assets.

The court *confirmed* the alteration, *holding* that the proposed power of sale did not involve a sale of the undertaking but merely of assets, and, in view of the extension of the company's business, was germane to its operations as an investment company.

Objects: alteration of objects: not limited to objects clause

The Incorporated Glasgow Dental Hospital v. Lord Advocate
1927 S.C. 400

A dental association, which had been instituted for benevolent purposes, presented a petition for confirmation of an alteration of its memorandum of association, one effect of which was to increase the number of the paid members of its governing body from three to five. This involved an alteration of a clause in the memorandum other than the " objects " clause.

Held that the statutory provision did not limit alteration to an alteration of the objects clause, since the whole objects were not necessarily contained in that clause; and, as the proposed alteration was designed for the better attainment of the objects of the association, petition *granted.*

LORD HUNTER (at p. 406): " The real question is: What is the proper construction of section 9 of the Act of 1908? I do not think that the intention of that section was that a company should necessarily be limited, in connection with the alteration of its memorandum, to an alteration only on what is described as the objects clause of the company. It is quite clear that the whole objects of the company may not necessarily be contained in a single clause, and that, even in the objects clause, you necessarily have material that deals with the objects only in the sense of enabling the proper attainment of these objects to be arrived at. Now, in this case, when Article VI of the memorandum is looked at and read along with Article III, it appears to me that it is just such a clause as might quite properly have been found in Article III. The alteration that is desired to be made is, in effect, an alteration admittedly for the better attainment of the real object of this company."

NOTES

1. In this respect section 5 of the Companies Act 1948 does not differ from section 9 of the Companies (Consolidation) Act 1908.

2. This case was followed in *Scottish Special Housing Association Ltd., Petitioners,* 1947 S.C. 17.

A company formed for the purpose of providing housing accommodation for members of the working classes presented a petition for confirmation of an alteration of clause IV of its memorandum—a clause which provided, *inter alia,* for the remuneration of the chairman and deputy chairman of its council of management. The purpose of the alteration was to enable the company to provide for the superannuation of the chairman and deputy chairman, as it had become necessary to appoint full-time salaried persons to these positions.

Held that the proposed alteration, although not an alteration of the objects clause, was an alteration with respect to the company's objects, since it would authorise the use of the company's funds for a purpose which would enable the objects to be better achieved; and prayer of petition *granted.*

Additional provisions in memorandum: alteration of such provisions

Liquidator of the Milford Haven Fishing Co. Ltd. v. Jones
(1895) 22 R. 577

The memorandum of association of M. Ltd. provided for the division of the capital of the company into preference shares bearing a cumulative preferential dividend and ordinary shares, with power to divide the capital into different classes to be held on terms prescribed by the articles or by special resolution.

The articles contained no provisions as to division of shares into different classes.

By special resolution the company purported to confer priority as to capital on the preference shares.

Held that the special resolution was *ultra vires* of the company, since it was inconsistent with the clause in the memorandum which, by providing for preference in regard to dividends, implied that all the shareholders were to have equal rights on the distribution of capital.

LORD KINNEAR (at p. 582): " I think that the resolution was invalid and ineffectual, both because it is against the contract already made with the existing shareholders, for the company could have no more right to deprive the ordinary shareholders of their equality of distribution than to deprive the preference shareholders of their priority in dividend; and also because it is inconsistent with the conditions of the memorandum, which provide by implication that the ultimate distribution of assets shall be equal, just as clearly as they provide in express terms that there shall be a certain priority of dividend. I think further . . . that those provisions of the memorandum as to a preferential dividend on the one hand and the equal distribution of the surplus assets on the other hand were essential conditions within the meaning of the 12th section of the Act of 1862, and therefore that the resolutions of 1st and 16th March are *ultra vires* and ineffectual."

NOTE

Section 12 of the Companies Act 1862 provided that a company might modify the conditions contained in its memorandum of association for specified purposes (*e.g.* to increase its capital), and concluded with the words " but, save as aforesaid, . . . no alteration shall be made by any company on the conditions contained in its memorandum of association."

Cf. section 4 of the Companies Act 1948: " A company may not alter the conditions contained in its memorandum except in the cases, in the mode and to the extent for which express provision is made in this Act."

CHAPTER 4

ARTICLES OF ASSOCIATION

Relationship between memorandum of association and articles of association

Liquidator of The Humboldt Redwood Co. Ltd. v. Coats
1908 S.C. 751

The memorandum of association of H. Ltd. provided for the division of the capital into ordinary shares and deferred shares. Its articles of association provided that the ordinary shares should have a preferential ranking as to dividend and that on a winding up the shares should be repaid " in the order in which the shares . . . are entitled to rank for payment of dividend."

In the winding up, the deferred shareholders maintained that the provision in the articles for the preferential ranking of the ordinary shareholders in a winding up was inconsistent with the memorandum and therefore invalid, and that the surplus assets fell to be distributed equally among all the shareholders.

Held that there was no inconsistency between the articles and the memorandum, and that in the winding up the ordinary shareholders were entitled to payment of their capital in full before the deferred shareholders received anything on account of their capital.

LORD PRESIDENT (DUNEDIN) (at p. 753): " The argument is that these provisions in the articles of association are bad as being contrary to the terms of the memorandum, and the well-known doctrine is invoked that the memorandum is the ruling document and overrides anything in the articles of association that may be contrary to its provisions.

" As far as I can see there is no inconsistency between the two documents here. The memorandum only states that the capital of the Company is to be divided in certain proportions between two classes of shares. . . . It leaves it to the articles of association to prescribe their respective rights."

NOTES

1. Contrast *Liquidator of the Milford Haven Fishing Co. Ltd.* v. *Jones* (p. 64, above), where the memorandum itself fixed the rights.

2. See also *The Oban and Aultmore-Glenlivet Distilleries Ltd., Petitioners* (p. 167, below): memorandum and articles are contemporaneous documents and are to be read together.

Article not binding if contrary to public policy

St. Johnstone Football Club Ltd v.
Scottish Football Association Ltd.
1965 S.L.T. 171 (O.H.)

A football club brought an action against an association of football clubs, of which it was itself a member, seeking declarator that a censure and fine imposed by the association upon the club was invalid.

Both the football club and the association were limited companies, and the articles of association of the association prohibited any member from taking legal proceedings on any matter except with the previous consent of the Council of the association.

The association pleaded that the club was precluded from bringing the action because it had not had the prior consent of the Council of the association.

Held that the article in question was not wide enough to debar the club's action, and that, if it were, it was contrary to public policy and consequently not binding.

LORD KILBRANDON (at p. 175): " A literal interpretation would lead to an absurdity. . . . I would say that on a construction of Rule 75 the pursuers did not agree to accept as final and binding the decision of the Council on all cases of dispute even between a member and the association itself in which the member was maintaining that the association was in breach of the implied terms of the rules themselves. Secondly, I would say that even if the members had so agreed, then they would not be bound in law by any such agreement as being contrary to public policy. Public policy must surely insist upon a rule that when a new judicial tribunal is set up, albeit by a contract between private persons voluntarily entered into, with privative jurisdiction, then since that tribunal must accept the obligation of conducting its proceedings in accordance with the rules of natural justice, the privative nature of the jurisdiction cannot be permitted to prevent the Court from stepping in to enforce those rules."

Non-member not entitled to found on articles

National Bank of Scotland Glasgow Nominees Ltd. v. Adamson
1932 S.L.T. 492 (O.H.)

Wilkie, the holder of 700 £1 shares in Askit Ltd., was indebted to his bank, and on February 10, 1931, transferred his shares so as to give the bank security over them. He urged the secretary of the company to put the transfer through as soon as possible.

The transfer was registered in the company's books on the same day, with the assent of three directors, but no formal meeting of the directors had been held to pass the transfer.

Wilkie was also indebted to Scottish Amalgamated Silks Ltd., and on February 13, 1931, Adamson and Sharp, the joint liquidators of that company, attempted to arrest Wilkie's 700 shares in the hands of Askit Ltd. They argued that there had been a breach of the articles of Askit Ltd. in the manner in which the transfer of the shares out of Wilkie's name had been made.

Held, in an action brought by the transferee against these liquidators, that the right to the shares had vested in the transferee.

LORD MONCRIEFF (at p. 494): " In the present case the objection is pleaded by a stranger to the company. I am not prepared to hold that in an ordinary case an outside party is entitled to avoid such an administrative act of the company as the passing of a transfer upon an assertion of mere irregularities in matters of domestic management of which members of the company do not complain. . . . Even on the assumption that formal meetings were not held which were required, this was a domestic irregularity of which it is *jus tertii* for the defenders to complain."

Irregularity in alteration of articles: articles as altered incorporated into contract between company and third party

Muirhead v. Forth and North Sea Steamboat Mutual Insurance Association
(1893), 21 R.(H.L.) 1; (1893) 20 R. 442

A mutual insurance company resolved to alter one of its articles by adding to it " that it shall be a condition of insurance that the assured shall keep one-fifth (of the ship) uninsured." The provisions of the Companies Acts were not complied with, but the articles as altered were registered, and were printed on the back of each policy as rules of the insurance. The policy bore *in gremio* that the " articles of association shall be deemed and considered part of this policy."

M. brought an action against the company on a policy granted by the company, and in defence the company stated that M. had violated the condition quoted in that he had insured the vessel for £4,000 altogether, being £250 more than its declared value. The ship was lost at sea.

Held that the articles of association referred to in the policy must be held to be the registered articles, and that the altered article was a valid condition of the insurance.

LORD WATSON (at p. 4): " I . . . am of opinion that according to the right construction of this contract the articles of association referred to in the policy must be taken to be those articles which had been duly registered, and under which the company was trading at the date of the contract. I am not prepared to hold that in a question with a person in the position of this appellant these articles were in any sense invalid. . . . On account of an irregularity in the passing of the resolution, the article might be open to exception at the instance of members of the company in a question with their directors; but in a question between the company and those who *bona fide* traded with it through its directors, these articles were valid in this sense, that the directors could bind the company, and the company could take no exception to a contract made by them on the ground that there had been an irregularity in the manner in which the resolutions were passed.

" . . . The question as between validity and invalidity arising from an irregularity is, to my mind, purely a domestic matter; it is a matter which concerns the company and its directors, and not one which concerns the company dealing with *bona fide* third parties outside."

NOTE

In the extract from Lord Watson's speech, M. is treated as a third party. Since, however, the company was a mutual insurance company, M. was also a member. M. had, therefore, two capacities—that of a third party contracting with the company and that of member. This point is brought out in opinions in the Court of Session.

Alteration of articles: clarification of special rights

Caledonian Insurance Co. v.
Scottish American Investment Co. Ltd.
1951 S.L.T. 23 (O.H.)

The capital of a company was divided into " A " ordinary stock, " B " ordinary stock, and preference stock. Under the articles it was not clear whether the holders of the " B " ordinary stock had any right in surplus assets beyond the payment annually of a preferential dividend of 10 per cent.

Resolutions were passed approving new articles to make it clear that the " B " stock would more properly be described as

" preferential " than as " ordinary," and also for payment of 1s. for every £1 of " B " stock held.

Trustees for debenture stockholders, who were also holders of " A " ordinary stock, brought an action for reduction of the resolutions and for interdict against payment of the 1s.

Held that the resolutions were valid, and decree of *absolvitor* pronounced.

LORD BIRNAM (at p. 24): " I reach the conclusion . . . , without difficulty, that it is in the interests of the company as a whole that the respective rights of the holders of ' A ' and ' B ' ordinary stock should be clarified and that any money which it may be necessary to expend in doing so will be spent for a purpose which is reasonably incidental to the carrying on of the business of the company. The directors are best able to determine what form the clarification should take and they have decided that in the interests of the company it should be made clear that the right to an allocation of new capital should be confined to the holders of ' A ' stock who are truly the only ' ordinary ' members of the company. Clarification in this direction involves the abandonment by the holders of ' B 'ordinary stock of their possible rights under . . . the existing articles of association, and it is admitted by the pursuers that without a cash payment being made to them the ' B ' stockholders would not consent to the proposed alterations.

" It follows from what I have said that in my judgment the proposed payment to the ' B ' stockholders is not a gratuitous payment and that it will not be without benefit to the company. . . . I see nothing illegal or *ultra vires* in what is proposed.

" . . . By making the payment in question to the ' B ' stockholders the result will be not merely to remove any ambiguity from the articles of association but to simplify the administration of the company's affairs."

Alteration of articles: prejudicing minority

Crookston ᴠ. Lindsay, Crookston & Co. Ltd.
1922 S.L.T. 62 (O.H.)

C. was a director and shareholder of L. Ltd., a private company. C. and three other directors held amongst them the whole of the issued shares.

L. Ltd. altered its articles so as to include a provision that any member desiring to sell his shares had first to offer them to the directors at par.

C., alleging that the alteration of the articles had been devised to enable the other three directors ultimately to acquire C.'s shares at a price far below their fair value, sought to interdict the alteration.

Held that the alteration was valid, even although it might have the effect of prejudicing C.'s rights under the original articles.

LORD ASHMORE (at p. 63): "For the complainer it was maintained that the power of alteration conferred by section 13 of the Act of 1908 is not absolute; that there is an implied condition that the power shall be exercised in good faith for the benefit of the company as a whole, whereas in this case what has been averred by the complainer shews that the respondents' actings in the matter are inconsistent with good faith and are really for the purpose of enabling the complainer's fellow directors to acquire his shares to his prejudice; that the proposed alterations are unnecessary for any company purpose and are not conceived for any company benefit. . . .

" . . . The following general comment seems to me to be well founded on the decisions in this branch of the law, *viz.* that an alteration under section 13 of the Act is not invalid merely because it may have the effect of prejudicing the rights under the original articles of a particular shareholder or class of shareholders."

NOTE

The provision of section 13 of the Act of 1908 referred to is now in section 10 of the Companies Act 1948.

Alterations of articles: alteration refused retrospective effect

Liquidator of W. & A. McArthur Ltd. v. The Gulf Line Ltd.
1909 S.C. 732

The articles of G. Ltd. provided " The Company shall have a first and paramount lien and charge on all the shares not fully paid, registered in the name of a member . . . for all calls due on such shares."

M. (South Africa) Ltd., a holder of both fully paid shares and partly paid shares in G. Ltd., transferred the fully paid shares to M. Ltd. at a time when a call was due on the partly paid shares.

The secretary of G. Ltd. refused to recognise the transfer unless M. Ltd. paid the calls due by M. (South Africa) Ltd. on its partly paid shares.

G. Ltd. thereafter altered its articles to the effect of giving it a lien on all shares registered in the name of a member for all calls due on any shares registered in the name of such member.

M. Ltd. presented a petition for rectification of the register.

Held that M. Ltd. was not affected by the subsequent alteration of the articles, and was entitled to have its name placed on the register in accordance with the articles in force at the time when the transfer had been presented.

LORD LOW (at p. 735): " The only statutory authority relied upon was the 50th section of the Companies Act of 1862, which gives a company power to 'alter... the articles of association....' That section makes it competent to alter the regulations during the existence of the Company, and declares the altered regulations to be as valid as if they had been original regulations, but it does not provide that an altered regulation shall be held to have come into force as at the date when the Company was formed. The alteration comes into force at its own date . . . . There is also this further element that the alteration was made, not so much because the directors deemed it to be an alteration required in the general interests of the Company, as simply in order to meet the particular case of the petitioner's transfer."

NOTES

1. Section 50 of the Act of 1862 corresponds to section 10 of the Companies Act 1948.

2. *Allen* v. *Gold Reefs of West Africa Ltd.* [1900] 1 Ch. 656 was referred to by the respondents, but was not mentioned in the opinions.

3. *Allen's* case had been commented on in *Moir* v. *Duff & Co. Ltd.* (1900) 2 F. 1265, in which the question was raised, but did not require to be decided, whether a new article confirmed by the company after an action had been raised could affect the pursuer's right to be registered.

Held that the pursuer, even under the original articles, was not entitled to insist on registration.

CHAPTER 5

PROMOTERS

Fiduciary position: company entitled to recover promoter's profit

Henderson v. The Huntington Copper and Sulphur Co. Ltd.
(1877) 5 R.(H.L.) 1; (1877) 4 R. 294

A company formed for the purchase of certain mines in Canada at the price of £125,000 issued a prospectus in which H. was named as a director.

H. received £10,000 from the vendor of the mines, in consideration, as H. alleged, of certain services rendered and to be rendered by him to the company.

The company brought an action against H. for repetition of the £10,000.

Held that the company was entitled to recover, since (1) the true price of the mines was only £115,000, (2) H., standing in a fiduciary relation to the company from the date when he agreed to become a director, could not enter into a contract with the vendor for his own benefit, and (3) in fact H. had not rendered or come under any obligation to render services worth £10,000 to the company.

LORD CHANCELLOR (CAIRNS) (at p. 4): "There is nothing better settled upon the authority of the cases . . . than that in a case of this kind and under circumstances of this kind no payment by him who is selling to a public company, made to those who are to be the directors and managers of the company, can stand if the consideration for the payment be their affording their services as the fiduciaries, the trustees, the directors of the company."

LORD O'HAGAN (at p. 7): "The arrangement was made in contemplation of the formation of a company, of which company the appellant was to be a director. . . .

"The appellant, relying upon that arrangement, cannot refuse to take the consequences of it, and one of those consequences undoubtedly was to place him in the fiduciary position, *eo instanti* that the arrangement was made. What was the effect of that? . . . It appears to me that the effect of it was, in the first place, with reference to the directorship, to make this payment of £10,000, if it were to be made at all, a mere bribe to the appellant to induce him to take the position of director."

The opinions of the Court of Session judges were approved of in the House of Lords.

LORD PRESIDENT (INGLIS) (at p. 307): "The position of the defender is that he received £10,000 for giving his name as a director, and for getting up the company along with those other persons. . . . I think . . . that he just accepted the £10,000 as a bribe to induce him to bring this company into existence, and to make himself a director of the company— he accepted the £10,000 as the consideration upon which he was to perform that office for the vendors of the mine, and thus he placed himself in the position of having a trust duty to perform and a personal interest directly conflicting with that trust duty."

LORD MURE (at p. 306): "It appears to me that this is a very clear case for applying the general rule which runs through all the cases on the subject, *viz.,* that parties in the position of trustees are not permitted to make profit by that position. . . . Now, I think, in the circumstances of this case, the defender was substantially a trustee, and his duty was to endeavour to acquire the copper mine at as low a price as possible from the parties who were selling it to the company. His duty was to beat down the price to be paid to the lowest possible figure for which the property could be acquired. This was his duty as a trustee. But, on the other hand, he was only to get this £10,000, as I understand the case, if the company was floated; so that he had a material interest to get the company started, whatever the cost might be to the other shareholders, in order to get the £10,000. His interests were therefore plainly in conflict with his duty; and on that ground alone he is not, as I apprehend, entitled to retain the £10,000."

NOTES

1. The principle of this case was extended to the situation where the profit was to go to the prospective director's firm in *Scottish Pacific Coast Mining Co. Ltd.* v. *Falkner, Bell, & Co.* (p. 75, below).

2. A comparable case, relating to a statutory company, is *Mann* v. *Edinburgh Northern Tramways Co.* (1892) (p. 76, below), but at the later stage of that case—*Edinburgh Northern Tramways Co.* v. *Mann* (1896) (p. 76, below)—doubts were expressed as to the analogy between the positions of an ordinary trustee and a promoter.

Profit to promoter's firm: no disclosure to shareholders

Scottish Pacific Coast Mining Co. Ltd. v. Falkner, Bell, & Co.
(1888) 15 R. 290

Sutherland, being desirous of selling certain mines in California, entered into an agreement with F. & Co. under which half of any profit on the sale of the mines would be paid by Sutherland to F. & Co.

Thereafter a mining company was incorporated to purchase the mines, and Walker, a partner of F. & Co., was named in the company's prospectus as a provisional director, and he subsequently acted as one of the company's first directors.

The agreement between Sutherland and F. & Co. was never communicated to the shareholders.

Held that, as Walker had, with the knowledge of his firm, occupied a fiduciary position towards the company in the purchase of the mines, the firm was bound to repay £7,000, its share of the profit, to the company.

LORD MURE (at p. 303): "The case is, I think, clear, and distinctly ruled, in so far as Mr. Walker is concerned, by the decision of this court in the case of the *Huntington Copper Company*. . . .

"The circumstance that the question is here raised with the firm of Falkner, Bell, & Company and not directly with Mr. Walker, which is the main distinction I see between this and the case of *Huntington*, cannot, in my opinion, be held to make any difference in the application of the general rule, more particularly in a case where, as here, the firm were throughout quite well aware that their leading partner was acting as a director of the company. The firm, in a question of this description cannot, in the view I take of it, be in any better position than the partner himself who assumed the fiduciary character."

LORD ADAM (at p. 305): "There is a great deal of parole and other evidence upon this point, as to whether or not it is proved that Mr. Walker communicated his position with reference to the vendor to his co-directors. . . . Now, my view of the evidence on this point is, that it is entirely immaterial whether he did or did not communicate his position to his co-directors. What I think is material is, that he concealed his position— that he was to make a profit out of the transaction—from the company. Whether he concealed that, not from his co-directors, but from the company, is the question. In my opinion no amount of disclosure to his co-directors would relieve him from liability in respect of concealment from the company."

NOTE

For the *Huntington* case referred to, see p. 73, above.

Payment to promoters: lump sum for promotion distinguished from remuneration for professional services: statutory company

Mann v. Edinburgh Northern Tramways Co.
(1892) 20 R.(H.L.) 7; (1891) 18 R. 1140

and

Edinburgh Northern Tramways Co. v. Mann
(1896) 23 R. 1056

The special Act incorporating a tramway company provided that " the company shall pay all costs, charges, and expenses of and incident to the preparing for obtaining and passing of this Act, or otherwise in relation thereto."

Mann and Beattie were the principal promoters of the Act, and afterwards became solicitor and engineer respectively of the company.

Shortly after the Act had been obtained, Mann and Beattie, on behalf of the company, entered into a contract with a cable company by which the cable company was, for the sum of £93,000, to make the required tramways and to pay the expense of obtaining the Act.

The following day Mann and Beattie as individuals entered into an agreement with the cable company by which, for the sum of £17,000, Mann and Beattie were to relieve the cable company of the obligation to pay the expense of obtaining the Act.

Held (1892) that the two agreements were to be regarded as one transaction and that in so far as the second agreement authorised Mann and Beattie to retain any part of the £17,000 beyond the actual expenses incurred in obtaining the Act it was illegal.

Held (1896) that Mann and Beattie were not barred from receiving remuneration for professional services rendered by them, by reason of their having been promoters of the Act at the time when the services were rendered.

(*1892*)

LORD CHANCELLOR (HERSCHELL) (at p. 9): "The real effect of the transaction . . . was this, that one is to treat £76,000 as paid for works, and £17,000 . . . as paid in effect to Messrs. Mann and Beattie in order that out of it they might pay the expenses incurred in obtaining the Act, and keep the residue for themselves.

". . . The only question is, whether they are bound to account and shew how much they have so expended, or whether they can keep the residue, however great it may be beyond those expenses, for their own benefit.

". . . This is a company created by Act of Parliament which has no right to spend a penny of its money except in the manner provided by the Act of Parliament. . . .

"Now in the present case the 78th section . . . has sanctioned expenses, costs, and charges coming within the definition of that section. But the payment of any money whatsoever to Messrs. Mann and Beattie not necessary for the discharge of those obligations is a payment out of the assets of the company—that is in effect the money of the company . . . , which the company have no right to apply in the manner in which they do apply it if Messrs. Mann and Beattie keep anything beyond the sum necessary to discharge those expenses."

LORD WATSON (at p. 11): "It would be intolerable that persons employed by a company to make a contract on its behalf should be able either directly or indirectly to secure a pecuniary advantage to themselves, for which they have given no consideration, at the company's expense. . . .

". . . It is beyond the power either of promoters or of directors or of shareholders to apply the moneys of the company which are devoted by statute to special purposes to any purpose which is not sanctioned by the provisions of the Act of incorporation."

(*1896*)

LORD McLAREN (at p. 1066): "It may not be strictly accurate to describe the promoter of a private bill as an agent for a company which does not exist until the bill becomes an Act; but if Parliament thinks fit to recognise his services in obtaining the Act, and gives him a claim against the company for his costs and charges, I think it is a condition of his claim that he must put himself in the position of an agent for the company which he has promoted, and must regulate his relations towards the company according to the duty of an agent. . . . But I do not find in the opinions delivered in the House of Lords, or in this Court, any expressions which imply that the defenders were disentitled to fair professional remuneration for services of which the company had the benefit. To say that they were trustees is to assume the question. Persons who agree to act as trustees are understood to give their services gratuitously. . . . But in the present case there is no trust. The defenders never agreed to undertake any fiduciary duties that I know of, and I venture to think that it is only in a very remote and unreal sense that the language of trust law can be used with reference to the relation of a company to its promoters. I think that the services of promoters and especially these professional services, are fairly within the scope of such a clause as this 78th section, which authorises the payment of costs and charges connected with obtaining the Act.

" On the subject of the decisions which touch this point, I have nothing material to add, because I agree in the Lord Ordinary's statement of their import."

Lord Ordinary (Kincairney) (at p. 1059): " I do not think that the point now raised, viz., whether a promoter is entitled to credit for professional charges, was decided in the Court of Session in the case of *The Huntington Copper Company*. Neither do I think that any distinct opinion on the point was expressed in the House of Lords. . . .

" I think that the analogy between a trustee and a promoter is defective, and that all the principles and practice applicable to a trustee cannot be applied to a promoter. Mann and Beattie were not in a strict sense trustees when they were engaged in promoting the company. They could not be, because they had no constituent or beneficiary. . . . It cannot be affirmed that, during the whole time when a promoter is concerned with the promotion of a company, he is under the disabilities of a trustee. . . .

" There is no doubt that a promoter cannot make secret profits, and that all promotion money is illegal. But I cannot affirm that his duties towards the company he promotes are the same as the duties of a trustee towards the trust-estate, or towards the beneficiaries under the trust law, and I think that it is stretching the analogy of trust law too far to affirm that a promoter can never be paid for his professional services in virtue of a clause which requires the company to pay the costs, charges, and expenses incident to the obtaining of the Act. . . .

" On the whole, I come to the conclusion that there is no sufficient authority for applying to the case of a promoter the rule that a trustee cannot be allowed his professional charges, and that such charges may be allowed under the words ' costs, charges, and expenses ' in the 78th section of the pursuers' Act."

NOTES

1. For the case of *The Huntington Copper Company* referred to, see p. 73, above.

2. A similar distinction between promotion money and professional remuneration may be seen by a contrast of two cases decided in 1903 —*Muir* v. *Forman's Trustees* (1903) 5 F. 546 and *Mason's Trustees* v. *Poole & Robinson* (1903) 5 F. 789.

Muir v. *Forman's Trustees*: The special Act incorporating a railway company provided that if the undertaking were abandoned, then the Parliamentary deposit " shall be applied in the discretion of the Court as part of the assets of the Company for the benefit of the creditors thereof . . . ," and that " all costs, charges and expenses of and incident to the preparing for, obtaining, and passing of this Act, or otherwise in relation thereto, shall be paid by the Company."

The undertaking was abandoned, and a process was raised to determine the rights of parties to the Parliamentary deposit fund—the only asset of the company.

Held that (1) solicitors and engineers who had given their professional services in preparing and carrying through Parliament the Bill for the creation of the company were creditors of the company and entitled to recover payment of their accounts out of the deposit fund, although they had given their services, not on the employment of anyone, but solely in the prospect of being remunerated by the company when formed; and (2) in the exercise of its discretion in the distribution of the assets the court could give direct effect to the claims of professional persons who had given their services in the promotion of the company on the employment of the professional promoters.

Lord President (Kinross) (at p. 565): " The fact of a man being a promoter does not, *per se*, form a ground for holding that he is not entitled to remuneration for professional services rendered in obtaining an Act of Parliament for the Company—*Edinburgh Northern Tramways Company* v. *Mann*."

Mason's Trustees v. *Poole & Robinson*: The special Act incorporating the Dundee Suburban Railway Company anthorised payment from the funds of the company of the cost of obtaining the Act.

Shortly after its incorporation the company granted an acknowledgment of indebtedness for £5,000, being 2 per cent. on its authorised capital, to M., an expert on railway matters, for services rendered under an agreement which had been entered into between M. and the promoters and under which M. had agreed to aid in the obtaining of the special Act and in negotiations with neighbouring railways.

The undertaking was abandoned, and proceedings were raised for distribution of the company's assets.

Held that the agreement to pay a lump sum for M.'s services, irrespective of their value, and not subject to official taxation or audit, was *ultra vires* of the company and that M. was not entitled to claim as a creditor upon its funds.

Lord President (Kinross) (at p. 798): " It is to be observed that Mr. Mason did not belong to any of the professions the members of which have known rights and are subject to known responsibilities and liabilities."

Expenses of promotion: whether promoters or company liable

Welsh & Forbes v. Johnston
(1906) 8 F. 453

W. & F., a firm of law-agents, brought an action against partners of a dissolved firm for an account incurred for work done in connection with the transfer of the dissolved firm's business to a new limited company, the whole transaction, including the formation and flotation of the company having been undertaken by W. & F.

Opinions that W. & F. were entitled to charge a commission on the flotation against the promoters, but not against the sellers.

LORD PRESIDENT (DUNEDIN) (at p. 457): " When a company is promoted, somebody of course must promote it, and he is generally known as a promoter; and in promoting a company he of course incurs a certain amount, it may possibly be a great deal, of expense. Presumably it is all with a view to his own future advantage in some way; but he, the promoter, or the band of promoters, whoever they may be, are the only people who are liable for that expense, though of course they may take any other person bound to relieve them of that expense. . . . If they chose to do the work of promoting the company themselves and employed a law-agent, they must of course be liable to that law-agent for what he had done; but then they would be liable directly as promoters themselves, and not in any way as the sellers of the subjects. To go on to the next step, of course promoters do not get up companies to benefit the world generally, but to benefit themselves, and therefore a very usual stipulation to put in the articles of association of the new company, and a very natural and proper one, is to make the new company relieve the promoters of the expense they have incurred in the promotion of the company. There have been plenty of decisions on that subject, and it has been perfectly well settled that a new company can never be liable in any expenses incurred before its birth, unless that liability is assumed by the instrument which brings it into the world, namely, the memorandum and articles of association."

LORD McLAREN (at p. 459): " I think that the real promoters should pay the promotion expenses, unless they are able to induce the shareholders whom they take into their company to accept that liability as an element in the constitution of the company."

NOTES

1. *Scott* v. *Money Order Co. of Great Britain and Ireland Ltd.* (1870) 42 Sc.Jur. 212 is an instance of liability being assumed by the company's constitution.

The articles provided: " The capital may be applied . . . in discharge of all the expenses of and incident to the promotion . . . and all preliminary expenses of the company, and for the general purposes of the company, as the board may think fit."

Held that S., the patentee of inventions which the company had been incorporated to work, was entitled to constitute against the company in liquidation a debt of £400 which he alleged was remuneration due to him for services rendered to the company by him before its incorporation.

2. In *J. M. & J. H. Robertson* v. *Beatson, McLeod, & Co. Ltd.,* 1908 S.C. 921, where a company, B. Ltd., had engaged Fulton, a C.A., to carry out an amalgamation of B. Ltd. with another company, and Fulton employed R. & Co., a firm of solicitors, for part of the work, R. & Co. were held to have no enforceable claim against B. Ltd. for their charges, expenses and outlays, on the ground that Fulton had had no authority from B. Ltd. to employ the solicitors.

Lord McLaren drew a parallel between amalgamation and promotion, saying (at p. 928): " If this had been the ordinary case of the promotion of a company, the law is perfectly well settled. Wherever, in order to establish a new commercial undertaking, it is necessary that law-agents, engineers, or other experts, should be employed by the promoters, these persons have a claim against the promoters who are liable to them, and against no other person unless that person can be shewn to have taken over the obligation. It is not unusual in such cases that the company undertakes to relieve the promoters of their obligation, and to pay the preliminary expenses. I suppose there are few companies that do not give some undertaking of the kind; but supposing that they do not choose to do it, the experts employed by the promoters have no claim except against the person who employed them. I do not think the principle is varied by the fact that in this case the object proposed was an amalgamation of two existing companies in order to form a third; because the question still remains, who employed this law-agent?"

CHAPTER 6

PROSPECTUS

Definition: not issued to the public generally: not containing an invitation to take shares

Sleigh v. The Glasgow and Transvaal Options Ltd.
(1904) 6 F. 420

Before the formation of G. Ltd., S. received from Dalzell, to whom he was personally known, a document relating to the proposed company and naming Dalzell as one of six provisional directors. Accompanying the document was a letter advising S. to apply for shares.

About 40 copies of the document were similarly distributed by the provisional directors to their business friends, who were in turn requested to place it before their friends or clients.

The document itself contained no invitation to take shares, and it stated that the proposed company was to be a private one.

S. applied for and was allotted shares, but subsequently presented a petition for rectification of the register by the removal of his name on the ground that the document in question was a prospectus, that he had applied for his shares on the faith of it and that it contained misrepresentations and omitted information required to be stated in a prospectus.

G. Ltd. denied that the document was a prospectus.

It was not proved that G. Ltd. after its formation had adopted or issued copies of the document.

Held that (1) the document was not a prospectus within the meaning of the statutory provisions, since it was not issued to the public generally and did not contain an invitation to take shares, and (2) G. Ltd., not having adopted the document, was not responsible for its contents.

LORD PRESIDENT (KINROSS) (at p. 426): "In section 30 of the Act of 1900, it is declared that unless the context otherwise requires, the expression 'prospectus' means any prospectus 'notice, circular, advertisement, or other invitation, offering to the public for subscription or purchase, any shares or debentures of a company.' Two main things are here required, (1) it must be an offer of shares, and (2) it must be an offer to the public, *i.e.*, to the public generally. . . . The document to which the present question relates . . . is a short typewritten document, not signed by anyone, and the proper inference which I think is to be drawn from its character and tenor . . . is, that it was not intended to be a prospectus in the statutory sense, or to be issued to the public. It bears that ' the Company will be a private one,' and if the document in question had been a ' prospectus ' in the sense of the Act, it would undoubtedly have been disconform to the Act of 1900. . . .

" I am . . . , *separatim,* of opinion that, upon the evidence adduced, it is not established that the petitioner applied for the shares which he holds in reliance upon anything contained in the so-called prospectus. He was a friend of Mr. Dalzell . . . and I think the proper inference from the evidence is that he (the petitioner) became a shareholder in consequence of the information which he received from Mr. Dalzell."

NOTES

1. " Private company " in the context of this case does not refer to the statutory form of private company—which was not introduced until the Companies Act 1907.

2. For the second ground given by the Lord President—reliance on the so-called prospectus—see *McMorland's Trustees* v. *Fraser* (p. 88, below).

Rescission for material misrepresentation

Blakiston v. The London and Scottish Banking and Discount Corporation Ltd.
(1894) 21 R. 417

A prospectus relating to the formation of L. Ltd. stated that Scrafton was to be one of the directors.

On March 8, B., relying on that statement, applied for shares, and on March 14 received a letter of allotment.

On March 11, however, Scrafton had withdrawn his consent to become a director.

B. subsequently presented a petition for rectification of the register of L. Ltd. by the removal of his name and for repayment of the sum paid by him for the shares.

Held that B. was entitled to have his petition granted.

LORD KINNEAR (at p. 425): " If it be proved—and I think it is proved—that Mr. Blakiston made his offer in reliance on the reputation of Mr. Scrafton, and that at the time his offer was accepted by the allotment of shares the administration of the company were perfectly well aware that Mr. Scrafton had not agreed, and did not intend to agree, to be a director, then I think the petitioner has made out his case, that he has been induced to make this contract in reliance on representations material to induce to that result, and that that representation was made by the company in the knowledge that it was in fact untrue. I am therefore of opinion that the prayer of the petition should be granted."

NOTE

Contrast *Chambers* v. *The Edinburgh and Glasgow Aerated Bread Co. Ltd.* (1891) 18 R. 1039.

The prospectus stated that Mr. Esslemont, M.P., was to be the chairman and Dr. Clark, M.P., one of the directors of a company.

The company was wound up because of a mistake in the memorandum as to the registered office.

A new company was formed, and in a circular sent along with the prospectus of the new company to persons who had applied for shares in the original company there was a statement that " as the company will now fall to be managed in Glasgow, Messrs. Esslemont and Clark, the two Members of Parliament (whose parliamentary duties will prevent their attendance at the board), . . . have retired."

C. and a number of other persons who had applied for shares in the original company applied for shares in the new company after receiving that circular, but later sought to have their names removed from the register of members on the ground that the statement in the circular was false, the true reason why Esslemont and Clark had retired being that they were dissatisfied with the prospects of the company.

Held that, as the shareholders concerned had applied for shares after the distinct statement that Esslemont and Clark were not to be on the board, it was irrelevant to inquire into the truth of the reasons stated in the circular for their retirement.

Lord McLaren (at p. 1046): " The fact that Messrs. Esslemont and Clark had retired was all that the public had any legitimate concern with, and that fact having been duly intimated, the petitioners cannot be said to have taken their shares in reliance upon these gentlemen being on the board."

(In relation to the civil liability for mis-statements in a prospectus provided for in s. 43 of the Companies Act 1948, a person who has consented to become a director and who, after the issue of the prospectus and before allotment, becomes aware of any untrue statement and withdraws his consent, is required—in order to escape liability—to give reasonable public notice of the withdrawal *and of the reason for it*.)

Discrepancy between prospectus and memorandum: misrepresentation which was not material

The City of Edinburgh Brewery Co. Ltd. v. Gibson's Trustee
(1869) 7 M. 886

The prospectus of a proposed brewery company set forth the special advantage in the trade of a large capital, and that the company's capital would be £50,000, " with power to increase."

The memorandum stated the nominal capital at £50,000, " to be varied, reduced, or increased in the manner provided by the articles."

Held that the discrepancy between the prospectus and the memorandum was not such as to entitle G., who had taken shares, to have his name removed from the register.

The prospectus set forth that " a large number of gentlemen in the trade and others have become shareholders."

When the register was made up, there were 55 shareholders, of whom 10 or 12 were connected with the trade.

Held that there was here no such misrepresentation as to entitle G. to have his name removed from the register.

LORD PRESIDENT (INGLIS) (at p. 890): " The defender maintains that Mr. Gibson was, and that his representative is, entitled to be relieved from all liability as a partner, on two grounds—(1) that the company, as constituted, by the articles of association and memorandum of association, was essentially different from the company proposed by the prospectus; and (2) that Mr. Gibson was induced to take the shares by fraudulent representations contained in the prospectus.

" As regards the first of these defences, . . . I entertain no doubt that if the business of a company should be described in the prospectus as being of one distinctive character, and the business as ultimately fixed by the memorandum of a clearly different character, the person who has been induced on the faith of the prospectus to take shares will, as soon as he discovers the variance, be entitled to have his name removed from the register, because the company of which he undertook to become a partner is not the company of which he has been made a partner by the insertion of his name in the register. And the same would hold if the extent of the business undertaken by the company as incorporated were greatly in excess of what was proposed by the prospectus, though of the same kind. . . .

" In the present case, however, . . . it is, I think, quite clear that the difference between the prospectus and the memorandum is not such as to entitle the defender to the relief he seeks. The power to diminish the capital of the company neither changes the character of the business, nor exposes the partners to any indefinite extension of the business or of the risk; it is nothing else than a power (very prudently as it seems to me) reserved to the company to limit the extent of the capital, if they find that they cannot advantageously employ the whole of it in the business of the company.

" The defence founded on allegations of fraudulent representations in the prospectus stands in a different position. If this can be established, there can be no doubt that the defender is entitled to be liberated from his obligations as a partner, provided he can shew that these representations induced him to take the shares, and that they were material to the risk he was thereby undertaking, and either that they were false, within the knowledge of the partners, or were made by the promoters in ignorance of whether they were false or true.

" But here, again, the facts as proved are quite insufficient to let in the application of this rule. . . . The gentlemen in the trade were . . . about 20 per cent of the whole existing shareholders, and if this proportion, or anything like it, had been maintained in giving off the remainder of the 5,000 shares, it could hardly be said that there was not a large proportion of the shareholders engaged in the trade. . . . It seems out of the question to hold this to be a fraudulent representation in any relevant or available sense of the term. The law will not allow persons who have become partners in such a company to escape from liability merely on account of some high colouring or grandiloquence in a statement of the prospectus which is substantially true."

NOTE

Cf. Liverpool Palace of Varieties Ltd. v. Miller (1896) 4 S.L.T. 153 (O.H.), an action for calls on 200 shares allotted to M.

In defence M. alleged that statements in the prospectus as to the highly profitable nature of variety companies contained misleading figures. He averred that statements such as " The property to be taken over by the Company is the only first-class fully licensed variety theatre in Liverpool " were untrue, the theatre being a very second-class establishment and of undoubtedly bad fame.

Held that M. had no relevant defence, since his allegations related to matters of opinion and belief, and were too vague and general to be remitted to proof.

Rescission for fraudulent misrepresentation: company not entitled to take benefit from fraudulent statements of director in prospectus

Mair v. The Rio Grande Rubber Estates Ltd.
(1913) S.C.(H.L.) 74

R. Ltd., formed for acquiring a rubber estate in the Philippines, issued a prospectus in which was quoted a report on the natural advantages of the estate by Littler, one of the directors of R. Ltd. Littler was stated to be acquainted with the locality. The prospectus also bore that no portion of the price of the estate would be paid until the directors had received an independent report confirming Littler's statements.

M., who had received the prospectus and had applied for and been allotted 200 shares, brought an action against R. Ltd. for removal of his name from the register of members and for repayment of the price of the shares, on the ground that he had been induced to apply for them by the statements in the report quoted in the prospectus, which statements he averred were false and fraudulent.

R. Ltd. maintained that the action was irrelevant, the directors having in the prospectus not only not vouched for, but expressly refrained from committing themselves to, the truth of the statements made in the report.

Held that M. had stated a relevant case, since the prospectus had been put forward by the company as an inducement to take shares and the company could therefore not take benefit from the false and fraudulent statements of their agent which it contained.

Opinion (*per* Lord Shaw) that M. would have been entitled to succeed if the statements had been merely false without being fraudulent.

Lord Chancellor (Haldane) (at p. 77): " The representation here was a continuing one, and the Company authorised it to be put forward as made by Mr. Littler, and if it was false and fraudulent on his part the Company which authorised it to be made can no more retain money subscribed on the faith of it than it could had the whole board of directors been guilty."

Lord Shaw of Dunfermline (at p. 80): " Each and every director is the agent of the Company to make the representations which the prospectus contains, and to induce applications for shares on the basis of those representations. . . .

" The representations accordingly being taken to emanate from the Company, and the whole body of directors or signatories of the prospectus, the case becomes a simple one. In the view which I take of it, it is sufficient in such circumstances that the material representations, or any of them, inducing the contract were untrue, and it is not necessary separately and substantially to establish fraud in such a case. Fraud is averred on the record. . . . For rescission of a contract to take shares, on the ground of misrepresentation in the prospectus, it is not necessary to prove a knowledge by the directors or signatories of that document of its untruth. This is in entire accord with a whole body of case law on the subject in recent times."

Rescission: " on the faith of " the prospectus

McMorland's Trustees v. Fraser
(1896) 24 R. 65

M. applied for shares " upon the terms of the prospectus," and shares were allotted to him.

Later, M.'s representatives brought an action against the directors of the company for the purpose of obtaining compensation provided for by the Companies Act 1867. The statutory provision was restricted to persons who had taken shares " on the faith of " a prospectus.

M.'s representatives founded on the terms of M.'s application, and proved that the prospectus had been widely advertised in Glasgow where M. had been living.

There was, however, no direct evidence that M. had read the prospectus, and the directors were able to prove that M. had applied for the shares in reliance on advice of one of the directors who had been a personal friend of M.

Held that M.'s representatives, having failed to prove that the shares had been applied for on the faith of the prospectus, were not entitled to claim the statutory compensation.

Lord Trayner (at p. 78): " I agree . . . with the Lord Ordinary in thinking that there is not sufficient evidence to shew that Mr. McMorland took his shares on the faith of the prospectus. I think one might go farther, and say that there is no evidence in support of the view that he did so. That Mr. McMorland saw the prospectus in some newspaper is probable, but by no means certain. Still less is it certain that he ever read it or relied on it in applying for shares. My opinion on this matter is, that Mr. McMorland applied for shares solely on the ground that Mr. McKillop represented it to be, what he thought it was, an investment which promised favourable results."

NOTES

1. Reliance on the prospectus is equally essential to a common law action for rescission.

2. For the statutory provision, see now Companies Act 1948, s. 43.

3. See also *Sleigh* v. *The Glasgow and Transvaal Options Ltd.* (p. 82, above).

Rescission for misrepresentation: shareholders must act timeously

Caledonian Debenture Co. Ltd. v. Bernard
(1898) 5 S.L.T. 392 (O.H.)

Shortly before the formation of C. Ltd., B. received a draft prospectus, which contained a reference to the possibility of some subscribers being willing to pay their shares in full, in which case it was stated that the amount so paid in advance would rank for a cumulative preferential dividend of 5 per cent.

On the faith of this document, B., on February 8, 1894, applied for 400 shares of £5 each.

On February 20, a memorandum of association was issued which provided that those shareholders who paid up their shares in full were to have a preference over capital.

On the same day, B. signed a regular application form " with reference to the memorandum of association," and received an allotment.

On being sued for calls, B. argued that he had never truly agreed to become a shareholder because he understood from the prospectus that shareholders who paid up their shares in full were to have only a preference for dividends, whereas he had found that by the memorandum they were to have a preference over capital.

Held that B. was liable for the calls, since he had delayed too long.

LORD STORMONTH DARLING (at p. 393): " The general principle applicable to all cases of this kind is that any man who seeks to rescind his contract as a shareholder must exercise his right of repudiation within a reasonable time. . . . But where the claim to repudiate is based on variance between the prospectus and the memorandum, there is a further rule, which has been repeatedly announced . . . *viz.,* that a shareholder who has the means of immediate access to the memorandum, or who knows that within a very short time he must have it, because no company can be registered without one, is bound to use all reasonable despatch in informing himself of the terms of . . . 'the charter of the Company.' . . . The duty of a shareholder in the position of the defender, to take active steps for having his name removed from the register, if he discovers that he has grounds for doing so, is just as precise and stringent as the duty timeously to examine the memorandum of association. . . . The rule is founded on the principle that it is unfair for a man, who thinks he has a claim of this kind, to leave his name on a register, and thereby mislead his fellow-shareholders and the creditors of the Company. The present case is unusually strong for applying the rule. There is evidence that the presence of the defender's name, he being a man of substance, was an element in inducing the bank, at the outset of the Company, to lend money to it. The defender's defence comes too late, both on the ground that he ought to have examined the articles of association sooner than he did, and also on the ground that, after he did examine it, he ought to have taken effective steps to have his name removed from the register."

NOTES

1. In *The City of Edinburgh Brewery Co. Ltd.* v. *Gibson's Trustee* (p. 85, above), which also concerned a discrepancy between a prospectus and the memorandum, Lord President Inglis said (at 7 M. 891): "In the absence of fraud, it may be greatly doubted whether the applicant for shares is not bound to make himself acquainted with the terms of the memorandum of association as soon as it is registered, and whether, if he allows his name to be put on the register after this, he is not bound by the terms of the memorandum."

In that case, however, it is not necessary to decide that question, since the difference between the prospectus and the memorandum was held to be not sufficiently material.

2. Liquidation puts an end to the right to rescind, *e.g.* in *The Western Bank of Scotland* v. *Addie* (1867) 5 M.(H.L.) 80, in which A. attempted to reduce a sale of shares to him by the company but not until after the company had converted itself from a common law company into a registered company for the purposes of winding up, Lord Chancellor (Chelmsford) said (at p. 86): "It is clear. however, upon the authorities, that, after the crisis had arrived of the failure of the company, and the order for winding it up had been made, the time for rescinding the contract was gone."

See also *Houldsworth* v. *The City of Glasgow Bank* (p. 91, below).

*No action of damages for fraud against company without
rescission*

Houldsworth v. The City of Glasgow Bank
(1880) 7 R.(H.L.) 53; (1879) 6 R. 1164

In 1877 H. purchased stock of an unlimited banking company
from the company. In 1878 the company stopped payment
and went into liquidation.

H. thereafter raised an action for damages against the company
and its liquidators, the amount claimed being (1) £9,046 5s. 3d.,
the purchase price of the stock, (2) £20,000, the call already made
on H. as a contributory, and (3) £200,000, the anticipated amount
of future calls. H.'s ground of action was that he had been
induced to purchase the stock by fraudulent misrepresentations
of the manager and directors.

Held that, as rescission of the contract was admittedly impossible and H. was therefore obliged to remain a member, H.'s
action of damages against the company was irrelevant.

LORD CHANCELLOR (CAIRNS) (at p. 56): " He is making a claim
which is inconsistent with the contract into which he has entered,
and by which he wishes to abide. In other words, he is in
substance, if not in form, taking the course which is described
as approbating and reprobating—a course which is not allowed
either in Scotch or English law."

LORD SELBORNE (at p. 59): " Rescission of the contract in
such a case is the only remedy for which there is any precedent,
and it is, in my opinion, the only way in which the company could
justly be made answerable for a fraud of this kind; but for
rescission the appellant is confessedly too late."

LORD HATHERLEY (at p. 60): " The Lord Ordinary held that the
case was concluded by *Addie*'s case, and the same view was entertained by three of the Judges in the Court of Session. The principal
difference between the present case and that of *Addie* is that in
Addie's case the company was not incorporated at the time of the
purchase, but became so before the liquidation, whereas in the
present case the company was incorporated before the time
when the purchase was made by the appellant and he became
a shareholder. . . . I do not consider that difference to be one
which should render relief possible in this case if it was proper
to withhold it in the case of *Addie*. It appears to me to be fatal
to the appellant's right to the relief he asks that he is still,

or was at the date of the liquidation, a shareholder in the company against which he asks it. . . .

" . . . In truth, the appellant is trying to reconcile two inconsistent positions, namely, that of shareholder and that of creditor of the whole body of shareholders, including himself."

NOTES

1. In the Inner House, Lord Shand dissented.

2. The case of *Addie* referred to was *The Western Bank of Scotland* v. *Addie* (1867) 5 M.(H.L.) 80, in which the House of Lords reversed the judgment of the Court of Session.

A., who had bought shares in a banking company from the company in 1850, raised in 1860 an action against the company, concluding for reduction of the sale and for *restitutio in integrum*, on the allegation that at the date of purchase the shares, instead of being of the value of £76 per share, the price paid by A., were worthless, that the purchase had been induced by the fraudulent misrepresentations of the directors in their annual report, and that A. had only come to know of the fraud after the stoppage of the bank in 1857.

When the bank stopped payment, the shareholders resolved to have it registered under the Joint Stock Companies Act 1857, for the purpose of having it wound up under the Joint Stock Companies Act 1856, and the company was registered accordingly.

Held that A. was not entitled to an issue of restitution since his own statements showed that restitution on his part was impossible.

Lord Chancellor (Chelmsford) (at p. 86): "Whether the change of the company from an unincorporated to an incorporated banking company, for the purpose of more conveniently winding up its affairs under the Joint Stock Companies Act 1856, so changed the nature and character of the shares purchased by the pursuer as to render a *restitutio in integrum* impracticable, is a question, if it were necessary to determine, I should wish to consider more carefully. . . .

"It is clear, however, upon the authorities, that, after the crisis had arrived of the failure of the company, and the order for winding it up had been made, the time for rescinding the contract was gone."

Lord Cranworth (at p. 89): "He cannot insist on *restitutio in integrum* unless he is in a condition to restore the shares which he so purchased. But this is impossible. The purchase was made by him in 1855, and in 1857 he was party to a proceeding whereby the company from which the purchase was made was put an end to. It ceased to be an unincorporated and became an incorporated company, with many statutable incidents connected with it which did not exist before the incorporation. This new company is now in course of being wound up; but even if that were not so, if it still were carrying on the business of bankers, *restitutio in integrum* would have been impossible. . . . The time had gone by during which the respondent could repudiate the contract. . . . The circumstance that the shares, from mismanagement or otherwise, had become depreciated in value subsequently to the purchase by the pursuer, would of itself have been of no importance. He might still have been able to restore that which he was fraudulently induced to purchase. But what in fact took place was not a depreciation, but a destruction of the thing purchased; the unincorporated company in which he had been induced to purchase shares no longer existed."

Action of damages for fraud against directors: *directors relying in bona fide on statements by officials*

Lees v. Tod, &c.
(1882) 9 R. 807

L. raised an action of damages against T. and others, former directors of the Caledonian Heritable Security Co. Ltd., on the ground that he had been induced to purchase shares in the company through the false and fraudulent representations of the directors contained in the published reports and balance-sheets.

Held that, as the directors had issued the reports and balance-sheets *in bona fide,* and on the faith of statements by the officials of the company, on which they were entitled to rely, they were not liable.

LORD DEAS (at p. 833): " The reports and balance-sheets are addressed only to the shareholders, but I agree with the Lord Ordinary that they must be considered to be put into the hands of the public as well as into the hands of the share-holders, and that the pursuer is consequently quite entitled to say that he purchased on the faith of them. . . .

" . . . The directors must be held to have been in good faith in relying on the reports and balance-sheets till the contrary is proved. The pursuer must prove clearly and unequivocally that they did not believe them to be true. Of that I can find no proof whatever. . . .

" Mr. Tod says, ' Throughout we had perfect confidence in our manager, and also in the auditor.' And he adds, ' I never gave any instructions as to how transactions were to be entered in the books or grouped in the balance-sheet. I left that to the manager and the examination of the auditor.' "

NOTES

1. *Boyd & Forrest* v. *The Glasgow and South-Western Railway Co.*, 1912 S.C.(H.L.) 93, is authoritative on the nature of fraud.

An engineer who had compiled information which he believed to be true was held not to have acted fraudulently.

2. Mere non-disclosure, even of a material fact, does not amount to fraud, unless the non-disclosure makes that which is stated absolutely false.

Honeyman v. *Dickson* (1896) 34 S.L.R. 230, 4 S.L.T. 150 (O.H.): H. sued the directors of the Employers Insurance Company of Great Britain Ltd., then in liquidation, for damages, on the ground that he had been induced to take shares in the company by the false and fraudulent representations of the directors. A prospectus, H. complained, had not disclosed that the company had been registered for nearly 18 months, during which time it had changed its name, and been unable to place its shares.

Held that H.'s action was irrelevant.

Lord Stormonth Darling (at 34 S.L.R. p. 231, 4 S.L.T. p. 150): " The pursuer ... says in this action that he was induced to take these shares by the false and fraudulent representations of the directors, and he sues them for damages accordingly.... The action is laid entirely on fraud.... An action laid on so serious a ground must be very precise in its averments.

" ... Mere concealment, even of a material fact, will not ground an action for fraudulent misrepresentation, unless, in the oft-quoted words of Lord Cairns in *Peek* v. *Gurney* (1873) L.R., 6 Eng. and Ir. App., at p. 403—' the withholding of that which is not stated makes that which is stated absolutely false.' I look in vain for any statement in this prospectus which is falsified by the mere non-disclosure of these two not very important facts.

" ... Vague general statements ... will not sustain a charge of fraud."

Action of damages for fraud against directors: measure of damages

Davidson v. Tulloch
(1860) 3 Macq. 783; 22 D.(H.L.) 7

D. had been governor of the Banking Company of Aberdeen. T., professor of mathematics in King's College, Aberdeen, had held shares in that company.

After both D. and T. were dead, T.'s representatives brought an action against D.'s representatives based on alleged fraud of D. and concluding for £1,910 (the price paid by T. for the shares in 1834) and £250 (the amount of calls paid by T. in 1843), and alternatively for £3,000, or such sum as might be ascertained to be the amount of the loss sustained by T.

Held that D.'s representatives were liable to compensate T.'s representatives, the measure of damages being the difference between the price paid by T. and the true value of the shares at the time when T. purchased them.

LORD CHANCELLOR (CAMPBELL) (at p. 789): "The gist of [the action] is this, that Davidson, now deceased, by false and fraudulent misrepresentations induced Dr. Tulloch to buy his shares, whereby he was injured. . . .

"The proper mode of measuring the damages is to ascertain the difference between the purchase-money and what would have been a fair price to be paid for the shares in the circumstances of the Company at the time of the purchase. . . .

" . . . The action lies against executors just as much as if it had been brought against Mr. Davidson himself."

NOTE

This case was referred to in *Davidson and Another* v. *Hamilton* (below).

Statutory action for compensation against directors: measure of damages

Davidson and Another v. Hamilton
(1904) 12 S.L.T. 353 (O.H.)

Davidson and Murray, two of the original shareholders of the Silver City Steam Trawling Co. Ltd., brought an action under the Directors' Liability Act 1890 against H., the promoter and one of the directors of the company, alleging that the prospectus of the company contained misstatements, and claiming respectively £225 and £200, the par value of the shares for which they had subscribed.

The Lord Ordinary *decerned* for £56 5s. in favour of Davidson and £50 in favour of Murray.

LORD STORMONTH DARLING (at p. 353): "Now, the question is considerably simplified at the outset by the defender's admission that the two statements complained of—*viz.*, that the vessels had been valued, with outfit complete, by Messrs. John Duthie, Sons, & Company, Shipbuilders, Aberdeen, at £21,500, and that they had gone through their special survey, No. 2, for Lloyd's Register—were untrue, or (to put it in a less invidious form) inaccurate. It is also admitted that the defender, jointly with others, was responsible for the whole prospectus. That being so, and on its being further established by the pursuers that the statements were material, and were relied on, the Directors' Liability Act throws on the defender the *onus* of proving that he had reason to believe, and did believe, in the truth of the statements. If he fails in discharging that *onus,* his liability for what the Act calls 'compensation' directly arises. . . .

" The *onus* of proof thus being shifted, I proceed to inquire whether the defender has succeeded in shewing that he believed, and had reason to believe, that the statement about the valuation by the firm was true. . . .

" . . . I reach the conclusion that the defender had no justification for making the statement complained of. . . .

" There remains only the question of the measure of damages which is one of legal interest, and not without difficulty in the method of its application. The principle is clear enough. I agree . . . that there is no difference between England and Scotland in this matter, the best proof of which is that the leading case, to which all English decisions go back, is the case decided by the House of Lords on appeal from Scotland. *Davidson* v. *Tulloch* (1860), 3 Macq. 783. . . . The measure of damages must be the difference between the price and the *real* value of the shares immediately after allotment. The principle is not inconsistent with the measure of damages I adopted without objection in the case of *Smith* v. *Moncrieff*, in 1894 (one of the earliest cases under the Directors' Liability Act . . .), for there the share were admittedly without value from the date of issue, except such as might be recovered in the liquidation out of surplus assets."

NOTES

1. The provisions of the Directors' Liability Act 1890 are now represented by s. 43 of the Companies Act 1948 (" Civil liability for mis-statements in prospectus ").

2. The case of *Smith* v. *Moncrieff and others* (1894) 2 S.L.T. 140 (O.H.) was an action, based on the Directors' Liability Act 1890, against directors to have them ordained to pay to the pursuer the sum which he had been induced to invest in the Edinburgh Employers' Liability and General Assurance Co. Ltd.

Lord Stormonth Darling's conclusion (at p. 142) " was that the defenders had not reasonable ground for believing that the material statements in the prospectus represented the true state of the company's affairs, even as at the date of the last balance-sheet."

3. Another early action based on the statutory provisions for compensation was *Gray* v. *The Central Finance Corporation Ltd.* (1903) 11 S.L.T. 309 (O.H.).

G., an original holder of 400 ordinary shares of £1 each in L. P. Johannessen Ltd., sued C. Ltd. and other promoters and directors of L. P. Johannessen Ltd. for £400 as compensation for damage sustained by him by reason of alleged untrue statements contained in a prospectus on the faith of which he had subscribed for his shares.

The Lord Ordinary (Stormonth Darling) *assoilzied* the defenders other than two of them.

Lord Stormonth Darling (at p. 310): "Mistakes in judgment there may have been, but the Act of 1890 was not passed to afford a remedy against mistakes in judgment. The one thing against which it does afford a remedy is an untrue statement of a material kind in the prospectus; and from the consequences even of that the persons responsible for the prospectus can relieve themselves by showing that they had reasonable ground for believing, and did up to the time of allotment believe, that the statement was true, or in the case of a true copy of a report or valuation by an expert, that they had reasonable ground to believe that the person making the report or valuation was competent to make it."

CHAPTER 7

COMMISSIONS AND DISCOUNTS

Shares may not be issued at a discount

Klenck v. East India Co. for Exploration and Mining Ltd.
(1888) 16 R. 271

The memorandum and also the articles of E. Ltd. provided that the company's shares might be issued at par or at a discount or at a premium.

K., to whom 300 £1 shares had been allotted at a discount of 12s. 6d. per share so that the liability on each share was to be only 7s. 6d., presented a petition for rectification of the register of members by the deletion of his name and for an order on E. Ltd. for repayment of £15, being 1s. per share paid by K. to the company.

The court *granted* the prayer of the petition on the ground that the issue of shares at a discount was *ultra vires* of the company under the provisions of the Companies Acts.

LORD PRESIDENT (INGLIS) (at p. 276): " The question whether this resolution of the company was illegal, and whether the issuing of the shares at a discount was *ultra vires* and therefore void, is a question of very great importance, and depends, I think, truly upon the clauses of the Companies Acts, particularly upon the clauses of the Act of 1862. . . . There is no such thing as limited liability at common law. . . . The limitation that we are dealing with here is a limitation which is ' to the amount, if any, unpaid on the shares respectively held ' by the members. . . . Nobody can have a greater amount of limitation of liability than is prescribed here. . . . That his liability extends to every shilling that remains unpaid is clear. . . .

" . . . The issue of shares at a discount involves this, that whereas the share capital of the company is all divided into £1 shares . . . , in point of fact the company has given a discharge to those who took the shares at a discount of a considerable portion of that which *ex facie* of the share they are bound to pay. That seems to me to be exactly the same thing in principle as the company buying its own shares. It is just a diminution of the apparent capital of the company. In the one case—the case of purchasing its own shares, and holding them without re-issue—the company just returns to the shareholder the whole or a portion of the capital which he has paid; and in the other, instead of returning a portion of the capital which he has paid, they fail to lay him under an obligation to pay up the unpaid portion of the shares, or rather they grant him a discharge of it, without consideration, to a certain amount. In short, both cases violate the principle of the statute exactly in the same way. The memorandum sets out—and is bound to set out—the precise amount of the capital of the company divided into shares of a certain fixed amount, and the effect of that is to shew to the public and the creditors dealing with the company, what is the amount of fixed capital upon which they are entitled to rely in so dealing with the company. But if by either of the means I have suggested—either the purchase by the company of its own shares, or the issuing of shares at a discount —the public and the creditors are misled entirely, then the memorandum is set at naught, and the provision of the memorandum is for all the purposes for which it was intended practically useless. These are the grounds upon which it appears to me that the issue of shares at a discount cannot possibly be maintained to be legal.

" . . . The case of the *Almada Company* (1888) L.R., 38 Chan.Div. 415) appears to me to be upon all-fours with the present. . . . But there is another and perhaps still more authoritative guide which we have in the present case, and that is the judgment of the House of Lords in the case of *Trevor* v. *Whitworth* ((1887) L.R. 12 App.Cas. 409). That was a case where the company had purchased up its own shares and held them without re-issue, and the House of Lords found that that was an entirely illegal and void transaction, and must be set aside upon the ground which I have already indicated as being the ground of judgment in the present case. . . . The two cases—the case of the purchase of shares by the company, and the case of issuing shares at a discount—I think depend entirely upon the same principle.

" There is just one other point to which it is necessary to advert in disposing of this petition. It is maintained upon the part of the respondents that they are entitled to issue shares at a discount, because they have a power to do so within the memorandum of association itself, whereas in the cases that have been decided, both in the *Almada* case and in the case of *Trevor* v.

Whitworth, the power was not in the memorandum of association, but in the articles of association. I do not think that that makes any difference in the case at all, because if the power to issue shares at a discount be inconsistent with setting forth the precise amount of the capital of the company, divided into a certain number of shares of fixed amount, then that is to superadd to the memorandum of association something that takes away its value, or rather something that utterly contradicts its most important provision. The point was dealt with . . . by Lord Macnaghten in the case of *Trevor* v. *Whitworth,* and as expressing my own views of the question, although it did not actually arise for decision in *Trevor* v. *Whitworth,* I am prepared to adopt Lord Macnaghten's views as there expressed. He says, ' It seems to me that if a power to purchase its own shares were found in the memorandum of association of a limited company it would necessarily be void.'. . . I cannot better express my own opinion than in the words there used by the noble and learned Lord. I think that if you add to the memorandum of association anything that derogates from or annuls one of the statutory requisites, that must necessarily be an illegal condition. Upon these grounds I am for granting the prayer of this petition, removing the petitioner's name from the register of shareholders, and ordering the company . . . to repay the £15.''

NOTES

1. On the same day, December 21, 1888, the First Division also held, in *General Property Investment Co. Ltd. and Liquidator* v. *Matheson's Trustees* (p. 128, below), that it was *ultra vires* of a registered limited company to purchase its own shares.

2. For the circumstances in which it is lawful to issue shares at a discount, see Companies Act 1948, s. 57.

3. It is not unlawful for a company to issue shares at a premium less than the premium which could be obtained in the market— *Cameron* v. *The Glenmorangie Distillery Co. Ltd.* (p. 249, below).

A general meeting of the shareholders of G. Ltd resolved to authorise the directors to allot to Maitland, the company's managing director, 200 of the company's unissued shares at a premium of £1 per share over their par value.

C., a shareholder, complained that the premium was inadequate, and presented a note of suspension and interdict to prevent the allotment.

Held that the resolution was not incompetent.

Sub-underwriting contract: sub-underwriter not entitled to repudiate allotment

The Premier Briquette Co. Ltd. v. Gray
1922 S.C. 329

P. Ltd. was incorporated in 1919 and entered into an underwriting agreement with the Mining, Commercial, and General Trust Ltd., whereby the latter company agreed to underwrite 100,000 of P. Ltd.'s shares.

In a sub-underwriting letter addressed by G. to the underwriter, G. offered to subscribe for 500 of the shares. G. also signed an application for 500 shares. The letter declared that the sub-underwriting contract and the application were to be irrevocable on G.'s part. G. forwarded both documents to the underwriter.

The underwriter signed a docquet of acceptance printed on the sub-underwriting letter, but did not intimate this acceptance to G. G.'s application for shares was passed by the underwriter to P. Ltd., and P. Ltd. allotted 500 shares to G.

Thereafter G. refused to pay instalments, on the ground that the underwriter, having failed to intimate acceptance of his offer, had had no authority to transmit his application to the company.

Held that G. was not entitled to repudiate the sub-underwriting contract on that ground, and that the allotment to him was valid.

LORD JUSTICE-CLERK (SCOTT DICKSON) (at p. 343): " On the face of the documents, I think that the proceedings of the pursuers have been in order, to the effect of warranting the entry of the defender's name on their share register for 500 shares. . . .

" It was urged that the whole allotment to the defender was radically vitiated, because the acceptance of the underwriting had never been intimated to him. In my opinion any such defence fails on two grounds: (1) In law, because it is not open to be pleaded against the pursuers. In my view the letter of application cannot, as in a question with the pursuers, be held to have been conditioned by the sub-underwriting letter; the letter of application was, on the face of it, free from all conditions, and was in fact at first dealt with by the pursuers as a firm application, and I think so dealt with in perfect *bona fides*. In my opinion, as in a question between the pursuers and the defender, it was a firm application. (2) On the facts, and having regard to article 5 of the sub-underwriting letter,

. . . the letter of allotment and the subsequent correspondence with the defender were, I think, sufficient intimation to the defender of the contract between him and the Mining Trust. In any event, the terms of the sub-underwriting letter, and particularly article 5 thereof, precluded the defender from objecting to the directors of the pursuers' Company allotting the 500 shares to him and entering his name on the register in respect thereof."

NOTE

Article 5 declared the contract and application to be irrevocable on G.'s part.

CHAPTER 8

APPLICATION AND ALLOTMENT

Application must be unconditional: "willingness to take" shares not sufficient

Mason v. The Benhar Coal Co. Ltd.
(1882) 9 R. 883

M., a shareholder of B. Ltd., completed a schedule which had been sent to him by the company and which was in these terms: " I, . . . hereby express my willingness to take . . . of the proposed new preference shares."

After a general meeting of the company had resolved to create the new preference shares, a second document was sent to shareholders. It was in these terms: " I, . . . hereby apply for . . . shares of the new preference stock."

M. sent no reply to this document, but the directors of B. Ltd., proceeding on M.'s completion of the earlier document, allotted 50 of the new preference shares to him.

There was a conflict of evidence as to whether M. ever received an allotment letter, but he admitted that he received, and paid no attention to, several call-letters.

B. Ltd. went into liquidation, and the liquidators entered M.'s name in the list of contributories in respect of these shares.

Held that M.'s expression of willingness to take the proposed shares was not sufficient to bind him to become a shareholder, and that his name had therefore to be struck off the list of contributories.

LORD SHAND (at p. 887): " The liquidators have placed the name of Mr. Mason, the petitioner, on the list of contributories, . . . and the question is, whether he agreed to become a shareholder in respect of these shares? . . . I have come to be of opinion that the schedule signed by Mr. Mason was not a direct application for shares, such as, on being accepted by the company, can bind him. . . . The whole arrangement then contemplated was tentative. The stock was not yet created, though its creation was contemplated. The creditors were not arranged with. Unless the arrangement was satisfactory to all parties it was to fall through. . . .

" . . . I think that Mr. Mason was not bound as an applicant for shares, and was entitled, when the subsequent circular was

103

issued, to consider whether he was satisfied as to the position of the creditors, the number of shareholders who were willing to take the new stock, the new directors, and so on. . . . I am very far from saying that the words 'I hereby express my willingness to take fifty shares' might not, in other circumstances, have been held a sufficient offer to take shares. . . But the peculiarity here is, that accompanying the schedule for replies was a circular which informed the person to whom it was sent that the whole matter was tentative, and that the issuing or not issuing of the stock was to be resolved upon at a future meeting; and that when the meeting was held, and the resolution creating stock had been passed, a circular having annexed to it a schedule in the usual form for replies making application for stock was sent out. I think Mr. Mason is entitled in law to say that he did not make application for the new preference shares, and that he cannot be put upon the register. . . .

" As to the question whether notice of allotment was received or not, there is a considerable difficulty. . . . But it is not necessary to decide the question. I shall only say that, assuming the true inference from the proof to be that delivery is not proved, I should not hold that the contract was completed by the mere posting of the notice of allotment. I should concur on that point in the opinion of Lord Justice Bramwell in the case of the *Household Fire Insurance Company* (1879) L.R. 4 Exch. Div. 218."

NOTES

1. Similarly, in *Goldie* v. *Torrance* (1882) 10 R. 174, G., the official liquidator of the Glenduffhill Coal Co. Ltd., was held not entitled to have T.'s name placed upon the list of contributories, since it could not be proved that T. had ever applied for shares.

Lord President (Inglis) (at p. 174): " The issue of fact to be determined in this case is whether the respondent agreed to become a member of the Glenduffhill Coal Company or not, and that is a question to be determined upon the evidence."

Lord Shand (at p. 176): " The usual—indeed, the almost invariable —way in which a person becomes a member of a joint stock company is by an application for an allotment of shares, or by assenting in some other form by writing to become a partner. Where, as here, the agreement to take shares rests upon an alleged verbal agreement only, I am clearly of opinion that very distinct evidence is required to instruct it. That being the view I take of the law, I think the evidence in this case is insufficient. . . . Torrance really appears to have gone no further length than that of saying that he intended to take shares. . . . I think the agreement to take shares has not been made out."

2. In *Liquidator of the Florida Mortgage and Investment Co. Ltd. v. Bayley* (1890) 17 R. 525, there were special circumstances in which a person who had signed a transfer of shares which had been registered in his name was held nevertheless not to have been a shareholder.

B. had agreed with F. Ltd. to take shares and debentures in the company in part payment of property sold by him to the company. B. was allotted 300 £5 shares, on which £1 per share had been paid up, and a debenture for £130. B. refused to accept these shares, but, without his knowledge or consent, his name was put on the register as holder of them.

Subsequently, B. arranged with the secretary of F. Ltd. to sign a transfer of the 300 shares in favour of Doyle, B.'s coachman.

When F. Ltd. went into liquidation, the liquidator sought to have the register rectified by the restoration of B.'s name in place of Doyle's name.

Held that, as B. had never agreed to be a shareholder, the entry of his name on the register and his signing the transfer merely for the purpose of having his name removed did not make him a shareholder.

Lord President (Inglis) (at p. 533): " I am of opinion that Mr. Bayley never agreed to become a member of this company. . . .

" . . . Bayley was under no obligation or agreement to become a member of the company, except upon the footing that he was to have fully paid-up shares. . . .

" . . . If we are to believe Bayley, what was arranged was that he was not to become a member, but that Doyle, the man of straw, was to be accepted in his place. . . . There is no doubt that . . . Bayley signed the transfer. He did sign the transfer with a protest that he did so on the distinct understanding that he was to be under no liability to the company. My opinion accordingly is . . . that Bayley never was a member of the company, that his name was put upon the register in order that he might transfer the shares *unico contextu* to another, and for the purpose of carrying through the arrangement with Caesar [the secretary]."

3. *Curror's Trustee* v. *The Caledonian Heritable Security Co. Ltd.* (1880) 7 R. 479 shows that a person may make a binding application for shares without writing.

A report was made by directors of C. Ltd. to its shareholders stating that the directors had agreed to take up among themselves the unaccepted balance of a new issue of shares. That report was approved at a general meeting of the shareholders.

Held that, as this was an agreement which the directors were bound to fulfil, C. Ltd. was entitled to enter the name of C., one of the directors, on its register in respect of his share—one-eighth—of the unaccepted shares.

Lord Gifford (at p. 482): " The report by the directors sets forth shortly, but quite sufficiently, all the essentials of an agreement among the directors to take the unaccepted shares. . . . Such undertakings by the directors of a company must be carried out in the highest good faith, and the directors cannot be allowed to escape liabilities which they have fairly assumed under arrangement sufficiently embodied in their minutes or in the formal reports to which they were parties, and which were submitted to the shareholders and acted upon."

4. In *The Swedish Match Co. Ltd.* v. *Seivwright* (1889) 16 R. 989 a condition attached to a letter of application was held to have been fulfilled.

The prospectus of S. Ltd. stated: "Share capital, £100,000, in 20,000 shares of £5 each. First issue £80,000, in 16,000 £5 shares. In addition to the above shares, £30,000 of six per cent. debentures to be issued. . . . The consideration to be paid by the company for the . . . property . . . has been fixed by the vendor at £90,000, of which £55,000 is payable in cash, and the balance, £35,000, in fully paid-up shares, debentures, or cash, or partly in each, at the option of the directors."

On applying for 120 shares, S. added to his letter of application the condition: "If capital all subscribed for."

At the time of the letter of allotment to S., about 13,600 of the first 16,000 shares had been allotted to the general public, and it was in the option of the company to allot 2,400 to the vendor in part payment of the price of the property. The whole of the debentures had not been subscribed for.

S. Ltd. brought an action for payment of calls against S., and S. pleaded that, as his application had been subject to a condition which had not been fulfilled at the date of the allotment, he was entitled to be assoilzied.

Held that the condition had been fulfilled, and that S. was therefore liable to pay the calls.

Lord Justice-Clerk (J. H. A. Macdonald) (at p. 991): "I take the stipulation in the defender's letter of application, 'if capital all subscribed for,' to apply alone to the capital which was then offered for subscription. I cannot accept the Sheriff-substitute's view that it was intended to refer to the whole capital of the company, whether then issued for subscription or not; nor can I accept the view of the Sheriff that the word 'capital,' while it was intended to include only the amount then offered for subscription, included not merely the share capital, but a large amount of debentures. According to the ordinary use of language debentures are not capital. . . .

"Now, there is no doubt that 13,000 odd shares were subscribed for by the public before the day of allotment, and as regards the balance, the question is whether the 2,400 allotted to the vendor must be held to be shares subscribed for or not. In my opinion they were. They were shares which the company could allot to the vendor if they pleased. He was not in a position to insist on having them allotted to him, for the company might have paid him in cash if they had the money, but he was bound to take the shares if the company chose to allot them to him. I think therefore that the whole capital of the company was subscribed for in the sense of the defender's letter of application, and that he is in consequence bound."

5. In contrast, in *Cowan* v. *Gowans* (1877) 15 S.L.R. 195, a condition attached to an undertaking to take shares was held not to have been fulfilled.

This was a petition by C., official liquidator of the Edinburgh Theatre Co. Ltd., to settle a list of contributories.

G., a creditor who had a large shareholding, objected that the directors had bound themselves to double their original holdings and that C. had not given effect to that obligation in the proposed list.

The directors answered that their undertaking had been conditional, depending on whether or not the rest of the capital was subscribed.

Held that, as the directors' undertaking had been subject to a condition which had not been fulfilled, C. had been right not to include their names on the list of contributories in respect of additional shares.

6. In *The National House Property Investment Co. Ltd.* v. *Watson*, 1908 S.C. 888, W.'s letter of application contained the following condition: "This application is made on the distinct understanding . . . that my firm is appointed surveyors to this company over an average radius of thirty miles from Edinburgh . . . and that my firm is also appointed advisory surveyors to the Advisory Board for Scotland at fees to be adjusted."

W. obtained the first appointment, but not the second because the company went into liquidation before the Board referred to had been constituted.

Opinions that W.'s application was one for an immediate allotment provided the company agreed to the conditions, and that the condition as to the advisory surveyorship was not a condition precedent but subsequent and collateral to the contract.

Lord Low (at p. 892): "I read the application as being an application for an immediate allotment of shares if the pursuers agreed to the conditions annexed."

7. In *The Waverley Hydropathic Co. Ltd.* v. *Barrowman* (1895) 23 R. 138, where a company purported to allot to B. preference shares which it had no power to allot, B. was held not to be the holder of ordinary shares, since his application had been for preference, not for ordinary, shares. See Note 1 to *Life Association of Scotland* v. *Caledonian Heritable Security Co. Ltd. in Liquidation*, p. 52, above.

Allotment must be unconditional

Liquidator of the Consolidated Copper Co. of Canada Ltd. v. Peddie, &c.
(1877) 5 R. 393

C. Ltd., formed for the purpose of purchasing and working certain mines in Canada, issued a prospectus inviting applications for shares.

A large number of shares were applied for on the usual unconditional terms.

Before allotment, the directors of C. Ltd. and the vendors of the mines entered into an agreement whereby the purchase of the mines was to depend on the report made by a deputation sent to Canada to inspect the mines.

Letters of allotment were issued, requesting payment of £1 per share payable on allotment, and at the end of each letter of allotment there was the following note: " After this payment no further call will be made till the deputation of directors shall have reported on the mines. If the board resolve not to purchase the mines the money will be returned to the shareholders without deduction."

The deputation reported unfavourably, and the directors resolved not to complete the purchase of the mines. This resolution was approved of at a meeting of the allottees, and the money paid on application and allotment was returned.

In a petition to settle the list of contributories in the liquidation of C. Ltd., *held* that the letters of allotment, since they contained a suspensive condition, did not make the allottees shareholders of the company.

LORD GIFFORD (at p. 401): " The question is, What was meant to be carried out by the directors when they issued those letters? Upon that view, and looking rather to the substance of the letter than to its mere accidental form, I think it was not intended that the gentlemen to whom those letters were addressed should be to every intent and purpose present members of the company, but that it had in view a contingent event, upon the occurrence of which alone their membership should take place. . . . I have come, though not without difficulty, to think that this is a proper suspensive condition, meaning that the parties to whom the shares are allotted will become shareholders to that amount, and will be called upon to pay in reference thereto if the mines are purchased and not otherwise. . . .

" On the whole I am of opinion that they were not share-holders; that looking both to the carrying out of the bargain and the terms of the bargain itself they were never in truth members of this company; and therefore, that . . . in respect of those letters of allotment . . . no instant membership was constituted in favour of the parties to whom those letters were directed, and that if that is the only ground for putting them on the list of contributories, they should not be put on it."

LORD JUSTICE-CLERK (MONCREIFF) (at p. 405): " I agree with Lord Gifford. I think there was an unconditional offer to become partners made by the respondents through the application for shares and the payment of the deposit, but that the offer never was unconditionally accepted, and until it was the contract was not complete.

" The question turns on the terms and effect of the letter of allotment, and the provision attached to it. . . .

" Now, I think it clear, both on the terms of the documents and on the real nature of the transaction, there never was, and never was intended to be, any such concluded contract, but that, on the contrary, it had been expressly conditioned from the first that these allottees should be accepted as partners if the mines were purchased, and that they should not be accepted if the purchase was not made.

" The words of the allotment letter bear this construction and as I think no other. . . . I think this means, we accept your application, if we purchase; if we do not, we decline, and return your money. The return of the money seems to me to be susceptible of no other interpretation. The money is returned because the person advancing it is to get no consideration for it. The only consideration he expected for his money was a partner-ship, and he got back his money because he had not received, and was not to receive, the counterpart. . . .

" I think . . . that this was a suspensive condition, and that unless the condition was purified there was no concluded con-tract.

" . . . I am therefore of opinion that the respondents . . . are not contributories, and ought not to be put on the list, in respect that they were never partners of the company."

NOTE

Contrast *Nelson and Another* v. *Fraser* (1906) 14 S.L.T. 513 (O.H.), in which a condition attached to an allotment was held to be not a condition precedent but a collateral condition subsequent.

Fraser, Ross & Co. Ltd. resolved to increase its capital by the issue of 5,000 shares of £1 each. At a directors' meeting the secretary intimated that 4,748 shares had been applied for. F., who was one of the directors, stated that he wished the balance of 252 shares to be kept for him till he would be able to pay for them. F.'s name was entered in the Allotment Book as having 252 shares allotted to him. F. denied having received any allotment letter. F.'s name was also entered in the register of shareholders and, in the liquidation of the company, in the list of contributories. The liquidators claimed payment from F. for instalments and calls unpaid on the shares. The Lord Ordinary (Dundas) gave decree for the sums sued for.

Lord Dundas (at p. 514): " The argument . . . is that there was here no contract requiring to be rescinded, because no intimation of any allotment of the shares in question was made to him by the Company at the time; and therefore, although his name appeared upon the register of shareholders as owner of the 252 shares, he was not, in the words of section 23 of the Companies Act 1862, a ' person who has agreed to become a member of ' the Company in respect of them. It becomes necessary . . . to consider what it was that the Directors, at their Meeting on February 11, 1902, agreed to do. The minute bears that the shares were ' to be kept for him until he would be able to pay for them.' . . . I am of opinion that what was agreed to was that the 252 shares should then be allotted to Mr. Fraser, with the adjected condition that he should not be called upon to make any present payment in respect of them; and not that the shares should be allotted to him, if and when he paid for them, and that until then they should be kept for him, and not issued to the public. In other words, I think that the minute imports a present agreement to allot, with a collateral condition subsequent attached to it, and not an agreement to allot, but only upon the fulfilment of a preliminary or precedent condition. . . . I am disposed to believe that written intimation of the allotment was made to, and received by, Mr. Fraser at the time. But, assuming this point to be doubtful, I am prepared to hold that sufficient intimation was made to him. . . . I consider that the proof discloses quite enough to have shewn Mr. Fraser that the Company had responded to his offer, and that he understood, or must be held to have understood, that this was so. . . . Mr. Fraser cannot be heard to say that there was no contract between him and the Company as regards the 252 shares. I think that they were duly allotted to him; that he was sufficiently apprised of the fact; that his name stood properly upon the register of shareholders as that of a ' person who has agreed to become a member of ' the Company; and that it was properly transferred to the list of contributories in the liquidation."

Letter of allotment not essential provided intimation of allotment is otherwise sufficient

Chapman v. Sulphite Pulp Co. Ltd.
(1892) 19 R. 837

C. applied for shores in S. Ltd. Shares were allotted to him, and his name was entered in the register of members. There was no conclusive proof that he had received a letter of allotment, but it was proved that he had been informed orally of the allotment by the company secretary and that he had received a circular to attend the first general meeting of the company.

C. presented a petition for the removal of his name from the register of members.

Held that C.'s name was properly on the register, since he had received sufficient notice of allotment.

LORD PRESIDENT (J. P. B. ROBERTSON) (at p. 839): " On two occasions in spring 1891, after he had been put on the register, Mr. Chapman was in communication with the officials of the company regarding those shares, and I think the result of the evidence is that, apart altogether from the disputed letters, he was then sufficiently apprised that the company had accepted him as a shareholder in terms of his application. . . .

" The other fact to which I refer is that, he being on the register, the company sent to the petitioner a circular calling him to a meeting of shareholders. This was, unless explained away, an intimation that the company treated him as a shareholder."

NOTES

1. In *Mason* v. *The Benhar Coal Co. Ld.* (p. 103, above), the question arose, but did not require to be decided, whether receipt of call-letters was sufficient notice of allotment.

2. See also *Nelson and Another* v. *Fraser* (Note to *Liquidator of the Consolidated Copper Co. of Canada Ltd.* v. *Peddie, &c.,* p. 109, above), in which there was held to have been sufficient notice of allotment.

Consideration for allotment: payment not in cash

Liquidators of Coustonholm Paper Mills Co. Ltd. v. Law
(1891) 18 R. 1076

L. agreed to sell his paper mills to Weir who was promoting a company to acquire them and to carry on the business.

Of the price of £12,000, L. consented to take £8,500 in fully paid-up shares of the company.

Held that L. was not to be regarded as having paid for his shares in cash.

LORD JUSTICE-CLERK (J. H. A. MACDONALD) (at p. 1081): " Where there is a money claim on the one side for property or services, and a money claim on the other side for shares subscribed for, it is not necessary in order to the shares being held to be paid for in cash that money should actually pass from hand to hand, either in specie or by notes or cheque. A ceremonial payment in cash is not necessary, if the truth of the transaction be that money claims have been satisfied on both sides, the price of the property or services being satisfied by the delivery of the shares as paid-up shares, to the extent of the money payable for the property or services. If that be the position of the transaction in this case, then undoubtedly Mr. Law has paid cash for his shares. . . .

" But is that the position of the transaction? I cannot hold it to be so. I find no trace in the agreement made between Law and Weir, or between Law and the company, of any contract under which the company became liable to pay any money to Mr. Law. . . . It is not a money price to which he is entitled under the agreement, but shares the nominal value of which corresponds to the money price. . . . He had a right to shares, and nothing else."

NOTES

1. This case was brought under section 25 of the Companies Act 1867, which provided that every share was to be deemed to have been issued subject to the payment of the whole amount of it in cash, unless a written contract was filed with the Registrar of Joint Stock Companies at or before the issue of the shares. The decision was therefore that the liquidators had been right in placing L.'s name on the list of contributories in the company's liquidation, with the same liability as that under which he would have been had he given no consideration for the allotment.

The statutory provision has since been altered.

For information required in the return of allotments in respect of shares allotted as fully or partly paid up otherwise than in cash, see now Companies Act 1948, s. 52.

2. In *The Liquidator of the Pelican Fire and Accident Insurance Co. Ltd.* v. *Bruce* (1904) 11 S.L.T. 658 (O.H.), Lord Kyllachy held that B.'s name ought to remain on the list of contributories.

B. had applied for 50 shares of £1 each in P. Ltd. on the footing that he would be appointed a medical officer of the company at a fee of £75 per annum. B. paid £25 to P. Ltd., and received a letter of allotment with the receipt appended: "Received the sum of £25, making the above shares now fully paid." This second £25 was a payment to account of B.'s salary as medical officer.

The liquidator argued that, since at the date of allotment there was no debt exigible by B. against P. Ltd., the alleged payment was bad in law, and that B.'s name had therefore to be put on the list of contributories.

3. In *The National House Property Investment Co. Ltd.* v. *Watson* (see Note 6 to *Mason* v. *The Benhar Coal Co. Ltd.*, p. 107, above), an agreement that the balance due on shares should be paid up by fees to be earned by the allottee for services to be performed for the company was held *ultra vires* of the directors, with the result that the allottee was not a shareholder, and was therefore not liable in the company's liquidation to pay what was unpaid on the shares.

W.'s letter of application included the condition: "I am to be at liberty, if I so desire it, to pay up the balance of my shares by allowing the fees to be earned by my firm to accumulate for this purpose." The court held that this third condition furnished a complete defence.

Lord Low (at p. 893): "I think . . . that the defender is entitled to absolvitor, because, in my opinion, the agreement in regard to fees was *ultra vires* of the directors. . . . But if that be so, then the whole contract is vitiated, and cannot be enforced either by or against the Company."

Consideration for allotment: court does not inquire into adequacy

Brownlie and others, Petitioners
(1898) 6 S.L.T. 249 (O.H.)

In 1877, the Scottish Heritages Co. Ltd. allocated the balance of profit to the shareholders in the shape of bonus shares upon which 10s. was paid up out of the profits.

In 1897, when the company was in liquidation, the liquidator made a call of 10s. on the bonus shares.

The liquidator claimed that the issue of bonus shares was *ultra vires* of the company, and asked for a proof in order that he might show that the profit taken credit for in 1876 had not truly been earned.

Held that the issue had not been *ultra vires,* and that the shareholders, not having paid for their shares in cash, were therefore liable. The liquidator's request for a proof was refused.

Lord Stormonth Darling (at p. 250): "Next it is urged that the issue of 'bonus' shares was an act *ultra vires* of the Company. . . . No doubt . . . the operation was a mere piece of book-keeping; no money passed. Accordingly, I . . . say . . . that the shareholders did not pay for their shares 'in cash.' But that is a very different thing from saying that the shares were issued without any consideration at all and, therefore, that the operation was *ultra vires* of the Company. . . .

" . . . The liquidator asks a proof in order that he may show that the profit taken credit for in 1876 was not truly earned. . . . He does not say that the estimate of profit was fraudulent or even extravagant, but that subsequent events proved it to have been too sanguine. Now that, I apprehend, is an irrelevant averment. Where a company, in good faith, issues shares as fully paid-up in consideration of property transferred or services rendered, the Court will not inquire into the value of that which was accepted by the Company as an equivalent of money. . . . I do not see why a different rule should be applied where a company in good faith . . . sets a certain amount of its estimated profit against an issue of new shares. . . . I reject this demand for proof."

Specific implement of undertaking to subscribe for shares: enforcement of undertaking against executrix

William Beardmore & Co. Ltd. v. Barry
1928 S.C.(H.L.) 47; 1928 S.C. 101

Park addressed a letter to the directors of B. Ltd., stating: " I agree at any time upon request by you to subscribe for or find subscribers to your satisfaction for 48,000 6 per cent. cumulative preference shares of £1 each."

No such request was made during Park's lifetime, but the directors called upon B., Park's executrix, to implement the agreement.

Held that (1) the undertaking, being neither personal to Park nor subject to the condition that the request should be made during Park's lifetime, transmitted in the ordinary way against his executrix, and (2) specific implement was an appropriate remedy since the executrix had not averred facts and circumstances which would have made the grant of that remedy inequitable.

VISCOUNT DUNEDIN (at p. 50): " There remains one question, and one only: is the obligation undertaken by the late Colonel Park to subscribe for 48,000 preference shares in the respondent's Company an obligation which binds his executrix?

" This depends upon the construction to be put upon the letter of October 19, 1920. . . .

" . . . Now, by the letter . . . he came under a contract . . . which was a contract of a very common description, namely an underwriting contract. Now, that an underwriting contract which in expression must necessarily be phrased personally, nevertheless is binding on executors is well settled. . . . The whole point, therefore, comes to depend on the words ' upon request by you.' Now, it is to be observed, first, that the words are preceded by the words ' at any time,' and, second, that it is ' upon request by you,' not ' upon request made to me.' That seems to me to point, keeping in view the ordinary nature of an underwriting contract, to this, that the request was not especially limited by the lifetime, and that it might be made to whoever was bound under the contract, that is here, the executrix."

LORD JUSTICE-CLERK (ALNESS) (at p. 108): " The first plea in law for the defender is: ' The action is incompetent, in respect that the Court cannot now order specific performance of the alleged obligation.'. . . That contention necessitates consideration of the law of Scotland with regard to a claim for specific performance. I do not think it is too much to say that our law, differing from the law of England, favours such a claim. . . . It cannot be contended in this case that the implement of the defender's obligation is unjust, and I am unable to affirm that it is inexpedient. I can see no valid reason why the defender should not be required to implement the obligation which the deceased, had he lived, would plainly have been bound to obtemper. There are, in this case, no special facts and circumstances averred which, as a matter of equity, would exclude the remedy which *prima facie* is within the pursuers' rights. The defender has more than sufficient estate in her hands as executrix to enable her to implement his obligation. She need not, unless she likes, go upon the register of the Company as a shareholder, for the shares in question may be allotted to her nominees. If she goes on the register, she can sell the shares on the following day; and it must not be forgotten that, as they are fully paid, no liability whatever would attach to her in respect of them. The defender can qualify no prejudice or hardship or difficulty if she should be required to carry out her author's obligation. Her resistance to the claim made appears to me to be of a purely technical and insubstantial character. In these circumstances I think the Lord Ordinary was right in repelling the first plea in law for the defender."

NOTE

The judgment of the Second Division as to the competency of specific implement was not challenged in the appeal to the House of Lords.

CHAPTER 9

MEMBERSHIP

NOTES

1. The general principle as to the constitution of membership is stated thus by Lord Deas in *Macdonald, &c.* v. *The City of Glasgow Bank* (1879) 6 R. 621 at p. 633: "Apart from the subscription to the memorandum of association . . . , two things are required by the 23d section of the Act of 1862 to make any one a member of the company—(1) He must have agreed to become a member, and (2) his name must be entered in the register of members."

The statutory provision is now in section 26 of the Companies Act 1948:

"(1) The subscribers of the memorandum of a company shall be deemed to have agreed to become members of the company, and on its registration shall be entered as members in its register of members.

"(2) Every other person who agrees to become a member of a company, and whose name is entered in its register of members, shall be a member of the company."

2. The general principle as to the effect of entry on the register of members is stated thus by Lord Sands in *Inland Revenue* v. *Wilson,* 1927 S.C. 733 at p. 737: "The ownership of the shares is recorded in a register open to public inspection, and subjected to such inspection for the public protection in view of the privileges accorded to a limited company. . . . The document of title is the register of the company. The share certificate is not a document of title, it is merely an acknowledgment on the part of the officials of the company that the name of the person mentioned in it is duly recorded in the proper document of title, the company's register. This is illustrated by the fact that dividend warrants are issued to the shareholders whose names are on the company's register, without any inquiry or concern as to whether the shareholder is in possession of the share certificate. The register of the company bears, in this aspect, a certain resemblance to the Register of Sasines as regards land."

Minors as members

Hill v. The City of Glasgow Bank
(1879) 7 R. 68

Lang left his estate, which included stock in an unlimited registered bank, to trustees for behoof of his widow in liferent and his children in fee.

In 1865, the original trustees assumed Lang's widow and children as trustees. One of the children, Janet, was then a minor. She accepted office by signing a deed of assumption.

In 1867, while still a minor, Janet sanctioned the transfer of the stock into the names of the assumed trustees including herself. This transfer was effected by mere production of the deed of assumption to the bank, without any deed of transfer being signed.

After majority, Janet acted three times as a trustee.

Held, in the liquidation of the bank in 1878, that Janet had been validly registered as a stockholder, and that, as no challenge had been brought during the *quadriennium utile*, she was properly made a contributory.

LORD PRESIDENT (INGLIS) (at p. 74): " The position of a *minor pubes* is very well understood in the law of Scotland. A *minor pubes* is certainly subject to no legal incapacity. . . . A pupil is under incapacity, and no act done by a pupil can have any effect whatever. But incapacity ends with the attainment of the age of puberty, and it may be said generally that after that time a minor is just as capable of contracting obligations, and of doing any other thing inferring liability, as is a person of full age. This general statement of the law is subject to certain qualifications. In the first place, a minor who has curators requires their consent to do certain acts, but a minor who has no curators may do all those things that I have been mentioning, and the circumstance that he has no curators will not make his acts one bit the less effectual in law than if they had been done with the consent of curators. Again, every act of a minor is liable to be reduced after he attains majority and within four years after his attainment of majority upon the ground of minority and lesion, but there must be distinct proof of lesion of the minor, and it is also absolutely indispensable as a condition of this remedy that the reduction be brought within four years of his attaining majority—*intra quadriennium utile.* If that be not attended to, the remedy is altogether gone, and the act of the minor stands as unchallengeable as if it had been done by a person of full age. Among the other things that a minor can do without curators, if he has none, and with the consent of curators if he has them, is the contraction of personal obligation, and particularly of the obligations of a deed of copartnership. There is nothing to prevent a *minor pubes* engaging in trade, either in an ordinary trading company, consisting of a few partners, or in a joint-stock company, and his act in becoming a partner of such a concern is in law like any other act contracting a personal obligation. It is perfectly valid, subject to the qualifications which I have just explained.

". . . Here was a lady of full age, in a position, if she thought fit, to challenge the transaction by which she had been made a partner of the bank . . . but instead of challenging the transaction she ratifies and confirms it. . . . After that she as a trustee attends meetings of the trust. . . . Now, it appears to me that in these circumstances Mrs. Hill, instead of availing herself of the privilege which undoubtedly belonged to her when she came of age, of challenging this transaction, did everything that she then could to confirm it, and that she remained accordingly a partner of the bank, along with the other trustees."

NOTE

Cf. Inland Revenue v. *Wilson,* 1928 S.C.(H.L.) 42, 1927 S.C. 733, in which there was held to have been a completed gift of shares by W. to his minor son, with the result that a claim for repayment of income tax on behalf of the son was sustained.

Shares in the Perth Garage Ltd. had been bought by W. with his own funds in 1920, when his son was still a pupil. At W.'s request, the son's name was entered in the register of members. Dividend warrants were issued in the son's name, and the claim for repayment of income tax deducted from the dividends was made for a period after the son had attained minority.

In the Court of Session *opinions reserved, per* Lord Sands and Lord Blackburn, as to whether a purchase of shares by a father in name of his pupil child could constitute a completed donation while the child remained in pupillarity.

Executors: not entered as members

Macdonald, &c. v. The City of Glasgow Bank
(1879) 6 R. 621

The estate of Hume, who had died in July 1878, included £400 of the City of Glasgow Bank stock.

Hume's executors gave their law-agent general instructions to do what was necessary.

The law-agent on September 17, 1878, sent the confirmation to the bank, with a request to transfer the stock from Hume's name to the name of the executors.

On October 2, 1878, the bank stopped payment, and on October 5 its hopeless insolvency was made public.

After October 11 a clerk of the bank entered the names of Hume's executors in the register of members.

Held that that entry could receive no effect, and that the executors were therefore entitled to have their names removed from the list of contributories in respect of personal liability.

LORD PRESIDENT (INGLIS) (at p. 628): " Persons in the position of the petitioners who succeed to shares belonging to a deceased member of the company, and who are entitled and bound to administer them as part of the executry estate, . . . are under no obligation to any one to become members of the company, and to allow their names to be put on the register. They owe no such duty either to the deceased or to his legatees, for they can, under the 24th section of the Act of 1862, realise and dispose of these shares as part of the executry estate, without the necessity of having them transferred to their own names. They may, no doubt, follow the latter course, and if they give authority for transferring shares into their names, and their names are in due course put on the register, they will become partners of the company. But this consequence will not follow from any antecedent obligation or agreement to become members, but only from their voluntary act in giving a mandate to the company to transfer the shares from the name of the deceased to those of his executors. . . . It seems to me to follow that, before the registration of the executors as partners, this voluntary and gratuitous mandate may at any moment be recalled. . . .

" . . . I am of opinion that the names of the petitioners ought to be removed from the register of shareholders, and from the first part of the list of contributories, and entered in the second part of the list as those of representatives of a deceased member, bound in a due course of administration to account for the deceased's estate."

LORD DEAS (at p. 635): " I am humbly of opinion that, in the absence of registration of the petitioners, in a character inferring personal liability on their part as shareholders prior to the hopeless and published insolvency of the bank, the petitioners cannot be placed on the register or upon the list of contributories in a character inferring such personal liability, but only in their representative character as executors of the deceased, and liable as in the course of a due administration to the extent of the estate of the deceased whom they represent in this liquidation."

NOTES

1. Lord Shand commented on the effect of the general instructions given to the law-agent, saying (at p. 639): " I am not prepared to

hold that a general instruction and authority of the kind given by Mr. Dickson was sufficient as authority to put his name on the register of the bank, and so make him a partner, liable as an individual for the debts of the company. A title to the stock of a joint stock company is properly made up by obtaining decree of confirmation. Such a decree gives a complete title for all purposes of administration . . . ; and a title so obtained is sufficient to enable executors under section 24 of the Act of 1862 to grant an effectual transfer of the stock to a purchaser, without themselves becoming members of the company. . . . Mr. Dickson . . . was not even made aware that the deceased held any such stock."

2. The provision in section 24 of the Act of 1862 is now represented by the provision in section 76 of the Act of 1948 (" Transfer by personal representative ").

3. In *Wishart, &c.* v. *The City of Glasgow Bank* (1879) 6 R. 1341, general instructions given to a law-agent to make up a title to the estate in the person of the executors were held not to have authorised the law-agent to transfer the stock of the bank to the names of the executors, with the result that, as the executors were not proved to have subsequently known of or adopted the law-agent's unauthorised act, they were not, as individuals, stockholders in the bank.

Lord Mure (at p. 1344): " The petitioners . . . as executors . . . were not entitled to hold bank stock, but were bound to realise the stock with a view to the reinvestment of the proceeds, as soon as they could conveniently do so within a reasonable time after the death of the truster. . . . What was it necessary for the agent to do in order to effect that object? Was it necessary not only to make up a title to the stock by confirmation, but also to have the petitioners registered as holders of the stock in the sense of being partners in the bank? Now, the answer to this question is to be found in the provisions of the 24th section of the . . . Companies Act 1862. . . . All, therefore, that it was necessary for the agent to do, in order that the executors should be able to avail themselves of this enactment, was to expede a confirmation to the personal estate of the deceased, including the bank stock in question, and exhibit that confirmation to the bank as their title to transfer the stock, and intimate their intention to dispose of it as soon as a purchaser was found."

Lord Shand (at p. 1349): " In this case we had a very full argument on questions of law arising out of the position of executors in regard to stock held by the deceased, whom they represent, particularly with reference to what fell from the noble and learned Lords in the case of *Buchan*, H. of L. cases, p. 44, which was recently decided on appeal. I confess I think that the law in such a case presents no difficulty whatever. Executors taking up the estate of a person deceased, in so far as consisting of shares in a joint stock company, have an alternative presented to them under section 24 of the statute of 1862. They may either simply make up a title by confirmation, and so vest themselves with a right or title to the shares, which will enable them to dispose of the shares without going on the register, and may intimate the fact of confirmation to the company as a mere notice that they have made up such a title; or they may, if they think fit, intimate the confirmation to the bank and request that the shares shall be transferred to their names, the legal result of which is that they thereby make up a title of ownership in themselves to the shares, and thereby become partners. ... Executors have a strong presumption in their favour which will not arise in the case of an ordinary transferree—as, *e.g.,* in the case of a purchase—and will not arise in the same degree in the case of trustees who are in the administration of a continuing trust— they have this strong presumption in their favour, where they do not intend to hold the stock, but intend to sell it within a short time—that they do not mean to put their names on the register, and so acquire a title of ownership in their own persons as individuals in the shares."

For the case of *Buchan* referred to, see below.

Executors: entered as members

Buchan v. The City of Glasgow Bank
(1879) 6 R. (H.L.) 44; (1879) 6 R. 567

The estate of Gibson, who died in 1854, included City of Glasgow Bank stock. B. and other trustees appointed by Gibson's trust disposition and settlement were confirmed executors, and the bank stock was transferred in the register from Gibson's name to the names of B. and the other trustees as "executors" of the deceased.

For 24 years thereafter, B. signed the dividend warrants on the stock, usually adding to his name the word "trustee," and in one instance adding the words "sole surviving executor."

In the liquidation of the bank, B. presented a petition for the rectification of the register and the list of contributories by deletion of his name.

Held that B. was personally liable, on the ground that he had authorised the transfer of the stock into his name, and had ever since acted as a stockholder.

LORD CHANCELLOR (CAIRNS) (at p. 45): " It appears to me impossible to say, looking to those facts, that the appellant did not authorise the placing of his name on the register, or that he did not agree to become a partner of the bank.

" I do not think it necessary to enter into an examination of the question whether the appellant ought properly to have been described as ' executor ' or ' trustee.' I rest the conclusion at which I arrive not upon any question of form, but upon the substance of the case namely, that the appellant upwards of twenty years ago had the stock transferred into his own name, and has ever since been upon the register of the bank as a partner, and that this state of things is, upon the principles laid down by this House in *Muir's* case (*supra,* p. 21) inconsistent with any conclusion but that of personal liability.

. . .

" An executor whose testator has held shares in a joint stock company has generally one of two courses open to him. He may have the shares transferred into his own name, and become to all intents and purposes a partner in the company; or he may, on the other hand, not wish to have the shares transferred into his name, and he ought then to have a reasonable time allowed him to sell the shares, and to produce a purchaser who will take a transfer of them."

LORD SELBORNE (at p. 50): " The case of trustees who take a transfer of shares into their names differs in principle from that of executors, who merely intimate their title as executors to a company in order to claim and exercise the rights which belong to them as the legal representatives of their testator.... Trustees have not, in any proper sense of the word, a representative character, but executors have. . . . Having representative rights, it is impossible that they should not be entitled to produce the legal evidence of them to the company, for the purpose of having their title in some way recorded and recognised, without making themselves personally liable. This would be a necessary preliminary, even to the exercise (since 1862) of the statutory right of transfer. . . .

" . . . However, . . . it cannot be said that executors (at all events when, as in this case, they are also disponees in trust) have not the power to transfer their testator's shares to themselves. . . . A request for a transfer made by executors who were also trustees, and who had full power to transfer as they thought fit, followed by an actual transfer in the stock ledger and the issue of stock certificates in accordance therewith, and acted upon afterwards (as in this case it has been for 24 years), cannot, I think, be satisfactorily distinguished, as to its legal effect, from any other transfer to trustees."

NOTES

1. For the case of *Muir* referred to, see p. 132, below.
2. *Shepherd's Trustees* v. *Shepherd* (p. 206, below) distinguishes

between transmission on death and transfer. The House of Lords held that an article which expressly gave to directors a right of pre-emption where there was a transfer of shares did not impliedly confer on them a right of pre-emption where there was only a transmission on death.

Lord Reid (at 1950 S.C. (H.L.) p. 70): " The first question for decision is whether this provision gives to the directors or any one of them any right to acquire shares which belonged to a deceased member of the company when his executors do not seek to transfer the shares to another person but only seek to have their own names registered as members in respect of the shares. . . . Transfer, if the word is used in its ordinary sense, means a transfer from one person to another and implies that there must be both a transferor and a transferee. But where an executor is registered in respect of shares forming part of the deceased's estate there is no transfer from one person to another; the executor, as is recognised by article 17, is already entitled to the shares when he makes application for registration of his name. . . . There is nothing illogical or even unreasonable in drawing a distinction between a case where an executor seeks to have his own name registered and a case where an executor seeks to transfer shares to someone else."

Trustee in bankruptcy

Myles v. The City of Glasgow Bank
(1879) 6 R. 718

M. was a trustee on the sequestrated estate of Kidston whose name stood on the register of the City of Glasgow Bank in respect of £100 of the bank's stock.

Brown's trustees, who were creditors on the sequestrated estate, claimed that they had a right in security over Kidston's stock, and an agreement was made between M. and Brown's trustees by which M. was to complete a title to the stock as trustee and then transfer it to Brown's trustees.

M. forwarded his act and warrant to the bank for registration, and a transfer by him to Brown's trustees was prepared. Before M.'s name had been entered in the register, however, the bank stopped payment.

Held that the liquidators were not entitled to retain M. on the list of contributories as a contributory in his own right.

LORD PRESIDENT (INGLIS) (at p. 725): : " The facts as regards this part of the case are almost identical with those which occurred in the case of *Macdonald, &c. (Hume's Executors, supra, p. 621)*, and some other cases recently decided by the Court. The name of the petitioner was not entered in the register till after the stoppage of the bank, at some indefinite time between

October 2 and 18, when, without any special authority or instructions, it was entered by the clerk. . . .

" For the reasons stated in the former cases I am of opinion that the entry was improperly made, and can receive no effect, and that the case must be dealt with as if that entry had never been made. . . . The petitioner consented in his agreement with Brown's trustees to complete a title to the bankrupt's stock in the bank only for the purpose of enabling him to transfer the stock to them. . . .

" . . . For the purpose of realising the bankrupt's interest in this concern the trustee has no occasion to become a partner of the company or incur any of the liabilities of a partner. If he does so he is going beyond his statutory powers and duties. But every species of moveable estate is so vested in the trustee by the 103rd section of the Bankruptcy Act 1856, that he can sell any portion of it without the necessity of a formal conveyance to himself. . . .

" . . . This was a binding agreement as between the petitioner and Brown's trustees; but the directors of the bank . . . had no interest in its being carried out. . . . They had no interest in the petitioner becoming, for a few days or a few hours, a holder of this stock for the purpose of transferring it to Brown's trustees. If, therefore, Brown's trustees and the petitioner had cancelled their agreement the bank had no *jus quaesitum* under which they could have enforced. But when the stoppage of the bank occurred without the agreement having been carried into execution, without the petitioner having been entered in the register of shareholders, without any transfer by him to Brown's trustees having been accepted or registered, the agreement between the petitioner and Brown's trustees fell to the ground; the subject of the agreement had become worse than valueless, and, if the only parties having any right or interest under the agreement did not seek to enforce it, the bank had no title or right to insist that it should be executed either in whole or in part."

NOTE

For the present provisions as to vesting of moveable estate in the trustee in a sequestration, see Bankruptcy (Scotland) Act 1913, s. 97.

Curator bonis *to insane person*

Lindsay's Curator v. The City of Glasgow Bank
(1879) 6 R. 671

L., the proprietor of £220 stock of the City of Glasgow Bank, became insane, and in March 1877 his brother-in-law, McLean, was appointed his *curator bonis*. Because of debts due by L., McLean found it necessary to sell £100 of the bank stock, and for the purpose of the transfer of this £100 to the purchaser the act and warrant appointing McLean curator was sent to the bank.

McLean's appointment was noted in the register of members, a stock certificate in McLean's own name for unsold stock was sent to him, and McLean subsequently received a dividend warrant on the whole balance of L.'s stock in his own name as *curator bonis* and signed a receipt upon it.

Held in the liquidation of the bank in 1878 that McLean, as he had never authorised the stock to be transferred from L.'s name to his own, was not personally liable.

LORD PRESIDENT (INGLIS) (at p. 674): " A *curator bonis* who sells a portion of his ward's estate does not necessarily become the proprietor of that estate in order to enable him to sell. He sells under the authority of the Court, and the Court gives him that authority because the ward is incapable himself of giving it. . . .

" . . . I can understand that, as a matter of mere convenience —as a memorandum—it may be a quite reasonable thing for the keeper of this stock ledger to note that the person who is to operate upon this stock in the way of drawing the dividends and otherwise is the *curator bonis*, and not the person in whose name the stock is registered. That is quite a reasonable and intelligible explanation of the entry being made. But that it can have any effect in transferring the stock from the person in whose name it stands to that of another person who has not by reason of the fact there stated acquired any title to it is not intelligible.

. . .

" Therefore I think we can give no sort of effect to this note, and the consequence of that is that Mr. McLean is not upon the register.

" . . . I do not think a man can be made a partner of a bank by receiving a dividend on a false narrative, or by receiving a certificate of stock with an inaccurate description, the fact being, behind all that, that the original owner of this stock, Mr. John Lindsay, is down to this day the only man upon the register in respect of that stock."

LORD MURE (at p. 677): " A good deal has been said about the case of *Lumsden* v. *Peddie* . . . , but it appears to me to be a totally different one from the present, in essential respects. The words of the transfer there were—'And I, the said Donald Smith Peddie, . . . as *curator bonis* foresaid hereby become a partner of the said bank'—and these were held to amount to a distinct acknowledgment on his part that when he took the transfer of shares to himself he, by so doing, intended to become a partner of the bank."

LORD SHAND (at p. 678): "The case of the bank really lies in these two things—the certificate and the dividend warrant. I am clearly of opinion that as the petitioner gave no warrant originally to put his name on the register, and had no reason to suppose this had been done, we cannot infer from the receipt of the first of these documents and the signature of the other that he adopted the act of putting his name on the register."

NOTE

The case of *Lumsden* v. *Peddie* (1866) 5 M. 34 referred to arose out of the liquidation of the Western Bank of Scotland. The *curator bonis* was held to be personally liable.

Lord Justice-Clerk (Inglis) (at p. 38): "The curator thought fit to enter into an arrangement with the executor, by which he . . . consented, in satisfaction of his ward's claim for that amount of money, to take over seven shares of the stock of the Western Bank . . . and to pay the difference . . . in cash to the executor, out of the first dividends received on the stock.

" . . . The arrangement was on the part of the curator entirely voluntary. He was entitled to . . . cash, and he preferred to take the value in Western Bank stock. . . .

" . . . The effect of these proceedings was to make the defender a partner of the company, to the extent of seven shares of the capital stock. . . . There cannot, we think, be the smallest doubt, that the defender could not make his ward a partner of the company, and that he did not intend, or even think of doing or attempting such a thing, and that he did in fact make himself a partner of the company.

" If this be so, it is in vain to allege that he became a partner of the company only as *curator bonis,* and is therefore not liable *ultra valorem* of the curator's estate; for it is now well settled. that in this or any the like company no one can become a partner with a limited liability, or with any other liabilities than such as are borne in common by all the partners."

Company may not be member of itself

General Property Investment Co. Ltd. and Liquidator
v. Matheson's Trustees
(1888) 16 R. 282

The articles of G. Ltd. provided: " IV. No shareholder shall transfer his shares until he has first made offer of them to the company at the then market price. V. Any shares acquired by the company to be retained as the property of the company, or disposed of in such manner as the company in general meeting thinks fit to direct."

M., an original shareholder of G. Ltd., transferred his 250 shares to the company in 1876 for £254 11s. 10d.

G. Ltd. went into liquidation in 1886, and along with its liquidator brought an action of reduction of the transfer and of the entry of the company's name as holder of the 250 shares. There was also a conclusion for payment of £3066 10s., made up of the price paid by the company, and calls on the shares, together with interest on both amounts. The action was brought against M.'s trustees, M. having died in 1877.

Held that the transfer fell to be reduced as having been *ab initio* void.

M.'s trustees were held bound to pay the purchase price, but with interest only as from citation in the action.

The names of M.'s trustees were placed on the list of contributories.

The question of liability for calls was reserved by the court, and was ultimately compromised.

LORD SHAND (at p. 290): " The Lord Ordinary . . . has found that it was *ultra vires* of the company, under the Joint Stock Companies Acts of 1862 and 1867, to become purchasers of their shares, and upon that ground he has found that the transaction was illegal, and that the price must be repaid. If there was any argument against that view of the Lord Ordinary, I have only to say that I think the point has been clearly settled by the decision in the case of *Trevor* v. *Whitworth* ((1887) L.R. App.Ca. 409), shortly before this action was raised, and as we have already had occasion to refer to that case very fully in the case of *Klenck* (*ante,* p. 271), I shall say no more than this, that I think it clearly decides that a transaction of this kind is not merely voidable, but is void, as being *ultra vires* of the company. It is a transaction which not only the directors had no right to enter upon, but which even the company themselves at a meeting of all the shareholders could not adopt, because it was directly in the teeth of the Statute of 1862. . . .

" . . . The transfer is . . . an absolute nullity. . . . A company of this kind, carried on under the statutes with the limited powers which these statutes confer, can no more by adoption or homologation make a proceeding of this kind legal than they can lawfully enter into the original transaction itself. It is a nullity originally, and the company cannot homologate or adopt a nullity, for that is equally *ultra vires*. . . . The views that I have now stated as to this transaction being clearly *ultra vires* of the company, and as to the effect of a transaction of that kind being such that it cannot be adopted even by homologation, I think are strongly borne out by the decision of the Court in the case of the *Ashbury Railway Carriage Company*, which has been so often referred in cases of this kind, regarding the powers of joint stock companies. . . . What I have said now leads, I think, first, . . . to the granting of a decree of reduction of the transfer, and, in the next place, to the putting of Mr. Matheson's executors on the register."

NOTES

1. For the case of *Klenck* referred to, see *Klenck* v. *East India Co. for Exploration and Mining Ltd.* (p. 98, above).

2. The case of *Ashbury Railway Carriage Company* referred to is *Ashbury Railway Carriage and Iron Co. Ltd.* v. *Riche* (1875) L.R. 7 H.L. 653.

3. The Companies Act 1948, s. 27 (1), provides that, with certain exceptions a company cannot be a member of its holding company, and that any allotment or transfer of shares in a company to its subsidiary shall be void.

That this provision does not prevent a subsidiary company from arresting the shares of its holding company for the purpose of founding jurisdiction was decided in *Stenhouse London Ltd.* v. *Allwright*, 1972 S.L.T. 255.

Stenhouse London Ltd., a company with its registered office in Glasgow, raised an action for £8,000 against A., who was resident in Somerset. A. was the registered holder of shares in Stenhouse Holdings Ltd., which was the holding company of Stenhouse London Ltd. and which had its registered office at the same address in Glasgow. A.'s shares were arrested by Stenhouse London Ltd. *ad fundandam jurisdictionem*.

If an arrestment to found jurisdiction is to be effective, the subjects arrested must be capable of being attached afterwards by arrestment in execution, and A. claimed that the court had no jurisdiction over him because, by s. 27 (1) of the Companies Act 1948, a transfer of the shares to Stenhouse London Ltd. would be void. *Held* that, as it was open to the subsidiary to conclude, not for the transfer of the shares, but for the sale of the shares to another party, with payment of the proceeds to itself, there was no contravention of s. 27 (1) and the arrestment of the shares was therefore effective.

Lord Justice-Clerk (Grant) (at p. 257): " It is clear, I think, both from practice and from authority, that it would be open to the pursuers in an action of furthcoming to conclude, not for transfer of the *shares* to themselves, but for sale of the shares (to such an extent as would satisfy their debt and expenses) and the payment to themselves of the *proceeds. . . .*

" . . . An arrestment is futile unless it can be followed up by an effective decree of furthcoming. . . . I am satisfied that the pursuers could obtain such a decree here. . . .

" The defender submitted a brief alternative argument that the arrestment was invalid inasmuch as Stenhouse Holdings Ltd., being the holding company of the pursuers, was not a third party. The two companies, however, are separate and distinct legal entities and no good reason was adduced to show that they should not be so treated for the purpose of the issue now in dispute."

4. An unlimited company may purchase its own shares: *Nelson Mitchell* v. *The City of Glasgow Bank* (1879) 6 R. (H.L.) 66; (1878) 6 R. 420.

On September 28 and 30 M. sold £2,500 of stock upon the Stock Exchange in the usual way. Settlement was to be on October 16. On October 11 M.'s brokers were informed that the purchaser was the bank itself. The bank had stopped payment on October 2, and the directors had on October 5 called a meeting to consider voluntary winding up on the ground of insolvency.

On October 16 M. executed a transfer of his stock to the bank, and on October 19 presented a petition for rectification of the register by the removal of his name and entry of the bank's name in its place.

Held that, as after October 5 the bank had not been entitled to alter the register, M. was not entitled to have his name removed from the register or from the list of contributories.

This being the decision, the remarks on the legality of a purchase by the bank of its own stock are *obiter.*

Lord Chancellor (Cairns) (at p. 67): " The brokers who bought, bought for the bank, and there is no doubt that the bank, who had authority to buy their own stock under their deed of copartnery, were the purchasers."

Lord President (Inglis) (at p. 429): " This is not the case of a sale by a partner of his shares to a third party outside the company, but it is a sale to the company itself. The directors of the company were, under ordinary circumstances, undoubtedly quite entitled to purchase the stock of their own bank, and they had been in the course of doing so apparently for some time to a large extent. This purchase was made by their brokers, not upon special instructions for that purpose, but upon general instructions as to the purchase of such stock."

5. Although a company is not entitled to hold its own shares, there is not the same objection to shares being held by a named person on behalf of the company: *Gardiners* v. *The Victoria Estates Co. Ltd.* (1885) 12 R. 1356.

In October 1878, James G. and William G. sold their shares in V. Ltd. The transfers bore that the sale was made to Drummond " for behoof of V. Ltd."

In November 1878 the Gardiners' names were removed from the register of members, and the shares were entered as held by V. Ltd.

In June 1884, the directors of V. Ltd., acting on legal advice that V. Ltd. had no power to purchase its own shares, restored the Gardiners' names to the register.

The Gardiners brought a petition for rectification of the register by the removal of their names.

Held that the Gardiners were entitled to have their names removed.

Lord Mure (at p. 1361): " According to the view I take of the case, the entry on the register ought to have been in the name of ' James Drummond as holding for behoof of the company.' But the circumstance that the entry of the transfer was not properly made cannot, as matters now stand, affect the right of the petitioners to have the register rectified; and upon the whole I am of opinion that the names of the petitioners were properly removed from the register in 1878, and that they were improperly replaced upon it in 1884."

This case, though earlier than the *General Property* case, is in accordance with the principle established by that case.

However, the later case of *Gill* v. *The Arizona Copper Co. Ltd.* (1900) 2 F. 843 appears not to be entirely reconcilable with *Gardiners'* case and the *General Property* case. It represents an attempt to establish that the rule which makes it illegal for a company to hold its own shares does not apply if the shares are fully paid. The facts of the case were, however, somewhat special.

A. Ltd. was formed to acquire certain copper mines in Arizona. Its capital consisted of preferred shares and deferred shares. The deferred shares were issued as fully paid to the vendors of the mines. The vendors sold some of these shares to other parties.

Thereafter A. Ltd. made certain claims against the vendors, and an agreement was entered into between A. Ltd. and the vendors, by which the claims were compromised on certain terms, one of which was that the vendors should transfer their deferred shares to the company " or its nominees, for behoof of the preferred shareholders."

G., a preferred shareholder, brought an action against A. Ltd. for declarator that the deferred shares were held in trust for the preferred shareholders. A. Ltd. maintained that the transaction was equivalent to a surrender of the shares to the company as a whole, and that it was *ultra vires* of the company to acquire and hold its own shares.

Held that, since the agreement had been of the nature of a compromise and since the shares were fully paid, it was not *ultra vires* of the company to acquire the shares as it did, and that the transaction was not equivalent to a surrender of the shares to the company, but that the company was bound to hold them in trust for the preferred shareholders.

Lord McLaren (at p. 859): " It was ... maintained ... that ... a company is legally incapable of holding its own shares. It is, of course, indisputable as a general rule that a company is disabled from acquiring shares in its own undertaking to which liability attaches. The reason is that by such purchase or acquisition the uncalled capital of the company is reduced, because in the event of the company going into liquidation, the liability of the insolvent company is substituted for that of a shareholder who is presumably solvent. . . .

" Now it is plain enough that a transfer of fully paid shares in a company to the company itself or its nominees does not in fact diminish the capital of the company available for distribution amongst its creditors, because, according to the hypothesis, the shares only represent a claim upon the income of the company, and the holders of the shares are not liable to be made contributories in liquidation. I therefore cannot hold that the judgment in *Trevor* v. *Whitworth* (1887) L.R. 12 App. Cas. 409, and the other cases cited, have any application to the case of a transfer of fully paid shares. There may be a theoretical difficulty as to a company holding fully paid shares in its own name; and in the case of an unqualified transfer perhaps the correct view would be that the shares are extinguished, as in the case of a transfer by an insolvent shareholder. But this is not the case of an unqualified transfer; the obligation, as I read it, is to transfer the shares to the company or its nominee in trust for a particular class of shareholders. . . . There is nothing to prevent the company from now registering these shares in the name of a nominee who would be willing to hold them and to execute a declaration of trust in favour of the preferred shareholders."

Trustees

Muir. &c. v. The City of Glasgow Bank
(1879) 6 R. (H.L.) 21; (1878) 6 R. 392

£6,000 stock of an unlimited bank had been transferred to M. and three other persons as " trust-disponees " of Mrs. Mary Murdoch or Syme and Mrs. Sophia Murdoch or Boyd. The entry in the bank's register of members was in the same form.

In the liquidation of the bank, the liquidators placed the names of M. and other trustees upon the first part of the list of contributories as "contributories in their own right," and made a call upon them individually and collectively of £500 per cent amounting to £30,000.

The trustees presented a petition for rectification of the list of contributories by the transfer of their names to the second part of the list of contributories who were representatives of others.

Held that the trustees were individually liable as "contributories in their own right."

LORD CHANCELLOR (CAIRNS) (at p. 23): "I will now ask your Lordships to bear in mind the general scope and provisions of the deed of partnership. . . .

" . . . The scheme of the deed is clear. . . . There is no limit of liability. If the partner is an individual he is absolutely liable, to the extent of his means as an individual, for the proportion of the debt of the bank attributable to his share. . . .

" . . . The appellants undertook, as they say, to be liable in the obligation incumbent on holders of stock to the extent only of the trust-funds under their administration. . . .

" . . . What would this be but the creation of shares with a limited liability? . . . This is just what the law would not permit to be done with regard to a joint stock company of this kind except by means of the constitution of a company with liability limited according to the statute; and such a company the City of Glasgow Bank never was. . . .

" . . . There is no difficulty whatever in assigning to the words ['as trust-disponees of Mrs. Syme and Mrs. Boyd'] a meaning and a purpose clear, intelligible, and within the limits of the contracting power of the directors. One object of these words, and one purpose served by them, is noticed in the judgments of the Lord President [Inglis] and Lord Shand. The Lord President says that the practice of using them and of entering them upon the register arose 'not for the purpose of altering the liability of the holders of such stock as compared with the other holders of stock in the same company, but only for the purpose of marking the stock as the property of the particular trust named in the transference and in the register.' The Lord President further observes that it was the Scotch practice of marking trust stock in this way which prevented the

Legislature extending to Scotland the enactment that no joint stock company should take notice of any trusts on its register of shares; and I may add there is no doubt that a permission to notice trusts on a register of shares is *prima facie* a permission introduced for the benefit of the beneficiaries and not of the trustees. Lord Shand observes that the law of Scotland as to the proof of trust is very stringent ' in requiring that in all cases the averment that property is held in trust shall be proved only by writing subscribed by the alleged trustee, or by his oath on reference; and that no more effectual way of avoiding the dangers of this limited mode of proof can exist than by having the title to the trust-property qualified by a declaration on its face that the property is held for behoof of others.' A second purpose served by the words is, that they make it clear that the shares are held upon a joint account with a right of survivorship, and that they do not belong to the persons named on the register as tenants in common. It is possible (I will not say more) that there may be a third purpose served by the words founded on the law of Scotland, which gives peculiar facility to a trustee for retiring from the trust, and which might justify in the case of a retiring trustee a simpler mode of removing his name from the register than in the case of another joint owner. . . .

" . . . The observations of the Lord Chancellor [Westbury] and of Lord Cranworth [in *Lumsden* v. *Buchanan* (1865) 3 M.(H.L.) 89, 4 Macq. 950] . . . appear to me to apply conclusively to the present case."

LORD PENZANCE (at p. 33): " In truth the present case is, in my opinion, governed in principle by the case of *Lumsden* v. *Buchanan.*

" What the principle involved in that decision was is, I think, rightly appreciated and declared by the learned Judges in the Court of Session. The Lord President said the rule of liability then established might be stated in a single sentence as follows: ' Persons becoming partners of a joint stock company such as the Western Bank, and being registered as such, cannot escape from the full liabilities of partners either in a question with creditors of the company or in the way of relief to their co-partners by reason of the fact that they hold their stock in trust for others, and are described as trustees in the register of partners and the other books and papers of the company.' And Lord Deas said that the grounds of decision in *Lumsden* v. *Buchanan* ' resolved themselves into this, that where trustees join in a contract of partnership for trading purposes, such as a contract for carrying on the business of banking, the mere designation of them as being trustees will not exempt them from the same personal liability as is undertaken by the other partners, or limit their liability to the value of the trust-estate.' "

NOTES

1. In *Lumsden* v. *Buchanan* (1865) 3 M.(H.L.) 89, the House of Lords reversed the judgment of the majority of the whole Court of Session ((1864) 2 M. 695).

The action was brought by the liquidators of the Western Bank of Scotland against B. and others for £7,500, the amount of calls made by the liquidators on 60 shares of £50 each held by the defenders as trustees under the marriage-contract of Charles Brown and Mrs. Ellen Buchanan or Brown.

The shares had been purchased by the defenders direct from the bank, and the defenders had signed a deed of accession which embodied the terms of the bank's original contract of copartnery. The testing clause of the deed of accession bore that the deed had been signed by B. and others, "trustees for Mrs. Ellen Brown, spouse of the said Charles Wilsons Brown, the majority surviving being a quorum." In the stock-ledger B. and the others were designed "trustees for Mrs. Ellen Brown, Glasgow."

Held (rev. judgment of the Court of Session) that B. and the other trustees who had signed the deed of accession were personally liable, since there was no special stipulation limiting their responsibility.

Held (aff. judgment of the Court of Session) that one of the trustees who had not signed the deed was not liable.

As the Western Bank of Scotland was at the time when the trustees purchased the shares a common law company formed under a contract of copartnery, there is more emphasis in this case on the contractual nature of shareholding than in *Muir's* case.

Lord Chancellor (Westbury) (at p. 92): "The trustees now contend that the legal effect and operation of this mode of executing the deed is, that they became parties to the deed of partnership, and therefore partners in the bank, as trustees only, without any personal liability. . . .

"It is obvious that the position thus claimed for themselves by the trustees is wholly at variance with the spirit and intent of the partnership contract. It is repugnant to the obligations they expressly entered into. . . .

"According to the argument of the trustees, there would be two distinct classes of partners. One of persons who became shareholders in the ordinary case, and who would be partners with unlimited liability, and the other of trustees who took shares in their fiduciary character, and who would be partners with limited liability. . . .

"A trustee may, both in England and in Scotland, so limit and restrict any contract he may enter into, as to exclude (as between himself and the other parties to such contract) personal liability. But this must be the result of express stipulation, and whether this be or be not the effect of any particular contract, is a question depending on the construction of the instrument, and the nature of the contract.

" In the present contract the parties bind themselves, their heirs, executors, and successors (which is the recognised style by which an individual binds himself so as to be personally liable), and in the words of the deed which I have cited, each partner personally obliges himself to contribute *pro rata* to the debts and losses of the company. There can be no question, therefore, as to the meaning, construction, and effect of the contract, as contained in the deed of partnership."

2. For the distinction between trustees and executors in this connection, see *Buchan* v. *The City of Glasgow Bank* (p. 122, above).

3. A trustee who had not signed any transfer but who had signed a dividend mandate which referred to the stock as standing in his name as trustee was held to have agreed to become a member of the company and to have acquiesced in his name being put on the register in *Cuninghame* v. *The City of Glasgow Bank, &c.* (1879) 6 R.(H.L.) 98, (1879) 6 R. 679.

Trustees under a marriage-contract, five in number, by minute signed by all, agreed to invest part of the trust-funds in the bank's stock. The deed of transfer was signed by three of the trustees as a quorum. The names of all the trustees were entered in the register of members. Later a dividend mandate, which described the stock as " standing in our names as trustees," was signed by the trustees, including C., a trustee who had not signed the transfer.

Held that C. was liable as a contributory.

Lord Chancellor (Cairns) (at p. 100): " Acceptance may be in many ways besides the execution of a deed. . . .

" . . . The only thing that can be suggested as not being present is the formal signature by the appellant of the deed of transfer. That, my Lords, seems to me to be the purest form, the merest ceremony, and the want of it can have no substantial operation whatever in the present case."

Lord O'Hagan (at p. 101): " We have here an antecedent sanction and authority given by this gentleman, with the other trustees, . . . distinctly approving of the investment. . . . That antecedent authority was followed by subsequent recognition in a letter of mandate . . . which at once establishes the appellant's full knowledge of the transaction which had been so antecedently authorised. Under those circumstances, I am clearly of opinion that we have no alternative in this case but to affirm the judgment of the Court below."

4. Another instance of a trustee who had not signed a transfer being held to have agreed to be a member occurs in *Roberts* v. *The City of Glasgow Bank* (1879) 6 R. 805.

Two of the three trustees under a marriage-contract purchased stock of the bank, and signed the transfer as a quorum. The other trustee, R., was not aware of the purchase. The names of the three trustees were entered on the register of members.

R. afterwards signed a minute of the trustees approving of the purchase and also a dividend mandate which described the stock as " belonging to us as trustees."

Held that R. was not entitled to have his name removed from the register.

5. Similarly, in *Smith, &c.* v. *The City of Glasgow Bank* (1879) 6 R. 1017, where the agent in the trust had, without the authority or knowledge of the trustees, caused the bank stock to be transferred to the trustees' names, the trustees were held, by the signing of a dividend mandate, to have adopted the act of their agent and so were not entitled to have their names removed from the list of contributories.

In this case the mandate did not describe the stock as standing in the names of the trustees, but as being stock of Mrs. S. A. Smith. Lord Shand said (at p. 1023): " In no case that has hitherto occurred has any party been held to be properly on the register on such slender evidence as is presented in the case of James Brown Smith. . . . The single piece of evidence against Mr. Smith in this case is that he signed a mandate." Lord Shand therefore dissented with regard to that trustee, while agreeing with the other three judges of the First Division in holding that the other four trustees, who had signed certain dividend warrants describing the stock as standing in the name of trustees under the marriage-contract of Mr. and Mrs. Smith were not entitled to have their names removed.

6. In *McEwen, &c.* v. *The City of Glasgow Bank* (1879) 6 R. 1315, trustees who were also executors and who resolved not to sell bank stock forming part of the executry estate were held not entitled to have their names removed from the list of contributories on which they had been placed as persons liable in their own right. They had held the stock for some five years before the liquidation, and during that time had signed a dividend mandate.

Lord President (Inglis) (at p. 1319): " It is quite within the power, no doubt, of the executors, by themselves or their agents, to say, ' We are sending you this confirmation merely for the purpose of satisfying you of the fact that we are confirmed, and we are going immediately to sell these shares in virtue of the power conferred upon us by the 24th section of the Companies Act 1862,' a procedure which, even before the passing of that Act, would, according to the law of Scotland, have been competent to executors in that position, because it was clearly an assignable interest, and I think by the law of Scotland every assignable interest could be made the subject of sale. . . . If they send it in without any qualification, they must just submit to the necessary consequence arising from the provisions of the contract. Now, that is what was done here . . . beyond all doubt. . . .

" But there is more in the case than this. . . . All of them signed the mandate, which certainly is abundantly clear in its terms. . . . Now, when you add to all that, that the administration of this trust goes on consistently in the same way for a period of five years, . . . it seems to me to be altogether out of the question to say that at the end of five years, merely because they now begin to find that what they have done and authorised to be done, and knowingly authorised to be done, is attended with personal liability of a very serious kind, they are to say—well, we did not understand all this, and therefore we cannot be subjected in that liability."

7. *Stott, &c.* v. *The City of Glasgow Bank* (1879) 6 R. 1126 offers a contrast to the last-mentioned case. Trustees who were also executors were held to have established by evidence that they had expressly instructed their agent not to make up a special title to the bank stock in such a way as to make them liable as members. They were accordingly held to be entitled to have their names removed from the register. The trustees had signed a dividend mandate, describing the stock as standing in their names as trustees, but the weight to be attached to the mandate was considered to be too small to contradict the other evidence.

8. New trustees assumed to act along with original trustees were held to have agreed to become members and therefore to be liable as contributories in *Bell, &c.* v. *The City of Glasgow Bank* (1879) 6 R.(H.L.) 55, (1879) 6 R. 548.

At a meeting of the trustees, it was agreed that the bank stock which stood in the names of the original trustees should be transferred to the names of the original and assumed trustees. No deed of transfer was executed, but to the entry of the names of the original trustees in the register of members a note was added stating that by deed of assumption the original trustees had assumed the new trustees, whose names and designations were then given. A new stock certificate in favour of the whole trustees, original and assumed, was issued by the bank and laid before the trustees at one of their meetings.

Lord Chancellor (Cairns) (at p. 56): " I cannot doubt but that on these facts your Lordships have a clear and complete case of the . . . appellants agreeing to have the bank stock placed in their names, and of this having been done in a form perfectly sufficient."

9. In *Dalgleish* v. *Land Feuing Co. Ltd.* (1885) 13 R. 223, the First Division (*diss.* Lord President Inglis) held that where one of several trustees resigned in terms of the Trusts (Scotland) Act 1867, s. 10, and intimated the minute of resignation to the company he had an absolute right to have his name removed from the register provided the company was not in liquidation.

Lord Mure (at p. 228): " When the respondents agreed to accept the trustees of Mr. Dalgleish as holders of the shares, they must be held to have done so in the knowledge that any one of those trustees had a right at any time to resign."

Lord Shand (at p. 231): " I am of opinion that in the ordinary case a resigning trustee is entitled to have effect given to the resignation duly intimated to the company without executing any deed of transfer, either by himself alone, or by himself and his co-trustees, in favour of them. I may add that, in my opinion, nothing which can be regarded as authority on the subject can be found in the judgments given on appeal in the cases of the City of Glasgow Bank Liquidation. Earl Cairns, in *Alexander Mitchell's* ((1879) 6 R.(H.L.) 60) case, spoke of a transfer, or something equivalent to a transfer, being presented to the company—indicating that there might be a mode of terminating liability by an equivalent to a transfer—and in my opinion an intimation of resignation of office is such an equivalent."

The City of Glasgow Bank cases there referred to were not authoritative on the subject because in those cases formal intimation of the resignation had not been made until the bank's liquidation was imminent.

In *Sinclair* v. *The City of Glasgow Bank* (1879) 6 R. 571, the minute of resignation had been recorded in terms of the Act of 1867, but had not been intimated either to the co-trustees or to the bank.

Held that the resigning trustee was not entitled to have his name removed from the register of members.

Lord President (Inglis) (at p. 572): " It seems to me that intimation of this resignation, whatever may be its legal effect otherwise, would be absolutely indispensable in order to entitle the bank to remove the name of the petitioner from the register of shareholders. Now, it is admitted that there never was intimation of any kind made to the bank.... The absence of such intimation in the present case is, I think, fatal to the case of the petitioner."

In *Tochetti* v. *The City of Glasgow Bank* (1879) 6 R. 789, no formal intimation of T.'s resignation had been given to the bank, but an entry in the bank's dividend register showed that, whereas before T.'s resignation dividend warrants had been signed by T. and Miller, another trustee, dividend warrants subsequent to T.'s resignation had been signed by Miller only.

Held that T. was liable as a contributory.

Lord President (Inglis) (at p. 791): " It is not a matter in the discretion of the officials of the bank to remove a name from the register, nor are they entitled to do so unless they have distinct authority for doing it."

Lord Deas (at p. 793): " There is no doubt, as I have had occasion to observe in former cases, that, in holding trustees personally liable as partners, we encountered this anomaly, that we could not practically carry out the principle by holding either the rights or liabilities of a partner to be transmitted to the personal representative of the trustee. It follows that the liability of a trustee may be terminated in ways which would not terminate the liability of a partner holding for his own behoof. The death of the trustee will do it, without any transfer either by his personal representative to the surviving trustees, or by them to themselves, and this without even the necessity of intimation of any kind. So we have already decided. On the other hand, a deed of assumption may result in the party assumed becoming a partner without any transfer. If, therefore, there had been in this case distinct evidence of intimation to the bank of the petitioner's resignation, I am, by no means, prepared to say that this would not have been sufficient without a transfer. We have never yet decided that a transfer, in such cases, is necessary, and there is a good deal which goes the other way. But the radical objection here is the want of satisfactory evidence either that the resignation had been intimated to the bank, or held as intimated by the bank."

Two cases on resignation reached the House of Lords:

Ker v. *The City of Glasgow Bank* (1879) 6 R.(H.L.) 52; (1879) 6 R. 575: In 1855, K. and three other persons had been appointed marriage-contract trustees. The agent in the trust, without consulting K., had the bank stock transferred into the names of the trustees. In 1856, K. signed a dividend warrant, adding the word " trustee " to his name. Later the same year he moved from Greenock to Liverpool, and took no further part in the affairs of the trust. He had never formally accepted the trust, and he did not attend any meeting of the trustees. On the husband's death in 1868, K. wrote to the agent in the trust, " declining " the office of trustee. This letter was not intimated to the bank.

Held that K. was liable as a contributory.

Lord Chancellor (Cairns) (at p. 53): " He was a trustee, he signed as a trustee, and he knew that the shares were registered in the names of the trustees. . . .

" . . . I should doubt whether the letter in question bore the formal character of a resignation of the trust; but even supposing it to have been a resignation, it was not in any manner intimated to or acted upon by the bank."

Alexander Mitchell v. *The City of Glasgow Bank* (1879) 6 R. (H.L.) 60; (1878) 6 R. 439: The minute of resignation in this case was dated October 16, 1878, and a certified copy of it was delivered to the secretary of the bank the following day. The bank had, however, stopped payment on October 2, and on October 5 the directors had issued a circular intimating that on October 22 a resolution would be proposed for winding up on the ground of the bank's liabilities.

Held that after October 5 the directors were precluded from assenting to any alteration in the status of members.

Lord Chancellor (Cairns) (at p. 61): " His resignation of his trusteeship alone would not terminate his liability to the bank. He ceased to be a trustee; but it remained for him to terminate his liability in respect of the bank by a transfer, or something equivalent to a transfer, of his shares."

Lord Hatherley (at p. 64): "Without going so far as to say that the suspension of business, on account of insolvency, would necessarily in all cases operate to suspend all the powers of the directorate respecting the transfer of shares—upon which I offer no opinion—it is, I think, clear that such powers could not be exercised without a dereliction of duty in a case like the present. It is common, I believe, to all systems of bankruptcy to take the act of closing the trader's doors and suspending his business as the dividing period of time, after which the rights of his creditors ought not to be compromised by any transaction of the bankrupt. This is entirely conformable with justice."

Lord Mure (at p. 442): "After October 5, when intimation was made that the company . . . was utterly insolvent, the register of shareholders could not be altered by the directors."

Lord Shand (at p. 442): "It appears to me that the directors of the bank were entitled and indeed bound to decline to register transfers after October 2, and at all events after October 5."

10. In *Oswald's Trustees* v. *The City of Glasgow Bank* (1879) 6 R. 461, the executors of a trustee who had died prior to liquidation were held not liable as members.

Lord President (Inglis) (at p. 463): "I think it cannot be disputed that trustees . . . are what may be called joint owners of the trust-estate, and that when one of them dies the trust does not come to an end, nor do his representatives take up any part of the trust-estate, but the entire trust-estate immediately devolves upon the survivors. . . .

" . . . There are many cases, I apprehend, in which the representatives of a deceased party are not at all aware of the trusts in which he was engaged. . . . And therefore it appears to me that if there was a duty on anybody to make intimation to the bank of the death of this trustee it was a duty laid on his co-trustees and not upon his executors. . . . But I am not prepared to say that there is any positive obligation incumbent upon these surviving trustees, or that this failure on their part to make such intimation can be followed by any important consequences. And therefore it really comes to this, that there being nobody in such circumstances upon whom there can be imposed any duty to make the intimation which is said here to be wanting, the bank must be left to find out in the best way they can when one of three co-trustees whom they have thought fit to register as partners of the bank dies and leaves the trust-estate vested for the future entirely in his surviving colleagues."

Lord Shand (at p. 467): "The effect of an entry of this kind is, that on the death of one of the body of trustees the continuing liability of the trustee who has died is at an end. . . . Death is equivalent to a transfer of all interest that was in the deceasing trustee to the survivors in the trust. . . . It is clear that after the death of one of a body of trustees his representatives can take no benefit from the shares. . . .

" We have not to consider the case of a last surviving trustee. But it is obvious, I think, that if a trustee were the last survivor, very different considerations must operate. You have not in that case the transfer operated by law in favour of any joint owners as survivors, as in the case of the death of one of a body of trustees. . . .

" . . . It appears to me that the clause of the statute which allows notice of trusts is not only useful in this country in ear-marking the property as belonging to the trust, but is also of use in such questions as we have now before us, in shewing that the property being held by the owners of the stock jointly, not as the beneficial owners for themselves, but in trust for others, there is necessarily on accrual of the title on the death of one of the trustees in favour of the others.

" . . . I do not think that this judgment in the slightest degree trenches upon the decision we have already pronounced in the case of the petition *Muir,* or in the previous case of *Lumsden* v. *Buchanan.* . . . The liability ceases, for this reason, that the title and interest in the stock is thereby transferred to the other joint holders of the stock."

11. The case of a last surviving trustee arose in *Low's Executors* v. *The City of Glasgow Bank* (1879) 6 R. 830.

L., who had for many years been secretary of the City of Glasgow Bank, retired from that post in 1870 and died in 1872.

On the failure of the bank in 1878, L.'s name was found to be upon the register as holder of £90 stock as trustee along with Thomson, who had died in or about 1864. L., therefore, at the time of his death had been the sole surviving trustee.

L.'s executors took out confirmation, and this was exhibited to, and recorded in the books of, the bank in 1873 for the purpose of payment of certain sums due by the bank to L. L.'s executors also transferred £595 of the stock of the bank, which had belonged to L., and the transfers were recognised by the bank. L.'s executors did not know, until the stoppage of the bank, that L. had also held stock as a trustee.

Held that L.'s estate remained liable, and that his executors' names had to be placed on the second part of the list of contributories in the liquidation as representing him.

12. Trustees are liable *singuli in solidum* and not merely *pro rata.*

In *Oswald's Trustees* v. *The City of Glasgow Bank* (1879) 6 R. 461, Lord President (Inglis) said (at p. 466): " Trustees while engaged in the management of a trust-estate, if they jointly contracted engagements on behalf of that estate, must always be jointly and severally liable."

In *Cuninghame* v. *The City of Glasgow Bank* (1879) 6 R. 679, in the Court of Session, the petitioners, as well as arguing that they had not entered into any agreement to become members, maintained alternatively that, in any event, they were not individually liable *in solidum* in respect of the whole stock but only rateably, each for an equal share along with his co-trustees.

Lord President (Inglis) (at p. 682): " I consider that question to be already decided, first, in the case of *Lumsden* v. *Buchanan,* and, subsequently, in the case of *Oswald.*"

Lord Shand (at p. 682): " I may add that . . . the acceptance or admission of partners liable only to contribute *pro rata* with other joint owners of shares to the payment of calls in respect of these shares would create a limited liability, and would have been *ultra vires* of the directors."

The point was not considered by the House of Lords ((1879) 6 R. (H.L.) 98). Lord Chancellor (Cairns) said (at p. 101): " I need not go into the other part of the case, as it was not relied upon at the bar."

13. Trustees are entitled to full relief from the trust-estate: *Cuningham, &c.* v. *Montgomerie, &c.* (1879) 6 R. 1333.

This case also arose out of the liquidation of the City of Glasgow Bank.

Part of the trust-funds of a marriage-contract trust was invested by the trustees in £1,000 of the City of Glasgow Bank stock. The trustees were found personally liable to the bank for calls made in the liquidation. The total amount of the calls was £27,500. The trustees were unable to meet this out of their own means but the liquidators agreed to give them a discharge on their making a full surrender of their whole means and making over the whole of the trust-funds in their hands, which amounted to between £12,000 and £13,000.

The spouses and their children sought a declarator that the trustees were not entitled to apply the trust-estate in payment of the calls or to appropriate any part of the trust-estate for the purpose of indemnifying themselves, to any further extent than they themselves had made payments to account of the calls out of their own means.

Held that the right of relief was not limited by the trustees' own actual payments or ability to pay.

Lord Deas (at p. 1339): " There can be no doubt about our law and practice that when a party is entitled to relief against an estate, the relief must be out and out."

A contrasting case is *Brownlie, &c.* v. *Brownlie's Trustees* (1879) 6 R. 1233, in which marriage-contract trustees, who had no power to hold City of Glasgow Bank stock, were held not entitled to apply the trust-funds in payment of calls.

14. In *Gillespie, &c.* v. *The City of Glasgow Bank* (1879) 6 R. (H.L.) 104, (1879) 6 R. 714, " for behoof of " was held equivalent to " in trust for."

The entry in the register of members was " John Gillespie and Thomas Paterson, and the survivor of them, for behoof of the firm of Gillespie & Paterson, W.S."

Held that these two named partners were liable as contributories jointly and severally, and not merely each for half the amount of stock held by them.

Lord Chancellor (Cairns) (at p. 107): " There is no magic . . . in the use of the word ' trust,' and it appears to me that words which say that one person holds property ' on behalf of ' or ' for behoof of ' another, are words which come up to and satisfy the idea of the word ' trust,' just as much as the word ' trust ' itself, if the circumstances of the case are consistent with that interpretation. Now, here the circumstances of the case not only appear to me to be consistent with that interpretation, but to be absolutely inconsistent with any other interpretation."

Lord Hatherley (at p. 108): " The case is reduced simply to this point; whether or not the words ' for behoof of ' a given person or persons are equivalent to ' in trust for.' I have heard nothing that to my mind gives an intelligent explanation of the words which are here used unless they are equivalent to ' in trust for.'

" . . . Whether you say you hold ' for behoof of ' some one, or you hold ' in trust for ' some one, there is no particular magic in the choice of words,—all these words indicate that you are not beneficially the owner. . . .

" . . . There is no distinction . . . between the words ' for behoof of ' and ' in trust for.' "

15. The case of *Gillespie, &c.* v. *The City of Glasgow Bank* also illustrates the point that the persons for whom shares are held in trust are not members.

" Gillespie & Paterson, the trustees for " had been placed on the list of contributories as holders of £1,000 stock, as well as the names of Gillespie and Paterson severally as holders of £1,000 stock, each described as " trustee for Gillespie & Paterson."

Lord President (Inglis) (at p. 716): " It is quite settled that persons for whom or for whose behoof shares are held by persons who are entered in the register in their own names cannot be made contributories in respect of the shares so held."

The Court of Session therefore directed the liquidators to remove the name of the firm from the list of contributories, and there was no appeal on that part of the case.

16. Trustees are as much entitled to the privileges of membership as they are liable to the obligations of membership: *The Galloway Saloon Steam Packet Co.* v. *Wallace* (1891) 19 R. 330.

At a directors' meeting of G. Co., Aitken and Jordan, the two directors who formed a quorum, resolved to make a call upon the shareholders of £1 each.

W., who held 804 shares, declined to pay the call, and G. Co. raised an action to enforce payment.

The articles of G. Co. required directors to hold a minimum of 10 shares each. Aitken was registered as the holder of 40 shares and Jordan as holder of 100 shares.

W. averred that Aitken and Jordan had no beneficial interest in these shares, and pleaded that, as the directors were not qualified, the call had not been validly made.

Held that this defence was irrelevant, because Aitken and Jordan were *ex facie* of the register holders of the shares.

Lord Trayner (at p. 333): " It is said, however, that the shares held by these directors are held by them in trust for the North British Railway or North British Packet Company, and that they have no beneficial right or interest in these shares which are registered in their names. I think this is a matter which is quite irrelevant to any question affecting the rights or obligations of persons who are registered as shareholders.

" . . . He is registered individually, and individually he is liable for all the obligations of a shareholder. I think the converse of this must equally obtain. He is registered individually, and individually he must be entitled to all the privileges or benefits arising from the fact of his being a registered shareholder."

Even if articles provide that quaification shares must be held by a director " in his own name and right," shares held by the director in trust can be treated as qualification shares: *Elliot* v. *J. W. Mackie & Sons Ltd.,* 1935 S.C. 81.

E. and another, beneficiaries in George Mackie's trust, presented a petition for rectification of the register of M. Ltd., alleging that the trustees had executed transfers of trust shares in M. Ltd. in favour of certain of their own number and another person in order to afford them a qualification to act as directors of M. Ltd. The share transfers bore that the beneficial interest remained in the transferors. The articles of M. Ltd. required qualification shares to be held by a director " in his own name and right."

Held that (1) even if the shares had been transferred in breach of trust, that was not a matter which concerned the company or invalidated the registration of the transferees' names, and (2) the terms of the article regarding qualification shares did not preclude the use for this purpose of shares held in trust without beneficial interest.

Lord President (Clyde) (at p. 90): " The shares transferred were undoubtedly held by the transferees in their own names, but it is said that they were not held ' in their own right ' within the meaning of article 86, because the transferees had no beneficial interest in them. But, according to a long and well-known line of authority in England, the expression ' in his own right ' (as used in this connection) is insufficient to prevent shares held in trust from constituting a director's qualification. ' Nominal ' holdings for the purpose of such qualifications are very familiar in practice on both sides of the Border, and there is no case in Scotland in which a view contrary to the established English practice has been expressed. . . . I think it is too late to open a question which (in England) authority and practice, and (in Scotland) practice conform to that authority, has closed. My opinion accordingly is that the petition should be refused."

Lord Morison (at p. 92): "All that the article requires is that the shares shall be in the director's name, and that the company can treat him as in right of the shares and deal with him as such—whatever his relations with third parties may be. I am quite clearly of opinion that any one of Mackie's trustees, if he is duly invested with 200 shares of the company in his own name, may competently be elected a director of the company."

17. In *Stewart's Trustees* v. *Evans* (1871) 9 M. 810, trustees who had paid away the trust-estate *in bona fide* to beneficiaries were held not liable for a call made on shares.

S., who died in 1849, had been proprietor of 20 shares of the Agricultural Cattle Insurance Co. In 1849 his trustees were required to pay calls on these shares. On paying £71 6s. 6d. they received from the secretary a receipt, discharging them and declaring that the shares had been forfeited.

The trustees subsequently divided the estate among the beneficiaries.

In 1861 the company was wound up, and the trustees' names were placed on the list of contributories on the ground that the discharge had been invalid.

Held that the trustees were not personally liable.

It appears that the trustees were in the position of executors in relation to the shares.

Lord Justice-Clerk (Moncreiff) (at p. 814): "The trustees are not, and never were, individual partners of this company. They are only holders of an estate which continues liable to the other partners. . . . The trustees were only liable for faithful administration."

Lord Cowan (at p. 816): "The claim against the trustees is not on the footing of their being personally and individually, or even as a body, partners or shareholders of the company. Had they purchased shares with the trust-funds and taken a transfer to them, the principle recognised in the House of Lords in the case of *Buchanan and Others* v. *The Western Banking Company*, might have been applicable. Not the trust-estate merely, but the trustees personally, must have been answerable as shareholders. The position of the parties here is essentially different. Their constituent was the holder of these shares, but his trustees were never registered as such. All that they were entitled to do, and all that they did, was to deal with this part of Mr. Stewart's estate as administrators. . . . No doubt the trust-estate must make payment of this call, so far as there are funds remaining in the hands of the trustees to meet it. Still, it is the trust-estate alone, and not the trustees, that is involved in this responsibility, and it is only in the character of administrators that they come to be involved in this question to any effect."

Liferenter and fiar

Wishart and Dalziel v. The City of Glasgow Bank
(1879) 6 R. 823

Skinner purchased £100 stock of the City of Glasgow Bank. The transfer was in favour of Peter Skinner in liferent and Miss Jane Skinner, his daughter, in fee The entry in the register of members was in the same terms.

In the liquidation of the bank, W., whom Jane Skinner had married, was placed on the list of contributories.

Held that W. was entitled to have his name removed from the list upon his surrendering any estate which he had obtained from his wife on the marriage.

Dalziel purchased £100 of the same stock. The transfer was in favour of George Dalziel in liferent and Miss Margaret Helen Dalziel, his daughter, in fee. The entry in the register of members was in the same terms.

Dalziel's name was on the list of contributories.

Held that he was not entitled to have his name removed from the list.

LORD PRESIDENT (INGLIS) (at p. 825): " I shall take, in the first place, the case of Wishart, because I think the judgment which I propose your Lordships should pronounce in that case will rule the other.

" . . . If both parties were to have a control over this stock in respect of their several interests in it, it was necessary that both should be put upon the register . . .

" . . . They were *de facto* both registered as shareholders. . . .

" The contention in Wishart's case is that the only partner is the liferenter; the contention in the case of Dalziel is that the only partner is the fiar. Of course there is a third view of the case, which has been contended for by the liquidators, and that is, that they are both partners; and I am humbly of opinion that that last view is the sound one. I do not see how it is possible for anybody having an undoubted right and interest in the stock accepting a transfer for his right and interest in that stock, and engaging to become a partner of the company, and subject to all the liabilities of such in the same way as if he had signed the contract of partnership, afterwards to say that he is not a partner of the company. To say that the only partner of the company is the fiar would lead to this very extraordinary result, that the one party (the liferenter) would be entitled exclusively to all the profits accruing to the shares, and the other party (the fiar) would be liable exclusively to all the losses. . . . On the other hand, it seems just as anomalous to say that the liferenter is the sole partner. He might very easily have been made so if the transfer had been taken to the liferenter; and if the right of the fiar had stood upon separate agreement, and the liferenter had been registered as the only partner, undoubtedly he would have been the only partner in respect of liability, whatever right of recourse he might have had against the fiar in respect of the separate arrangement by which the two interests were created. But in the present case that is not what has been done. They are both registered,—they have both become partners for their respective presently existing right of liferent and fee, and have undertaken in these characters all the liabilities of partners. And as in the case of the fiar therefore I think equally in the case of the liferenter it is impossible to hold that there is not a partnership created.

" Now, that, I think, disposes of the first question which is raised in the petition of Wishart, and disposes also of the question raised in the petition of Dalziel.

. . .

" Then with regard to the second question—the relief from liability by Mr. Wishart in respect of the provisions of the Married Women's Property Act of 1877—the question is, whether the liability of Mrs. Wishart in respect of her registration as a partner of this company is within the meaning of the words of the statute an ' antenuptial debt ' of hers, for which her husband is by the enactment not to be liable? . . . It means debts contracted by the wife before marriage; and therefore the question comes to be whether this debt—the debt contracted by Mrs. Wishart by becoming a partner of this company— was contracted before marriage? It was contended that the debt was not contracted till after the marriage, because it was only the stoppage of the bank that created the debt. . . . The obligation was contracted by Mrs. Wishart by becoming a partner of the company. No doubt the obligation was not prestable except when the bank or its creditors required it to be performed, but it was contracted at that date unquestionably. . . . It appears to me therefore that Mr. Wishart is entitled to be relieved of his obligation for this debt of his wife upon surrendering any sum of money or other valuable consideration which he obtained upon the occasion of the marriage."

Persons intending to place shares

Miln v. The North British Fresh Fish Supply Co. Ltd.
(1887) 15 R. 21

M. sent an application for 1,000 shares to the directors of N. Ltd. With the application he enclosed a letter to the secretary of N. Ltd., stating: "Please to put this application before your directors at their allotment meeting on the following conditions: I do not wish to invest my own money in the shares of your company up to that extent, but see my way to invest 1,000 shares amongst my friends and clients. . . . I authorise to forfeit the deposit sent you herewith in case I fail to place the shares I apply for within two months from this date. I intend to remit you as and when I sell the shares, which I will sell by transfer out of my name, giving you notice of every transfer I sign."

An allotment letter for 1,000 shares was sent to M., and M. was registered as holder of those shares.

M. failed to place the shares, and presented a petition for rectification of the register by removal of his name.

Held that M. was not entitled to have his name removed.

LORD PRESIDENT (INGLIS) (at p. 24): " The letter . . . , which accompanied the letter of application, and which was founded on . . . as implying . . . a suspensive condition, I think plainly contemplates that the petitioner's name was to be put on the register, and was not to be removed from the register except in one way, and that is by the petitioner executing a transfer or transfers in favour of other persons. Now, no one can execute a transfer of shares except a shareholder, and therefore I think that this letter proves very clearly that what was to be done—was necessarily to be done—was to register the petitioner's name, and to register it as that of a partner of this company. . . . I think the petitioner's meaning was just this, ' I do not intend to continue a partner after I can find other persons willing to take my shares, but I do intend to become a partner, and to do so with the view of being able to transfer my shares in regular and competent form to the other persons when I find them.' That being so, I am of opinion that the petitioner is not entitled to have his name removed from the register, and accordingly I am for refusing the petition."

LORD SHAND (at p. 25): " It is plain that this is a case in which the applicant requested that he should be registered as a shareholder at once, and unconditionally, for his intention, as stated in his letter, was to dispose of his shares after he was registered, and to transfer them to new shareholders; and so I think he is liable as a member."

Importance of register of members: register not subject to a lien

Liquidator of the Garpel Haematite Co. Ltd. v. Andrew
(1866) 4 M. 617

In the liquidation of G. Ltd., A., a solicitor in London, had in his possession the register of members and certain other books and papers of the company. A. refused to produce or deliver these to the liquidator, on the ground that he had a lien over them for a sum due to him by G. Ltd.

Held that A. had no valid lien.

LORD PRESIDENT (MCNEILL) (at p. 622): "Under the 23rd section of the statute the register is a book required to be deposited in the registered office of the company, . . . in order that not only members of the company, but all persons, may have access to it. . . . Two questions arise, 1st, Could the company consistently with the provisions of the statute, remove the register, not only from the office of the company, but from the jurisdiction within which that office is? Another question is this, whether, with or without removing the register beyond the jurisdiction, the company could so far destroy its character and utility towards the public as to pledge it for their own debts by giving a lien over it to any one? It appears to me that the company had no power or authority to do either the one or the other. . . . They had no power to destroy the right of access to the register, for that is a public purpose connected with the policy of the constitution of such companies, and the company had no power to interfere with the rights of the public by creating a lien over the register either in England or Scotland."

LORD CURRIEHILL (at p. 623): "This is one of a class of companies which are purely the creatures of the statute. They are not companies known to the common law. By creating such companies the Legislature has made a very important infringement on the rights of the public at common law. The liability of each partner of such a company for all the debts of the company has by this statute been limited to a certain specified amount. That is a very important limitation; and the Legislature, while conferring that limitation on the one hand, has, on the other hand, made provisions of a very important kind, in order that the public might have the means of protecting themselves. And the most important of the provisions so made is that by which a register is established, by referring to which the public may know who the partners of the company are— how far their credit is pledged for the debts of the company— and what the estate of the company may be from time to time. . . . The Legislature has recognised the right of the public to have a register of each company kept at a certain specified place; . . . it is imperative on the part of the company to have their register at that place at all times, and open there every day, to be inspected not only by the partners, but by every person whatsoever. I think that is a most important right given to the public to counterbalance the rights taken away by the statute; and that the directors had no power to deprive the public of their right, or to defeat the security given to them by this provision. I hold, therefore, that they had no power to transfer the register to any one even in Scotland, far less to send it out of the jurisdiction of the Courts of Scotland, where the registered office of the company is."

NOTES

1. For the present provisions relating to the place at which the register of members must be kept, see Companies Act 1948, s. 110 (2). It is now expressly provided that the register of a company registered in Scotland must not be kept at a place outside Scotland, although the place within Scotland at which the register is kept is not necessarily the company's registered office.

2. For the point that the register of members is the document of title to shares, see quotation from Lord Sands in *Inland Revenue* v. *Wilson* in Note 2 at the beginning of this chapter (p. 117, above).

Petition for rectification of register: whether procedure appropriate

Blaikie v. Coats
(1893) 21 R. 150

B. and others, shareholders in the British Mexican Railway Co. Ltd., presented a petition under section 35 of the Companies Act 1862 for rectification of the register by the deletion of the names of C. and others, on the ground that C. and the other respondents had been promoters of the company and that the allotment of shares to them had been contrary to their duties as promoters.

The respondents set forth complicated transactions, with a view to showing that they had not been promoters, that they had given value for the shares, and that the petitioners were barred in the circumstances.

Held that the case was not an appropriate one for disposal under the summary procedure of section 35 of the Act.

LORD ADAM (at p. 153): "It is not a case which is appropriate for being tried and disposed of under the 35th section of the Act. From all I have heard it does not appear to me to be a case fitted for summary procedure of this kind. It is a question between shareholders and shareholders; it is not a winding-up or a case of that kind. It is a case raising questions of fraud and other considerations. . . . While I do not say the application is incompetent under the 35th section, I say it is not convenient that the case should be tried under that section, or rather that the 35th section is not appropriate to its trial. Therefore I am of opinion that we should, I do not say dismiss the petition, but keep it alive and sist it until we see the result of such reduction or other process as the petitioners may choose to raise."

LORD MCLAREN (at p. 154): "When the right of the party claiming to be put on the register or to be taken off depends on written documents—it may be on a contract to take shares or a contract to transfer shares, or upon the question whether the directors have the power to decline to accept a transferee, or any other consideration which admits of instant verification from documents—it has undoubtedly been the practice to dispose of such questions under an application presented in terms of the 35th section. We have had cases also under that section that depended on proof—I think only where the proof did not involve matter affecting the constitution of the company—especially where, as in the case of the *Aerated Bread Company,* no interest except that of the shareholder making the application was involved. But while I agree with Lord Adam that the terms of the 35th section are so comprehensive that we should have jurisdiction to entertain and determine the merits of this case in the present application, yet that jurisdiction is not meant to be substituted for the ordinary jurisdiction of the Court where the matters in controversy depend upon fact, and raise questions extrinsic to the proper object of the petition—the rectification of the register.

"Probably no precise line can be drawn between the cases that are suitable for disposal in a summary form and those which are more appropriate for trial by action of declarator or reduction, but the present case is clearly one which is unsuited for investigation in a proceeding under the 35th section. . . . The facts set forth are such as can only be properly investigated in an ordinary action, and therefore this proceeding ought to be sisted, leaving the petitioner to seek redress in a different form."

NOTES

1. The case of *Aerated Bread Company* referred to was *Chambers* v. *The Edinburgh and Glasgow Aerated Bread Co. Ltd.* (1891) 18 R. 1039. See Note to *Blakiston* v. *The London and Scottish Banking and Discount Corporation Ltd.*, p. 84, above. The suitability of the procedure was not referred to in the opinions in *Chambers'* case.

2. Another instance of matters being held to be too complex for disposal under section 35 of the Companies Act 1862 is given in *Colquhoun's Trustee* v. *British Linen Co.* (1900) 2 F. 945.

C.'s estates had been sequestrated, and his trustee presented a petition for rectification of the register of J. M. Smith Ltd. by the removal of C.'s name and the entry of the trustee's name in its place. Answers were lodged by parties who averred that C.'s shares had been transferred to them before the sequestration.

The court *sisted* the process to allow all parties interested an opportunity to take other proceedings to have their respective rights determined.

Lord McLaren (at p. 948): " It is quite settled by decisions in the Courts of England and in this Court that there are cases which are not suitable for disposal in this summary manner, and I am of opinion that this is one of them."

3. In *Sleigh* v. *The Glasgow and Transvaal Options Ltd.* (1904) 6 F. 420, opinions were expressed that the summary petition procedure was not appropriate for the questions there raised.

Lord President (Kinross) (at p. 425): " The proceeding which it is provided shall be adopted under section 35 in Scotland is by summary petition in the Court of Session, implying that the grounds of the application are of such a character that they can speedily be either verified or disproved.

" The jurisdiction conferred by section 35, for the rectification of a register has frequently been judicially considered, and I think that the result of the decisions is, that although section 35 has often been made use of for determining equities between alleged shareholders and the Company, and sometimes also between members, or alleged members of the Company, the Court may, if the case is one of difficulty and complication, decline to proceed under the section, and may refuse the application, without prejudice to an action being brought. . . . I am of opinion that the procedure contemplated by the section is inappropriate, if not inapplicable to the complicated circumstances of such a case as the present, and that this would, *per se,* afford sufficient ground for dismissing the petition, or refusing to grant the prayer of it.

" But I consider, *separatim,* that if the petition is entertained and considered on its merits, no sufficient ground has been established for granting the prayer of it."

Other aspects of this case have been considered above in the chapter on Prospectus (p. 82, above).

4. An instance of a case which was suitable for disposal under the summary procedure of section 35 of the Companies Act 1862 is *Gowans* v. *Dundee Steam Navigation Co. Ltd.* (1904) 6 F. 613.

G. presented a petition for the removal of his name from the register of D. Ltd., alleging that he had applied for the shares in reliance on false statements made to him in a letter from the promoter.

The court *allowed* a proof.

Lord Kinnear (at p. 616): "In this case the question is a very short and narrow one; and I see nothing to prevent its being satisfactorily tried in this summary form."

5. In *Kinghorn* v. *The Glenyards Fireclay Co. Ltd.* (1907) 14 S.L.T. 683 (O.H.), the circumstances were such that an action, and not a petition under section 35 of the Companies Act 1862, was held to be the appropriate process.

Lord Ardwall (at p. 684): "One of the questions argued was whether this action was a proper proceeding for what may shortly be called rectification of the register of members of the defenders' company. It was maintained that such a proceeding was only competent by summary petition to the Inner House. I am of opinion that this contention is not well founded. The ordinary method of obtaining relief, whether in Engand or in Scotland, from the position of being a registered member of any company is by way of action, and the 35th section of the Companies Acts, which allows rectification to be applied for by summary petition, is a provision in favour of members, but it is applicable only to cases which do not require much, if any, investigation for their determination."

6. The present provisions for rectification of the register are in the Companies Act 1948, s. 116.

CHAPTER 10

CONTRACTS

Preliminary contract

Tinnevelly Sugar Refining Co. Ltd.
v. Mirrlees, Watson, & Yaryan Co. Ltd.
(1894) 21 R. 1009

On July 11, 1890, Darley & Butler, purporting to act on behalf of T. Ltd., which was registered on July 29 following, entered into a contract with M. Ltd. for the supply by M. Ltd. of certain machinery.

T. Ltd. raised an action of damages against M. Ltd. on the ground that the machinery supplied was defective and had caused great loss to T. Ltd.

Held that T. Ltd. had no title to sue M. Ltd., since Darley & Butler could not have acted as agents for T. Ltd. before it was in existence.

LORD PRESIDENT (J. P. B. ROBERTSON) (at p. 1013): "The defenders' first plea is, 'No title to sue.' . . .

"The company was registered on July 29, 1890, and accordingly was not in existence at the date of the contract. It is therefore legally impossible that the contract can bind the company unless the company, since its registration, has in some way acquired the rights and submitted itself to the obligations of the contract. . . .

" . . . Darley & Butler could not be the agents of a non-existent company. . . . If the company was to take the place of Darley & Butler it required—that is to say, the shareholders or their executive required—consciously to do so. In place of any such overt action on the part of the company things were allowed to rest on the original contract between Darley & Butler and the defenders, which was erroneously believed to bind the company. . . .

" . . . First of all, where there is no principal there can be no agent; there having been no Tinnevelly Company at the date of this contract, Darley & Butler were not agents of that company in entering into the contract. The next point is that, in order to bind the company to a contract not incumbent on it,

155

it is necessary that the company should voluntarily so contract; and it is not equivalent to this if the company merely acts as if, contrary to the fact, the contract had from the beginning been obligatory on it."

1. Similarly, in *Molleson and Grigor* v. *Fraser's Trustees* (1881) 8 R. 630, an agreement with promoters to take shares in a company was held not to be equivalent to an agreement with the company itself once registered.

F. and others, having acquired the Inverkeithing Foundry and Ship-building Yard, proposed to form a company to carry the works on.

In October 1876, F. signed a document on which £1,000 was entered opposite his signature.

The company's memorandum of association was signed by seven persons, including F., each for one share of £10. The company was registered on March 3, 1877, and the following day F. died.

Held that F. had incurred no liability to the company except as a party to the memorandum of association, by which he had bound himself to take one share.

Lord President (Inglis) (at p. 633): " It must be proved that the deceased had agreed to become a member of the company, and by that I mean that he had agreed with the company to become a member."

Lord Shand (at p. 636): " The point in which the case of the liquidator fails is that, if there was an agreement between the promoters themselves, there never was any with the company."

2. In *James Young & Sons Ltd. and Liquidator* v. *Gowans* (*James Young & Sons' Tr.*) (1902) 10 S.L.T. 85 (O.H.), a newly formed company was held to have adopted a preliminary contract.

In February 1899, an agreement was entered into between James Young & Sons, contractors, Edinburgh, and Robert Young, the sole partner of that firm, on the one part, and Drummond, C.A., Edinburgh, as trustee on behalf of a company to be incorporated under the name " James Young & Sons Ltd.," on the othe part.

The company was registered on March 2, 1899, and Robert Young became chairman and managing director of it.

The memorandum of association stated that the company's objects were to purchase and acquire the business and assets of James Young & Sons, and for that purpose to adopt and carry into effect, with or without modification, the agreement of February 1899.

The first meeting of directors was held on March 9, 1899, and the minute bore that the agreement had been submitted and adopted. The minute was signed by Robert Young.

The directors thereafter proceeded to carry on business on the footing that they had acquired the business and assets of James Young & Sons.

The company was not successful, and went into liquidation on September 15, 1899. The estates of the firm James Young & Sons and of Robert Young had been sequestrated in August 1899.

The firm had been tenant of a brickworks at Carluke, and certain plant and machinery and tenant's fixtures on the brickfield were sold. The question in the case was whether the pursuer or the defender was entitled to the proceeds.

It was argued for the defender that a fresh agreement would have been necessary after the incorporation of the company in order to confer on the company the right to the proceeds.

Held that the company had adopted the agreement and was therefore entitled to the proceeds.

Lord Low (at p. 85): " The resolution, in my opinion, implied an agreement between the Company on the one hand, and Robert Young on the other, that the provisional agreement should become the agreement of the Company and should be enforceable by or against them, just as if it had been made by them."

3. A company is not liable for a debt incurred prior to its incorporation: *F. J. Neale (Glasgow) Ltd.* v. *Vickery,* 1973 S.L.T. (Sh.Ct.) 88.

On March 1, 1972, V. obtained decree against N. Ltd. for an alleged debt. N. Ltd. changed its name to " P.J.N. (Stone Cleaning) Ltd." Its assets and goodwill were sold to Forrest, a civil engineer and company promoter, who registered a new company on March 30, 1972, to continue the business. In order to obtain the advantage of the goodwill, Forrest chose the name " N. Ltd." for the new company.

In September 1972, V. arrested funds due to the new company, and the company raised an action for the recall of the arrestments on the ground that it could not be liable for a debt incurred before its incorporation. V. argued that the new company was in fact one and the same with the original company.

Held that, as a company could not acquire its legal personality until the date of its incorporation, the decree could not be operated against the new company; and arrestments *recalled.*

The Sheriff (H. W. Pirie) (at p. 89): " The procurator for the pursuers submitted that . . . in law, a company could not acquire its legal personality until the date of its incorporation. . . . Mr. Forrest's company of F. J. Neale (Glasgow) Limited could not therefore be liable for something which had taken place before his company was formed and the decree could not be operated against the new company. . . . I have reluctantly reached the view that the argument for the pursuers is well-founded and that the arrestments must be recalled."

4. On liability for expenses of promotion, see *Welsh & Forbes* v. *Johnston* (p. 80, above).

5. See European Communities Act 1972, s. 9 (2).

Personal liability of officers

Brebner v. Henderson,
1925 S.C. 643

A promissory note was in the following form:

" Fraserburgh, 7th March 1923.
" £175 Stg.
" Four months after date we promise to pay to Mr. James Brebner, Retired Builder, Fraserburgh or Order, within the Office in Fraserburgh of the Clydesdale Bank Limited, the sum of one hundred and seventy five pounds sterling, value received.

" JAS. R. GORDON, Director
" ALEX HENDERSON, Secretary
" The Fraserburgh Empire Limited."

On payment having been refused, Brebner brought an action against Henderson and Gordon.

The defenders averred that the promissory note was one of a series granted to Brebner for joiner work in the erection of a picture house at Fraserburgh for the Fraserburgh Empire Ltd., which had gone into liquidation. They pleaded that, as they were not the makers of the promissory note, they were not liable to pay the sum contained in it.

Held that Henderson and Gordon were personally liable, the words added to their signatures being merely descriptive.

LORD PRESIDENT (CLYDE) (at p. 646): " The note runs simply, ' we promise ' and so on. *Prima facie* ' we ' refers to the two individuals who sign the note. The question is whether the words appended to their signatures, construed along with the rest of the document, are equivalent to some such clause as ' we, the limited company, promise,' or again, ' we, for the limited company, and as authorised by the said company, promise.'

. . .

" According to section 26 of the [Bills of Exchange] Act of 1882, where a person who signs a bill ' adds words to his signature, indicating that he signs for or on behalf of a principal, or in a representative character, he is not personally liable thereon; but the *mere addition* to his signature of words describing him as an agent, or as filling a representative character, does not exempt him from personal liability.' . . . The argument for the defenders was based, in the main, upon the view that the name of the company written at the bottom of the note was truly the signature of the company. . . . I am unable to understand how the name of the company written by the clerk who drew out the bill under the two spaces reserved for the signatures, and under the words ' Director ' and ' Secretary ' opposite those two spaces respectively, can be said to constitute a signature by the company. . . .

" The appellants presented a further argument on section 77 of the Companies (Consolidation) Act 1908. . . . The section says that a bill shall be deemed to have been made by a company if made ' in the name of, or by or on behalf or on account of, the company by any person acting under its authority.' . . . It seems to me to be plain, on the terms of this note, that it is neither expressly nor by implication made in the name or on behalf or on account of the limited company. . . . The note . . . binds, in my opinion, the signatories and not the limited company of which they designed themselves as director and secretary."

NOTES

1. Section 33 of the Companies Act 1948 is precisely the same as section 77 of the Companies (Consolidation) Act 1908.

On the form of contracts made on behalf of a company, see Companies Act 1948, s. 32.

2. A contrasting case is *McLean* v. *Stuart and Others*, 1970 S.L.T. (Notes) 77 (O.H.).

Three of the five directors of a limited company signed an acknowledgment of a loan containing conditions for repayment. The acknowledgment was written on the official notepaper of the company, and stated: " We as directors of the above Company accept the loan received today of £1,625 from Mr. J. McLean and agree to pay back as follows. £200 starting Friday, 8th December 1967, Then £200 every Friday until repayment of £2,000 has been made. J.W. Rennie, I.D. Young, Alex. Stuart."

The lender raised an action for repayment against the signatories, contending that they had signed as individuals and not as agents of the company.

Held that the document was binding on the company and that the signatories were not personally liable.

Lord Wheatley (at p. 77): " The question is whether the words used here, namely ' as directors of the above company ' are merely descriptive or qualify the capacity in which the signatories signed the document. Each case has to be examined in the light of its own circumstances, of the words used, and of the context in which they are used. . . . The words ' as directors ' in their context here are, in my opinion, clearly words of qualification and not of description. . . . If the words used had been simply ' we the directors of the above company ' a different result might have followed. The insertion of the word ' as ' is not only significant, it is crucial.''

CHAPTER 11

SHARE CAPITAL

Classes of share capital: preference shares: dividend prima facie
cumulative

Partick, Hillhead, and Maryhill Gas Co. Ltd. v. Taylor
(1888) 15 R. 711

T. was the holder of preference shares in P. Ltd. By the terms
of the issue the shares were "entitled to a preferential
dividend of 5½ per cent. per annum."

For about 12 years the dividend of 5½ per cent. was duly
paid. There were then two years during which no profits were
available to pay the dividend.

Held that the preference shareholders were entitled to payment of the arrears of dividend out of the first profits made
by the company but that they were not entitled to interest
on the arrears.

LORD PRESIDENT (INGLIS) (at p. 713): "The question is very
simple, and it seems to me to be settled by authority, and
settled in a way which to my mind is both plain and just.
The difference between preference and ordinary shareholders is
just this, that the one is entitled to be paid preferably to the
other. Given profits, the rule is that the preference shareholders
shall be paid first. . . .

"I cannot see that there would be any justice in a rule which
would limit the right of the preference shareholders to receive
5½ per cent. to years in which profits have been made, and
give them no right to their dividend if no profits have been
made during the year. It seems to me that they are clearly
entitled when profits are made to their dividend of 5½ per
cent., whether it is a past year's dividend or the dividend of
the present year. The question was very fully considered in
Henry's case. That case is a very high authority, the decision
having been given in the Court of Chancery by Lord Chancellor
Cranworth and two Lord Justices of high repute. . . . I should
hesitate even if I had any doubt as to the justice of that
decision in going against so high an authority; it is therefore
satisfactory to find that one's own impression is in accordance
with it.

. . .

161

" As regards the question of interest, . . . if there are no profits no dividends can be paid. . . . I cannot see how interest can be payable on a sum which ought not to have been paid at the time from which the interest is said to become due. Interest runs only from the date when the principal ought to have been paid."

LORD SHAND (at p. 715): " In order to restrict the preference shareholders' rights you must have something express. . . .
" With regard to the claim for interest on the arrears of preference dividends, it appears to me that it is an extravagant claim. If you have no profits you can have no dividend, and if you have no dividend declared you can have no interest running."

NOTES

1. The case of *Henry* referred to is *Henry* v. *Great Northern Railway Co.* (1857) 1 De G. & J. 606.

2. In *Miln* v. *The Arizona Copper Co. Ltd.* (1899) 1 F. 935, a clause in articles which expressly declared a preferential dividend to be cumulative but which also included words suggesting that the dividend was non-cumulative was construed as conferring a right to a cumulative dividend.

The articles of A. Ltd. provided that " the holders of preferred shares shall be entitled to receive out of the profits of each year a cumulative preferential dividend for such year, at the rate of 10 per cent. per annum on the amount for the time being paid up on the preferred shares held by them respectively, and the surplus profits in each year shall belong one half to the holders of the preferred shares, and the other half to the holders of the deferred shares."

M., a holder of deferred shares raised an action against A. Ltd. for a declaration that the holders of the preferred shares were not entitled to a cumulative preferential dividend, but only to a preferential dividend paid out of the profits of each year.

Held that the holders of the preferred shares were entitled to have any deficiency in the dividend of 10 per cent. in one year made up out of the profits of subsequent years before there could be any division of " surplus profits " between the preferred and deferred shareholders.

Staples v. *Eastern Photographic Materials Co.* [1896] 2 Ch. 303 (C.A.) was distinguished.

Lord McLaren (at p. 941): " I would say that we come to the consideration of a dividend clause in this form with the law clearly laid down that a preferential dividend, in the absence of expressions limiting the preference to a particular year, means a dividend having a preference over the whole income of the company during the whole period of its existence, or during as many years as may be necessary to satisfy the claim of dividend. . . . If a preference limited to a particular year is intended, then it must be made clear by express words that such a preference, and no more, is intended. . . . *Staples* is no doubt a very high authority, but the substance of it is this, that it points out a form of words which may be safely used where it is intended to limit the preferential right given to a certain class of shareholders to an annual preference—a preference for each year over the profits of that year; but I have no reason to suppose from the passages that were read to us that the learned Judges who decided that case woud have been prepared to apply the same rule of construction to a clause in which the dividend was declared not only to be preferential but to be cumulative, and on that ground I concur in the construction and in all the observations made by the Lord Ordinary on this part of the case."

Lord Ordinary (Pearson) (at p. 938): " The decision of the question must depend on the true construction of the articles. The 7th article, containing as it does the prominent and distinctive term ' cumulative,' seems at first sight to be free from doubt, but on closer examination it proves to be a model of ambiguity. . . .

" . . . Even where the holders were declared entitled to their preference dividend ' out of the net profits of each year,' this was held sufficient to exclude a claim for cumulative dividend in the case of *Staples*. . . . That case seems to me to go a considerable length, for after all the expression ' the net profits of each year ' might be regarded as merely descriptive of the only possible fund out of which any dividend, whether cumulative or non-cumulative, could be paid. But where (as here) the holders are to receive the dividend not only ' out of the profits of each year,' but ' for each such year,' then even if the dividend be declared preferential, it is not cumulative. The rule in short seems to be this, that where no particular year is alluded to, a preferential dividend is held to be cumulative . . . ; but that even a description of the preferential dividend as payable out of the net profits of each year will make it non-cumulative (*Staples, cit.*).

" This rule, however, was settled in a series of cases, in none of which was the word ' cumulative ' used, the question in all being whether a dividend admittedly preferential was also cumulative. Here it is expressly described as ' a cumulative preferential dividend.' "

3. In *Ferguson & Forrester Ltd.* v. *Buchanan*, 1920 S.C. 154, a preference dividend, not expressly declared to be cumulative, was held to be cumulative. even although the company also had other preference shares whose dividend was expressly declared to be cumulative.

F. Ltd. had " A " preference shares and " B " preference shares. The " A " preference shares entitled the holders to a " cumulative preferential dividend " of 8 per cent. as a first charge on the profits, and the " B " preference shares entitled the holders to a " preferential dividend " of 5 per cent. as a second and postponed charge on the profits.

Held that the dividend on the " B " shares was cumulative: the fact that it was not expressly described as cumulative (in contrast to the dividend on the " A " shares) was insufficient to displace the general rule that preference dividends are *prima facie* cumulative.

Lord Dundas (at p. 160): " I think the unexplained omission of the word ['cumulative ']—in itself unnecessary—although it does cause perplexity, should not lead us to derogate from the usual meaning of the word 'preferential.' If that had been the intention, it would have been easy to insert the word 'non-cumulative' as regards ' B ' shareholders."

Lord Guthrie (at p. 161): " The case must be treated . . . as a pure question of construction. . . . So treating the case, I am of opinion that the unexplained insertion of the word 'cumulative' in one clause and not in two others is not sufficient to displace the *prima facie* meaning and effect of the word 'preferential.' "

4. In *Robertson-Durham* v. *Inches,* 1917, 1 S.L.T. 267 (O.H.), arrears of a cumulative preferential dividend were held not to be payable out of the assets in the company's liquidation.

In the liquidation of Robertson, Sanderson & Co. Ltd., the liquidator, R.-D., presented a note to the court for the determination of the question whether preference shareholders were entitled to payment of arrears of cumulative preferential dividend in priority to any repayment of capital to the ordinary shareholders. Answers were lodged by I. and others, holders of preference shares.

Preferential dividends had been declared out of profits down to March 31, 1914. The date of the commencement of the winding up was January 6, 1916. The preference shareholders alleged that between these two dates there had been great appreciation in the value of the stock of whisky held by the company, with the result that, if a profit and loss account had been made up as at the date of the commencement of the winding up, it would have disclosed a large profit earned during the period March 31, 1914, to January 6, 1916.

Lord Cullen (at p. 269): " The short and final answer to the contention of the preference shareholders . . . is to be found in Article 138. . . . It says that the . . . remaining assets are to be devoted, in the first place, to paying out to the preference shareholders the paid-up amounts of their shareholdings, and that the residual balance is to be paid to the holders of ordinary shares. . . . Now, the assets of the company in liquidation—taking the word 'assets' in its natural sense—mean all the things, of one kind or another, belonging to the company which passed under the administration of the liquidator in consequence of the winding up. . . .

" In my opinion, . . . Article 138 on its own terms excludes the claim of the preference shareholders."

Classes of share capital: preference shares: prima facie, *no priority for repayment of capital in winding up*

Monkland Iron and Coal Co. Ltd. v. Henderson, &c.
(1883) 10 R. 494

Preference shareholders in M. Ltd. were entitled to a cumulative dividend of 7 per cent. "guaranteed by the ordinary shares."

After failing to pay the 7 per cent. dividend for several years, M. Ltd. was wound up. The company's debts were paid and the liquidators presented a petition to the court for the determination of the question of how the sums remaining in their hands should be distributed as between preference and ordinary shareholders.

Answers were lodged by H. and others, preference shareholders, claiming that they were entitled to an entire preference over the ordinary shareholders in the distribution.

Held that the sums fell to be divided among all the shareholders in proportion to the number of shares held.

LORD PRESIDENT (INGLIS) (at p. 497): "The argument simply comes to this, that if this 7 per cent. dividend cannot be earned by the company, it must be paid out of capital. Now, the 80th article of association provides that ' no dividend shall be payable except out of profits arising from the business of the company. . . .' How it is possible in the face of that to contend that the dividend is to be paid out of capital I am quite at a loss to understand.

" . . . There is not anywhere in the articles a reference of any kind to the company being wound up."

LORD MURE (at p. 498): "The words ' guaranteed by the ordinary shares' refer to the guarantee fund raised out of surplus profits, but which is not to be called into operation except when in any year there were no other profits out of which to pay the preferential dividend. . . . The question now raised . . . seems never to have come within the contemplation of the parties who framed the articles, and who left the winding-up to the action of common law. That being so, I am of opinion that all the shareholders are entitled to rank *pari passu* on the surplus assets."

Classes of share capital: preference shares: prima facie, *surplus funds in winding up divisible rateably among all classes of shareholders*

Liquidators of Williamson-Buchanan Steamers Ltd., Petitioners
1936 S.L.T. 106 (O.H.)

W. Ltd., which had both preference and ordinary shares, went into liquidation in 1935, and after all liabilities had been discharged and all paid-up capital repaid to both classes of shareholders, the liquidators had in their hands a surplus of at least £100,000.

The liquidators presented a petition to the court for the determination of the question whether the preference shareholders were entitled to participate equally with the ordinary shareholders in the distribution of the surplus assets.

Held that the preference shareholders were entitled to participate in the surplus.

LORD CARMONT (at p. 107): " I refrain from calling this surplus 'surplus assets,' for that description was thought by Lord Macnaghten in the case of *Birch* v. *Cropper* ((1889) 14 A.C. 525) apt to lead to confusion. The phrase has been said to be ambiguous and to have no fixed legal meaning . . . , and that it should not be used in the case of a solvent concern. . . . The money has lost all definite characteristics such as would enable one to apply the word 'capital' to it or to call it a dividend fund. . . . I shall therefore refer to the surplus money in question as the 'surplus funds.'

. . .

". . . All shareholders are entitled to equal treatment unless and to the extent that their rights are modified by the contract under which they hold their shares.

. . .

" I am satisfied that there is nothing in the present case to shew that the preference shareholders, as corporators, are precluded from participating in the surplus funds along with the ordinary shareholders.

" After altering the last word in the question asked to ' funds ' (instead of assets) I answer the question in the affirmative."

NOTES

1. For a liquidator's power to apply to court to have questions in a voluntary winding up determined, see now Companies Act 1948, s. 307.

2. The decision is of limited authority, because of the rule, subsequently established, that a statement of the rights attaching to a special class of shares is *prima facie* exhaustive; see *Wilsons and Clyde Coal Co. Ltd.* v. *Scottish Insurance Corporation Ltd.* (p. 183, below). Lord Carmont referred to this rule as a " view," and himself preferred the contrary view—on which he based his decision.

3. A similar case was *Town and Gown Association Ltd., Liquidator, Petitioner,* 1948 S.L.T. (Notes) 71 (O.H.).

T. Ltd., incorporated in 1896 to provide accommodation for students in residential premises in Edinburgh, went into liquidation in 1948. Its issued capital amounted to £34,675, and the assets in the liquidation were valued at £60,000. The liquidator presented a petition to have questions of distribution determined by the court.

Held by Lord Sorn that, in the absence of express provision to the contrary in the articles of association, after all the shareholders had been repaid their paid-up capital, preference shareholders were entitled to participate with ordinary shareholders in the final distribution.

This decision also is now of doubtful value.

Classes of share capital: variation of class rights: rights conferred by memorandum: modification of rights clause in articles

The Oban and Aultmore-Glenlivet Distilleries Ltd., Petitioners
(1903) 5 F. 1140

Preference shareholders in O. Ltd. were, under the company's memorandum of association, entitled to receive a fixed cumulative dividend of 5 per cent.

A clause in the articles provided that all or any of the rights attached to any class of shares might be modified by an extraordinary resolution passed at a general meeting of the holders of shares of that class.

Dividends on the preference shares were two years in arrear. A meeting of preference shareholders agreed to a scheme for reduction of capital, under which these arrears were to be cancelled and future profits distributable as dividend were to be appropriated to payment of (i) a cumulative dividend of 5 per cent. on the preference shares, (ii) 5 per cent. on the ordinary shares, and (iii) *pari passu* dividends to the holders of both classes of shares.

When the petition for reduction was before the court, the reporter doubted whether the right to cumulative preference dividends, being stated in the memorandum, could be extinguished in the way proposed.

The court confirmed the scheme.

LORD PRESIDENT (KINROSS) (at p. 1143): "This case is certainly a very special one, and unusually large powers are conferred by article 46 of the articles of association. That article, reasonably construed, seems to put it in the power of the majority to make the modification of the memorandum which is here proposed."

NOTES

1. This case was followed in *Marshall, Fleming & Co. Ltd., Petitioners,* 1938 S.C. 873 (O.H.), in which the authorities were considered by Lord Keith.

M. Ltd. presented a petition to the court for confirmation of reduction of capital and for sanction of a scheme of arrangement, and the main question raised by the petition was whether a scheme of arrangement and the sanction of the court to the scheme were necessary.

The company's memorandum divided the shares into cumulative preference shares and ordinary shares, with certain rights attached to each class. The articles contained a modification of rights clause.

Held that M. Ltd. could, by following the procedure prescribed in the articles, alter the rights of the different classes of shareholders as set forth in the memorandum, without the necessity of obtaining the sanction of the court to a scheme of arrangement.

The Lord Ordinary confirmed the reduction which had been resolved on.

Lord Keith (at p. 877): "The effect of these resolutions is to alter the rights attached to the capital of the Company as set forth in clause V of the memorandum, and the question is whether this alteration of the memorandum can be effected without a scheme of arrangement and the sanction of the Court under section 153 of the statute.

"... Some difference of opinion exists among text writers on this subject. There is one Scots case which supports the view that a scheme of arrangement is unnecessary, viz., *Oban and Aultmore-Glenlivet Distilleries, Limited* ..., and at least one English case to the opposite effect, viz., *Ashbury* v. *Watson* (1885) 30 Ch.D. 376. ... In no material respect does the present case differ from the *Oban* case, and I am bound, I think, to follow it and to hold that recourse to section 153 is unnecessary. I have considered, however, the provisions of the statute and a number of the English cases, and I think that, independently of the *Oban* case, I might have arrived at the same result.

"... I find it difficult ... to see why only an express reference in the memorandum should authorise the alteration under the articles of rights fixed by the memorandum. Where memorandum and articles of association are issued contemporaneously and the articles contain power to alter the rights of shareholders as set forth in

CLASSES OF SHARE CAPITAL

the memorandum, there is no room for doubt as to the intention. . . . English authority does not seem to be entirely consistent or logical in this matter, but the tendency of most recent decisions seems to be in favour of a construction of the statutory provisions which would support the decision in the *Oban* case."

2. Section 153 of the Companies Act 1929 is now represented by section 206 of the Companies Act 1948. For an instance of variation of class rights in a scheme of arrangement under the latter section, see *The City Property Investment Trust Corporation Ltd., Petitioners,* 1951 S.C. 570.

3. In *Frazer Brothers Ltd., Petitioners,* 1963 S.C. 139, variation was held to include abolition.

F. Ltd. presented a petition for confirmation of a reduction of capital, which involved the cancellation of all preference shares and the return to their holders of the sums paid up on them.

By its articles F. Ltd. had adopted certain regulations of Table A in the First Schedule to the Companies (Consolidation) Act 1908, including regulation 4, which provided for separate class meetings being held where the rights of any class of shareholders were to be " varied." (See now regulation 4 in Table A in the First Schedule to the Companies Act 1948.)

A separate meeting of preference shareholders had been convened and had sanctioned the reduction proposals.

The reporter to whom the petition was remitted raised the question whether that separate meeting had been required, since the reduction proposals involved, not variation of the rights of preference shareholders, but abolition of these rights.

Held that the procedure of holding a separate meeting had been correct.

Lord President (Clyde) (at p. 140): " In our opinion . . . a variation of the rights of preference shareholders includes a total abolition of such rights. The purpose of requiring a separate meeting of a class of shareholders where a reduction of capital involves an alteration of their rights is to ensure that their legitimate interests are not swamped by the votes of other members of the company in general meeting. *A fortiori,* where their rights are not merely being altered but are being wholly abolished, this protection of a separate class meeting is all the more necessary. This conclusion is confirmed by the provision of subsection (6) of section 72 of the Companies Act 1948 (compare s. 61 (6) of the 1929 Act), whereby it is provided that the expression ' variation ' in this connection includes abrogation and the expression ' varied ' is to be construed accordingly. In our opinion, therefore, the separate class meeting of preference shareholders was correctly held.

" We shall therefore confirm the reduction in the present case."

Reduction of capital: procedure: remit to reporter

Fowlers (Aberdeen) Ltd., Petitioners
1928 S.C. 186

F. Ltd. presented a petition for confirmation of a reduction of capital which did not involve either the diminution of liability for any unpaid share capital or the payment of any paid-up share capital to shareholders. The rights of creditors were not affected in any way, and all the shareholders had consented to the proposed reduction.

The court, without delivering opinions, *dispensed* with a remit to a reporter, and *granted* the prayer of the petition.

NOTES

1. This case was followed and commented on in the similar case of *The Scottish Stamping and Engineering Co. Ltd., Petitioners,* 1928 S.C. 484.

Lord Anderson (at p. 487): "Although we decide in this case—as we decided in the case of *Fowlers (Aberdeen), Limited*—that the prayer of the petition may be granted without a remit to a reporter, I think the profession ought to keep clearly in mind, in these cases, that a report, as a rule, will be called for."

2. In *J. Hay & Sons Ltd., Petitioners,* 1928 S.C. 622, the court *refused* a motion to dispense with a remit to a reporter, although the petition did not differ from that of Fowlers (Aberdeen) Ltd. as summarised above except that letters were produced as evidence of the shareholders' consent. The case, therefore, taken along with that mentioned in Note 1 above, clearly establishes what the normal procedure must be.

Lord Justice-Clerk (Alness) (at p. 624): "We think that no sufficient cause has been shown for deviating from ordinary practice in these petitions, which is that there ought to be a remit to a reporter before granting the prayer. That course will be adopted here."

Reduction of capital: specific power to reduce

John Avery & Co. Ltd., Petitioners
(1890) 17 R. 1101

The memorandum of A. Ltd. gave the company power " to increase or reduce the capital, as provided by the articles."

The articles provided for increase of capital, but made no mention of reduction.

A. Ltd. passed a special resolution to reduce its capital.

In a petition under the Companies Act 1867 for confirmation

of the reduction, the court *refused* to grant the prayer of the petition.

NOTES

1. The reporter stated that, as the original articles did not include power to reduce capital, these articles had first to be altered so as to give the company such power; the company had merely passed a special resolution to reduce the capital, whereas two resolutions were required—the first one to alter the articles and the second to reduce the capital. The reporter's view, therefore, was that there had not been sufficient compliance with the statutory provisions.

2. Another case which illustrates the need for two separate special resolutions in such a situation is *The Oregon Mortgage Co. Ltd., Petitioners,* 1910 S.C. 964. Under the Companies (Consolidation) Act 1908, which was then in force, a special resolution required to be confirmed at a subsequent meeting.

At a meeting on November 19, 1908, O. Ltd. passed two resolutions, one to add power to reduce to its original articles and the other to reduce capital. Both resolutions were confirmed at a meeting held on December 10, 1908.

O. Ltd. then presented a petition to the court for confirmation of the reduction.

Held that the procedure had been irregular since, at the time when the special resolution for reduction had been passed, the company had had no power to reduce its capital.

Lord Justice-Clerk (J. H. A. MacDonald) (at p. 965): " Under its articles of association the Company had no power to reduce its capital. If the capital was to be reduced, it was necessary first that the articles should be altered so as to increase the powers of the Company. That could only be done in one way—by the passing of a resolution at an extraordinary general meeting of the Company, and the confirmation of that resolution at a subsequent extraordinary meeting called for the purpose. Now, could any procedure be taken under that resolution until the second meeting was held? I do not think it could."

Reduction of capital: confirmation by court: nobile officium *not available*

Alexander Henderson Ltd., Petitioners
1967 S.L.T. (Notes) 17

On December 22, 1965, at an extraordinary general meeting of H. Ltd. a special resolution was passed for reduction of capital by repayment of the whole of the preference shares at par. Repayment was made before the petition for confirmation was presented to the court. The petition was presented under sections

66 to 69 of the Companies Act 1948 and to the *nobile officium*. On November 23, 1966, the court *refused* the prayer of the petition.

LORD PRESIDENT (CLYDE) (at p. 17): "Clearly this payment was *ultra vires* and this court cannot condone an illegal step of that nature, nor have we power under the Companies Acts to grant approval *ex post facto* to a repayment of capital which the statutes do not authorise. A limited company has no power to reduce its capital at its own hand. . . . It can only do so in the manner allowed by law. . . .

"The petitioners sought to overcome their diffculties by invoking the *nobile officium*. We could not exercise this power unless intimation had been made to the Lord Advocate in the public interest. . . . But apart from this the *nobile officium* jurisdiction is not available to enable this Court to substitute a new provision for that contained in an Act of Parliament and if we were to invoke the *nobile officium* jurisdiction here that is just what we should be doing."

Reduction of capital: *modes of reduction*

Scottish Vulcanite Co. Ltd., Petitioners
(1894) 21 R. 752

S. Ltd. passed a special resolution by which 10 per cent. of its capital was to be returned to its shareholders "upon the footing that the amounts returned, or any part thereof, may be called up again."

Held that the reduction was competent and fell to be confirmed.

NOTES

1. In view of certain errors in the procedure the court accepted the reporter's suggestion that intimation and advertisement should be made of new before the prayer of the petition was granted.

2. This case was commented on and followed in *William Brown, Sons, & Co. Ltd., Petitioners*, 1931 S.C. 701.

B. Ltd. resolved that, in respect of each fully-paid £1 share of its issued capital, the sum of 2s. 6d. should be paid off "upon the footing that the amount so returned or any part thereof may be again called up."

Held that this form of reduction was competent.

Lord President (Clyde) (at p. 702): "The reason for the reduction of capital is that the Company's capital requirements are less than formerly. . . .

" . . . The capital of a company is equally reduced whether the reduction affects paid-up capital or uncalled capital; but I find it very difficult to understand how, or in what respect, the capital of a company can be said to be reduced by paying back part of the paid-up capital, and at the same time substituting therefor a corresponding uncalled liability. The capital does not appear to me to be reduced at all by an operation of this kind.

" We were referred to the case of the *Scottish Vulcanite Co.*, in which a resolution, similar in terms and effect to that which we are now asked to sanction, was confirmed. No opinions were delivered, notwithstanding that the reporter drew the attention of the Court to the remarkable characer of the resolution; and so far as reported cases in Scotland are concerned, the case stands alone. . . .

" . . . I think we must follow the *Scottish Vulcanite Co.*'s case, however doubtful the weight which should be attached to it as a precedent. If an opportunity of reconsidering it should occur, I think the opportunity should be taken."

Lord Morison (at p. 704): " The words of the section [s. 55 of the Companies Act 1929] are perfectly general, and its scope is in the widest terms, *viz.*, ' in any way.' I think that the effect of the resolution is to reduce immediately the paid-up capital of the Company, and that it therefore requires the sanction of the Court. It seems to be immaterial that, attached to the reduction resolution, there is a declaration that the portion of the share capital returned may be again called up. A resolution in these terms is, in my view, one way of effecting the reduction of the company's paid-up capital, and I think it ought to be confirmed."

3. Another case involving the same point was *Stevenson, Anderson & Co. Ltd., Petitioners*, 1951 S.C. 346, from which it would appear that there is no longer any ground for the doubt expressed in Lord President Clyde's opinion in 1931.

S. Ltd. resolved that, in respect of each fully-paid share of £1 of its issued capital, the sum of 10s. be paid off " upon the footing that the amount so returned or any part thereof may be again called up."

Held that this form of reduction was competent.

Lord Patrick (at p. 349): " The statute which now governs the matter is the Companies Act 1948. That Act was preceded by an exhaustive inquiry into existing company law and practice. Nevertheless Parliament took no steps to give effect to the doubts which Lord President Clyde had expressed. In these circumstances I think it is out of the question that we should now disturb a construction of the relevant sections of the various Companies Acts which has stood for 60 years and which has been frequently exemplified in the practice of both countries during that period."

4. In *Doloi Tea Co. Ltd., Petitioners,* 1961 S.L.T. 168, the reporter drew the court's attention to a composite resolution in a form not then in common use in Scotland.

The resolution provided for (a) reduction of the paid-up capital from £48,000 stock to £36,000 consisting of 96,000 shares of 10s. each paid up to the extent of 7s. 6d. per share, (b) return of paid-up capital to the extent of 2s. 6d. in respect of each 10s. of the stock, (c) immediately before the reduction took effect reconversion of the £48,000 stock into 96,000 shares of 10s. each, (d) capitalisation of £12,000 of the amount then standing at credit of profit and loss account and the application of this sum in paying up the 2s. 6d. on each of the 96,000 shares, and (e) conversion of the 96,000 fully-paid shares into £48,000 stock transferable in multiples of 10s.

For the petitioners it was argued that what was proposed, although it did not involve a reduction of nominal capital, was a competent method of reducing the capital, that the method, involving distribution of accumulated profits amongst the shareholders in reduction of paid-up capital, had been approved in *William Brown, Sons, & Co. Ltd., Petitioners,* and in *Stevenson, Anderson & Co. Ltd., Petitioners,* and that the only difference in this case was that, after the reduction, reserves were to be capitalised in order to make the shares fully paid again. This form of reduction was said to have been used in England since 1957.

The court, without delivering opinions, pronounced an order *confirming* the reduction.

5. On the other hand, in *W. Morrison & Co. Ltd., Petitioners* (1892) 19 R. 1049, the court held that a proposed reduction was incompetent where the real purpose of it was to raise new capital.

M. Ltd. had been registered with a capital of £2,000, in 2,000 £1 shares, all issued and fully paid up. The resolution, which narrated that the capital had been lost to the extent of £500, bore that the paid-up capital was to be reduced from £2,000 to £1,500 by the conversion of the £1 fully paid shares into £1 shares with only 15s. paid up.

The reporter raised the objection that the resolution involved not only a reduction of the company's capital, which was competent, but also the creation, in an irregular manner, of £500 of new capital to be called up, with the imposition upon the shareholders of an additional liability, which they did not formerly have.

Lord Kinnear (at p. 1051): "It is clear from the report that the real proposal is not to reduce capital but to raise £500 of new capital to replace capital which has disappeared. . . . I do not say that the company may not obtain the result which they desire, but that can only be by following the very explicit and precise provisions of the Companies Acts, and they are not entitled under colour of doing one thing to do something entirely different."

Lord Adam (at p. 1051): "It appears to me that what is here

called a resolution to reduce capital is not a resolution to reduce capital at all. . . . The result of the act would be to leave the amount of the capital exactly the same as it was before, the only difference being that at the end of the operation while the amount of the capital would be the same, only £1,500 would be paid up, while £500 would remain uncalled. I cannot see how this can be described as a reduction of capital."

6. Similarly, in *The Walker Steam Trawl Fishing Co. Ltd. (and Reduced), Petitioners,* 1908 S.C. 123, the court refused to confirm a resolution which would have effected a conversion or re-allocation of capital rather than a reduction of capital.

W. Ltd. had a capital of £50,000, divided into 50,000 shares of £1 each. All the shares had been issued, and 12s. 6d. had been paid up on each share.

The court was asked to confirm one or other of two alternative modes of reduction.

The first was that the capital should be converted into 31,250 fully paid £1 shares, leaving 18,750 to be issued at the discretion of the directors. The conversion was to be effected by re-allocating the capital among the shareholders, crediting to each of them one £1 share for each pound sterling at his credit in the share capital account.

The alternative was that the capital should be reduced to £31,250 divided into 50,000 shares of 12s. 6d. each fully paid. This was to be effected by extinguishing the liability in respect of uncalled capital to the extent of 7s. 6d. per share.

The reporter's view was that the first resolution could not be confirmed as a " reduction " of capital: there was to be a " conversion " or " re-allocation " of capital; he found nothing in the Acts or in the authorities to suggest that such a resolution was competent as a " reduction " of capital. He found that the alternative resolution clearly imported a reduction of capital.

The court *refused* to confirm the first resolution, and *confirmed* the alternative resolution.

Lord Stormonth-Darling (at p. 126): " The safer course will be to walk by the strict words of the statute, and confirm the second alternative resolution."

Lord Ardwall (at p. 126): " I am of opinion that no reasons of expediency can justify the Court in departing by a hair's breadth from the provisions of the statutes under which alone they have jurisdiction to make alterations in the capital of a company that has been incorporated under the Companies Acts."

7. A reduction may be competent, although effected, not by cash payment, but by distribution among the shareholders of certain of the company's assets (*e.g.* shares in another company): *The Westburn Sugar Refineries Ltd., Petitioners* (p. 187, below).

Reduction of capital: questions for the court: court's reluctance to interfere in company's financial affairs

Hoggan, &c. v. The Tharsis Sulphur and Copper Co. Ltd.
(1882) 9 R. 1191

The nominal capital of T. Ltd. consisted of 92,566 £10 shares, which, so far as issued, had been fully paid up, and of 31,100 new £10 shares issued at par to shareholders on which only £7 had been called up.

T. Ltd. passed resolutions (i) to reduce the capital by reducing the liability on each of the 31,100 shares "after £1 shall have been called up and paid," to the extent of £2 per share, and exchanging four paid-up shares of £10 for five of the £8 shares, and then (ii) to increase the capital by the issue of 8,224 £10 shares to be sold to the public.

T. Ltd.'s fully-paid shares were at the time selling in the market at a premium of about £30.

Certain holders of the shares on which only £7 had been called up brought a reduction of the resolutions on the ground that they were *ultra vires* of the company and unjust, as the pursuers were entitled to have the unpaid capital on their shares called up before the company raised capital otherwise.

Held (1) that the resolutions were not incompetent, and (2) that they did not prejudice any rights of the pursuers, since the pursuers had no right to insist that the unpaid capital on their shares should be called up and since no injury was done to them by a restriction of their liability.

LORD PRESIDENT (INGLIS) (at p. 1209): "It may be very expedient for a company to reduce one kind of capital and increase another kind of capital. . . . I think that may be quite legitimately done in many cases. The pursuers, however, say that this has been done to their detriment, and distinctly and purposely in order to injure them. Now, as to the purpose of injury, I confess I do not see any evidence of that. There may be, in one sense of the word, some injury done to the pursuer, and yet it may not be an injury of which he is entitled to complain. If the resolutions which have been adopted by the company are really in the interests of the company itself, and conducive to the prosperity of the company, I cannot affirm the proposition that every thing that indirectly affects the interests of a particular class of shareholders injuriously must necessarily be illegal; I do not think there is any authority for that. I can quite understand that a certain class of shareholders may be placed in a more unfavourable position than they were before, by a new financial arrangement of the company's affairs, and yet have no title to complain, the vast majority of the company being satisfied with the change which has been introduced, legally introduced in so far as statutory powers are concerned, and being for the great advantage of the company. But waiving that in the meantime, we must see whether there was any real injury inflicted upon the pursuers which they can have any title to complain of. . . .

" . . . It must be obvious that the unpaid capital of the company is the proper capital to reduce, in the first instance at least, and the most easy and natural way of effecting a reduction. . . . The complaint of the pursuer is, that the consequence of this is, 'that I shall never be called upon for the £2, and so shall never have my interest in the company in the shape of paid-up capital increased to £10.' Well, that was originally quite a natural expectation no doubt; but was it anything more than an expectation? Was it anything in the nature of a right? I cannot help thinking that it is very clearly not of the nature of a right, but only of the nature of a liability. . . . ; the position of a holder of such shares is, in respect of unpaid capital, one of liability merely, and not of right. . . .

" . . . One cannot have very much sympathy with the pursuers in the attempt they are making to prevent the company from carrying through a scheme which, it is thought, will very much advance the interests of the company. . . .

" I think companies of this kind must be left, in the main, to manage their own affairs in their own way. I do not like active and constant interference by the Court with the financial concerns of a company of this kind, who must understand their own financial affairs a great deal better than any Court of justice can; and therefore, unless they transgress the rules of the statute under which they are incorporated, and proceed to exercise powers not given to them, or to do things that are prohibited by statute, *prima facie,* I think the Court will not interfere. I do not say that there may not be cases in which, without any formal or statutory objection being stated, it may be shewn that a tyrannical majority of a company are unscrupulously sacrificing the interests of a minority to promote their own ends; and if a case of that kind were made, I am very far from saying that the Court should not interfere; but it does not appear to me that anything like that has occurred here."

Reduction of capital: questions for the court: court's power to confirm is not limited by provisions in company's memorandum

Balmenach-Glenlivet Distillery Ltd. v. Croall
(1906) 8 F. 1135

The memorandum of association of B. Ltd. provided that the capital should consist of 6,000 preference shares of £10 each and 6,000 ordinary shares of £10 each, the preference shares to be entitled to a cumulative preferential dividend of 5 per cent. and to priority of repayment of capital in a winding up.

In a scheme for reduction of capital, the preference shares were to be reduced from £10 to £5 10s., and the ordinary shares from £10 to £1.

The petition for confirmation of this reduction was opposed by certain preference shareholders, who contended that it was *ultra vires* of the court to confirm a scheme which violated the provisions of the memorandum as to shareholders' rights *inter se,* and, further, that the scheme was not just and equitable.

The court *confirmed* the reduction, *holding* that the court had power to do so and that the scheme was a just and equitable one.

LORD PRESIDENT (DUNEDIN) (at p. 1141): " The real authority on the matter is, I think, the case in which the last word has been said, the *British and American Finance Corporation* v. *Couper,* decided in the House of Lords, and reported in [1894] A.C. 399. I cannot read that case without coming to the conclusion that it really has settled, in a way that we must certainly follow, that, so far as the question of *intra vires* is concerned, there really is no limit to what the Court can do. It may confirm any resolution, however much against any provision of the Company it may be, provided always, of course, that that resolution is really for a reduction of capital, and subject also to this very great safeguard that the Court is not to do so unless it thinks that on the whole the new arrangement is a just and equitable arrangement. . . .

" . . . I am not wishing to throw the slightest doubt upon the view that, in ordinary circumstances, where there is a preference on capital in liquidation in favour of one set of shares against another, and where capital is lost, you should make the loss fall first of all on those who come last in the liquidation. But there are obviously cases where a desolating logic would defeat

itself, and I am bound to say I think this is one of them. . . .
The ordinary shareholders here represent the managing persons
of the Company; and it is not in human nature to suppose that,
if by arrangement the ordinary shareholders were wiped out of
existence, they would go on working to make the Company
prosperous for the preference shareholders. . . . I have come
to the conclusion that the arrangement proposed is a just and
equitable one, as being in the true interests of the shareholders
of the Company, and as being the only thing that stands between
them and utter ruin."

NOTE

The trend set by this and other cases was commented on by
Lord President Cooper in *Wilsons and Clyde Coal Co. Ltd.* v.
Scottish Insurance Corporation Ltd. (p. 183, below) (at 1948 S.C.
p. 375) as follows:

"Every major Companies Act, beginning with the Act of 1867,
has required that reduction of share capital (except by certain
methods which are not in point) should be confirmed by the Court.
In the early days the Courts took this jurisdiction very seriously
and refused to confirm many reductions of capital, often on the
dubious ground that they were *ultra vires*. This tendency was cor-
rected in *British and American Trustee Corporation* ([1894] A.C.
399); *Balmenach-Glenlivet Distillery; Poole* v. *National Bank of
China* ([1907] A.C. 229); and *Caldwell & Co.* (1916 S.C.(H.L.) 120),
which progressively narrowed the scope of the Court's powers, and
inaugurated in company practice what might be called an era of
self-determination and *laissez-faire*. Nevertheless, emphasis was again
and again laid by the House of Lords upon the proposition that the
Courts had a 'discretion' to confirm or not to confirm, which it
was their duty to apply in 'every proper case,' and that this discretion fell to be exercised by reference to the test of whether the
scheme would be 'fair and equitable,' 'just and equitable,' 'fair
and reasonable' or 'not unjust or inequitable,' expressions sometimes qualified and explained by the addition of the words, 'in the
ordinary sense of the term' or 'as a matter of business.' . . . It is
abundantly plain from these decisions that the Court's jurisdiction
is a discretionary one, not confined to verifying the technical correctness of the formal procedure, nor even to determining according
to strict law the precise rights of the contending parties, but involving the application of broad standards of fairness, reasonableness
and equity, and the avoidance of what Lord Dunedin once described
as 'a desolating logic' (*Balmenach-Glenlivet Distillery* (at p. 1142)."

Reduction of capital: questions for the court: alleged loss of capital: whether evidence of loss is required

Caldwell & Co. Ltd. v. Caldwell

1916 S.C. (H.L.) 120; 1915 S.C. 527

The capital of C. Ltd. was £50,000, divided into 50,000 shares of £1 each, all issued and fully paid.

After a fire at its works, C. Ltd. resolved to reduce its capital to £37,500, divided into 50,000 shares of 15s. each, by cancelling 5s. per share as capital which had been lost or was unrepresented by available assets.

Answers to C. Ltd.'s petition for confirmation of this resolution were lodged by C., a shareholder, who denied that capital had been lost or was unrepresented by available assets.

The opinion of the reporter was that no capital had in fact been lost.

The Court of Session *confirmed* the resolution for reduction, and the House of Lords *dismissed* an appeal against this decision.

LORD PARKER OF WADDINGTON (at p. 121): " It was decided by this House in *Poole* v. *National Bank of China* ([1907] A.C. 229) that whenever a company, having the necessary powers in that behalf, has passed a special resolution for the reduction of capital the Court has jurisdiction to confirm such reduction. In cases where the rights of creditors are not affected, that is to say, when the proposed reduction does not involve either diminution of liability in respect of unpaid share capital, or the payment to any shareholder of any paid-up share capital the only relevant considerations are (1) whether the Court ought to refuse its sanction out of regard to those members of the public who might subsequently become shareholders in the company; and (2) whether the reduction is fair and equitable as between the different classes of existing shareholders. . . .

" It often happens that the special resolution for the reduction of a company's capital refers to the amount by which the capital is to be reduced as lost or unrepresented by available assets. In such cases I understand that, since the decision of the case above referred to, the practice of the Courts in Scotland has been to dispense with proof of the facts referred to in the resolution, provided, at any rate, that there is no reason to suspect the *bona fides* of the parties. The practice of the High Court of Justice in England has not been uniform. Some Judges have dispensed altogether with such proof, as not being essential to the exercise of the jurisdiction of the Court. Others have insisted on the production of some evidence on the point. My own practice was to insist on *prima facie* evidence of the existence of the state of facts referred to in the resolution. . . .

" . . . In the present case . . . having regard to the effect of prolonged cessation of business upon the value, if any, of the goodwill, and to the fact that the amount of the actual loss by fire is seldom, if ever, covered by the amounts recovered under policies of insurance, I think that there was strong *prima facie* evidence that at least £12,500 of the Company's capital had been lost or was unrepresented by available assets, and the *bona fide* belief of the directors that this was so is not disputed."

LORD SHAW OF DUNFERMLINE (at p. 125): " In Scotland the procedure upon such application is by way of remit to a ' man of business,' that is to a solicitor of standing. No one can doubt . . . that the matter has been thoroughly inquired into and the fullest consideration has been given to every objection. . . . There is therefore in Scotland no question of procedure such as that which has given rise to the variety alluded to in the opinion of my noble and learned friend Lord Parker."

Reduction of capital: questions for the court: surplus capital: order of repayment

William Dixon Ltd., Petitioners
1948 S.C. 511

D. Ltd., a coal company, found itself, after the Coal Industry Nationalisation Act 1946, with capital in excess of its requirements.

The company had both preference and ordinary stock, and proposed to reduce its capital by returning to each preference and ordinary stockholder 6s. 8d. in respect of each £1 unit of stock held. By the articles of association preference stockholders had priority for repayment of capital in a winding up, and the reporter drew attention to the fact that the proposed repayment was not in accordance with the *prima facie* legal position that preference stockholders were entitled to the same priority in a reduction as in a winding up.

The court *confirmed* the reduction.

LORD PRESIDENT (COOPER) (at p. 516): " The learned reporter, founding upon a previous case in 1945, and with a citation of a number of earlier decisions, draws our attention to the fact that

' the *prima facie* legal position,' when any reduction of capital takes place, is that any loss should be thrown in the first instance on the ordinary shares, and that any capital repaid should be so repaid in the first instance to the preference shares; but that the *prima facie* legal position, as many instances show, may be departed from in any case where the Court feels disposed so to do. I wish to add that most observations which have been made in the past on the subject of what the reporter describes as ' the *prima facie* legal position ' have evidently been made with an eye to the risks which attend the perilling of capital in a going concern, and the possibility, never capable of being entirely excluded, of eventual loss or insolvency. In such cases the preference shareholder is normally entitled to the first place in the queue of those who wish to leave the sinking ship. But in this case, and in a number of the other coal cases which have come before us, there is no sinking ship. The company is not embarrassed in any way except by excess of riches. The competition is not to leave the ship for the stormy sea, but to stay on the ship. I feel therefore that in such a fundamentally altered position the observations previously made with regard to the *prima facie* legal position fall to be read *cum nota* and against a very different background. In this case there are no respondents, and there has not been at any stage any criticism of the proposal except by the holder of £100 of preference stock out of a total of £300,000. . . . In so far as the rights of preference shareholders in this company fall to be considered in isolation, they have been treated in the scheme with full justice, if not with generosity. My proposal therefore would be that there is no obstacle to our granting our confirmation to the reduction proposed."

NOTES

1. One of the other " coal cases " referred to was *Wilsons and Clyde Coal Co. Ltd.* v. *Scottish Insurance Corporation Ltd.* (p. 183, below).

2. The case in 1945 to which the reporter referred was *The Donaldson Line Ltd., Petitioners,* 1945 S.C. 162, in which the court granted the prayer of a petition for reduction, without delivering opinions. The reduction in that case was to be effected by the return to ordinary shareholders of 16s. in respect of each £1 share held. No provision was made for any repayment to preference shareholders, but a second special resolution, passed subject to the court's approval of the reduction, gave the preference shareholders new rights in the winding up of the company.

The reporter in *The Donaldson Line Ltd., Petitioners,* stated: " Your Lordships are . . . being asked to confirm a reduction of capital which is not in accordance with the general law. *Prima facie* a reduction of capital should be an all-round one. Where capital, however, is to be paid off, *prima facie* the same percentage should be paid off each share. . . . Where, however, there are preference shares with a priority as regards capital in a winding up, as in the present case . . . , the *prima facie* legal position appears to be that any loss should be thrown in the first instance on the ordinary shares, and on similar reasoning that, in the case of repayment of capital, preference shares are entitled to be paid in full before any repayment is made in respect of the ordinary shares. . . . It appears, however, that the Court has power to confirm any kind of reduction even if the strict legal rights of one class of shareholders are departed from."

Reduction of capital: questions for the court: fairness as between different classes of shareholders

Wilsons and Clyde Coal Co. Ltd. v. Scottish Insurance Corporation Ltd.
1949 S.C. (H.L.) 90; 1948 S.C. 360

W. Ltd. presented a petition for confirmation of a reduction of capital which involved the return to preference stockholders of their capital at its par value.

On account of the Coal Industry Nationalisation Act 1946, W. Ltd. was about to go into liquidation, and the reduction petition was opposed by 45 per cent. of the preference stockholders on the ground that the proposed reduction was unfair and inequitable to them since (i) it would deprive them prematurely of a high-yielding and well-secured investment, (ii) it would deprive them of their right to share in the surplus funds to be distributed in the approaching liquidation, and (iii) it would deprive them of the compensation provided for under section 25 of the Act of 1946.

Held that the reduction was to be confirmed because (i) the fact that liquidation was inevitable did not affect the right of the company to act under its articles at any time prior to liquidation, (ii) there was no provision in the articles conferring on preference stockholders the right to share in surplus funds on a liquidation, and (iii) the objectors had failed to show that there was any reasonable probability that on liquidation their position would be advantageously affected by the statutory provisions for compensation.

LORD SIMONDS (at p. 103): " Important though [the Court's] task is to see that the procedure by which a reduction is carried through is formally correct and that creditors are not prejudiced, it has the further duty of satisfying itself that the scheme is fair and equitable between the different classes of shareholders. . . .

" . . . Whether a man lends money to a company at 7 per cent. or subscribes for its shares carrying a cumulative preferential dividend at that rate, I do not think that he can complain of unfairness if the company, being in a position lawfully to do so, proposes to pay him off. . . . So long as the company can lawfully repay him, whether it be months or years before a contemplated liquidation, I see no ground for the Court refusing its confirmation. . . .

" . . . Reading the relevant articles as a whole, I come to the conclusion that articles 159 and 160 are exhaustive of the rights of the preference stockholders in a winding-up. . . .

" . . . The words of the specifically relevant articles, ' rank before the other shares . . . on the property of the company to the extent of repayment of the amounts called up and paid thereon,' appear to me apt to define exhaustively the rights of the preference stockholders in a winding-up. . . .

" . . . Funds being available for payment off of capital, the natural order is to pay off that capital which has priority, and I see no glimmer of unfairness in the company doing so at the earliest possible moment. . . .

" . . . The Court should in the exercise of its jurisdiction regard the provisions of section 25 as a factor to be included in its consideration of the fairness of a proposed reduction, but no more than that. . . .

" The section looks forward to regulations to be made in due course, which are to provide facilities for adjusting the respective interests of different classes in the company's assets. . . . At the date of the proceedings in the Court of Session, no regulations had been made. . . . Regulations have now been made, but they do not illumine the darkness. The Court therefore has . . . to take into account . . . the factor that the preference stockholders might at long last get something better than they are now getting, i.e., repayment in full of their capital, a possibility resting not on any sure guidance in the section or regulations, but on the speculative hope that, since there is no guidance, anything may happen."

LORD NORMAND (at p. 113): " The company is not bound to satisfy the Court that its proposals are not unfair. It has brought forward proposals which are *intra vires,* regular on the face of them, and in conformity with the usual practice. . . . If the objectors can find in the provisions of section 25 or of the regulations anything which should stand in the way of the Court's approval, it is for them to disclose it. If they fail to do this, the Court has no material before it which would warrant a finding that the proposed reduction is unfair."

NOTE

In the House of Lords Lord Morton of Henryton, and in the Court of Session Lord President Cooper, dissented.

Lord Morton of Henryton (at p. 114): " My reasons . . . are as follows: (1) In my view the preference stockholders have, under the company's memorandum and articles, a right to share in the surplus assets in a winding up. (2) The company's substratum is gone and a winding up is inevitable. Thus the scheme does not serve any useful business purpose connected with the carrying on of the company. The only results which will follow from it are (*a*) the preference stockholders will forthwith cease to receive their interest at 7 per cent., instead of continuing to receive it until winding up; (*b*) the preference stockholders will be excluded from any share in the surplus assets on a winding up. The ordinary shareholders have used their voting power in order to secure these results, and for no other purpose; there is no other reason why the company should not proceed to liquidation without taking this preliminary step. (3) The opposition to the scheme does not come from a small or factious minority but from a substantial minority who have excellent reasons for wishing to oppose the scheme. (4) It is possibly of some importance that the scheme cuts out the preference stockholders from any chance of getting favourable adjustment of their interests in the company's assets under section 25 of the Coal Industry Nationalisation Act 1946. . . . However, I attach very little weight to this point.

" My first reason is of great importance. If the preference stockholders are not entitled to share in the surplus assets, the scheme at once assumes a different aspect. . . .

" . . . I think that if it had been intended to exclude the preference shareholders from any share in the surplus assets, express words of exclusion would have been inserted in articles 159 and 160. . . .

" . . . I fall back upon that inherent equality which is, to my mind, in no way disturbed by the regulations of the company."

(In the course of reviewing some cases, Lord Morton said that he agreed with the reasoning and the decision in *Williamson-Buchanan Steamers Ltd.* (p. 166, above).)

. . .

"I now come to my second reason . . . , and I should like to adopt,
respectfully, the summary of the situation given by the learned Lord
President: 'What are the admitted facts? This company's capital
structure consists of preference and ordinary stock in the ratio of
roughly 1: 13. Its business was coal mining, and on January 1, 1947,
its collieries and working assets passed to the National Coal Board
in exchange for a share, as yet undetermined, in the global sum
of compensation. Liquidation is inevitable. The company's substratum is gone. Its remaining assets, consisting of investments and
cash, can no longer be employed in prosecuting the objects for
which it was formed. No resumption of business is in contemplation.
It survives, with one foot in the grave, solely for the purpose of
being wound up, and it will be wound up as soon as the compensation has been ascertained. . . . This company's future is behind it.
Its creditors are provided for. There is only one active controversy,
viz., the division of the assets amongst the shareholders. . . . There
are bound to be considerable surplus assets. Faced with this
situation . . . , this company determined to wind up by instalments
and to die by inches. . . . The proposal is to pay off the whole
preference stock at par and to return 10s. in the £ to the ordinary
stockholders, who, if the scheme is approved, will be left in undisputed possession of the field. . . . Confirmation is now opposed not
by a single obstructive shareholder or a small coterie of dissen-
tients, but by 71 preference stockholders holding 45 per cent. of
the preference stock.' Later, the Lord President said: ' . . . Both
parties see that, if there is no "first step" of a reduction of
capital to extinguish the preference stock at par, the surplus assets
will have to be divided between all the shareholders, whereas, if
this reduction is confirmed, the whole of the surplus assets will be
appropriated by the ordinary stockholders, and the preference stockholders will get nothing but the par value of their stock. The
ordinary stockholders have used their voting predominance with the
object of cutting the preference stockholders out, and the question
for us is whether in the circumstances that is, in a business sense,
fair and equitable.' Finally, he observed: ' . . . it can make no
appreciable difference to these ordinary stockholders whether they
get 10s. in the £ now at the "first step" in the winding up, or
whether the relative investments continue to be held by the company
until the "formal liquidation." . . . The preference stockholders . . .
are being bought off for less than a just equivalent, and this loss
is being inflicted upon them not in the interests of the company
but solely in order that the ordinary stockholders may eventually
appropriate 13/13ths of the surplus assets instead of 12/13ths. This
is not my idea of what is just or equitable, and I do not believe that
any jury of business men would so regard it.'

. . .

"My third reason, as to the nature of the opposition to the
scheme, is also dealt with in the passages quoted above. I would

only add that it is not of course to be supposed that the holders of the remaining 55 per cent. of preference stock support the scheme, merely because they have not appeared in these proceedings. Indeed, I find it difficult to imagine that any well-informed preference stockholder would support the scheme, unless he were also a still larger holder of ordinary stock.

" I do not place much weight on my fourth reason, because it is imposible to foretell with any accuracy what (if any) adjustment of interests will ultimately be made under section 25 of the Act of 1946, if the preference stock continues in being."

In the Court of Session Lord Cooper referred to the changed attitude of the courts towards their duty in connection with confirmation of reductions of capital: see Note to *Balmenach-Glenlivet Distillery Ltd.* v. *Croall* (p. 179, above).

" Nothing," said Lord Cooper (at p. 376), " could be clearer and more reassuring than these formulations of the duties of the Court. Nothing could be more disappointing than the reported instances of their subsequent exercise. . . .

" . . . If the Court's discretion to refuse to confirm a reduction of capital has still real value, the present is a clear case for its exercise. The grant of confirmation proposed by your Lordships will be a direct invitation to every other company in a like position (and there must be many) to apply a similar device, and a preliminary reduction of capital will become a recognised precursor to a winding-up resolution."

Lord Cooper referred to *The Alloa Coal Co. Ltd., Petitioners,* 1947 S.C. 651, in which the First Division had confirmed an unopposed all-round reduction in the case of another coal company. " Perhaps," he said, " we were incautious in so doing."

Reduction of capital: questions for the court: distribution of assets having a book value equal to the amount of capital to be repaid: threatened nationalisation

The Westburn Sugar Refineries Ltd., Petitioners
1951 S.C. (H.L.) 57.

W. Ltd. proposed to reduce its capital, not by a cash payment, but by distributing among the shareholders certain assets, *viz.,* shares of another company which, in W. Ltd.'s balance-sheet, had a book value equal to the amount of capital to be repaid, but whose true value was reasonably believed to be considerably in excess of their book value.

Held that, as the financial position of the company disclosed that the interests of creditors, shareholders and the general public could not be prejudiced by the proposed reduction, the reduction fell to be confirmed by the court, and further that the possibility that it might have been adopted in view of a threatened nationalisation of the sugar industry afforded no reason for the court to withhold its sanction.

LORD NORMAND (at p. 58): " The general rule is that the prescribed majority of the shareholders are entitled to decide whether there should be a reduction of capital and, if so, in what manner and to what extent it should be carried into effect. . . . But the powers of the shareholders must be exercised so as to safeguard the rights of creditors, the just and equitable treatment of shareholders, and the interests of the investing public. . . .

" . . . In an arrangement in which assets are taken at balance-sheet values there is the possibility that the scheme of reduction may be used as a means of defeating or injuring the rights of creditors or deceiving future investors. . . .

" . . . The material matter is, not the value of the investments which the company proposes to transfer, but the value of those assets which it will retain."

LORD REID (at p. 60): " There is nothing novel in paying off capital otherwise than with money; it has long been recognised that this is not incompetent.

" The real questions in this case are whether it is competent in a reduction of capital to pay off share capital by transferring assets whose value clearly exceeds the amount by which the capital of the company is reduced; and, if this is competent, whether it is proper in this case to allow it to be done. . . .

" What, then, is the duty of the Court in considering a matter of this kind? In the first place the interests of creditors must be safeguarded; but here that has been done. Secondly, the interests of shareholders may have to be considered; but in this case there has been no opposition by any shareholder at any time and it is difficult to see how there could be any prejudice to any single shareholder. And thirdly there is the public interest to consider. . . . It appears to me to be proper to consider what assets the company will retain if the proposed reduction of capital is confirmed. In this case the assets to be distributed taken at their real value form only a comparatively small part of the total assets of the company. . . .

" It has been said that there are other matters concerning the public interest to be taken into account in this case. Lord Carmont took the view that there is or may be an ulterior object behind the present petition, namely to avoid in part the consequences of future legislation. The fact that the petitioners may have such an ulterior object may be a good reason for making quite certain that the existing law is complied with in every respect, but it cannot, in my judgment, be by itself a ground for dismissing the petition. The petition must be judged by the law as it exists to-day."

LORD RADCLIFFE (at p. 63): " The consideration of what is unfair or inequitable cannot well extend beyond consideration of the interests of creditors, shareholders and the general public, by which term is, I think, meant persons who may in the future have dealings with the company or may be minded to invest in its securities. . . .

" . . . I do not think that the contingency of nationalisation has any relevance to the public policy that Courts of Justice should support."

NOTES

1. In the Court of Session (1951 S.C. 190), the leading opinion was given by Lord Carmont. Lord Russell dissented. Lord President Cooper said that he found the case one of serious difficulty; he concluded (at p. 200): " In the absence of clear authority or the guidance of practice, I cannot take the responsibility of lending the approval of the Court to a novel expedient which seems to me to open a wide door to the most dangerous possibilities."

2. *Cf. David Bell Ltd., Petitioners,* below.

Reduction of capital: questions for the court: avoidance of taxation

David Bell Ltd., Petitioners
1954 S.C. 33

B. Ltd., a private company with paid-up capital of £120,000, proposed to reduce its capital to £90,000 by returning 5s. on each £1 share.

The reporter to whom the petition for confirmation was re-mitted pointed out that the company could have distributed £30,000 among its shareholders without reducing its capital, as the amount at credit of its profit and loss account was largely in excess of that sum. He further pointed out that such a course would have involved the company in increased liability for profits tax and might have involved shareholders in liability for surtax.

Held that the decision of the House of Lords in *The Westburn Sugar Refineries Ltd., Petitioners*, had removed any possible doubt; and confirmation *granted*.

LORD PRESIDENT (COOPER) (at p. 34): " In this petition for reduction of capital, which presents no specialty not to be found in many petitions with which we have dealt, the reporter has pointed out that a possible difficulty might be created by the decision in the case of *A. & D. Fraser*. We feel, however, that the subsequent decision of the House of Lords in *Westburn Sugar Refineries* removes any doubt that might be created by the previous decision in the case of *Fraser*. We shall therefore grant the prayer of the petition."

NOTES

1. For the *Westburn Sugar Refineries* case, see p. 187, above.
2. The other case referred to by the reporter and by Lord President Cooper was *A. & D. Fraser Ltd., Petitioners*, 1951 S.C. 394, which was decided by the First Division on March 16, 1951, *i.e.* after the decision of the *Westburn Sugar Refineries* case by the same Division (December 8, 1950), but before that decision was reversed by the House of Lords (April 5, 1951).

F. Ltd., a private company with a paid-up capital of £50,000, passed resolutions whereby the capital was increased to £100,000 and whereby reserves were capitalised and applied in payment of the additional capital which was then issued to the existing shareholders. Immediately afterwards, the company passed a special resolution to reduce its capital from £100,000 to £25,000, by the return of £75,000 to the shareholders.

The court (*diss.* Lord President Cooper) *refused* to confirm the reduction, *holding* that, although the requirements of the Companies Act 1948 had been formally complied with, the court nevertheless had a discretion in the matter of confirmation, and that it would not be proper to confirm a reduction the sole purpose and effect of which appeared to be the distribution of accumulated profits in such a way as to avoid taxation.

3. The law of taxation includes express provisions aimed at preventing tax avoidance. In particular, certain rules are made to apply to any " qualifying distribution," and " distribution " has a wide definition: the term includes, *e.g.*, certain capitalisation issues and certain reductions of capital.

The case of *David Bell Ltd., Petitioners,* is, therefore, not to be taken as authoritative on the law of taxation at the present day: its authority is limited to the point that avoidance of taxation is not a factor to be taken into consideration by the court in petitions for reduction under the Companies Acts.

Reduction of capital: questions for the court: protection of creditors

The Palace Billiard Rooms Ltd. v.
The City Property Investment Trust Corporation Ltd.
1912 S.C. 5

P. Ltd., occupying premises under a lease of which four years had still to run, presented a petition for confirmation of a reduction of capital which was to be effected by the cancellation of a liability of 10s. on each £1 share.

The landlord of the premises objected to the reduction unless provision were made to secure the payment of the rent for the remainder of the lease.

P. Ltd. offered to appropriate in security a sum less than the full amount of the rent which would become due, and maintained that, as the landlord's debt was contingent, the court should approve of the offer as sufficient.

Held that, as the company admitted the full amount of the debt, and as that amount was neither contingent nor unascertained, the company was bound, by the statutory provisions, to provide security for the full amount.

Since the company stated that it was not prepared to do this, the court *dismissed* the petition.

LORD PRESIDENT (DUNEDIN) (at p. 8): " The whole question . . . depends upon section 49 of the Companies (Consolidation) Act 1908. That section provides . . . , by subsection (3), ' Where a creditor entered on the list whose debt or claim is not discharged or determined does not consent to the reduction, the Court, may, if it thinks fit, dispense with the consent of that creditor,' —now, that is what we are asked to do; the Court is asked to grant the privilege of dispensing with the consent of a person who does not wish to consent—' on the company securing payment of his debt or claim by appropriating, as the Court may direct the following amount.' Now, it seems to me that that is quite absolute. The Court can only do it ' on the company securing payment of his debt or claim by appropriating . . . the following amount,' and then come two alternatives: ' (i.) If the company admits the full amount of his debt or claim, or, though not admitting it, is willing to provide for it, then the full amount of the debt or claim; (ii.) if the company does not admit or is not willing to provide for the full amount of the debt or claim, or if the amount is contingent or not ascertained, then an amount fixed by the Court after the like inquiry and adjudication as if the company were being wound up by the Court.'

" . . . I think that this is a case where the Company does admit the full amount of debt or claim. They do not say that the rent will not be due at the terms when they come, and consequently I think the matter falls within subsection (3) (i.). I do not think that it can be held to fall within subsection (3) (ii.). It does not fall under the first part, because the Company does not 'not admit,' and it cannot fall under the second part, because, in my view, it is not a contingent debt. It is a perfectly certain debt, a future debt but not a contingent debt."

NOTES

1. The statutory provisions are now in section 67 of the Companies Act 1948.

2. The provisions of section 67 (2) of the Act of 1948 apply " where the proposed reduction of share capital involves either diminution of liability in respect of unpaid share capital or the payment to any shareholder of any paid-up share capital, and in any other case if the court so directs."

In *Lawrie & Symington Ltd., Petitioners,* 1969 S.L.T. 221, the court held that the replacement of preference shares with loan stock did involve payment to a shareholder of paid-up share capital for the purposes of that provision.

L. Ltd., whose issued share capital was 120,000 ordinary shares of £1 each and 32,400 6 per cent. cumulative preference shares of £1 each, proposed to reduce its capital by cancelling the preference shares and allotting to the holders of such shares £1 7 per cent. unsecured loan stock for each £1 share.

The court made a direction under section 67 (3) of the Act that, in view of the special circumstances of the case, section 67 (2) should not apply.

Lord President (Clyde) (delivering the opinion of the Court) (at p. 223): " In our opinion the replacement of preference shares with loan stock does involve payment to a shareholder of paid up share capital within the meaning of section 67 (2) of the 1948 Act. It is, of course, true that no immediate payment to a shareholder will occur, but the loan stock falls to be repaid on a future date, and therefore the company is assuming a liability to repay at a future date. If so, section 67 (2) is wide enough to cover such a case.

" In our view, therefore, section 67 (2) does apply. But in the light of the detailed figures regarding current assets and liabilities as explained and certified by the secretary of the company we consider that this is a case in which we should exercise the powers conferred on us by section 67 (3) to direct that subsection (2) shall not apply as regards the creditors of the company or any class of them."

3. In *New Duff House Sanitarium Ltd., Petitioners*, 1931 S.L.T. 337 (O.H.), the court dispensed with settlement of a list of creditors on the ground that creditors were not being prejudiced.

The proposal was to redeem or cancel 500 "A" preference shares and then increase the capital by the creation of 500 redeemable " A " preference shares to be issued to the holders of the shares which were to be redeemed.

Lord Anderson (at p. 339): " The interests of the creditors are in no whit impaired or prejudiced. The £5,000 will still be available for the purpose of paying the company's debts, and, in effect, there will be no reduction of capital at all."

4. Settlement of a list of creditors was also found to be unnecessary in *Cadzow Coal Co. Ltd., Petitioners*, 1931 S.C. 272.

The creditors, other than the Inland Revenue, had consented to the proposed reduction. The Inspector of Taxes had stated no objection to the proposed reduction, and had explained that it was departmental practice to decline to sign consents in such circumstances. The company's liquid assets afforded ample security for the outstanding liabilities.

5. A sum representing debts due to a company may be taken into account when the court is deciding whether to dispense with the provisions of subsection (2) of section 67 of the Act of 1948: *Anderson, Brown & Co. Ltd., Petitioners*, 1965 S.C. 81.

Reduction was to be by way of repaying to preference shareholders the whole paid-up capital of their shares. The cash and gilt-edged securities of the company fell short of the total of the liabilities plus the proposed repayment, but if the sum due to the company by sundry debtors (written down to provide for bad debts) was added to the value of the cash and gilt-edged securities, the result was a substantial excess over the total of the liabilities plus the proposed repayment. In the past the vast majority of the company's debtors had settled their debts regularly and punctually, and the company's obligations to its creditors had been regularly met.

The court *dispensed* with the making up of a list of creditors.

Lord President (Clyde) (at p. 83): " Although there is no reported decision of this court on the matter, it has long been our practice not necessarily to limit the assets to be taken into account to cash and gilt-edged securities. The issue under section 67 (3) is whether, having regard to the special circumstances of the case, it is proper to dispense with the inquiry provided for in subsection (2). In my view this confers upon the court a certain element of discretion."

Reduction of capital: questions for the court: form of minute

D. Simpson Ltd. and Reduced, Petitioners
1929 S.C. 65

D. Ltd. had passed resolutions to reduce its capital by cancelling capital which had been lost or was unrepresented by available assets and then to increase its capital by the creation of further shares.

Held that the minute required by the statutory provisions should set forth (1) the state of the company's capital after the reduction and (2) the state of its capital as increased.

LORD JUSTICE-CLERK (ALNESS) (at p. 67): " The reporter has raised the question whether, when a company has passed the necessary resolutions (1) to reduce its capital subject to the approval of the Court, and (2), on the approval of this Court of such reduction, to increase its capital, the minute required under section 51 should merely record (in accordance with existing practice) the state of the company's capital, after giving effect both to the reduction as sanctioned and to the increase made conditionally on the sanction of the reduction; or whether it should record separately (1) the state of the company's capital after giving effect to the reduction as sanctioned, and (2) the consequential resolution to increase the company's capital.

" After consultation with the other Division, we think the latter form of minute (which accords with the practice in England) is preferable. The form of the minute in the present case will therefore be as follows: ' The capital of the Company, D. Simpson, Limited, was, by virtue of a special resolution, and with the sanction of an order of the Court, dated 10th November 1928, reduced from £8,000, divided into 8,000 shares of £1 each, to £2,600, divided into 8,000 shares of 6s. 6d. each. Ordinary and special resolutions have been passed and confirmed by the Company to the effect that, on such reduction taking effect, the capital of the Company shall be increased to £7,600, divided into 10,400 preference shares of 5s. each, all issued and fully paid, and 20,000 unissued ordinary shares of 5s. each.' "

NOTES

1. The statutory provisions before the court in the case were those of the Companies (Consolidation) Act 1908, s. 51 (1). These provisions are now in the Companies Act 1948, s. 69 (1).

2. This case was referred to by Lord President Clyde in *William Brown, Sons, & Co. Ltd., Petitioners,* 1931 S.C. 701 (see Note 2 to *Scottish Vulcanite Co. Ltd., Petitioners,* p. 172, above), at p. 703: " The difficulty of regarding the resolution as one by which the capital of the Company can be said to be reduced in any way is shown by the circumstance that the form of minute recently adjusted with the other Division (*D. Simpson, Limited*) as the form to be followed in all cases of reduction of capital is incapable of adaptation to the resolution here. I think the best course in the special circumstances

of the present case is to follow the form of minute given in the latest edition of Palmer's Company Precedents ((13th ed.), Pt. I., p. 1187) as applicable to such a resolution as this: ' The capital of William Brown, Sons, & Co., Ltd., is £100,000 divided into shares of £1 each, of which 80,000 have been issued. At the time of the registration of this Minute, the whole of the said 80,000 shares have been issued, upon each of which £1 has been paid; but in respect of each of the said shares, the Company is empowered to pay off or return 2s. 6d. of the amount so paid up, upon the footing that the amount paid off or returned, or any part thereof, may be called up again.' "

CHAPTER 12

SHARES

Statements in share certificate: personal bar

Clavering, Son & Co. v. Goodwins, Jardine, & Co. Ltd.
(1891) 18 R. 652

J. borrowed £4,500 from C., giving to C. as security a share certificate bearing that J. had a certain number of fully paid shares in a company of which J. was a managing director. J. also delivered to C. an excuted transfer of the shares.

The shares were, to J.'s knowledge, not fully paid. The certificate had been issued in error by the secretary who, at J.'s request, had allowed J. to retain it.

J. failed to repay his loan within the stipulated time, and C. lodged the executed transfer, along with the certificate, with the secretary, requesting that the shares be registered in C.'s name. The secretary refused to do so.

C. raised an action for damages against the company.

Held that C. had been entitled to rely on the validity of the certificate, and that the company was therefore liable in damages.

Lord Justice-Clerk (J. H. A. Macdonald) (at p. 661): " The defence maintained upon the part of the company is that the secretary was not acting within his duty as their servant in doing what he did, and that as what was done was a fraud, they are not liable for his fraud. I cannot accept that. Their servant the secretary was authorised by them to conduct their business, and it was his duty to issue such certificates as were issued in this case, and he did issue the certificate, which is duly signed by two directors, as being a certificate for these shares. . . . I hold that he was acting as the representative of the company whose duty it was to do such acts, and that the company must be responsible for the acts so done."

Lord Young (at p. 662): " The pursuer was informed that the directors declined to recognise the transfer in his favour at all, and declined to put it upon the register.

" . . . They were bound to put the transfer upon the register . . . in November 1889; I think that was their obligation, and that they cannot be permitted to allege that the 500 shares were not fully paid up, in the face of the certificate of their own directors and secretary that they were fully paid up. I think they were estopped, or barred, or whatever term you choose to use, from pleading that they were not fully paid up. The pursuer proceeded, as he was entitled to do, in reliance upon a certificate under the hands of the proper officers of this mercantile company to the effect that they were fully paid up. . . . I therefore regard . . . the failure of the company to register when they were requested to do so in the month of November as a wrong committed by them upon the pursuer, and for that wrong he is entitled to compensation in damages.

" . . . If registration had taken place on the 20th of November the pursuer might have realised those shares which are now worthless.

" . . . The pursuer is, in my opinion, agreeing with your Lordship and the Lord Ordinary, entitled to be recompensed with the sum of £4,000 of damages, of course with the expenses of this process."

LORD ORDINARY (KYLLACHY) (at p. 656): " It will be, in the first place, convenient to see what are the relative rights which arise upon the issue in regular course of a certificate of shares or stock in a limited company.

" Such certificate . . . is a statutory document—that is to say, it is recognised by the Companies Acts. By section 31 of the Act of 1862 it is provided, ' A certificate under the common seal of the company specifying any share or shares or stock held by any member of the company shall be *prima facie* evidence of the title of the member to the share or shares or stock therein specified.'

" And by the articles of association of this (the defender's) company, section 11, it is provided, ' Every member shall be entitled to receive, gratis, a certificate under the common seal of the company, specifying the share or shares held by him, and the amount paid up thereon.'

" The certificate here, therefore, is a certificate by the company, and is a document by which the company is bound as by any other document issued in the course of its business. And, looking to the terms of the document, there seems no difficulty in carrying its operation and effect at least this length, that it implied, if it did not express, a contract as between the company and the person to whom the certificate was issued that the company should recognise the latter as a shareholder to the extent set forth in the certificate, or otherwise, should make good to him the pecuniary value of that position. In short,

M.P.C.—8

as between the company and the recipient of the certificate in regular course, it seems not doubtful that the company impliedly warrants the facts set forth in the certificate. On the other hand, of course, the recipient is open to all exceptions arising from his own conduct or his own knowledge. If, for example, . . . the transfer in his (the recipient's) favour, on the faith of which he has been registered and obtained his certificate, turns out, although unknown to him, to be a forgery, or if he has obtained the issue of the certificate by fraud, or if he is in any way open to any other personal exception,—in all such cases the company is free, and has a good answer to any action at the instance of the recipient of the certificate. All this is probably clear enough.

" But *quid juris* when the question arises, not with the recipient of the certificate, but as here, with a second transferree—a third party—to whom the certificate has not been issued, who has no communication with the company, but to whom the certificate has been handed or exhibited, and who in reliance thereon and the relative transfer—and in good faith—has made an advance of money—is he, when he lodges his transfer and demands registration according to the certificate, to be held open to all the exceptions pleadable against his transferrer? . . .

" On principle, and if the question were open, I acknowledge that there seems much to be said against putting a certificate of shares in the position practically of a negotiable instrument. The statute only declares that it shall be *prima facie* evidence, and it may be doubted whether a proposed transferree ought to be in safety to rely on such *prima facie* evidence, and ought not to be required for his safety to take the precaution of consulting the company's register.

" It appears, however, to be settled by a long course of decisions in England, and as I see no reason to doubt, on sound views of commercial expediency, that a certificate of shares, once regularly issued, is a document binding the company to make good its representation to any *bona fide* transferee for value into whose hands it (the certificate) comes. The way it is expressed is that the company is ' estopped ' in a question with such transferree from disputing the truth of the certificate, and the translation of that seems to be that the company is held to warrant the truth of the statements which the certificate makes, and so to be liable *ex contractu,* in specific performance, if that is possible, or in pecuniary reparation if that is impossible. . . .

" . . . The question which remains, and on which the case really turns, is whether the fact that the certificate was irregularly or fraudulently issued by the officials of the company can affect the legal operativeness of the document, as an obligation of the company, duly signed and sealed and put in circulation by the negligence or fraud of the company's officials.

" I confess I am unable to see how the pursuers can be affected by these considerations. . . . A negotiable instrument or document of title—say to goods—duly executed by a company, would not, I apprehend, be the less binding on the company—I mean in the hands of a *bona fide* holder for value—because it had been issued by the company's officials in violation of their duty, or for a fraudulent purpose of their own. And although of course a certificate of shares is not properly a negotiable instrument, nor in a proper sense a document of title, it is yet, as we have seen, substantially in the same position, so far as regards what in this question is the essential matter—*viz.,* the company's inability to plead against a *bona fide* transferree for value that he has no better title than his transferrer."

NOTES

1. The provision quoted from section 31 of the Companies Act 1862 is now section 81 of the Companies Act 1948.

The duty of a company to issue share certificates is dealt with in section 80 of the Act of 1948.

2. A case which emphasises the *prima facie* nature of the evidence provided by a share certificate is *Woodhouse & Rawson Ltd.* v. *Hosack* (1894) 2 S.L.T. 279 (O.H.).

W. Ltd. had offered for allotment 13,000 preference shares of £5 each. H. had applied for 100 shares, and these had been duly allotted to him. H. had paid the sums due on the shares at the times when they had been declared payable, except for a last instalment of £1 10s. on each share.

W. Ltd. sued H. for £150, and H. averred that he had paid the full amount. He produced a share certificate which acknowledged that there had been paid up the full sum of £5.

It was argued for H. that W. Ltd. was barred, by the terms of the share certificate, from insisting in the claim, and that the share certificate had to receive effect until it was reduced.

Held (by Lord Stormonth Darling) that, as the share certificate was only *prima facie* evidence, reduction of the share certificate was unnecessary and that a proof had to be allowed, in which H. would be entitled to the benefit of every presumption which his possession of the share certificate might create.

3. In *Waterhouse* v. *Jamieson* (1870) 8 M.(H.L.) 88, the House of Lords held that statements in the memorandum and articles, which

also appeared in share certificates, as to the amount paid up on shares could not be contradicted by the liquidator.

Lord Westbury (at p. 98) " Has the liquidator, standing in the place of the company, a right to recover from a shareholder to whom the company has given a certificate declaring that the whole amount, save £5, has been paid upon his shares—can the liquidator impeach the memorandum, set aside the articles, reduce the certificate, and recover in the right of the company that which the company could not for one moment, as against a *bona fide* shareholder, be entitled to recover?

". . . Here the appellant is a *bona fide* holder of shares, upon which, no doubt, there was a false statement made by the company, of which he had no knowledge, and as to which he was under no obligation to inquire, and therefore he cannot be subjected to liability by having imputed to him a knowledge of the falsehood. Could the company recover against him? If there had never been a winding-up order the question would not have admitted of a moment's doubt; and the winding-up order does not place the liquidator in a better position against the shareholders than the company were in."

4. In *Liquidator of Scottish Heritages Co. Ltd.* (1898) 5 S.L.T. 336 (O.H.), Brewis, the liquidator, obtained the decision of the court on whether different classes of holders of bonus shares were liable to pay a call of 10s. per share.

The bonus shareholders were divided into five classes:

    (1) original allottees of bonus shares;
    (2) original allottees who were also transferees of other bonus shares and whose share certificates bore that the shares were paid up to the extent of 15s. per share;
    (3) original allottees of bonus shares, who were also transferees of other bonus shares and whose share certificates did not bear that any particular sum was paid up thereon;
    (4) transferees of bonus shares, whose share certificates did not bear that any particular sum was paid up thereon;
    (5) transferees of bonus shares, whose share certificates bore that the shares were paid up to the extent of 15s. per share.

Held that the shareholders in classes (1), (2) and (3) were liable in payment of the call, but not those in classes (4) and (5).

Lord Stormonth Darling (at p. 338): " In a question with a transferee for valuable consideration, a liquidator is barred, as representing the Company, from denying the truth of the representation which the Company has made with regard to the amount paid up on the shares. This would not help the transferee if he had notice that the shares were not actually paid up in cash, but the burden of proving such notice lies on the liquidator. . . . As regards original allottees, their presumed knowledge of the flaw in the constitution of the bonus shares made it necessary for them to inquire what they were buying. But no such duty can be imputed to members of the public. The only inquiry which they could be expected to make was as to the amount which had been paid up on the shares; and it is not alleged that the public statements made on the authority of the Company gave any information beyond the amounts. . . . It is no objection to a call of this kind that the money is partly required for the adjustment of the rights of contributories *inter se*."

5. In *The Penang Foundry Co. Ltd.* v. *Gardiner,* 1913 S.C. 1203 (O.H.), there were circumstances in which even an original allottee was held entitled to rely on statements in share certificates.

The partners in a foundry, with the object of forming a syndicate to acquire the business, obtained deposits from several persons including G.

The project of forming a syndicate was abandoned, and the partners floated a limited company instead. Depositors were offered shares in the new company in proportion to the amounts of their deposits. G. received share certificates which bore that the shares allotted to him were fully paid, though in fact they were not.

In the liquidation of the company, the liquidators sued G. for the price of his shares.

Held that, as G. had accepted the shares in *bona fide* reliance on the statements in the certificates that the shares were fully paid, the company was barred from maintaining that the shares were not fully paid; and defender *assoilzied*.

Lord Cullen (at p. 1206): " The principle of bar or estoppel is a general one of the common law and, in this connection, cannot be limited to transferees of shares unless the conditions of its application are only possible in the case of transferees. But this, in my opinion, is not sound. It is true that an allottee will not often be in the position of not knowing the footing on which shares which he accepts have been allotted to him. But he may be, and if, in such circumstances, he accepts shares in reliance on the Company's representation that they are fully paid up, and without notice to the contrary, he is, I think, as much entitled to hold the Company to that representation as a transferee acquiring right from him without notice would be. . . .

" In the present case, the defender did not make an application to the Company for an allotment of shares. . . . He acted in perfectly good faith. . . . He is entitled to plead the Company's . . . representation against their present demand. . . . The defender simply accepted the shares when offered to him by the Company, and he accepted them on the footing on which the Company tendered them to him, namely, that they were fully paid up, and fully believing in the truth of the Company's representation to that effect."

Transfer of shares: restrictions on transfer: exercise by directors of discretion to refuse registration of transfer

Stewart v. James Keiller & Sons Ltd.
(1902) 4 F. 657

The articles of association of K. Ltd. permitted the directors to decline to register any transfer of shares to any person provided they named another person willing to purchase the shares at a price fixed by a valuation procedure laid down in the articles.

The widow of a shareholder, claiming her legal rights in her deceased husband's estate, received from his executors a transfer which the directors refused to register.

The widow raised an action for decree ordaining the directors to register the transfer. She alleged that the directors' refusal was corrupt and fraudulent, and in any case that the valuation was far below the true value of the shares.

Held, after a proof, that the directors had not acted corruptly or capriciously, and that the valuation was not unreasonable.

LORD TRAYNER (at p. 678): " The directors must exercise the power . . . conferred on them fairly and reasonably; they must not act in the exercise of that power capriciously or corruptly. . . . The power given to the directors to ' decline to recognise or register any transfer ' is absolute—it is not a power to be exercised only on cause shewn, or a power the exercise of which must be justified by reasons sufficient in the judgment of the transferee or of the Court to which the transferee appeals. . . . The reasons . . . for the directors' action . . . all appear to me to have a bearing upon the interests of the company, and such as might reasonably affect the minds of the directors in coming to the conclusion that the pursuer should not be allowed to increase her holding in the company. Whether the reasons assigned by the directors for what they did are such as we should consider satisfactory or sufficient is not the question. I think that the directors did not act corruptly or through mere caprice; and that being so, the reasons which the directors considered sufficient for their action must, I think, be regarded by us as sufficient. The directors' opinions and reasons are not subject to our review. . . .

" . . . The . . . evidence shews that the directors have valued the shares fairly and honestly. . . . It is not for the Court to inquire whether the shares might be valued at something more than £20. It was left by contract to the directors to fix a value which should determine and regulate all questions as to the value which might arise, and having done that fairly and honestly according to their own judgment (supported as that is by experts of skill) I am of opinion that we cannot review or alter that determination."

NOTES

1. The general rule is that shares are transferable; restrictions are treated as exceptional.

O'Meara v. *The El Palmar Rubber Estates Ltd.*, 1913 1 S.L.T. 383 (O.H.) was an action by O. against the company to have transfers in which O. was the transferee registered by the company. The transferor was Barnes.

The company had raised an action against O. in New York, and it claimed a lien over the shares.

The Lord Ordinary (Dewar) granted decree *ordaining* the company to register the transfers.

Lord Dewar (at p. 384): " By section 22 of the Companies (Consolidation) Act 1908 it is provided that the shares in a company shall be transferable in manner provided by the Articles of the Company; and it is settled that unless the Articles otherwise provide, a shareholder has a right to transfer to whom he will. . . . Now the only restriction on the right of transference in the Articles in the present case is contained in Article 26, which provides that ' the directors may refuse to register any transfer of shares upon which the company has a lien. . . .' . . . The only question is whether the defenders have a lien over these shares.

"*Prima facie* a company has no lien on the shares of a member, and although the Articles may, and generally do, provide that the Company shall have a paramount lien on the shares of a member for his debts due to the Company, there is no such provision in these Articles. But the defenders maintained that there is in Scotland a lien at common law, and I was referred to the case of *Bell's Tr.* (1886, 14 R. 246), where it was decided that there is a right of retention on the part of a company where shares stand in the name of a shareholder in satisfaction of debts due by the shareholder to the company. But that does not appear to me to assist the defenders. The shareholder here is Mr. Barnes, and they do not aver that there is any debt due by him."

The case of *Bell's Tr.* referred to is *Bell's Trustee* v. *Coatbridge Tinplate Co. Ltd.* (p. 223, below).

2. Provisions entitling a company to refuse to register transfers are construed restrictively: *Furness & Co.* v. *Liquidators of " Cynthiana " Steamship Co. Ltd.* (1893) 21 R. 239.

The articles of C. Ltd. provided that the company might decline, in respect of any shares not fully paid up, to register any transfer made to a " bankrupt."

Held that C. Ltd. was not entitled to refuse to register a transfer made to a person who was insolvent but not bankrupt, even although the transfer was made for the purpose of freeing the transferor from liability.

3. The *onus* of proof that directors were actuated by corrupt motives in refusing to register a transfer lies on the person who makes that allegation: *Kennedy* v. *The North British Wireless Schools Ltd.*, 1915 1 S.L.T. 196 (O.H.), affd. 1916 1 S.L.T. 407.

One of the articles of association of N. Ltd. provided that the directors might, without assigning a reason, refuse to register any transfer where they were of opinion that the transfer would not be conducive to the interests of the company or where they considered that the proposed transferee was a person whom it was not desirable to admit to membership.

In connection with an action brought against Mayne, a shareholder in N. Ltd., Mayne's shares had been arrested and were later sold. The purchaser was K.

When K. applied to the directors of N. Ltd. to have his name registered as owner of the shares, the directors intimated to him that they refused to register his name.

K. brought an action against N. Ltd. to have the company ordained to register the transfer.

The Lord Ordinary (Anderson) *assoilzied* N. Ltd. The First Division *adhered*.

Lord Anderson (at p. 198): " As the article absolves the directors from assigning reasons for their decision they are practically masters of the situation, and it is incompetent to shew that the personality of the proposed transferee is unexceptionable, or that it would really be beneficial and not detrimental to the interests of the company to have his name on the register. . . .

(After quoting from Lord Trayner in *Stewart* v. *James Keiller & Sons Ltd.*) " A pursuer accordingly may make a relevant case against the directors of a company in a question of this nature by alleging that they were actuated by corrupt motives in passing the resolution complained of. That is the case which the pursuer makes in the present action. His averment against the directors is that in passing the resolution which is challenged they abused their powers solely for the purpose of enabling one of their own members to acquire the said shares at less than their true value. . . . It is proper to keep in view (1) that the *onus* of proof is on the pursuer, and the gravity of that *onus* is emphasised by the fact that the Lord Ordinary (Cullen), in the interlocutor allowing a proof, has ordained the pursuer to lead; (2) there is a presumption that the directors in the matter in question have acted *in bona fide* and reasonably . . .; (3) the pursuer is attacking the conduct of the whole body of directors.

". . . I have reached the conclusion that the pursuer has failed to prove the case he sets out to establish against the chairman, and that he has led no evidence whatever to implicate the other directors."

4. In *The Property Investment Co. of Scotland Ltd.* v. *Duncan* (1887) 14 R. 299, the court dealt with a petition for rectification of the register of P. Ltd., presented by D., a shareholder who had intimated to the company a transfer of his shares to his wife. The transfer had been intimated to the company in December 1883; it had not been considered at the first meeting of the directors, which took place in the following January; and at the next meeting, which took place in April, the directors, in the exercise of a power given to them by the articles of association, declined, without cause assigned, to register the transfer. D.'s petition was on the ground that there had been " unnecessary delay " within the meaning of the Companies Act 1862, s. 35 (corresponding to Companies Act 1948, s. 116).

Held (1) that there had been " unnecessary delay," but that this did not of itself entitle D. to have the transfer registered; and (2) that although D. might have been entitled to have the register rectified if he could have shown that he had been prejudiced by the delay, he had failed to prove such prejudice, since the shares had been unsaleable during the whole time.

The court therefore gave decree against D. for calls, and refused his petition.

Lord President (Inglis) (at p. 302): " Unnecessary delay does not in itself constitute a ground for rectification of the register. . . . The mere occurrence of unnecessary delay will certainly not be a good ground for an order by the Court upon the directors to register a transfer executed by a member, and the company must always be entitled to shew that although there has been unnecessary delay sufficient to justify an application to the Court, there are good reasons for not having the transfer registered. . . .

" But . . . I think that if the petitioner can shew that he was prejudiced by the unnecessary delay which occurred, that might be a very good reason for insisting upon a rectification of the register. If the petitioner was in a position to say that had the transfer been considered at the first meeting after it was sent in, and the refusal then intimated, he could have found a purchaser who would have been unobjectionable, he would thus have been able to put forward a strong case of hardship which might have afforded ground for a rectification of the register. But this is not the state of the facts. The shares were entirely unsaleable, and could not have been disposed of by the petitioner even if the refusal by the directors had been timeously made. The prejudice therefore to the petitioner is entirely imaginary and fanciful."

5. In *National Bank of Scotland Glasgow Nominees Ltd.* v. *Adamson* (p. 67, above), an arrester of shares was held not entitled to found on an alleged irregularity in the procedure for approving a transfer and for waiver of a right of pre-emption.

Lord Moncrieff (Ordinary) (at 1932 S.L.T. 495): " By sending the transfer properly executed to the company the pursuers conclusively applied to be admitted *inter socios* as members of the company. In view of the non-exercise by the directors of their right of pre-emption of the shares, and in further view of what I regard as their waiver of the power of veto of the transferee, the completion of the pursuers' membership of the company depended merely on the execution of purely formal acts. In such circumstances, in a question with a stranger to the company, it may be said that *res incepta pro finita habetur*. Such a stranger has no title to intervene so as to interrupt the execution of such acts."

6. See also *Shepherd's Trustees v. Shepherd* (p. 206, below).

Transfer of shares: restrictions on transfer: pre-emption clauses

Shepherd's Trustees v. Shepherd
1950 S.C.(H.L.) 60

One of the articles of association of a private company provided: " It shall be in the absolute discretion of the directors to refuse to register any transfer of shares of which they do not approve."

Of two directors in the company one was in favour of, and the other against, granting an application by the trustees and executors of a deceased member for the registration in the trustees' names of shares held by the member at the time of his death and conveyed to the trustees by his trust-disposition and settlement.

The objecting director claimed a right of pre-emption.

No registration was made, and the trustees presented a petition for rectification of the register.

Held that they were entitled to be registered because (1) as no resolution had been passed by the directors, there had been no refusal to register, and (2) an article which expressly gave the directors a right of pre-emption where there had been a transfer did not impliedly confer on them a right of pre-emption where there had been only a transmission on death.

LORD PORTER (at p. 65): " Powers of restriction upon the the right of the transfer or transmission of shares from one person to another are a serious restriction upon the rights of holders of shares in a company, even though that company be a private one. No doubt in such a case it may well be desirable for the directors to have control over the transfer of shares to outside persons, but that construction does not necessarily apply to the transmission of shares from a holder to his personal representatives, and, if it is desired to control such a transmission, it should be done in plain terms.

" . . . The mere failure to pass a resolution is not a formal active exercise of the right to decline. . . . In my view, a formal active exercise of the right of refusal to register is required before the company is authorised to refuse to register the shares in the names of those to whom they have been transmitted."

LORD NORMAND (at p. 66): " The right of pre-emption is a heavy burden on the rights of shareholders, and, though it is not doubtful that it may be created by implication as well as by the express terms of the articles, an inference from ambiguous data will not do; it must be a clear implication."

LORD REID (at p. 70): "Transfer, if the word is used in its ordinary sense, means a transfer from one person to another and implies that there must be both a transferor and a transferee. But where an executor is registered in respect of shares forming part of the deceased's estate there is no transfer from one person to another; the executor . . . is already entitled to the shares when he makes application for registration of his name. This distinction between transfer and transmission on death is well recognised in company law, and I can find nothing in any of the articles . . . to suggest that in these articles the word transfer is used in any but its ordinary sense. . . . Where there is in question a power which so severely limits a right of property as does a right of pre-emption I would not be prepared to base its existence on implication except perhaps in a very clear case. . . . There is nothing illogical or even unreasonable in drawing a distinction between a case where an executor seeks to have his name registered and a case where an executor seeks to transfer shares to someone else. . . .

" . . . Directors can only exercise their right to decline registration by passing a resolution to that effect."

NOTES

1. On the distinction between transfer and transmission, see *Buchan* v. *The City of Glasgow Bank* (p. 122, above).

2. *Neilson* v. *Ayr Race Meetings Syndicate Ltd.*, 1918 1 S.L.T. 63 (O.H.) also illustrates the restrictive construction given to pre-emption clauses.

The articles of association of A. Ltd. provided that a transferor was bound to offer his shares to the directors for purchase, and that the directors were bound to exercise their option to purchase within three weeks of the offer.

In this case the directors neither accepted nor refused an offer within the stipulated time.

Held that the directors had lost their right to insist on the shares being sold to themselves.

3. In *J. M. Smith Ltd.* v. *Colquhoun's Trustee* (1901) 3 F. 981, there were circumstances in which a shareholder was held to have validly withdrawn an offer of shares which he had made to the company in virtue of a pre-emption clause in the articles.

The pre-emption clause provided that any holder of B shares who wished to sell his shares had, before doing so, to offer them to the company in writing, specifying the price which he was willing to accept for them, whereupon the directors were either to take the shares on behalf of the company at that price or intimate the offer to the other B shareholders who were entitled to lodge sealed offers with the company specifying the price which they were willing to pay.

The shareholder withdrew his offer before the company had either intimated its acceptance to him or intimated to the other B shareholders that the offer had been made.

Lord Moncreiff (at p. 991): " There is no doubt that at common law a person who has made an offer to sell is entitled to withdraw the offer at any time before acceptance, unless he has bound himself to leave the offer open for a specified time. I cannot find anything in article 4 to introduce a condition altering the common law on this point."

4. The decision in *Lyle & Scott Ltd.* v. *Scott's Trustees*, 1959 S.C.(H.L.) 64 turned on the interpretation of the phrase " desirous of transferring " occurring in a pre-emption clause.

The private company, L. & S. Ltd., carried on a knitwear and hosiery business in Hawick. Its articles of association provided that no holder of more than 1 per cent. of the issued ordinary share capital could transfer his shares so long as any other ordinary shareholder was willing to purchase them at a price fixed by agreement between the transferor and the directors or, failing agreement, at a price fixed by the auditors; any such ordinary shareholder who was " desirous of transferring " his ordinary shares was required to inform the secretary of the number of shares which he desired to transfer, and the price was then to be fixed in the way described.

Hugh Fraser sent letters to all the shareholders, offering to purchase their shares. A number of ordinary shareholders holding more than 1 per cent. of the issued ordinary share capital accepted Hugh Fraser's offer of £3 for each ordinary share, and bound themselves to vote as he desired in order to put him as fully in control of the company as they could without registering transfers.

L. & S. Ltd. brought actions against these shareholders to have them ordained to implement the pre-emption clause.

Held that the actings of the shareholders were sufficient to show that they were " desirous of transferring " their shares within the meaning of the pre-emption clause, and that they were therefore bound to implement it.

5. See also *Stewart* v. *James Keiller & Sons Ltd.*, and Notes thereon (pp. 201–205, above).

Transfer of shares: completion of title by entry on register

Morrison v. Harrison, &c.
(1876) 3 R. 406

In 1885 Merrett executed a transfer of shares in the Forth and Clyde Junction Railway Company in favour of Harrison. In 1856 Merrett's estates were sequestrated. In 1857 the transfer was entered in the railway company's register of transfers in accordance with the Companies Clauses Consolidation (Scotland) Act 1845.

In 1875 Morrison, the then trustee in the sequestration claimed the shares on the ground that by virtue of his act and warrant the shares had vested in him at the date of the sequestration.

Held that, although the trustee at the date of the sequestration had been in a position to complete a title to the shares, he had not complied with the statutory forms and could not now displace Harrison whose name had duly been entered in the railway company's register.

LORD JUSTICE-CLERK (MONCREIFF) (at p. 409): " That which is essential under the statute is that the transferee shall be put on the register of shareholders. . . .

" . . . The trustee . . . says that he holds an intimated assignation, and that is the case. He might so acquire a right to become a partner of the company, but the question is whether he is a partner. . . . It is quite plain . . . that an assignation to shares, though intimated, will not make the assignee a partner of the company."

LORD ORMIDALE (at p. 410): " Mr. Harrison, having got his right and title to the disputed shares duly completed by registration before the trustee or any one else, must, having regard to the statutory provisions bearing on the matter, be held to be the owner of them—keeping in view that there was nothing unfair or fraudulent in anything he did."

LORD GIFFORD (at p. 411): " The true completion of a transfer of shares in a joint stock or railway company, constituted under the public general statutes regulating railway and joint stock companies, appears to me to be the reception of the transferee as a shareholder of the company, so as to give him the rights and subject him to the liabilities of a partner. There may be a contract to convey shares in the company and to accept thereof and to become a shareholder, but that remains a mere contract or obligation until it is completed by the party actually becoming a shareholder. . . . Bare intimation to the company, not followed by the transferee becoming and being received as a partner, is not the criterion of completion of the rights of the transferee."

NOTES

1. The principle in this case does not apply to the situation where there is a competition between a transferee and an arrester whose arrestment is lodged with the company after the transfer has been received by the company but before it has been registered by the

company: *Harvey's Yoker Distillery Ltd.* v. *Singleton and others* (1901) 8 S.L.T. 369 (O.H.).

The fund *in medio* in this case was 3,000 preference shares of H. Ltd. registered in S.'s name and a dividend of £80 16s. 10d. declared on the shares on April 28, 1899.

On January 16, 1899, S. had transferred 1,000 shares to Mrs. Fletcher, and the transfer had been duly received by the secretary of the company on February 2, 1899.

On January 17, 1899, S. had transferred 200 shares to Marsden, and that transfer had been received by the secretary on January 19, 1899. Neither transfer was registered because a bank had, on November 8, 1898, lodged an arrestment against S. in the hands of the company, and that arrestment was not withdrawn until September 11, 1899.

On March 30, 1899, arrestments on the dependence of an action were executed by Dempster against S. in the hands of the company. Dempster obtained decree in his action on June 20, 1899.

The Lord Ordinary (Stormonth Darling) referred to *Thomson* v. *Fullarton* (1842) 5 D. 379 and to *Morrison* v. *Harrison, &c.* Of the former case, which related to shares in a railway company, he said (at p. 370): "The circumstances . . . were very like those of the present case . . . That seems to me to be a decision directly in point, and to be in accordance with the general principle that an arrestment can only attach property belonging truly and in substance to the common debtor." He continued: "Now these shares did not belong in substance to Singleton at the time of the arrestment, because he had by that time done all in his power to dispose of them by executing the transfers." He then referred to *Morrison* v. *Harrison, &c.*: "It may be quite true, as laid down in the case of *Morrison* v. *Harrison* . . . that 'the true criterion of the completion of a title upon a transfer of shares in a public company is not bare intimation to the company, but the reception of the transferee as a partner of the company according to the forms prescribed by the statute.' But that doctrine relates to a different chapter of the law, and has no bearing on the present case." He added: "Neither do I find the English cases to which I was referred at all instructive as to the effect of the purely Scottish diligence of arrestment."

2. Similarly, in *Jackson* v. *Elphick* (1902) 10 S.L.T. 146 (O.H.), intimation of an assignation of shares was held to exclude a subsequent arrestment of the shares.

J. and E. had carried on business together as manufacturers of baths. They afterwards transferred their interests in that business to a limited company, J. & E. Ltd., in return for shares in the company. J. and E. were the only shareholders, and were appointed managing directors.

Later, when the company was in liquidation, J. sought payment from E. of £112 10s. which J. alleged to be the balance due to him under an agreement entered into between J. and E. E. resided in London, and J. used arrestments *ad fundandam jurisdictionem* in the hands of J. & E. Ltd. and its liquidator.

E. was at the date of the execution of these arrestments the registered holder of preference and ordinary shares in the company, but he stated that prior to the date of the arrestments he had assigned to Murphy his whole right and interest in the company.

For J. it was argued that there was here no transfer but merely an assignation, and the argument was supported by a reference to the opinion of Lord Gifford in *Morrison* v. *Harrison, &c.*

The Lord Ordinary (Low) accepted E.'s contention that intimation of the assignation was sufficient to exclude a subsequent arrester, though it did not make the assignee a member or divest the registered member of his liabilities as a contributory.

3. *Morrison* v. *Harrison, &c.* was also referred to by Lord Moncrieff (Ordinary) in *National Bank of Scotland Glasgow Nominees Ltd.* v. *Adamson*, 1932 S.L.T. 492 (O.H.), at p. 495 (for the facts of the case, see p. 67, above) as authority for the statement: " Between applicants for membership of a company he will be preferred who first completes his title to its shares." Lord Moncrieff then added: " Where the competition arises, however, between an applicant for membership of the company on the one hand and an arrester on the other, as soon as a transfer has been lodged for registration the transferee will be preferred to the arrester."

Transfer of shares: company refusing to register transferee: transferor quasi-trustee for transferee

Stevenson v. Wilson
1907 S.C. 445

W. sold shares in J. M. Smith Ltd. to S. The company's articles of association gave the directors power to refuse to register any transfer of shares to any person not approved of by them.

S. paid the price of the shares to W. and received a transfer from W., but the company refused to register S. as owner of the shares. W. declined to receive from the company the dividends accruing on the shares.

In an action brought by S. against W., the court granted declarator (1) that S. had the sole beneficial right, title, and interest in the shares and the dividends thereon, and (2) that the shares were held by W. in trust for S. so long as W.'s name should remain on the register and S. continued to hold the beneficial interest in the shares, and also granted decree ordaining W. from time to time to pay to S. the dividends accruing on the shares.

LORD PRESIDENT (DUNEDIN) (at p. 454): " The defender . . . says that he ought not to be subject to the trouble and annoyance of being made a sort of perpetual trustee for the benefit of the pursuer. I am bound to say that his action . . . creates a complete deadlock. He admits that the pursuer is entitled to the beneficial right in the shares. He admits also that if he got any dividends on the shares he would be bound to hand them over to the pursuer. But he says, 'I am entitled to button my pockets and refuse to let dividends into them,' and accordingly when he got a dividend from the Company in the shape in which they generally come—a cheque—he said, 'I don't want any dividends; the shares don't belong to me. Please keep them.' The Company were equally unaccommodating to the pursuer, for they said, 'We are not bound to pay to any but a shareholder. You are not a shareholder, and therefore we are not bound to pay to you.'. . .

" . . . In an ordinary case there can be no doubt, if A and B enter into a contract for the sale of shares that belong to A, A executes the transfer, and B, I have no doubt, is bound, as part of the bargain, not only to accept that transfer, but to get the transfer registered so as to take A off the register. In the case of an unlimited company the interest is too plain, but even in a limited company I have no doubt that A is perfectly entitled as part of the bargain to get his name off the register. But when there is a stipulation in the articles of the company which allows the directors of the company to refuse at their own hand any particular transferee, then A and B, who are contracting, do so with their eyes open, and knowing that it may be the case that B will not be accepted as a transferee. It still becomes the duty of B, if he cannot get the defenders to register him, to find a transferee whom the defenders will register in order to free A, and I think, if he is entirely unable to do that, A can bring the bargain to an end. But I think he could only do so in the ordinary way by annulling the bargain—that is, giving back the money he got from B and bringing matters to their entirety. . . . Now, that is just what Mr. Wilson will not do; so far from annulling the bargain he raised an action in the Court of Session and got decree against Mr. Stevenson for the money, and he does not propose to give that money back. . . . The attitude of Mr. Wilson in this action is that he proposes to stick to the money, and at the same time not to have the trouble of acting as *quasi*-trustee in giving over the dividends. Now, I think that is an impossible position, and therefore so long as Mr. Wilson chooses, as he does still choose, not to try to avoid the bargain but to keep the money in his pocket, so long, I think, he must be content to fulfil this obligation of *quasi*-trustee."

NOTE

This case was held to be conclusive authority for the decision of *Tennant's Trustees* v. *Tennant*, 1946 S.C. 420.

T., of Innes, Elgin, died in 1941, leaving a will in which he bequeathed to trustees for certain trust purposes all his shares in Innes Estates Company. At the time when the will was made—1935— T. had held almost all the shares in an unlimited company whose actual name was " Innes Estates."

In 1939, a limited company, called "Innes Estates Holding Co. Ltd.," had been incorporated, and T. had sold his shares in Innes Estates to this new company. The transfer had been executed by T. and delivered to the company, but it was never stamped or registered.

The question was whether the bequest in the will had been adeemed.

Held that, as the sale of the shares had not been completed, the bequest had not been adeemed.

Lord Moncrieff (at p. 425): " By agreement for sale . . . the testator sold his 77,100 shares in Innes Estates to this holding company for £30,000. He received payment of this sum from the holding company. . . .

". . . It could scarcely be disputed that, if the sale had been completed, the testator would on its completion have been divested of his ownership of the 77,100 shares as effectively as if the holding company had been in a proper and practical sense an independent third party— *Salomon* v. *Salomon & Co.* ([1897] A.C. 22). The sale, however, was not completed. The testator, indeed, executed a transfer of the 77,100 shares and delivered this to the holding company, but this transfer was never stamped or registered. . . .

". . . A transfer of shares, as is stated in *Palmer's Company Law* (17th ed.), p. 115, remains incomplete until registered. Pending registration, as is stated by the learned author, the transferee has only an equitable right to the shares transferred to him; he does not become the legal owner until his name is entered on the register in respect of the shares transferred to him.

". . . . The case of *Stevenson* v. *Wilson* appears to me . . . to be conclusive of this question. . . . The case is an authority for the proposition that until registration of the transfer of shares the transferor's right of legal property remains undivested, although his property title may have become charged with trusts and contractual obligations in favour of persons upon whom the proprietor of the shares may have conferred such equitable rights. Such equities may clog the title of the proprietor, but do not divest it. . . . Though the legacy be not adeemed, a completed agreement for sale will stand, and the legatee may thus be entitled only to receive the price. . . .

". . . The mere agreement of sale did not operate ademption of the bequest. . . .

". . . Had I been of opinion that the sale to the holding company had been completed so as to pass the property in the shares, it might therefore have been necessary to consider whether or not the testator's control of the holding company was substantially and sufficiently an equivalent, though in a different shape, of his former personal property in the shares. In the view I have taken of these transactions this question, which might have required an extensive examination of the authorities, does not however arise."

Transfer of shares: company not concerned with objections to transferee's right

Shaw v. Caledonian Railway Co.
(1890) 17 R. 466

Rayner had deposited with S., a sharebroker, a certificate for certain railway stock and a signed transfer for the stock as security for a series of transactions. Rayner failed to pay the debit balance arising as a result of these transactions, and S. sold the railway stock.

Rayner objected to the registration of the transfer on the ground that it had been granted in security of a gambling debt.

Held that the transactions had been real and *bona fide* transactions and were not of a mere gambling nature. The court accordingly repelled Rayner's objection.

Question whether, even if the transactions had been of a gambling nature, this would have prevented registration of the transfer.

Opinion (*per* Lord McLaren) that the proper course was for the company to proceed to register the transfer unless the objector brought an interdict.

LORD McLAREN (at p. 482): "I rather think that where a company like the Caledonian Railway Company is called upon to register a transfer of stock, which is purely a ministerial proceeding, and they receive intimation from some other person that he has an interest in it, their true position is to say, 'Unless you follow up your intimation by an application for interdict or other legal measure, we will register the transfer.'"

NOTES

1. Directors may be justified in delaying registration of a transfer: *The Property Investment Co. of Scotland Ltd.* v. *Duncan* (1887) 14 R. 299 (Note 4 to *Stewart* v. *James Keiller & Sons Ltd.,* p. 204, above).

2. In *Elliot* v. *J. W. Mackie & Sons Ltd.,* 1935 S.C. 81 (Note 16 to *Muir, &c.* v. *The City of Glasgow Bank,* p. 145, above), the court held that the company was not concerned with the allegation that a transfer had been in breach of trust.

Assignation of shares in security: delivery of share certificate insufficient

Gourlay v. Mackie
(1887) 14 R. 403

On December 23, 1885, John Millen & Company, coalmasters, Glasgow, obtained a loan of £450 from Richard Mackie & Company, steamship owners, Leith. In exchange, John Millen & Company granted to Richard Mackie & Company a promissory note, and a letter stating that they were handing over as security 100 shares of £6 paid in the Holmes Oil Company and were binding themselves to transfer the shares at any time desired by the lenders. The share certificate was at that date delivered to the lenders.

On January 14, 1886, a circular was issued intimating that the affairs of John Millen & Company had become embarrassed. On the following day, the lenders obtained a transfer of the shares from John Millen & Company, and this transfer was immediately intimated to the company.

The estates of John Millen & Company were sequestrated on January 28, 1886, and G., the trustee in the sequestration, raised an action against the lenders concluding for reduction of the transfer.

Held that the transfer, having been granted to secure a prior debt within 60 days of bankruptcy, was reducible under the Bankruptcy Act 1696.

LORD JUSTICE-CLERK (MONCREIFF) (at p. 408): " I do not doubt that where the money is advanced on the faith of a specific security, stipulated for as part of a present transaction, it will not vitiate the security that it is formally completed within 60 days of the granter's bankruptcy. The security is in that case truly granted in fulfilment of a prior obligation. But this case, in my opinion, belongs to an opposite category. The money here was not advanced on the faith of a present or instant security. It was advanced without security and in the knowledge that there was none, but under a promise from the debtor that if and when the creditor desired it the shares in question should be transferred to him. The meaning of this is quite plain. It was a transaction separate from the advance, and was not absolute but conditional. So far as the parties were concerned, neither desired that any present or instant security should be then given."

NOTES

1. *Cf.* Lord Gifford in *Morrison* v. *Harrison, &c.* (p. 209, above.)

2. Contrast *Guild* v. *Young* (1884) 22 S.L.R. 520 (O.H.). In this case the debtor had executed and delivered transfers of the shares. with the result that the creditor was in a position to register the shares in his own name without further intervention of the debtor. The fact that the transfers were not registered until the debtor was on the eve of sequestration did not make them reducible under the Bankruptcy Act 1696. The date of the grant of security was taken to be the date of the delivery of the transfers to the creditor, not the date of their registration with the company.

Lord Kinnear (at p. 522): " There is nothing necessarily illegal in a transaction by which the lender may hold shares belonging to the borrower in security without becoming ostensibly the owner of such shares. . . . It is not a perfect security; and if it were completed, or required to be completed, by an act of the bankrupt, it might be struck at by the statute. But in the present case the bankrupt did nothing, and could do nothing, to give a further security to the defender beyond what he had obtained when the transaction was settled. . . . It is true that the transferee's right was not completed, for all purposes and against all the world, until he had obtained registration of the transfers. But as against the bankrupt and anyone in his right it was completed and made effectual by delivery of the transfers and certificates. . . . It is the debtor, and not the creditor, whose hands are tied by the statute; and it is impossible to hold that the act of the creditor in presenting his transfer for registration is the voluntary deed of the debtor within the meaning of the statute."

This was not a case where the transfers were blank in name of the transferees. Such transfers may be invalid under the Blank Bonds and Trusts Act 1696.

Arrestment of shares

Sinclair v. Staples, &c.
(1860) 22 D. 600

Staples having failed to pay a sum of money due by him to Sinclair, Sinclair raised an action of adjudication of Staples' shares in the Garpel Hematite Co. Ltd.

Staples pleaded that the shares were by the Joint Stock Companies Act 1856 and by the company's articles of association declared to be moveable estate and were therefore subject to the diligence of arrestment and not to the diligence of adjudication.

Held that it was incompetent to attach the shares by adjudication.

LORD JUSTICE-CLERK (INGLIS) (at p. 604): " The ground taken by the pursuer is, first, that there is no other diligence applicable to attach such property; and second, that according to a general principle of the law of Scotland, all rights may be attached by adjudication, to which no other diligence is applicable. The first point, therefore, that the pursuer has to make out is, that no other diligence is competent in the present case. Now, the property here being shares in a joint-stock company, is personal estate. The 15th section of the statute 19 & 20 Vict., c. 47, expressly provides that the shares of joint-stock companies ' shall be personal estate, and shall not be of the nature of real estate.' It is quite clear, therefore, that the property here is personal estate. There can be no doubt, as a general rule, that the proper diligence to attach moveable estate is arrestment and furthcoming. . . . It appears to me that the pursuer fails in that first proposition on which he relies—*viz.*, that arrestment is not a diligence applicable to this species of moveables. If he had made out that proposition, he would have required to satisfy us that the form of adjudication which he has resorted to is competent."

LORD COWAN (at p. 605): " I cannot think it questionable in this case that arrestment is competent.

" The property sought to be attached consists of the shares of the stock of a joint-stock company, and in the hands of the company itself; and, therefore, the subject-matter of the debtor's interest in them is attachable in the hands of the company. . . .

" . . . I am clearly of opinion that arrestment is the proper diligence here, and that the diligence of adjudication is incompetent."

NOTES

1. Section 73 of the Companies Act 1948 provides that shares " shall be personal estate . . . and shall not be of the nature of real estate." By section 455 (1) of that Act "' real ' and ' personal,' as respects Scotland, mean respectively heritable and moveable."

2. This case was followed in *The American Mortgage Company of Scotland Ltd.* v. *Sidway*, 1908 S.C. 500, in which S.'s shares in the Missouri Land and Live Stock Co. Ltd., which had its registered office in Edinburgh, were arrested by A. Ltd. for the purpose of founding jurisdiction in an action for payment raised by A. Ltd. against S., who resided in Chicago.

This arrestment *ad fundandam jurisdictionem* made S. liable to the jurisdiction of the Court of Session.

Lord President (Dunedin) (at p. 503): "It is a somewhat startling proposition to find at this time of day, over forty years after 1862, that the practice, which has certainly been going on all this time, of arresting shares of limited companies, is radically wrong. Although there may not have been many cases of arrestment of shares *jurisdictionis fundandae causa,* there certainly have been countless cases of arrestment in execution; and it is quite evident that the two matters depend upon the same principles. . . . I think that, as a mere matter of authority, the question is decided by the case of *Sinclair* v. *Staples.* . . . The case there was put, so to speak, the other way. . . . The action of adjudication was dismissed upon the ground that arrestment was competent. . . . It is a direct authority. . . .

". . . The doctrine that the partnership assets do not belong to the partners but belong to the partnership has always been held quite consistent with our well-established Scottish doctrine that a share in a common law partnership is perfectly well arrestable. It seems to me that the point put by Mr. Bell (2 Com. p. 71) is the true criterion. It is the obligation to account which is the subject of attachment, and the obligation to account does not mean that there is then and there a debt due in the sense of something due and payable. . . .

". . . There is a separate *persona* in a Scottish partnership which corresponds exactly with the separate *persona* of an incorporated company. I am of opinion that it would be a great pity to alter the law, and I do not think there is any reason for doing so. The case of *Sinclair* v. *Staples,* which has ruled the practice for nearly half a century, ought, I think, to be followed here."

Lord McLaren (at p. 505): "In this case the subject is said to be arrestable in the hands of the Company because of the principle of accountability to a shareholder by the Company. In Scotland we are not embarrassed by a distinction between a private partnership and a public company, because the law of Scotland recognises a separate *persona* in a private partnership. . . . There is nothing but a formal difference between the right of a partner in a private partnership and the right of a shareholder in a company incorporated under the Companies Acts."

3. *Valentine* v. *Grangemouth Coal Co. Ltd.* (1897) 35 S.L.R. 12 (O.H.) is an instance of a competent action of furthcoming following on an arrestment in the hands of G. Ltd. of shares belonging to Aitken. The conclusions of the action were that G. Ltd. should be decerned to pay to the pursuer £100, or such sum as might be owing by G. Ltd. to Aitken, or otherwise should transfer to the pursuer the shares of G. Ltd. belonging to Aitken, to the end that the pursuer might sell as much of the shares as would satisfy his claim.

Lord Kincairney granted warrant to sell the shares accordingly.

4. See also *Harvey's Yoker Distillery Ltd.* v. *Singleton and others, Jackson* v. *Elphick,* and *National Bank of Scotland Glasgow Nominees Ltd.* v. *Adamson* in Notes 1, 2, and 3 respectively to *Morrison* v. *Harrison, &c.* (pp. 209–211, above).

Calls on shares: general nature of calls

Wryghte v. Lindsay
(1860) 22 D. (H.L.) 5; (1856) 19 D. 55

Sir Francis Walker Drummond at his death in 1844 held 140 shares of £50 each in the Royal Bank of Australia, an English joint-stock company.

The Bank later became financially embarrassed, and W. was appointed official manager for the purpose of winding up its affairs under the Joint-Stock Companies' Winding up Acts 1848 and 1849.

W. made a call of £14,000 on the executry estate, and on this call not being paid applied for sequestration of the estate. This application was resisted by L., who had been appointed judicial factor on the estate.

Held that, as the call was not a debt which had been due by the deceased, sequestration was incompetent.

LORD PRESIDENT (McNEILL) (at p. 62): " Mr. Wryghte is the official manager appointed under the Winding-up Acts, and the £14,000, as I trace it, is the amount of a call made by him in virtue of the powers conferred on him by these Acts, to make calls on those persons whom the statute describes as contributories. . . .

" A call so made is a statutory demand of a very peculiar kind. The liability for it is a statutory liability. The right to make it, and the liability to satisfy it, both spring from statute. They had no legal existence before the date of the statute, so far as has been explained to us. The Company was an English Company, but we have not been told, as matter of fact, that, according to the law of England, such a demand could have been made and enforced before the date of the statute. We know that, by the law of Scotland, it certainly could not. The statute does not extend to Scotland, except in certain portions of it. . . .

" . . . It appears that the sum of £14,000, upon which Mr. Wryghte rests his title, is the amount of a call made by him under the authority of the statute. . . . The call of £14,000 is clearly not a debt due by the deceased Sir Francis Walker Drummond. . . . But the case must be brought up to that point. Sir Francis must have been a deceased debtor in that £14,000. I cannot see any way of construing the facts, so as to bring matters into that position, nor can I see how this £14,000 had any shape or subsistence while Sir Francis was alive. It was the creature of statute, brought into existence after his death."

NOTE

In *Waterhouse* v. *Jamieson* (1870) 8 M. (H.L.) 88, the House of Lords, reversing the judgment of the majority of the whole Court of Session, held that where the official liquidator of the Garpel Haematite Co. Ltd. alleged that statements in the memorandum and articles of association as to the amount of capital which had been paid up were false the court would not make a call upon a person who had not himself been an original shareholder for an amount exceeding the amount per share appearing *ex facie* of the memorandum and articles to be unpaid.

Calls on shares: action to enforce payment of calls

Scottish Amalgamated Silks Ltd. v. Macalister
1930 S.L.T. 593 (O.H.)

S. Ltd. brought an action against M. for payment of calls. M. alleged that her application for shares had been made on the faith of statements in a prospectus which were false, fraudulent and misleading in material respects.

The Lord Ordinary (Fleming) *continued* the cause to give M. an opportunity of presenting an application to the Inner House for the rectification of the register.

LORD FLEMING (at p. 595): " I was not referred to any case in Scotland where, in an action at the instance of a company against a person on the register for calls due in respect of shares allotted to him, the defender put forward a defence similar to that put forward in this case. . . . The pursuers founded strongly upon the case of the *First National Reinsurance Co. Ltd.* v. *Greenfield* ([1921] 2 K.B. 260). . . . I may summarise the ground of judgment in that case as follows: the obligation to pay calls is a statutory obligation which is imposed upon persons who have agreed to take shares in a company, have had shares allotted to them, and whose names are on the register of shareholders. The only proper defence which such a person has to an action for calls is in substance that he is not a shareholder. . . . I think . . . that some caution must be observed in applying this case to Scottish procedure. Applications for rectification of the register under the statutory provisions must be presented to the Inner House. . . . I agree, however, with the views expressed in the *First National Reinsurance Co.* v. *Greenfield* . . . that in answer to an action for payment of calls against a registered shareholder a defence of repudiation on the ground of fraud is not sufficient, and that the defender must also aver that he has taken steps, or at least comes under an obligation to take steps, to get rid of the entry of his name in the register. The defender says that she has done what is tantamount to that, for she pleads that the agreement to take the shares and the allotment following thereon should be set aside *ope exceptionis*. . . . But even if it be competent in this Court to set aside the entry in the register of members by exception, the Court has under the Act of Sederunt a discretion in the matter, and I think in the present case I ought not to allow the matter to be raised by way of exception unless the defender is prepared to present a petition for rectification of the register."

NOTE

No such question arises where the action for payment is against a former member whose shares have been forfeited for non-payment of calls: *Liquidators of the Mount Morgan (West) Gold Mine Ltd.* v. *McMahon* (1891) 18 R. 772.

M.'s shares in M. Ltd. had been forfeited for non-payment of calls. M. Ltd. went into liquidation, and an action for payment of the calls was brought by the liquidators against M. as a debtor to the company.

Held that M. was entitled to state in defence that he had been induced to take the shares by fraudulent misrepresentations in the prospectus.

Lord Kinnear (at p. 780): " That, then, was the position of the defender, according to the form of the documents, after the forfeiture of his shares. He had ceased to be a member of the company, but he had not ceased to be liable for the calls which he had already declined to pay. . . .

". . . If the defender was not a member but a mere debtor of the company, then I am unable to see how the fact of the liquidation can in any way affect the respective rights and liabilities of the parties. . . . A liquidator . . . has no higher right against the company's debtors than the company itself possessed, and if the persons whom he may sue as debtors have a good answer to the claim by the company, it appears to me of no consequence to them whether the proceedings are instituted against them by the directors, while the company subsists for its original purpose, or by the liquidator, when it subsists only for the purpose of winding up. They cannot be deprived of their right to state a valid defence against an alleged claim of debt by the voluntary resolution of the company to wind up its affairs."

SHARES

Calls on shares: distinction between calls made during winding up and other calls

Mitchell, Petitioner
(1863) 1 M. 1116

The directors of the Lochwinnoch Consols Copper Mining Co. Ltd. had during the company's active existence made three calls, which were duly paid by a large number of shareholders. The company went into voluntary liquidation.

Held that the statutory provisions relating to enforcement of calls made during a winding up did not apply to such of the calls made during the company's active existence as had not been paid.

LORD BENHOLME (at p. 1120): " This is a case which required a very careful analysis of the Acts of Parliament—the difficulty arising from the ambiguous use of the word ' call.' Calls may be made during the flourishing subsistence of the company, by the directors, in the course of their ordinary management; and calls may also be made when the company is insolvent, in the course of winding up, in order to pay off its debts. But although these two operations go under the same name, it is manifest that they are very different in their nature, and it is demonstrable from the clauses of the Act of Parliament, that they are very different also in the mode of their recovery. . . .

" . . . Liquidators are appointed, who are officers in some respects analogous to the Roman dictators, appointed on emergencies, who are invested with immediate powers, which are not to be lightly interfered with, in respect of the extreme urgency of the case. In particular, they are invested with the power of calling up discretionary contributions from the shareholders, in order to pay off the debts of the insolvent company. These dictatorial powers are enforced in particular forms; and, among others, the clause founded on enables the liquidators, by giving in a list of the contributories, and of the sums they ought to pay, to obtain an immediate enforcement of the calls made by them, for paying off the debts of the insolvent company. . . . We must look with very great jealousy to any extension of so summary a power; and an analysis of the sections founded on makes it perfectly clear that this summary procedure was only intended to apply to calls made during the course of winding up, and not to those previously made by directors in the ordinary course of their management."

LORD NEAVES (at p. 1121): " A sum claimed as an arrear under a call made by the directors of the company while it carried on business, and a sum demanded by the liquidators under a call made in the course of winding up the company, are quite different things. The one is of the nature of an outstanding debt to the company, the other is a contribution to the assets of the company for the purpose of paying its debts."

NOTES

1. The sections of the Companies Act 1862—sections 121 and 138—analysed in this case correspond to sections 275 and 307 respectively of the Companies Act 1948.

2. The same point of distinction arose in relation to a compulsory winding up in *Liquidators of the Benhar Coal Co. Ltd., Petitioners* (1882) 9 R. 763. The liquidators were held entitled to obtain decree for payment of calls made after the commencement of the liquidation without notice to the persons from whom payment was sought, but in respect of calls made by directors prior to the commencement of the liquidation, notice by registered letter to each person from whom payment was sought was *ordered.*

Calls on shares: payment in advance of calls

Myles, Petitioner
(1893) 1 S.L.T. 90 (O.H.)

The liquidator of the General Property Investment Co. Ltd. presented a petition for audit of his accounts and dissolution of the company. A remit was made to an accountant to audit and report.

Interest had been paid out of capital sums paid up on shares in advance of calls, but this had not prejudiced the general creditors because, if the calls had not been paid up in advance, overdraft interest would have had to be paid to a bank.

The question was whether the liquidator was required to call for repayment of the interest.

Held (by Lord Stormonth Darling) that the interest paid did not fall to be recovered from the contributories by the liquidator.

Lien on shares

Bell's Trustee v. Coatbridge Tinplate Co. Ltd.
(1886) 14 R. 246

The estates of B. were sequestrated at a time when B. held 248 shares in C. Ltd. The trustee in the sequestration sought to have his name entered on the register of members as holder of these shares, but C. Ltd. claimed a lien in respect of a debt of £7,038 2s. 9d. due to it by B.

Held that C. Ltd. had a lien, both at common law and under its articles, and was therefore entitled to refuse the trustee's application for registration.

LORD PRESIDENT (INGLIS) (at p. 248): " Three things are provided for in the 11th article. First, it is provided that the company are to have a preferential permanent lien for debts due. In the second place, in the case of a transfer, the company is to be entitled to refuse to register a transfer by any member who may then happen to be in debt to the company until the debt is paid. In the third place, there is provision for working out the lien by notice and sale. . . .

" . . . The only point is whether the lien is good or not.

" I must say that I have not seen any reason for refusing effect to the lien. The right is one which is quite in conformity with the law prior to the passing of the Joint Stock Companies Acts. We are familiar with this in connection with the law dealing with the management of banks. There is one well-known case—*Hotchkis* (*Keir's Trustee*) v. *The Royal Bank,* 1797, M. 2673, which was affirmed on appeal, 3 Paton 618. In that case Bertram, Gardner, & Company became bankrupt, deeply indebted to the Royal Bank of Scotland. The by-law of 1728 really created such a lien as we are dealing with here, and it was maintained by the trustee for the creditors of Bertram, Gardner, & Company that the by-law was *ultra vires* of the bank, and it is very important to observe how that contention was met. The answer was that the right of retention was good at common law independently of the by-law, and this was the ground upon which the Court decided the case. It was observed that the by-law was merely corroborative of the common law.

" No less than three cases were decided at the same time, and all upon the same ground. It was thus established that by the common law of Scotland there is a right of retention on the part of a company, where shares stand in the name of a shareholder, in satisfaction of debts due by the shareholder to the company.

" The same thing occurred in connection with another bank— *Burns (Manager of Central Bank)* v. *Lawrie's Trustees,* July 7, 1840, 2 D. 1348—where the doctrine laid down in the case of *Hotchkis* was dealt with as a fixed rule of law. . . . The application of these authorities is very apparent, and even without them the creation of this lien would be a perfectly lawful stipulation in the constitution of the company. It is therefore clear that the company have this lien, and that they are entitled to retain the shares, because an incorporated society such as the present is on the same footing as a private trading company.

" It is inconsistent with this right of lien that the shares should be transferred to the name of the trustee, and therefore the trustee's demand is quite untenable. . . . I am of opinion that the company's lien is good, and that they are entitled to retain the shares that they may realise them in satisfaction of the debt which is due to them."

NOTES

1. In *Hotchkis* v. *Royal Bank* (1797) 3 Paton 618; (1797) Mor. 2673, no opinions are reported from either the House of Lords or the Court of Session.

Keir had been a stockholder in the Royal Bank of Scotland to the extent of £2,000, and the bank objected to the stock being sold. The by-law provided that no proprietor who was indebted to the bank should be allowed to transfer his stock until he found security.

The action was an action of declarator brought by the trustee to have it found and declared that the bank had no right of retention on the stock but that it belonged to him as trustee for behoof of Keir's creditors.

2. In *Burns* v. *Lawrie's Trustees* (1840) 2 D. 1348, the Central Bank of Scotland was held entitled to retain shares in satisfaction of debts due to it by a shareholder.

The Lord Ordinary (Moncreiff), in a passage from which Lord President Inglis quoted in *Bell's Trustee* v. *Coatbridge Tinplate Co. Ltd.*, said (at p. 1351): " There are three practical questions in this case: 1. Whether the Central Bank have a right to retain the shares of stock standing in the name of Peter Rae, in satisfaction of debts due to them by Rae? . . . 1. The Lord Ordinary thinks, that there is no doubt or difficulty in the *first* question. . . . By the constitution of that Company . . . it was an intrinsic quality or condition of the right of every holder of such stock, that the bank should be entitled to retain it for payment of whatever debts he might in any way contract to the bank."

3. Where articles confer a lien on shares for debts due by " the holder " of the shares, " the holder " is the registered holder: *Paul's Trustee* v. *Thomas Justice & Sons Ltd.*, 1912 S.C. 1303.

P., a Dundee solicitor, had owned certain shares in J. Ltd. At the date of P.'s death, certain of these shares stood registered in P.'s name; others, however, stood registered in the names of nominees of the Bank of Scotland and the British Linen Bank in security of sums due by P. to the banks.

After P.'s death, his estates were sequestrated. The banks, having recovered payment of the debts due to them from other securities, were prepared to transfer the shares to the trustee in the sequestration.

J. Ltd., however, which had a claim in the sequestration amounting to £3,854 8s. 3d., sought to exercise a lien on all the shares which had been owned by P. J. Ltd. relied on a provision in its articles of association which gave it a right of lien on its shares for all debts due to it from a " holder " of the shares.

Held that J. Ltd. had no lien over the shares which stood in the names of the banks' nominees.

Lord Guthrie (at p. 1304): " The only question . . . is whether the word ' holder ' in article 27 . . . includes owners of the shares—those having the radical right, whether registered or not—at the date when the question arises, or at any time. . . .

" The word ' holder ' does not seem to me applicable in any sense, either popular or technical, to the late Mr. Paul, in regard to shares, which were either never registered in his name, or which, having been at one time registered in his name, had been subsequently registered in the names of others. In the one case, he never held the shares; in the other case he had ceased to hold them."

Lord Dundas (at p. 1307): " It seems to me to be quite plain that ' holder ' in article 27 does mean ' registered holder,' and that the word cannot, in any reasonable sense or upon any stateable ground, be held to apply to or include a person who may have the radical right to shares, but whose name does not appear upon the Company's register as holding them."

4. Other cases on lien already noted above are *Liquidator of W. & A. McArthur Ltd.* v. *The Gulf Line Ltd.*, and *O'Meara* v. *The El Palmar Rubber Estates Ltd.* (pp. 71 and 202, above).

Forfeiture of shares

Ferguson v. Central Halls Co. Ltd.
(1881) 8 R. 997

The articles of association of C. Ltd. provided that 21 days' notice had to be given of the time and place for payment of every call, and also that any shareholder whose shares had been forfeited was to remain liable to pay to the company all calls due at the time of the forfeiture.

A call was made on June 14, payable in two equal instalments on July 21 and August 23.

On June 28 (before notice of the calls of June 14 was required to be given to shareholders), shares held by Yuill were forfeited for non-payment of earlier calls. Yuill received no notice of the call of June 14 untill August 13.

Held that Yuill was liable to pay the call of June 14, being no longer entitled to insist on 21 days' notice because he was no longer a shareholder.

LORD PRESIDENT (INGLIS) (at p. 1001): "It appears to me that the twenty-one days' notice is a privilege of the shareholders, and a very important privilege. For if they had not twenty-one days' notice of the time and place of the call they might incur the risk of forfeiture. . . .

"But the question here is, whether one who has ceased to be a shareholder is entitled to that privilege which belongs to existing shareholders? And I think . . . that at the date of the forfeiture there was a debt due, not only for calls then payable, but also for calls of which the terms of payment had not arrived. They were debts due by the bankrupt, but due by him not as a shareholder, but as having been a shareholder. . . . Every man is entitled to some notice as to when and where he is to pay his debts. And notice of this kind the bankrupt has had. On August 13 a circular was sent to him intimating that a call had been made, payable in equal instalments on July 21 and August 23, and requiring payment. That is not notice in terms of the articles of association, but it is a perfectly sufficient intimation to any ordinary debtor, and having ceased to be a shareholder the bankrupt is just in the position of an ordinary debtor. Therefore I am of opinion that this is a debt due by the bankrupt, or, rather, a debt in his sequestration, which may be enforced in the ordinary way."

NOTES

1. Ferguson was the trustee on Yuill's sequestrated estate.

2. On liability after forfeiture, see also *Liquidator of the Mount Morgan (West) Gold Mine Ltd.* v. *McMahon* (Note to *Scottish Amalgamated Silks Ltd.* v. *Macalister*, p. 221, above).

Surrender of shares

General Property Investment Co. Ltd. and Liquidator v. Craig
(1890) 18 R. 389

C. held 250 shares of £10 each in G. Ltd. The amount paid up was £2 per share. A further call of £2 per share was intimated in December 1878, at which time C. was insolvent.

In April 1879, in order to be relieved of liability for the shares, C. executed a transfer of the shares to the company.

In 1886 G. Ltd. became insolvent, and went into liquidation.

In 1889 G. Ltd. and its liquidator brought an action against C. for reduction of the transfer and for payment of £1,533, being the amount of calls on the 250 shares less the amount paid on 108 of the shares, which had been reissued by the company.

Held that the surrender of the shares had been valid.

LORD MCLAREN (at p. 395): " The question in this case is, whether the transfer of Mr. Craig's shares to the company is void, as falling under the general rule that a company constituted under the Companies Acts is not entitled to purchase its own shares. There can be no doubt as to the justice of the rule or as to its obligatory character. It is a condition of the constitution of every limited company that there shall be individual liability to the extent defined by its memorandum and articles of association, and it is evident that the purchase of its own shares by such a company is equivalent to a reduction of its uncalled capital, or, in other words, is an extinction of individual liability to the extent of the value of the shares purchased by the company. This is the ground of the judgments of the House of Lords in *Trevor* v. *Whitworth*, and of this Court in the case of *The Property Investment Company* v. *Matheson.*

" An exception to this rule of company law is indicated in the opinion of the Lords of Appeal who advised the case of *Trevor* v. *Whitworth*. . . . The exception is that, where the company is in a position to forfeit the shares, a surrender of the shares to the company may be valid. By a surrender I understand a transfer of the shares to the company without consideration. . . .

" . . . The acceptance of a surrender from a solvent shareholder on a tacit understanding that he was to be released from his obligation to pay the calls already made would, in my apprehension, be undistinguishable in principle from a purchase of the shares, because it would amount to a surrender by the company of a part of the capital which ought to be available for the payment of its debts. But if the shareholder be insolvent, and if the transaction he entered into is in good faith, I think it is within the spirit of the exception indicated in the case of *Trevor* v. *Whitworth*. In the present case there can be no doubt that Mr. Craig was insolvent when he surrendered his shares to the company. . . .

" . . . Mr. Craig . . . proposed to transfer his shares in the Investment Company to the company by way of surrender. His proposal was accepted, and he executed a gratuitous transfer accordingly. . . . The company could not get anything out of Mr. Craig's estate without making him bankrupt, and I rather think that the argument for the pursuer must be carried this length, that it is the duty of a company in such a case to make its shareholder bankrupt on the chance of recovering a dividend. . . . The other view is, that the surrender was a fair settlement with an insolvent debtor such as the law will support, and in no true sense a purchase of the company's shares or a giving away of the company's capital. The latter is in my opinion the true character of the transaction."

NOTES

1. For *General Property Investment Co. Ltd. and Liquidator* v. *Matheson's Trustees* and *Trevor* v. *Whitworth*, see pp. 128–132 above.

2. In *Gill* v. *The Arizona Copper Co. Ltd.* (1900) 2 F. 843 (Note 5 to *General Property Investment Co. Ltd. and Liquidator* v. *Matheson's Trustees*, p. 131, above) a transaction was held not to be equivalent to a surrender of shares to the company.

Lord McLaren (at p. 859): " It is, of course, indisputable as a general rule that a company is disabled from acquiring shares in its own undertaking to which liability attaches. The reason is that by such purchase or acquisition the uncalled capital of the company is reduced, because in the event of the company going into liquidation, the liability of the insolvent company is substituted for that of a shareholder who is presumably solvent. An exception is admitted in the case where a shareholder, being unable to pay calls which are due, surrenders his shares, but this is only an apparent exception; in the case supposed creditors are not prejudiced, because the extinction of the obligation of a bankrupt shareholder can injure nobody."

Chapter 13

GENERAL MEETINGS

Kinds of general meeting: convening of extraordinary general meeting on requisition

Thyne v. Lauder
1925 S.N. 123 (O.H.)

The capital of A. & R. Scott Ltd., oat-flour manufacturers, consisted of ordinary and preference shares. The company had four directors, including T. and L. T. and his friends held a majority of the ordinary and preference shares combined, but L. and his friends held a majority of the ordinary shares. T. and L. were joint managing directors. T. was chairman of the board of directors.

Disagreement arose between T. and L. To settle the dispute both T. along with his friends and L. along with his friends had recourse to the statutory power of requisitioning an extraordinary general meeting.

The articles of association confined the right of voting at general meetings to holders of ordinary shares, except where " the directors or a majority of them decided that the holders of preference shares should attend and vote." The articles also provided that a quorum of directors was three, and that the chairman had a casting vote.

Two meetings of directors were called to consider whether preference shareholders should be admitted to the extraordinary general meeting. L., with his supporting co-director, Taylor, did not attend these board meetings, and, as there was no quorum present, no business could be transacted. As a result, the right to convene the extraordinary general meeting devolved upon the requisitionists themselves, and the meeting would consist of ordinary shareholders only.

T. and his supporting co-director of the same surname presented a note of suspension and interdict to have L. restrained from convening the general meeting.

L. and Taylor contended that L. had an absolute statutory right to convene the meeting following the directors' failure to do so, and they maintained that their abstention from the board meetings had been justified by the knowledge that T. intended to use his casting vote to admit preference shareholders to the general meeting in furtherance of his personal interests in the dispute.

The Lord Ordinary (Constable) *granted* the interdict, *holding* that while L., as an ordinary shareholder, would in normal circumstances have been entitled to convene the meeting, his right to do so had been abrogated by the fact that his opportunity for doing so arose out of his abstention from attending board meetings—conduct contrary to his duty under the statutory provisions and the articles in question, and further involving possible injustice to a substantial body of shareholders.

NOTES

1. The statutory provisions, now in section 132 of the Companies Act 1948, were at the date of this case in section 66 of the Companies (Consolidation) Act 1908.

2. According to the opinion of Lord Hill Watson (Ordinary) in *Ball* v. *Metal Industries Ltd.*, 1957 S.C. 315 (O.H.), business other than that specified in the requisition could competently be placed before an extraordinary general meeting convened on requisition.

An extraordinary general meeting of M. Ltd. was convened by requisition to appoint three new directors. Included in the agenda was a further resolution, proposed by a shareholder, that B., a director, should be removed from his office under section 184 of the Companies Act 1948. B. contended that this proposed resolution could not competently be put before the meeting and he sought an interdict.

Held that the proposed resolution was incompetent, since it was not included in the objects of the requisition and could not otherwise, under the articles of M. Ltd., be considered except at an " ordinary " meeting (*i.e.* an annual general meeting).

Lord Hill Watson (at p. 316): " I think it would be perfectly competent for the board of a company, when they are sending out a notice convening an extraordinary general meeting pursuant to section 132 to incorporate in the notice provisions relating to business which could have competently been put before the company by the directors at an extraordinary general meeting of the company in terms of the Act of Parliament and the articles of association of the company concerned."

Kinds of general meeting: power of court to order meeting

**The Edinburgh Workmen's Houses Improvement Co. Ltd.,
Petitioners**
1935 S.C. 56

The articles of association of E. Ltd. provided that the quorum for general meetings was 13 shareholders personally present.

Two extraordinary general meetings were called for the same day, (1) to alter the articles so as to authorise the company to reduce its capital and (2) to reduce the capital. Only two shareholders were personally present, but they proceeded to pass the resolutions. All of the 21 proxies received were in favour of the resolutions.

The company presented a petition for confirmation of the proposed reduction.

The reporter to whom the petition was remitted pointed out that the resolutions had not been validly passed, but added that, as only 14 shareholders resided in the Edinburgh area, it would be difficult to obtain the required quorum and that, since the presentation of the petition, all except five of the 54 shareholders had given their written assent to the resolutions.

The court *held* that in the circumstances it was impracticable to conduct the meetings in the manner prescribed by the articles, *ordered* further meetings to be called, *directed* that at these meetings the quorum should be five shareholders personally present and *continued* the petition to await the result of the meetings.

LORD PRESIDENT (CLYDE) (at p. 59): " I think it is the case that an irregularity of procedure under the Companies Acts can be cured if you get the consent of every shareholder. The attempt to get a unanimous consent has been very largely successful, but just falls short of complete success; and I am afraid that the remedy which depends upon getting the consent of every shareholder remains beyond the Company's reach, seeing that there are some shareholders whose consent has not been secured. There is in these circumstances no waiver of the statutory conditions. . . .

[Referring to s. 115 of the Companies Act 1929] " I think the expression ' impracticable . . . to *conduct* the meeting of the company in manner prescribed by the articles ' is sufficient to cover a case in which it is impracticable, owing to the terms of the Articles and the state of shareholding in the Company, to get a quorum present."

NOTE

The statutory provisions are now in section 135 of the Companies Act 1948.

Notice of general meetings: length of notice

The Aberdeen Comb Works Co. Ltd., Petitioners
(1902) 10 S.L.T. 210

The articles of association of A. Ltd. provided that (i) seven days' notice should be given for general meetings, (ii) notice sent by post was to be deemed to have been served on the day after posting, and (iii) " when any number of days is mentioned for the . . . giving of any notice, such number of days shall be reckoned excluding the first and including the last of such days."

Meetings were called for the purpose of a reduction of capital. The notices were posted on March 11, and the meetings were held on March 19.

In the petition for confirmation by the court, the reporter stated (at p. 210): " I am not aware of any reported case in which the computation of days under the Companies Acts is dealt with by the Courts in Scotland, but I may refer your Lordships to the case of the *Railway Sleepers Supply Co.* (1885, 29 Chan.Div. 204), from which it would appear that where so many days' notice ' at least ' is to be given, the day of the meeting, resolution, or other matter, would not be counted. . . . " Otherwise his report was favourable to the petition being granted.

Held that due notice had been given; reduction *confirmed.*

LORD PRESIDENT (KINROSS) (at p. 211): " It is quite proper that Sir Charles Logan should bring this question under our notice, because the article is very peculiarly worded. . . .

" The meeting to which the question relates required seven days' notice, and that notice was given, if the day on which the meeting was held is included, which I think may be done, even although the meeting was held before the close of the day. The clause declares that the last day is to be included, even although the whole day has not expired. It is very like the rule expressed in the maxim *dies inceptus pro completo habetur.*"

NOTES

1. *Cf. Neil McLeod & Sons Ltd., Petitioners* (p. 237, below).
2. Under section 133 (1) of the Companies Act 1948, a provision in a limited company's articles requiring only seven days' notice for the calling of general meetings would be void.

Quorum at general meetings: members entitled to vote

Henderson v. James Louttit & Co. Ltd.
(1894) 21 R. 674

The articles of association of L. Ltd. included the provision: " No business shall be transacted at any general meeting, except the declaration of a dividend, unless a quorum of members is present at the time when the meeting proceeds to transact business." The quorum, calculated in accordance with further provisions in the articles, was 13 members.

At a meeting convened to consider voluntary winding up only 12 members entitled to vote at the meeting presented themselves. Georgeson, who had acquired shares in the company on the day before the meeting, was also present, but by one of the articles of association he was disqualified from voting because he had not held his shares for a period of three months. Ten of the 12 qualified members took the view that Georgeson could not be counted towards the quorum, and they then left the place of the meeting. The two remaining qualified members and Georgeson then purported to pass a resolution which would have had the effect of putting the company into voluntary liquidation.

Subsequently a petition was presented to court to have the voluntary liquidation continued subject to the supervision of the court.

Held that (1) " members " in the provision quoted from the articles meant members entitled to vote, and (2) a quorum was required not only at the commencement of the meeting but also at the time when the business was transacted, and that there was therefore no liquidation in existence which could be continued subject to the supervision of the court; petition *refused.*

LORD PRESIDENT (J. P. B. ROBERTSON) (at p. 676): " It is impossible to hold that when the word ' quorum ' is used it has any other sense than a quorum of effective members—members qualified to take part in and to decide upon questions brought before the meeting. Accordingly, it appears to me that in regard to the meeting in question the proceedings disclose two fatal faults: First, Mr. Georgeson was not a member qualified to vote, and could not therefore, in my view, count as a member in ascertaining the quorum. Second, when the meeting proceeded to the business for which it had been called there were present only two members qualified to vote, and I think it would never do to construe section 37 of Table A as the petitioners propose. It would be a highly inconvenient, not to say unnatural meaning to attribute to it, to hold that all that is necessary to the validity of the proceedings is, that at the earliest stage of the meeting a quorum should be present, but that after the real business of the meeting is started and under consideration the quorum might go away."

NOTES

1. The company had been incorporated without registering articles of association, and consequently Table A of the Companies Act 1862 formed the articles of the company.

Regulation 53 of Table A in the First Schedule to the Companies Act 1948 provides: " No business shall be transacted at any general meeting unless a quorum of members is present at the time when the meeting proceeds to business; save as herein otherwise provided, three members present in person shall be a quorum."

2. In *Re Hartley Baird Ltd.* [1955] Ch. 142, the English court held that this statutory form of article was satisfied if a quorum was present merely at the beginning of the meeting.

Quorum at general meetings: one individual not sufficient

James Prain & Sons Ltd., Petitioners
1947 S.C. 325

The articles of association of P. Ltd. provided that two or more members present in person or by proxy should be a quorum for a general meeting.

At an extraordinary general meeting convened to consider reduction of capital, P., the chairman of the company, was the only member present in person, but he was also there as a trustee in two trusts which held shares in the company and as a proxy for another member.

In the petition for confirmation of the special resolution which P. had purported to pass, the court *declined* to confirm the reduction, *holding* that, unless the word " meeting " could have assigned to it some special meaning, a meeting could not consist of one individual.

LORD PRESIDENT (COOPER) (at p. 327): " At the company meeting at which the special resolutions were submitted for approval only one person was present, although that person was present in more than one capacity. . . . But notwithstanding the multiple capacities in which he was present, the fact remains that the ' meeting' consisted of him and of him alone.

" . . . The submission was pressed upon us that, as there

were notionally present at this meeting two persons in person or by proxy, though actually only one individual, the requirements of the articles and of the law were satisfied. I am not prepared to accept that view.

" Since the case of *Sharp* v. *Dawes* (2 Q.B.D. 26) in 1876 the view has been held . . . that a ' meeting ' is an assemblage where two or more persons meet, and that, unless the word ' meeting ' can have assigned to it some special meaning, a meeting cannot be composed of one individual. . . .

" Putting decisions aside, I turn next to the textbook writers on the subject of company practice; and, so far as they reveal, the rule in *Sharp* v. *Dawes* has held the field down to the date of the publication of the latest editions of these works.

" The point before us may seem a technical point, and so in a sense it is; but I cannot feel that it is wise or safe for the first time after over 80 years of company practice to give in this Court an authoritative recognition of a principle which has never hitherto been laid down, but has, on the contrary, been frowned upon as incompatible with the substance of the statutory provisions under which companies are administered. . . . In this case there was no serious difficulty in securing the attendance of a second member, and in all such cases it is easy enough to adopt the familiar expedient of transferring a qualification holding to selected individuals."

NOTES

1. This case was distinguished in *Neil McLeod & Sons Ltd.*, *Petitioners*, 1967 S.C. 16 (see also p. 237, below).

The articles of association of McL. Ltd. provided that at a general meeting a quorum should be three members personally present.

At a meeting convened to pass a special resolution, only two members were present, but one of them held shares both as an individual and as a trustee in a trust which held shares.

Held that a quorum had been present.

Lord President (Clyde) (at p. 21): " The requirement for a quorum is three members personally present, not three individuals. One individual may be present at a meeting in more than one capacity, and there were in fact present at this meeting three *personae*, each of whom was a member, namely, Mrs. Lord, Mr. Brydie as a member holding shares in his own right and the same Mr. Brydie as a member entitled to vote in person in respect of a trust holding. The case of *Prain & Sons* was referred to. But this case merely decided that a meeting is not properly constituted if only one individual is present, for there is no-one for him to meet. It therefore does not affect the present question."

2. Where the court orders a meeting to be held under section

135 (1) of the Companies Act 1948, the court may give a direction that one member present in person or by proxy shall be deemed to constitute a meeting.

Quorum at general meetings: interpretation of " present "

M. Harris Ltd., Petitioners
1956 S.C. 207

The articles of association of H. Ltd. provided: " No business shall be transacted at any general meeting . . . unless a quorum of members is present. . . . Such quorum shall consist of two members of the company, of whom Edith Bloch or Harris . . . shall be one."

At a general meeting convened to consider reduction of capital, the named person was not personally present but was represented by an attorney.

Held that " present " meant " personally present " and that there had therefore been no quorum at the meeting.

LORD PRESIDENT (CLYDE) (at p. 208): " Mrs. Harris, who has remarried, is now Mrs. Gompertz. She resides in the United States of America. Her health will not permit her to travel to this country. . . . Prior to going to the United States she executed a power of attorney in favour of Mr. Levy, in terms of which he was authorised, among other things, to attend, act and vote for her at all meetings of any corporation in which she held shares. . . . But, in my opinion what the article contemplates is a specified number of members being present, one of whom must be Mrs. Gompertz. . . . The article, as I read it, requires for the constitution of a quorum the presence of Mrs. Gompertz herself, and neither a proxy nor an attorney for her will form a proper substitute for her actual presence. . . .

" . . . If it had been intended that a proxy or an attorney could enable a quorum to be completed, I should have expected the words ' personally or by proxy ' to appear in the articles, as these words frequently do in other connections. In the absence of such words, ' members present ' must mean ' personally present.' "

Special resolution: " not less than twenty-one days' notice "

Neil McLeod & Sons Ltd., Petitioners
1967 S.C. 16

On June 15, 1966, McL. Ltd. passed a special resolution for reduction of capital. The notice calling the meeting had been posted on May 24, 1966, and so, by the terms of the articles of association, was deemed to have been served on May 25. There were, therefore, only 20 clear days between the date of service and the date of the meeting.

Held that, since the period of "not less than 21 days" was to be computed by excluding the day on which the notice was served but including the day on which the meeting was held, the notice had been timeously served.

LORD PRESIDENT (CLYDE) (at p. 19): "Section 141 (2) of the Companies Act 1948 . . . provides, *inter alia,* that a resolution shall be a special resolution when it has been passed at a general meeting of which not less than twenty-one days' notice specifying the intention to propose the resoultion has been given.

"For the purpose of computing the period of not less than twenty-one days' notice it is clear that the day on which the notice reached the shareholders (*i.e.* May 25) cannot be counted. It follows from this that the meeting in the present case took place on the twenty-first day after the day on which the notices reached the shareholders. The issue in the present case is whether this amounted to not less than twenty-one days' notice, in which case the notice was good, or whether twenty-one clear days must intervene between the receipt of the notice and the day on which the meeting was to take place. In that event the notice was bad.

"I shall consider first of all the case where the requirement is simply a twenty-one day notice. In that case the normal rule in Scotland is that the day on which the notice is received is not counted, but the last of the succeeding twenty-one days is included. Running days are not periods of twenty-four hours but calendar days. This general rule was laid down in *Parish Council of Cavers* v. *Parish Council of Smailholm* (1909 S.C. 195) in ascertaining what amounted to a three-year residential settlement. As Lord President Dunedin said (at p. 197): ' I think three years must be three years according to the calendar. . . . I do not think . . . the Court will ever be concerned with the question of what happens inside a day; . . . the maxim *dies inceptus pro completo habetur* is applicable.'

"In the second place it appears to me that a period of twenty-one days' notice and a period of not less than twenty-one days' notice must in the present connection be computed in the same way. . . .

" It follows from this that if the general rule applies in the present case, the notice is timeous.

" It may well be that the terms of a particular statute or regulation are such as to show that a specified number of clear days must intervene between the receipt of the notice and the day on which the meeting is held. . . . I can find no warrant in Scotland for treating the present case as falling outside the general rule. If the legislature had wished twenty-one clear days to elapse between the receipt of the notice and the date of the meeting, it would have been easy to say so.

" We were referred to the decision of Bennett J. in the case of *In re Hector Whaling Ld.* ([1936] Ch. 208). That case was concerned with the provision in the Companies Act 1929 corresponding to section 141 (2) of the 1948 Act. In that case the learned judge held that the words ' not less than twenty-one days' meant ' twenty-one clear days exclusive of the day of service and exclusive of the day on which the meeting is to be held.' In reaching this conclusion he relied upon two English cases. . . . These latter cases were concerned with the interpretation of the language used in quite different statutes, and in my opinion there is nothing in the language or content of section 141 (2) to show that twenty-one clear days were intended. In my opinion, therefore, the rule laid down by Lord President Dunedin in *Parish Council of Cavers* is applicable, and the notice given in the present case was timeous. In Scotland the requisite notice under section 141 (2) of the Companies Act 1948 means a notice of not less than twenty-one days computed by excluding the day on which the notice is received by the shareholder but including the day on which the meeting is to be held."

NOTES

1. For another point in this case, see Note 1 to *James Prain & Sons Ltd., Petitioners* (p. 236, above).

2. Where a company's articles are in the form of Table A, clear days' notice is required: regulation 50 provides: " The notice shall be exclusive of the day on which it is served or deemed to be served and of the day for which it is given."

3. See also *The Aberdeen Comb Works Co. Ltd., Petitioners* (p. 233, above).

4. In *Parish Council of Cavers* v. *Parish Council of Smailholm* the decision of the court was that, where a person had commenced to reside in the parish of S. on the afternoon of May 29, 1900, and had left that parish on the morning of May 28, 1903, he had not resided in the parish for three years.

*Special and extraordinary resolutions: requirement to specify
the intention to propose the resolution as a special or
extraordinary resolution*

Rennie v. Crichton's (Strichen) Ltd.
1927 S.L.T. 459 (O.H.)

At a meeting of C. Ltd., the following extraordinary resolution
was unanimously passed: " That the company be voluntarily
wound up in consequence of its being unable to continue its
business by reason of its liabilities, and that it is advisable to
wind up."

The notice by which the meeting had been convened did
not specify that that resolution was to be proposed *as an extraordinary resolution.*

Held that the notice was invalid, and that the company was
therefore not in liquidation.

LORD CONSTABLE (ORDINARY) (at p. 460): " The notice was
in the following terms: ' An extraordinary general meeting . . .
will be held . . . to pass a resolution . . . that the meeting resolves:
" That the company be voluntarily wound up in consequence of
its being unable to continue its business by reason of its liabilities
and that it is advisable to wind up." The sanction for the resolution was section 182 (3) of the statute, which provides that
' A company may be wound up voluntarily— . . . (3) if the
company resolves by extraordinary resolution to the effect that
it cannot by reason of its liabilities continue its business, and
that it is advisable to wind up '; and the statutory requirements
as to notice are contained in section 69, which provides that
' (1) A resolution shall be an extraordinary resolution when it
has been passed by a majority of not less than three-fourths of
such members entitled to vote as are present in person or
by proxy (where proxies are allowed) at a general meeting of
which notice specifying the intention to propose the resolution
as an extraordinary resolution has been duly given."

" The objection is that the notice did not specify the intention
to propose the resolution *as an extraordinary resolution.* The
answer is that the substance of the resolution quoted in the
notice was sufficient to shew by reference to section 182 that
an extraordinary resolution was intended, and that section 69
was therefore sufficiently complied with.

" . . . The effect of section 69 (1) was carefully considered by
Sargant J. in *MacConnell* v. *E. Prill & Co.* ([1916] 2 Ch. 57),
and he held that . . . in the case of an extraordinary resolution,

express notice must be given that the resolution will be proposed as an extraordinary resolution. I agree with this decision and with the reasoning upon which it is based. . . . The perfectly definite language of that provision appears to me to leave no room for construction and to require that in the notice the resolution shall be expressly specified as an extraordinary resolution."

NOTE

The statute in force at the date of this case was the Companies (Consolidation) Act 1908.

For the statutory provisions now corresponding to sections 69 (1) and 182 (3) of that Act, see the Companies Act 1948, sections 141 (1) and 278 (1), respectively.

Special and extraordinary resolutions: chairman's declaration: contradictory evidence on the face of the minute

Cowan v. The Scottish Publishing Co. Ltd.
(1892) 19 R. 437

A meeting of S. Ltd. had before it a special resolution for voluntary winding up. Certain shareholders, including Forbes, were not in favour of the resolution.

The minute of the meeting stated: " Mr. Forbes' amendment being then put against the proposed resolution, and a shew of hands being taken, there voted for the former four, and for the latter eight. The resolution therefore became the decision of the meeting, and the chairman declared it carried. No poll was demanded in either case." That minute was signed by the chairman.

Held that, as the minute showed that the resolution had not been passed by the necessary statutory majority, the resolution was of no effect.

LORD PRESIDENT (J. P. B. ROBERTSON) (at p. 439): " The minute bears that the figures for the resolution and amendment are eight and four respectively. These figures do not shew a majority of three-fourths; but upon the footing that these are the *media,* as I think they purport to be, by which the conclusion is reached, the minute goes on to state, ' The resolution therefore became the decision of the meeting, and the chairman declared it carried.' It is true that the section I have referred to bears that ' a declaration of the chairman that the resolution has been carried shall be deemed conclusive evidence of the fact, without proof of the number or proportion of the votes recorded in favour of or against the same.' But in the present case we find a minute under the hand of the chairman which is evidence not corroborative but contradictory of the validity of the resolution. Now, the section merely dispenses with the need of proving the numbers, but it does not suggest that, when they are proved, under the hand of the chairman and in the very minute founded on, the chairman's declaration is to overrule and nullify them. Accordingly, . . . I think the case must be treated as one where there is no voluntary liquidation."

NOTES

1. The section in question was section 51 of the Companies Act 1862. The corresponding statutory provision is now in section 141 of the Companies Act 1948.

2. *Cf. John T. Clark & Co. Ltd., Petitioners*, 1911 S.C. 243: A meeting had been convened to consider a special resolution for reduction of capital. The minute of the meeting recorded that of the 12 shareholders present eight voted for the resolution, two voted against it, and two abstained from voting, and that the chairman had declared the resolution carried.

Held that the resolution could not receive effect, since it was plain on the face of the proceedings that the majority then required by the statutory provisions had not been obtained.

The case was concerned with section 69 of the Companies (Consolidation) Act 1908, by which a three-fourths majority of the shareholders who were present was required for the passing of a special or an extraordinary resolution. For the purposes of sections 141 (1) and (2) of the Companies Act 1948, only those who actually vote are reckoned in computing the three-fourths majority. To this extent, the decision in *John T. Clark & Co. Ltd., Petitioners,* is outdated.

Lord Justice-Clerk (J. H. A. Macdonald) (at p. 245): "The provision in subsection (3) of section 69, that a declaration of the chairman that the resolution is carried shall . . . be conclusive evidence of the fact, does not legalise the proceedings if it is plain upon the face of them that no such thing has happened."

3. The provision in section 117 (3) of the Companies Act 1929 as to the conclusiveness of the chairman's declaration was given effect to in *Grahams' Morocco Co. Ltd., Petitioners*, 1932 S.C. 269.

Among the majority voting in favour of a special resolution were two shareholders who were, under the articles, disqualified from voting because they had held their shares for less than one month. If their votes had not been included, the necessary majority would not have been obtained.

Lord Blackburn (at p. 273): "No poll was demanded, and the petitioners are accordingly, in my opinion, entitled to invoke the strict terms of section 117 (3) of the Act. Had the mistake which has occurred been apparent *ex facie* of the minute itself, then perhaps we should have been constrained, by the decision of the other Division in

J. T. Clark & Co., to hold that the declaration of the chairman was not conclusive and might be reconsidered. But the circumstances of this case are entirely different. . . . The words of the section are imperative, and . . . the chairman's declaration that the resolution was duly passed is conclusive, and not *prima facie,* evidence."

Lord President (Clyde) (dissenting) (at p. 275): " I find nothing in the statutory enactment to extend the chairman's finality to questions of the qualifications or legal competency of the persons present at the meeting to take part in the show of hands at all."

4. See also *The Citizens Theatre Ltd., Petitioners,* below.

Resolutions: articles of association requiring show of hands: minutes not recording that show of hands had been taken

The Citizens Theatre Ltd., Petitioners
1946 S.C. 14

A meeting of C. Ltd. had before it special resolutions to alter provisions of its memorandum and articles of association. The chairman moved the resolutions, and the motion was seconded.

The minute of the meeting recorded that, there being no counter motion or amendments, the chairman declared that the resolutions had been duly passed as special resolutions.

The articles of association of C. Ltd. provided that at general meetings resolutions should be decided on a show of hands.

Held that the resolutions had not been duly submitted to the meeting, and that the chairman's declaration that they had been passed was therefore not conclusive.

Lord President (Normand) (at p. 17): " The company has by article 17 declared the method by which a resolution is to be approved. . . . The prescribed formalities are . . . some safeguard against fraud or error or too hasty judgment, and, in any event, the chairman has no power to waive the prescribed method of taking the vote. Since there was no show of hands, there could be, and there was, no declaration by the chairman and no entry in the minute book conforming to the requirements of the article.

" It was suggested that section 117 (3) of the Companies Act might help the petitioners. . . . The effectiveness of the chairman's declaration, however, is conditional, and it depends upon the resolution having been submitted to be passed. In the present case the question is whether the resolution was duly submitted, and, according to the articles, the answer is that it was not. Therefore section 117 (3) does not help the petitioners."

Lord Moncrieff (at p. 18): " I incline to think that, had

the company not imposed special requirements upon itself as regards procedure in its articles of association, what took place at the meeting as recorded in the minute would have satisfied the requirements of the Companies Act 1929. It might well have been maintained, apart from the articles, that what had so occurred had amounted to the submitting of the resolution to the meeting in order that it might be passed; because when a resolution is moved and seconded and no counter motion is made within the observation of the chairman, it may be assumed, so far as the statutory requirements are concerned, that such a resolution has not only been passed but has been submitted so as to satisfy all that is required in section 117 (3) of the Act. The procedure may, however, of course be governed by further requirements which the company may impose upon itself in the articles of association; and in article 17 . . . it is made perfectly clear that the resolution can only be submitted for decision upon a show of hands. . . . I think the Court must hold that the resolution was in this case not ' submitted ' in terms of the requirements of the articles."

NOTES

1. Section 141 (3) of the Companies Act 1948 now corresponds to section 117 (3) of the Companies Act 1929. Regulations 58 and 15 of Tables A and C respectively in the Act of 1948 contain similar provisions regarding a show of hands to the provisions considered by the court in this case.

2. Contrast *The Fraserburgh Commercial Co. Ltd., Petitioners,* 1946 S.C. 444: A special resolution for reduction of capital had been passed, but the minute did not record that it had been carried on a show of hands, as required by the articles of association. There was, however, lodged in process a letter from the chairman stating that the resolution had in fact been carried on a show of hands.

Held that the chairman's letter was sufficient evidence; and petition *granted.*

Minutes: member's right of inspection

McCusker v. McRae
1966 S.C. 253

McC., one of the two directors and shareholders of Rob Roy Highland Motels Ltd., presented a petition for an order on the company to make available on inspection by himself " and by such men of skill as he may instruct to assist him " the minutes of all proceedings of general meetings.

McC.'s application was opposed by McR., the other director and shareholder of the company.

At the court's suggestion, the prayer of the petition was amended so that there was substituted for the words " such men of skill as he may instruct to assist him " the name and designation of a specific accountant.

The court *granted* the prayer of the petition, as amended.

NOTES

1. No opinions were delivered.

2. The petition was under section 146 (4) of the Companies Act 1948, which expressly confers power on the court to order inspection of the minutes of general meetings. Contrast the other part of this case, relating to inspection of minutes of board meetings and of books of account (p. 268, below).

Chapter 14

MAJORITY RULE AND MINORITY PROTECTION

Majority rule: directors not liable to account to individual shareholders: statutory company

Orr v. Glasgow, Airdrie, and Monklands Junction Railway Co.
(1860) 3 Macq. 799; 22 D.(H.L.) 10; (1857) 20 D. 327

O. and others, individual shareholders of the G. Railway Co. incorporated by special Act of Parliament, brought an action against the directors of the company concluding for count and reckoning and repetition of so much of the deposit paid by the pursuers as should be found due to them.

Held that the directors were not liable to account to the individual shareholders but only to the company itself.

LORD CHANCELLOR (CAMPBELL) (at p. 802): "It must be observed that this is not, as was the case in *Tulloch* v. *Davidson* ((1860) 3 Macq. 783), an action founded *ex delicto* for damages in respect of a deceitful representation, or damages in respect of fraudulent conduct. It is for count and reckoning, it is with a view to surcharge and falsify accounts which have been rendered.

" . . . Here you have a Joint Stock Company, a corporation, and . . . there are special opportunities and means given to all the shareholders from time to time to see that proper accounts are rendered, and that their affairs are properly conducted; and the accounts are to be periodically submitted to the general meetings of shareholders and balances are to be struck.

"Now, it seems to me that under these circumstances, until there has been a complaint made, and until there has been an effort made to obtain justice by applying to the Company, this mode of bringing an action at the suit of one or of several of the shareholders is incompetent. . . . Here there has been no complaint at any public meeting of the Company, as far as we know, and no attempt to make any such complaint of the accounts rendered, or to call a meeting for the purpose. There are means of calling a meeting, but none of them have been resorted to. But this action is brought by several gentlemen against the Company and against the Directors of the Company, and I think that according to the analogy of the cases that have been decided in England, which rest upon principles that

246

are equally applicable to Scotland, this ought not to be permitted. If one shareholder is allowed to bring such an action, then each individual who has a different complaint of his own on different parts of the accounts which have been rendered may follow the example, and the Company may be torn in pieces, and utterly ruined by the litigation in which it is involved.

" . . . I do not find here anything which might not have been ratified and adopted by the Company if they had thought fit. . . . Although the acts that were done by the Directors were *ultra vires* of the Directors, I do not think it was necessarily *ultra vires* of the Company to have condoned the acts done by the Directors, and to have adopted them."

LORD CRANWORTH (at p. 804): "Where there are shareholders in any incorporated body who have, or think they have, a right to complain of the conduct of those who are managing the affairs of that body, their remedy is not directly against the Managers, but through the Company against the Managers, and through the Company only. And upon very obvious principles; the Managers are the servants not of the individual shareholders, but of the Company; and the course, therefore, that any share-holder must take if he is aggrieved is to call upon the employers of those Managers to bring them to account, and then, that being done, to get relief from the Company itself. If, indeed, there be any collusion that can be suggested, or any specialty, to show that the ordinary course being pursued would lead to injustice, that would give rise to different considerations; but nothing of that sort occurs here."

NOTE

For *Tulloch* v. *Davidson,* see *Davidson* v. *Tulloch* (p. 94, above).

Another case in the same category as *Davidson* v. *Tulloch* was *Leslie's Representatives* v. *Lumsden* (1851) 14 D. 213.

L. had been a shareholder in the Banking Company of Aberdeen, which was dissolved in 1849. L.'s representatives brought an action against five of the 12 former directors to make good the loss caused by their alleged fraud.

Held that L.'s representatives were entitled to sue without making the other shareholders or the company parties to the action.

Instances of actions brought by a company (and its liquidators) against directors are to be found in *Liquidators of the Western Bank of Scotland* v. *Douglas, &c.* (1860) 22 D. 447, and in *The Western Bank of Scotland* v. *Baird's Trustees* (1872) 11 M. 96.

In the former case the Lord Ordinary (Kinloch) said (at p. 487): " If any action can be clearly said to be a proper company action, it is that which is brought by the company against its administrators for restitution of money lost to the company funds by malversation in office. The directors were the servants of the company. . . . They held of the company, and to the company they were responsible. What is now charged on them is, that money was improperly paid away by them out of the coffers of the company. What is demanded is simply that the money should be replaced in these coffers. It is to be so placed, as part of the proper assets of the company, for discharge in the first instance of the company debts; and then, and then only, for division amongst the partners, whose claim is against the company administrators for mere distribution of the balance after the creditors are satisfied."

Lord Justice-Clerk (Inglis) said (at p. 499): " Lastly, the defenders urge with much earnestness, that the claim in this summons is not a company claim, and consequently, that neither the incorporated company nor the liquidators have any title to sue for its recovery. The plea is rested on what appears to be a total misunderstanding of the judgment of this Court, and of the House of Lords, in the recent case of *Tulloch* v. *Davidson*; where, under certain circumstances, an individual shareholder of a joint-stock banking company was found entitled to sue directors, accused of fraudulent malversation in office, for the loss thence arising to his own personal estate, as an owner of shares in the company. . . .

" It appears to the Court that when damage has been sustained by the company, through acts of the directors, for the consequences of which they are legally responsible, the company is, primarily at least, the party to sue the directors for reparation, to the effect of restoring the company's estate against the loss it has sustained, whatever may be the nature otherwise of the acts of the directors inferring such liability."

In *The Western Bank of Scotland* v. *Baird's Trustees*, Lord Justice-Clerk (Moncreiff) said (at p. 109): " It is . . . fixed in this case, and is a material element as regards some important points involved in it, that the title on which the summons is rested is that of the company itself, and that the debt sued for is a debt due to the bank."

Majority rule: shareholder's action against director for sums advanced to officials

Lee v. Crawford
(1890) 17 R. 1094

L., a shareholder in the Scottish Provident Investment Co. Ltd., raised an action " on behalf of himself and all other shareholders " of the company, against C., one of the directors, to have C. ordained to make payment to the company of company funds lent by C. and his co-directors to a managing director, a secretary, and other officials of the company.

C. contended that the action was incompetent, since the company itself was the true creditor.

The court *dismissed* the action.

LORD YOUNG (at p. 1097): " As to whether such a question can be tried in an action by one shareholder against one of the directors alone, the general rule is that stated by Sir G. Jessel in the case of *Russell,* that an action to have money replaced in the company's coffers must, as a general rule, be at the instance of the company itself, and be laid against the directors as a body. The Master of the Rolls says, ' The rule is a general one, but it does not apply to a case where the interests of justice require the rule to be dispensed with.' I cannot find in the circumstances of this case any case of necessity, in the ' interests of justice,' which ought to introduce an exception to the rule, and allow this pursuer to sue Mr. Crawford (or indeed all the directors) to restore this alleged balance due by the managing director."

LORD LEE (at p. 1098): " As to demand for repayment by the defender to the company, I think there is a clear distinction between this case and that of *Leslie* v. *Lumsden.* There the pursuer asked that money which he had paid for his shares should be restored. Such an action could only be raised by an individual shareholder. Here the pursuer demands that the defender shall pay money into the coffers of the company."

NOTES

1. The case of *Russell* referred to was *Russell* v. *Wakefield Waterworks Co.* (1875) L.R. 20 Eq. 474.

Counsel for the defender also relied on *Orr* v. *Glasgow, Airdrie, and Monklands Junction Railway Co.* (p. 246, above).

2. For *Leslie* v. *Lumsden*, see Note to last-mentioned case (p. 247, above).

Majority rule: shareholder seeking to interdict company from issuing shares to managing director on favourable terms

Cameron v. The Glenmorangie Distillery Co. Ltd.
(1896) 23 R. 1092

At an extraordinary general meeting of G. Ltd., a resolution was passed to issue to Maitland, the managing director, 200 shares of £10 each at a premium of £1 each (*i.e.* at the price of £11 each). C., a shareholder who was also one of the directors, dissented.

Thereafter, C. presented a note of suspension and interdict against the company, his co-directors and the secretary, to have them interdicted from acting upon the resolution.

The prayer of the note was *refused*.

LORD ORDINARY (KYLLACHY) (at p. 1094): "The ground of complaint is that the premium was inadequate, so that the shares were allotted at a price below their true value—that there was thus made to Mr. Maitland a present of large amount —and that the transaction was not justified by any interest of the company, but was, on the contrary, prejudicial to the company's interests. . . .

"The respondents' case, on the other hand, is that Mr. Maitland's services had been specially valuable to the company . . . , that it was desired to add to his interest in the concern . . . , and that the allotment wase made with that object. . . .

" . . . The proof having been led, the result, in my opinion, is, that the complainer has failed to shew either that the transaction was *ultra vires* of the company, or that being *intra vires,* it involved any abuse of power by the majority of the shareholders.

"It is, I think, quite clear that the transaction was not *ultra vires.* I do not know that it would have been *intra vires* of the directors. But it was certainly *intra vires* of the company. It is within the company's power to allot, as the shareholders here did, unissued shares forming part of the authorised capital. It is also within its power to fix the premium, if any, at which such shares shall be issued. It is also within its power to select the allottees. . . . There is no suggestion that the transaction in any way diminished the capital of the company. Neither is there any room for challenge on the ground that the act of the company was *intra vires* but irregular. There is no dispute that the meetings were duly called and duly held, and that everything done was done formally and regularly.

"The complainer therefore requires to make out a case of what I have called abuse of power; and I do not doubt that such cases occur, and that when they do, the Court may interfere. It is always, however, a delicate matter to interfere as between a majority and minority of shareholders of a going company, with respect to matters connected with the conduct of the company's business, and as to which the shareholders have come to a resolution. *Prima facie,* the shareholders are the best judges of their own affairs, and it is only where it appears that some sinister motive has operated, or that interests other than the interest of the company have plainly prevailed, that the Court will entertain a complaint. The test always is—Is the thing complained of a thing done in the interest of the company?—or, to put it perhaps more accurately— Is the action of the majority irreconcilable with their having proceeded upon any reasonable view of the company's interest?

" Now, in this point of view, it requires only a glance at the evidence to see that the complainer's case fails. The allotment to Mr. Maitland of 200 additional shares was, I see no reason to doubt, a proceeding which was in the interests of the company."

The First Division adhered.

NOTE

On this case, see also Note 3 to *Klenck* v. *East India Co. for Exploration and Mining Co. Ltd.* (p. 98, above).

Majority rule: shareholder's action against directors for their alleged recklessness in commencing business before sufficient capital had been subscribed

Brown v. Stewart
(1898) 1 F. 316

The articles of association of the Thistle Mechanical Milking Machine Co. Ltd. provided: " The company . . . may commence and carry on business when, in the judgment of the directors, a sufficient number of shares shall have been subscribed for to justify them in so doing."

B. applied for and had allotted to him 400 shares in the company shortly after its formation.

After the publication of the company's first balance-sheet, however, B. raised an action against those who had been directors at the date of the allotment to have them ordained to accept a transfer of the shares and to repay to him the amount of his subscription. B. averred that the directors had been reckless in proceeding to allotment and commencing business before sufficient capital had been subscribed.

Held that B. was not entitled to sue the directors in respect of an alleged wrong done by them to the company, there being no allegation that B. had called the attention of the company to the matter.

LORD KINNEAR (at p. 324): " By the articles of association it is provided that the directors are to have a discretion in commencing business according to their judgment. I agree that this is a discretion which imposed a duty, and if, instead of exercising an honest judgment upon the question submitted to them, they began business, as the pursuer alleges, with insufficient capital in circumstances in which no reasonably prudent and honest man would have done so, I do not doubt that they may be made responsible for consequent loss to the company, whether they acted from indirect motives or from mere negligence. But whether an individual shareholder can recover damages as for a separate wrong to himself while the company is still a going concern, is a very different question. . . . The principle upon which that question must be solved is that established by the cases of *Foss* v. *Harbottle* ((1843) 2 Hare 461), and *Orr* v. *The Monkland Railway Company* ((1860) 3 Macq. 799), and others of the same class. There can be no question that the commencement of business, whether prudent or not, might have been sanctioned and confirmed by the company. If the company are satisfied to carry on the business, as it would appear that they are, the Court cannot interfere in the management of their private affairs. . . . It is said that the defenders had a preponderating holding in the shares, and are able to out-vote independent shareholders. But the averment on this head is vague and general. There is no specific statement to support it; and the pursuer has made no attempt to ascertain the views of the other shareholders, and is therefore not in a position to allege that he has been out-voted by the influence of the defenders. . . . Everything complained of is a wrong to the company as such, nor does the pursuer seek to protect the interests either of a majority or a minority, or to restrain proceedings which he avers to be illegal. It is an entirely different case therefore from those in which it has been held that when an apparent majority has used its influence to pass a vote against an injured minority, the Court will interfere upon the application of the minority to restrain something that is *ultra vires*. . . . The principle explained by Lord Cranworth in the case of *Orr* seems to me to be directly applicable. The directors were not acting as the servants of the pursuer in beginning business, but as the servants of the company. It is for the company to call them to account; and if the pursuer as a shareholder has suffered damage with the other shareholders, he may obtain redress through the company. But we cannot entertain an inquiry of the kind at the instance of a single shareholder, and in the absence of the company."

LORD ORDINARY (STORMONTH-DARLING) (at p. 320): "Now,

the pursuer has not adopted any means of taking the sense of the company, which is a going company. . . . He is, therefore, not in a position to allege either that a majority of the other shareholders agree with him, or that he has been outvoted by interested parties. . . . He makes, it is true, an averment that the defenders as a body have a preponderating holding in the shares of the company, and that . . . they are able to outvote the independent shareholders and to control the company. But he is not in a position to say that he has tried to obtain redress within the company and has failed. He is not even able to say what is the view of those ' independent shareholders ' whose existence he admits."

NOTE

For *Orr's* case, see p. 246, above.

Minority protection: fraud on minority

Rixon v. Edinburgh Northern Tramways Co.
(1889) 16 R. 653

R., a shareholder in a company incorporated by special Act of Parliament, brought an action against the company concluding for reduction of an agreement entered into by the company and three other parties. R. averred that the agreement had been entered into wholly irrespective of the interests of the company, and to the prejudice of the independent shareholders including himself, that it had been entered into " fraudently and collusively," that, if carried out, it would seriously depreciate the value of the shares of the independent shareholders, and that it was *ultra vires* of the company.

Held that R. had a title to sue.

LORD PRESIDENT (INGLIS) (at p. 657): " There is a distinct and intelligible ground of reduction stated here, namely, fraud, in respect of which it cannot be said that one or more of the shareholders cannot sue though the company can do so. I think, therefore, that the Lord Ordinary is wrong."

NOTES

1. The opinion of the Lord Ordinary (Kinnear) included the following passage (at p. 655): " It is well-settled law that a single shareholder can have no title to sue such an action, except on the ground that the contract which he challenges is *ultra vires* not of the

directors only, but of the company as such, or on the ground of fraud upon himself."

2. At a later stage of the case (*Rixon* v. *Edinburgh Northern Tramways Co.* (1890) 18 R. 264), the First Division held that, although a minority of the shareholders had a title to plead fraud, it had not been proved that there had been any fraud practised by the majority upon the minority, or that a bad bargain had been made knowingly or in disregard of the company's interests, with the intent to sacrifice the interests of the company and of the minority. This judgment was affirmed by the House of Lords (*Rixon* v. *Edinburgh Northern Tramways Co.* (1893) 20 R.(H.L.) 53), on the ground that no cause had been shown for disturbing the concurrent judgments of the Lord Ordinary and the First Division on questions of fact.

At this later stage of the case, the Lord Ordinary (Kincairney) said (at p. 271): " It does not seem doubtful that . . . where a contract amounts to a fraud by a majority of shareholders on the minority, such a contract may be reduced at the instance of any shareholder who has been so defrauded. . . .

" The present is clearly a case to which that principle is applicable."

3. *Hannay* v. *Muir* (1898) 1 F. 306 was an action brought by minority shareholders against directors of their company and against two firms in both of which M., one of the directors of the company, was virtually the sole partner. M. also commanded a majority of the shares and votes of the company. The pursuers sought payment into the coffers of the company of sums which they alleged had been overcharges of commission allowed to the two firms. The pursuers averred that M. had defrauded the company and had used his voting power to prevent the pursuers from getting redress through the company.

Held, per Lord Low, Ordinary, and acquiesced in, that the pursuers had a title to sue.

Lord Low (at p. 310): " There is no doubt that the general rule is that for which the defenders contend. Directors and managers are servants of the company, and it is the company who has the title to call them to account (*Orr* v. *Glasgow, &c. Railway Company*, 3 Macq. 799). Further, if the complaint relates to a matter of internal management which it is competent for a majority to sanction, an action by individual shareholders will not be sustained. . . .

" But to these general rules there are exceptions.

" Thus if a company is defrauded by a person who can command a majority of votes, and who thereby stifles inquiry, a minority of the shareholders, or even a single shareholder, can sue."

4. In *Harris* v. *A. Harris Ltd.*, 1936 S.C. 183, two of the three judges in the Second Division held that there were circumstances in which no element of fraud had been proved and that the resolution complained of by a minority shareholder was not *ultra vires*, with the result that the court refused to interfere with the actings of the majority.

Two shareholders, who were also joint managing directors, had used their majority shareholding to pass a resolution, the effect of which was to increase their remuneration as directors. A minority shareholder brought an action for reduction of the resolution against the company and the joint managing directors as individuals, maintaining that the resolution had been passed from an oblique motive in fraud of the pursuer's interests.

Lord Hunter (after quoting from Lord Davey who had delivered the judgment of the Privy Council in *Burland* v. *Earle* [1902] A.C. 83, at p. 93) said (at p. 196): " The enunciation of the principles of law contained in Lord Davey's opinion in the case of *Burland* appears to me to afford a complete guide for the determination of the legal question involved in the present case."

Lord Anderson (at p. 199): " In the leading case of *Burland* v. *Earle* Lord Davey, at page 93, enunciates certain principles of company law which seem to be pertinent to the decision of the present case. He points out (1) that the Court will not interfere with the internal management of companies acting within their powers. In the present case the pursuer's attack is directed against the Company; it is a resolution of the Company passed in general meeting which is complained of, and not the actings of the managing directors as such. (2) A minority of shareholders complaining of what has been done by the majority can succeed only if they establish that the acts complained of are of a fraudulent character, or beyond the powers of the Company. (3) Unless otherwise provided by the regulations of the Company, a shareholder is not debarred from voting, or using his voting power to carry a resolution, by the circumstances of his having a particular interest in the subject-matter of the vote. . . .

" The resolution seems to be *intra vires* in this sense, that it does not conflict with any part of the constitution of the Company as disclosed in the memorandum and articles of association; no part of it involves alteration of any article. The pursuer endeavoured to assimilate this case to those in which a majority of shareholders had used their voting powers for the purpose of appropriating to themselves property belonging to the minority. . . . In these and similar cases, however, the minority received no counterpart for the expropriation of their property; the transaction was unilateral; there was no *quid pro quo*. In the present case the transaction proposed is bilateral. The resolution, in its three branches, is concerned with additional work to be performed by the managing directors, and additional remuneration to be payable to them in consideration thereof. These seem to me to be matters peculiarly domestic, and matters which the shareholders, in general meeting, were best qualified to decide. . . . The Lord Ordinary was thus, in my opinion, well founded in holding that the resolution was not *ultra vires*.

" The decision of the Lord Ordinary seems to me to be equally sound in so far as it negatives fraud. . . .

" The Lord Ordinary, in order to determine whether the actings complained of were fraudulent, applies this test to each of the three branches of the resolution—Whether it can be held to be so oppressive

and extravagant that no reasonable man could consider it to be for
the benefit of the Company? . . . The Lord Ordinary reaches the
conclusion that fraud has not been established against the defenders
in connection with the resolution. I entirely agree with this result."

The Lord Ordinary was Lord Wark.

Lord Murray, the third judge in the Inner House, reached the
same conclusion as the other judges but on a different ground.

Lord Murray (at p. 202): " I take a different view of the test by
which the conduct of the defenders falls to be tried. . . . I am of
opinion that the true test to be applied is not whether the pursuer
has or has not established that the defenders were guilty of fraud in
the common law sense; I adopt as the true test a higher standard of
conduct, whether they were or were not in breach of a fiduciary duty
to the Company and its constituent shareholders. It follows, if this
view be sound, that the case may become much more narrow for the
defence."

Applying this stricter test, Lord Murray concluded that the pursuer
had not established even breach of a fiduciary duty and so the court
could not interfere with the judgment of the majority of the shareholders.

5. In *Baird* v. *J. Baird & Co. (Falkirk) Ltd.*, 1949 S.L.T. 368
(O.H.), the case of *Harris* v. *A. Harris Ltd.* was referred to by the
Lord Ordinary (Guthrie) in support of the conclusion which he
reached as a matter of interpretation of the particular article founded
upon.

The case arose out of an annual general meeting of B. Ltd., at
which a shareholder moved that the directors should call up a loan
which B. Ltd. had made to B., who was the chairman of the meeting.
An amendment was moved that no action be taken on the matter.
The amendment was carried only because the votes of B. in respect of
the shares held by him were included.

In an action for reduction of the resolution, *held* that B. had been
entitled to vote.

Lord Guthrie (at p. 369): " The action . . . raises a question of
construction of Article 75. . . .

". . . The Article deals only with the position of the director in his
fiduciary capacity as director at meetings of the board. It does not
either expressly or impliedly impose any disqualification upon him at
meetings of members at which he is present in virtue of his membership of the company as a shareholder. As a shareholder at a general
meeting of the company he is not acting in any fiduciary capacity but
in furtherance of his own interests as a shareholder. Accordingly, as a
matter of construction of Article 75, I hold that the action is ill-
founded and that the pursuer's averments are irrelevant.

" While I have reached this conclusion as a matter of interpretation
of the particular article founded upon, I think it is supported by the
principles which have been laid down in a number of authoritative
decisions." (Lord Guthrie then referred to several cases, including
Harris v. *A. Harris Ltd.*)

Minority protection: ultra vires

Dunn v. Banknock Coal Co. Ltd.
(1901) 9 S.L.T. 51 (O.H.)

At an extraordinary general meeting of B. Ltd., two resolutions were passed relating to appointment and retiral of directors. The first of these resolutions was " That Mr. Robert Galloway ... and Mr. David Draper ... be elected directors of the Company; and that the board be empowered to elect one other member."

One of the existing directors, D., sought to interdict B. Ltd. and its board of directors from acting upon the resolutions.

Held that the resolutions were *ultra vires* and illegal, and that D. was entitled to interdict accordingly.

LORD STORMONTH DARLING (ORDINARY) (at p. 52): " The question which I have to decide ... simply is, whether the two resolutions complained of were, or were not, within the powers of the extraordinary general meeting which passed them.

" The first of these two resolutions was to the effect that two gentlemen should be elected directors of the Company, and that the board should be empowered to elect one other director. It is the last clause of this resolution that is attacked as *ultra vires,* and I am of opinion very clearly that it was. The power of electing directors is by the articles of association confided to general meetings of the Company. ... The board itself has no power to co-operate. ... This general meeting went beyond its powers in delegating the election of one director to the board. ... By the law of companies, the articles of association form a strict code which must be closely observed, and ... in this instance no warrant can be found in those articles for what this general meeting did."

NOTE

Lord Stormonth Darling further held that, as the second resolution included mention of the director who was to be elected by the board, that second resolution was also bad.

Minority protection: remedy alternative to winding up

Meyer v. The Scottish Co-operative Wholesale Society Ltd.
1958 S.C.(H.L.) 40; 1957 S.C. 110; 1954 S.C. 381

A private company, the Scottish Textile and Manufacturing Co. Ltd., had originally been formed by a co-operative wholesale society to enable the society to enter the rayon textile industry. The majority shareholder in the company was the society, and the minority shareholders were Meyer and Lucas, on whose connections, qualifications and experience the company was, at the time of its formation, dependent. Meyer and Lucas were joint managing directors of the company, and three other directors were nominated by the society.

After the company had earned substantial profits for several years, the society made an unsuccessful attempt to purchase the shares of Meyer and Lucas for less than their true value.

The society then proceeded, with the co-operation of its nominee directors on the company's board, to divert the company's trade to a new department within the society's own organisation. The result was a great reduction in the value of the company's shares.

Meyer and Lucas petitioned the court under section 210 of the Companies Act 1948.

Held that (1) the society's conduct amounted to oppression of the minority shareholders, and (2) winding up, though otherwise justified, would unfairly prejudice the minority shareholders; and *order made* on the society to purchase the petitioners' shares at the value which it was estimated that they would have had if there had been no oppression.

VISCOUNT SIMONDS (at p. 43): " Your Lordships have for the first time to consider a new and important section of the Companies Act 1948. . . .

" . . . It is common ground that at the date of presentation of the petition on July 13, 1953, it was—apart from prejudice to the respondents—' just and equitable that the company should be wound up.'. . . The only question is whether its affairs were being conducted in a manner oppressive to the respondents and, if so, whether the Court ordained the appropriate remedy. . . .

" Upon the facts . . . it appears to me incontrovertible that the society have behaved to the minority shareholders of the company in a manner which can justly be described as ' oppressive.' They had the majority power and they exercised their authority in a manner ' burdensome, harsh and wrongful '—I take the dictionary meaning of the word. . . . I do not think that my own views could be stated better than in the late Lord President Cooper's words on the first hearing of this case. ' In my view,' he said (1954 S.C. 381 at p. 391), ' this section warrants the Court in looking at the business realities of a situation and does not confine them to a narrow legalistic view. The truth is that, whenever a subsidiary is formed as in this case with an independent minority of shareholders, the parent company must, if it is engaged in the same class of business, accept as a result of having formed such a subsidiary an obligation so to conduct what are in a sense its own affairs as to deal fairly with its subsidiary.' At the opposite pole to this standard may be put the conduct of a parent company which says: ' Our subsidiary company has served its purpose, which is our purpose. Therefore let it die,' and, having thus pronounced sentence, is able to enforce it and does enforce it, not only by attack from without but also by support from within. If this section is inept to cover such a case, it will be a dead letter indeed. . . . This case . . . appears to me to be a glaring example of precisely the evil which Parliament intended to remedy."

LORD KEITH OF AVONHOLM (at p. 65): " Oppression under section 210 may take various forms. It suggests, to my mind, as I said in *Elder* v. *Elder and Watson* (1952 S.C. 49 at p. 60), a lack of probity and fair dealing in the affairs of a company to the prejudice of some portion of its members. The section introduces a wide power to the Court to deal with such a situation in an equitable manner which it did not have in the case of a company before the passing of the Act of 1948. The Court has here acted, in my opinion, within the powers conferred upon it.

" It was said that appeal could not be made to section 210, unless the company had a continuing life ahead of it, and that here it was clear that the company would have to be wound up. But that means that, if oppression is carried to the extent of destruction of the business of the company, no recourse can be had to the remedies of the section. This would be to defeat the whole purpose of the section. The present position is due to the oppression, and, but for the oppression, it must be assumed that the company would be an active and presumably flourishing concern. The section is, in my opinion, very apt to meet the situation which has arisen."

LORD DENNING (at p. 68): " The affairs of a company can, in my opinion, be conducted oppressively by the directors doing nothing to defend its interests when they ought to do something—just as they can conduct its affairs oppressively by doing something injurious to its interests when they ought not to do it. . . .

" Now, I quite agree that the words of the section do suggest that the Legislature had in mind some remedy whereby the company, instead of being wound up, might continue to operate. But it would be wrong to infer therefrom that the remedy under section 210 is limited to cases where the company is still in active business. The object of the remedy is to bring ' to an end the matters complained of,' that is, the oppression, and this can be done even though the business of the company has been brought to a standstill. ... Even though the oppressor by his oppression brings down the whole edifice—destroying the value of his own shares with those of everyone else—the injured shareholders have, I think, a remedy under section 210.

" ... The section gives a large discretion to the Court and it is well exercised in making an oppressor make compensation to those who have suffered at his hands.

" True it is that in this, as in other respects, your Lordships are giving a liberal interpretation to section 210. But it is a new section designed to suppress an acknowledged mischief. When it comes before this House for the first time it is, I believe, in accordance with long precedent ... that your Lordships should give such construction as shall advance the remedy. And that is what your Lordships do to-day."

Court of Session (1957)

LORD RUSSELL (at p. 137): " The ordinary meaning of the term ' oppression ' connotes the exercise of power in a tyrannical and unjust manner. I respectfully agree with what was stated by the Lord President (Cooper) in the case of *Elder* v. *Elder & Watson* at p. 55, that the word in its present context means the unfair abuse of powers, manifesting a visible departure from the standards of fair dealing. ...

" ... The society representatives on the company's board, wielding their powers as majority shareholders, are proved to have conducted the affairs of the company unfairly and in a manner ' oppressive ' to the petitioners as minority shareholders within the meaning of section 210."

Court of Session (1954)

LORD PRESIDENT (COOPER) (at p. 390): " The question is whether the petitioners are to be given an opportunity of proving [their story], or whether, even if proved to the hilt, the story would not fit the requirements of section 210 or justify the remedy asked. ...

" Finally, a point is taken with regard to the statutory requirement that the oppression must affect ' some part of the members,' the suggestion being that section 210 is not available in any case where all the members, as distinguished from a part, are in the same boat. In other words, it is maintained that the section has no operation where Samson destroys himself as well as the Philistines in a single catastrophe, the point being that in this case the society hold 4,000 of the shares the value of which they are said to have deliberately depressed. I have come to think that this is to give too narrow a meaning to this remedial provision, and to place on the words ' some part ' an emphasis which they were not intended to bear. . . . If the section bears the meaning suggested by the respondents, it will fail of effect in a class of case to which its spirit is plainly applicable. It is not essential for the application of section 210 that the oppressor should have made a profit as a result of his oppression, and I see no sufficient reason for inferring as a requirement that he must not *qua* shareholder have made a loss or the same loss *pro rata* as the complainer. The section is not concerned with the results to the oppressor but with the results to those who complain of the oppression."

NOTE

In *Elder* v. *Elder & Watson Ltd.*, 1952 S.C. 49, the petitioners, Elder and Glass, shareholders in a small private company, averred that they had suffered oppression at the hands of other shareholders who had used their combined voting powers to remove the petitioners from their offices as directors and from their employment as secretary and factory manager respectively.

The petition under section 210 of the Companies Act 1948 was *dismissed* as irrelevant, on the grounds that (1) section 210 was intended to apply in cases of oppression of members in their character as such, and in this case the matters complained of affected the petitioners solely in the character of director or employee, and (2) no facts had been averred which would have justified a winding-up order on ' just and equitable ' grounds.

Lord President (Cooper) (at p. 55): " The application for relief is . . . envisaged as one of an oppressed minority of shareholders. On such a petition the Court can only act under the section on being satisfied of three matters: (i) that the company's affairs are being conducted in a manner oppressive to some part of the members (including the petitioner); (ii) that to wind up the company would unfairly prejudice that part of the members; and (iii) that otherwise the facts would justify the making of a winding-up order under the ' just and equitable ' clause.

" In the present case it is conceded that . . . condition (ii) is satisfied. . . . The introduction into section 210 of condition (iii) refers us back to the pre-1947 practice under the ' just and equitable ' clause, and is a salutary reminder of the fact that the new remedy is not lightly to be accorded. . . . Where the 'just and equitable' jurisdiction has been applied in cases of this type, the circumstances have always, I think, been such as to warrant the inference that there has been, at least, an unfair abuse of powers and an impairment of confidence in the probity with which the company's affairs are being conducted, as distinguished from mere resentment on the part of a minority at being outvoted on some issue of domestic policy. . . . The essence of the matter seems to be that the conduct complained of should at the lowest involve a visible departure from the standards of fair dealing, and a violation of the conditions of fair play on which every shareholder who entrusts his money to a company is entitled to rely. . . .

". . . The true grievance is that . . . George Elder and James Glass have lost the positions which they formerly held as directors and officers of the company. I do not consider that section 210 was intended to meet any such case, the 'oppression' required by the section being oppression of members in their character as such. I do not think that a 'just and equitable' winding-up has ever yet been ordered merely because of changes effected in the board of directors or the dismissal of officers, and very strong grounds would be needed to justify such a step. . . .

". . . Conditions (i) and (iii) are not in my judgment satisfied."

Lord Keith (at p. 58): " Apart from the Board of Trade, . . . it is only a member who can invoke the section, and, in my opinion, this means a member in his capacity as member, and further, in my opinion, his only relevant ground of complaint is oppression of his rights as a member, because of the manner in which the affairs of the company are being conducted. An employee who has been treated oppressively has no remedy under this section and a member who is an employee can, in my opinion, have no recourse to this section merely because of treatment he has suffered as an employee. The same holds, in my opinion, of a member who is a director or holds other office in the company and whose only complaint is of deprivation of such office by whatever manner achieved. . . .

". . . Oppression involves, I think, at least an element of lack of probity or fair dealing to a member in the matter of his proprietary rights as a shareholder. . . .

". . . The company's affairs must be conducted in a manner oppressive to some part of the members, and that connotes to my mind an abuse of power by some person or persons controlling the company, resulting in injury to the rights of some part of its members. . . .

" In the present case I am satisfied that there are no circumstances avered in the petition relevant to infer oppression within the meaning of the section. . . . I can find . . . no suggestion that anything that was done was designed to injure the petitioners in their rights as shareholders or did in fact do so. At the most, the averments seem to me to disclose no more than differences of opinion as to the management of the company, giving rise perhaps to animosities and to exclusion of the first and second-named petitioners from office and employment in the company. There is nothing to suggest that the company is not being conducted efficiently by the existing board in the interests of the members as a whole. . . . Equally I find no relevant ground for holding that this would be a case for a winding-up under the ' just and equitable ' clause."

Chapter 15

DIRECTORS

Qualification shares

**Liquidator of the Consolidated Copper Co. of Canada Ltd.
v. Peddie, &c.
(1877) 5 R. 393**

The articles of association of C. Ltd. named certain persons as its first directors, and also provided that "no person shall be eligible to, or shall continue in, the office of director, unless he be the holder in his own right of shares representing at par the nominal sum of £300 in the capital of the company."

Held that this provision as to qualification shares applied only to directors subsequently elected, and that the directors nominated by the articles had therefore come under no implied agreement to take the minimum number of qualification shares.

LORD JUSTICE-CLERK (MONCREIFF) (at p. 408): "It is now said that these four gentlemen acted as directors of the company, and that in consequence of a clause in the articles of association relative to the qualification of directors they must be held to have been shareholders to the extent of the number of shares necessary to qualify them for the position of directors. The article to which I refer is the 18th article. . . . That provision follows immediately after the 17th article, in which certain persons are nominated to be the original and first directors, and the four persons as to whom the question now arises are all named there. . . .

" . . . I have come to a very clear impression . . . that the 18th clause in these articles of association does not apply and cannot apply, and never was intended to apply, to a nominated director."

NOTES

1. For another point raised by this case, see the chapter on Application and Allotment at p. 108, above.

2. In *The Kingsburgh Motor Construction Co. Ltd.* v. *Scott* (1902) 10 S.L.T. 424 (O.H.), Lord Stormonth Darling held that a director was bound to take qualification shares allotted to him, although he had in the meantime intimated his resignation.

The action was for payment of calls on shares which had been allotted to S. as qualification shares on December 1, 1900. S. had intimated his resignation of office on October 30, 1900, and by a clause in the articles his office thereby fell vacant after three months, *i.e.* on January 30, 1901.

Lord Stormonth Darling (at p. 425): " His resignation did not take effect until . . . January 30, 1901.

" . . . I cannot for a moment assent to the view that merely because he intimated his wish to retire from the office of director his colleagues could treat him as if he were no longer a director, or, in other words, could treat his office as vacant. . . . The directors were not only entitled but bound to allot these shares and to make this call."

3. Shares held in trust may count as qualification shares: *The Galloway Saloon Steam Packet Co.* v. *Wallace* (1891) 19 R. 320. This is so even where articles provide that the qualification shares must be held by the director " in his own name and right ": *Elliot* v. *J. W. Mackie & Sons Ltd.*, 1935 S.C. 81. For these cases see Note 16 to *Muir, &c.* v. *The City of Glasgow Bank* in the chapter on Membership (pp. 144, 145, above).

Remuneration and expenses

McNaughtan v. Brunton
(1882) 10 R. 111

The Musselburgh Wire Mills Co. Ltd. was incorporated in 1878. By its articles of association B. was appointed one of the first directors, his remuneration to be fixed by the board until otherwise determined by the company in general meeting.

At a meeting of the board B. intimated that if he were appointed managing director he would subscribe for 50 other shares and would undertake his duties gratuitously until the company was in a position to pay a dividend of 5 per cent. B. was appointed managing director.

In 1880, at a meeting of shareholders, a resolution was passed appointing B. and another director to advertise the mill for sale but in the meantime continue its business.

In 1881, the shareholders resolved that the company should be wound up voluntarily, and McN. was appointed liquidator.

B. retained a fee of £42 for his time and expenses in the years 1880-1881, and McN. presented a petition to court to have B. ordained to pay that sum.

The court *granted* the prayer of the petition, reserving any claim to B. for actual outlay incurred by him on the company's behalf.

Lord President (Inglis) (at p. 113): " These duties were

undertaken by Messrs. Brunton and Brown, as directors of the company, and it is for work done under that appointment that the claim is made. Now, it is clearly the law that where a party holds a fiduciary position, whether as a director of a company, or one of a body of trustees, no matter how he is appointed, unless there is some express provision in the contract under which he acts that he shall receive remuneration, he must do the work gratuitously. Applying that principle here, I think we are bound to give decree for the £42, but as there is some doubt as to whether that sum includes actual outlay incurred by Mr. Brunton, I think we may reserve any claim he may have on that score."

NOTES

1. In *Marmor Ltd.* v. *Alexander,* 1908 S.C. 78, a provision in articles of association giving directors a right to be indemnified by the company for expenses incurred in the execution of their offices was held not to cover expenses incurred by a director in travelling from his home in Glasgow to attend board meetings in London.

Lord President (Dunedin) (at p. 80): " I do not think that a payment to a director, in order to get from his own dwelling-house to where the Company has its meetings, is an expense which he is put to in the execution of his office. He only begins to execute his office for the Company at the directors' meetings. I am not doubting that a payment of travelling expenses could be perfectly well made to a director where the director, at the request of the other directors, undertakes any special visit of inspection, or undertakes to go anywhere where he would not naturally be in the interests of the Company. . . . But the ordinary expense which a man incurs in getting from where he himself chooses to live to the seat of the Company's business does not seem to me to be expense that is incurred in the execution of his office at all. . . . In a question with the Company he is bound to refund this illegal payment."

2. In *Harris* v. *A. Harris Ltd.,* 1936 S.C. 183, joint managing directors were held entitled to use their voting power as majority shareholders to pass a resolution at a general meeting with the effect of increasing their own remuneration, this resolution being neither a fraud on the minority nor *ultra vires* of the company. See Note 4 to *Rixon* v. *Edinburgh Northern Tramways Co.,* in the chapter on Majority Rule and Minority Protection at p. 254, above.

3. Where remuneration is stated as being " £X per annum " (as distinct from " at the rate of £X per annum "), the remuneration is payable only in respect of completed periods of one year, no apportionment being made in respect of lesser periods. This was held to be the position in Scots law in *Liquidator of the Fife Linoleum and Floorcloth Co. Ltd.* v. *Lornie* (1905) 12 S.L.T. 670 (O.H.).

The articles of association of F. Ltd. provided: " The members of the Board shall be entitled to set apart, and receive for their remuneration, such sum, not being less than four hundred guineas per annum, as the company may, in general meeting, determine. Such sum shall be divided amongst the members of the Board in equal shares —unless the Board shall otherwise determine amongst themselves.

L. had served upon the board for three years and seven months.

Lord Salvesen (Ordinary), following English authorities, held that L. was not entitled to remuneration for periods of service of less than one year.

Lord Salvesen also held, on an interpretation of the article quoted, that a resolution of the board was not a condition precedent to the right of a director to receive an equal share with his co-directors of the minimum lump sum stated in the article as the board's remuneration.

4. Expenses incurred in a successful defence to a criminal charge may not be covered by an indemnification clause in the articles: *Tomlinson* v. *Liquidators of Scottish Amalgamated Silks Ltd.*, 1935 S.C. (H.L.) 1; 1934 S.C. 85.

The articles of S. Ltd. provided for the indemnification of any director against all costs, losses and expenses which he might incur by reason of any act done by him as director.

S. Ltd. went into voluntary liquidation, and T., who had been a promoter and director, was tried for alleged fraud, the charges being that he had issued a fraudulent prospectus and had fraudulently misapplied funds of the company.

T. was acquitted, and thereupon lodged a claim in the liquidation for the expenses, amounting to £11,524 13s. 2d., incurred by him in his defence.

The liquidators rejected T.'s claim, and T. appealed to the court.

Held that T. was not entitled to his expenses either under the indemnity clause in the articles or at common law, since expenses incurred in defending himself against an allegation that he did something, which he did not in fact do and which it was not his duty to do, were not expenses incurred by him as a director or as an agent of the company in the discharge of his duties.

Articles indemnifying a director against liability for negligence, default, breach of duty or breach of trust in relation to the company are void under section 205 of the Companies Act 1948. There is, however, the proviso that a company may indemnify a director against any liability incurred by him in defending any proceedings, whether civil or criminal, in which judgment is given in his favour or in which he is acquitted. An application for relief may also be made to court under section 448 of the Act.

5. By section 189 of the Companies Act 1948, it is not lawful for a company to pay a director remuneration (whether as director or otherwise) free of income tax, and such a provision in a contract takes effect as if it provided for payment, as a gross sum subject to income tax, of the net sum for which it actually provides. *Owens* v. *Multilux Ltd.*, 1974 S.L.T. 189 (N.I.R.C.), involved an application of these provisions.

O. had been managing director of M. Ltd. in terms of an agreement under which his salary was to be "£2,500 per annum net of deductions." He had been paid £50 per week through the company secretary, and M. Ltd. had paid the stamps on O.'s national insurance card. Differences of opinion arose between O. and his fellow directors, and O.'s employment was terminated. O. had never been supplied with written particulars of the terms of his employment in accordance with the provisions of the Contracts of Employment Act 1972, and he applied to the industrial tribunal, for a determination by the tribunal of the " scale or rate of remuneration or the method of calculating remuneration," which ought to have been stated in the statutory particulars.

The tribunal held that the agreement did not mean that the company would be liable for income tax. O. appealed to the National Industrial Relations Court against this decision.

Held that O.'s legal right was to payment of a gross sum of £2,500 per annum subject to income tax. Appeal *refused*.

Judgment of the National Industrial Relations Court (at p. 190): " In our view, . . . the terms of section 189 of the Companies Act 1948 are themselves conclusive against the appellant and it is not necessary to consider what the parties themselves believed to be the legal import of a salary of ' £2,500 net of deductions '."

Right to inspect minutes of board meetings and books of account: nobile officium

McCusker v. McRae
1966 S.C. 253

McC., one of the two directors of Rob Roy Highland Motels Ltd., presented a petition under the *nobile officium* for an order on the company to make available for inspection by himself " and by such men of skill as he may instruct to assist him " the minutes of all proceedings at directors' meetings kept under section 145 of the Companies Act 1948 and the books of account kept under section 147 of that Act.

Answers were lodged for McR., the other director.

At the court's suggestion, the prayer of the petition was amended so that there was substituted for the words " such men of skill as he may instruct to assist him " the name and designation of a specific accountant.

The court *granted* the prayer of the petition, as amended.

NOTES

1. No opinions were delivered.

2. The petition was under the *nobile officium* because the statutory provisions founded on did not expressly confer any right of inspection. Contrast the other part of this case, relating to inspection of minutes of general meetings (p. 244, above).

Managing director

Anderson v. James Sutherland (Peterhead) Ltd.
1941 S.C. 203

The articles of association of S. Ltd. conferred on the directors power to appoint and remove managing directors, and also provided that " whenever any member of the company who is employed by the company in any capacity is dismissed " for misconduct, the directors might resolve that such person should cease to be a member.

A., a managing director, was convicted of assault by the firing of a revolver at a directors' meeting, and the other directors passed two resolutions—(1) that A. be dismissed from his post as managing director, and (2) that A. should cease to be a member.

A. contested the validity of the second resolution, on the ground that as managing director he was not " employed " by the company.

Held that, for the purposes of the provision in the articles, A. was " employed " by the company, and that the resolution was therefore valid.

LORD CARMONT (at p. 213): " It appears to me significant that the language of article 14 is ' member employed by the company in any capacity,' for employment is of wider application than contract of service. . . .

" . . . The qualification of employment ' in any capacity ' removes any doubt. This view of the pursuer's position is in harmony with the decision of this Division of the Court in *Hindle* v. *John Cotton, Limited* ((1919) 56 S.L.R. 625 (H.L.)), which has been dragged by the industry of counsel for the defenders from some obscurity among the reports of cases on this point, although in other connections it has the importance of a House of Lords decision which reversed the Court below on other grounds. A good deal may turn on the particular wording of the articles in the case, but it seems to be clear that there is nothing to prevent a managing director being treated as being in the company's employment. There are *dicta* in the case of *Kerr* v. *Walker* (1933 S.C. 458) in regard to this matter, but they are in conflict *inter se*. A limited company which was empowered by its memorandum of association ' to give pensions to any person in the employment of the company and the widows of any such persons ' undertook to pay an annuity of fixed amount to the widow of a director who had held at the same time the position of a salaried manager (not being the managing director, which post was held by another director). The company went into liquidation, and the Court held that the terms of the agreement showed that the payment of the annuity was to be contingent on the continued existence of the company. That was sufficient for the decision of the case, but the various judges expressed views as to the position of the director manager. Lord Hunter said . . . 'I do not think that his co-directors were entitled to treat him as an employee so as to justify their making a gratuitous payment to his widow. . . . ' . . . Lord Murray thought on the other hand that . . . Kerr *qua* manager was an employee of the company and that the grant of the annuity was therefore *intra vires* of the board . . . The Lord Justice-Clerk (Alness) does not deal with the matter at all, and Lord Anderson reserves his opinion as to whether a director can ever be an employee albeit appointed manager. . . . I think the language of article 14 is so wide that it will cover under the phrase ' employment in any capacity ' the functions exercised by the pursuer, for which he was paid a salary, over and above his director's functions."

LORD PRESIDENT (NORMAND) (at p. 217): " I accept the view that a director as such is not the servant or employee of the company. . . . In my opinion . . . the managing director has two functions and two capacities. *Qua* managing director he is a party to a contract with the company, and this contract is a contract of employment. . . .

" . . . I . . . construe article 14 as applying to any member of the company, whether a director or not, who is employed by the company in any capacity, whether as managing director or in some humbler way, who has been guilty of conduct prejudicial to the company. Such a construction seems to me to give effect to every word of the article in its natural sense."

NOTES

1. *Hindle* v. *John Cotton Ltd.* (1919) 56 S.L.R. 625 (H.L.): The articles of association of C. Ltd. included a provision that whenever a member was dismissed from the " employment " of the company for breach of faith, misconduct, or other offence which the directors deemed prejudicial to the interests of the company, the directors might, at any time after the " employee " had been dismissed, resolve that he should cease to be a member.

The directors, having dismissed H., the managing director, resolved that he should cease to be a member, and they appropriated H.'s shares for the amount paid up on them, although the shares were said to be worth a large premium.

The Lord Ordinary (Ormidale) held that H.'s averments were relevant to infer that the directors had acted in bad faith in passing the resolution, and he allowed a proof.

On appeal, the First Division, holding that there were no averments of want of good faith on the part of the directors, dismissed the action.

The House of Lords reversed the interlocutor of the First Division and allowed a proof.

The Lord Ordinary, on the question whether H. was an employee, said (at p. 627): " In my opinion he was. . . . Article 115 provides for ' managing director' and ' manager' indifferently. I mean that the provisions of the article . . . are equally applicable to the holder of either office. The directors have identically the same powers as to the appointment, the remuneration, and the dismissal of both. These are the ordinary *indicia* of employment, and it seems to me that the pursuer having been appointed by the directors of the company, remunerated by them, and being liable to dismissal by them, was an employee of the company in the sense of article 36."

In the Inner House Lord President Strathclyde and Lord Mackenzie expressed agreement with the Lord Ordinary's view on that point.

In the House of Lords this question was not commented upon.

2. In *Kerr* v. *Walker,* 1933 S.C. 458, Walker was the liquidator of the company (R. S. Kerr (Glasgow) Ltd.).

3. In *Dunlop* v. *Donald* (1893) 21 R. 125, a managing director was held to be an " officer of the company " within the meaning of a statutory provision then in the Companies Act 1862, s. 100, and now in the Companies Act 1948, s. 258, under which the court may, at any time after making a winding-up order, require any contributory, trustee, receiver, banker, agent or " officer of the company " to pay or transfer to the liquidator any money or property in his hands to which the company is *prima facie* entitled.

Donald's Chlorine Co. Ltd. had been incorporated in 1890, one of its objects being to acquire and work patents, then held by Donald, for the manufacture of chlorine.

Under an agreement between Donald and the company, Donald had received fully paid shares and a cash sum, but had not assigned the patents to the company by 1893, when a winding-up order was made, Dunlop being appointed liquidator. Donald had been managing director of the company since its commencement.

Dunlop craved the court to ordain Donald to assign the patents to him, but Donald maintained that he was not an " officer of the company " within the meaning of the statutory provision.

Lord Adam (at p. 132): " No doubt, as manager his powers are limited to the technical or manufacturing department, but I see no reason why the manager of a company is not an officer of that company."

4. In *Allison* v. *Scotia Motor and Engineering Co. Ltd.* (1906) 14 S.L.T. 9 (O.H.), Lord Mackenzie held that Wark, the managing director of the company, had authority to engage a works manager, A., with the result that, when the company's affairs did not prosper and, on the directors' instructions, A. was dismissed by Wark without notice, A. was held entitled to damages from the company.

Lord Mackenzie (at p. 10): " There was no express delegation by Minute of the Board of any of their powers to Wark, as managing director, under Article 94. . . . In appointing the pursuer as works manager Wark took it upon himself, with the knowledge of the directors, to act for the Company. I think that the pursuer dealt in *bona fide* with Wark, and was entitled to assume that he had the power to make the agreement."

5. In *Caddies* v. *Harold Holdsworth & Co. (Wakefield) Ltd.*, 1955 S.C.(H.L.) 27, an agreement appointing C. as managing director for a period of five years was interpreted as permitting the board of directors to pass a resolution the effect of which was to confine C.'s activities to one of the company's subsidiaries. C. was therefore not entitled to damages for breach of contract.

The clause of the agreement being interpreted was in these terms: " Mr. Caddies shall be and he is hereby appointed a managing director of the company and as such managing director he shall perform the duties and exercise the powers in relation to the business of the company and the businesses (howsoever carried on) of its existing subsidiary companies at the date hereof which may from time to time be assigned to or vested in him by the board of directors of the company."

The House of Lords (*diss.* Lord Keith of Avonholm) reversed the judgment of the First Division.

Lord Chancellor (Kilmuir) (at p. 41): " I cannot find, either in the statute or in the cases in which the matter has been considered, anything to prevent a board of directors appointing a managing director and limiting his duties according to their own wishes."

Lord Reid (at p. 50): " The agreement of 1949 appoints the respondent a managing director (not the managing director) of the appellant company. The law does not specify the duties of a managing director and there is no averment that they were specified in the articles of association. . . .

". . . The parties are left to define his duties, and I can see nothing inconsistent in an agreement that a person shall be a managing director of a company but shall devote his attention to managing subsidiary companies."

Lord Keith of Avonholm (*diss.*) was of opinion that a proof was necessary to assess the whole surrounding facts and circumstances before the question of breach of the agreement could properly be decided.

Director's fiduciary duties

Aberdeen Railway Co. v. Blaikie Bros.
(1854) 1 Macq. 461

B., the managing partner of B. Bros., a firm of iron-founders, was also a director of the A. Railway Co.

B. Bros. brought an action against the A. Railway Co. for implement of a contract whereby the company had agreed to purchase certain iron chairs to be manufactured by B. Bros.

Held that B., being, as director, in the position of trustee for the company, was precluded from contracting on its behalf with a firm of which he was himself a partner.

LORD CHANCELLOR (CRANWORTH) (at p. 471): " The Directors are a body to whom is delegated the duty of managing the general affairs of the Company.

" A corporate body can only act by agents, and it is of course the duty of those agents so to act as best to promote the interests of the corporation whose affairs they are conducting. Such agents have duties to discharge of a fiduciary nature towards their principal. And it is a rule of universal application, that no one, having such duties to discharge, shall be allowed to enter into engagements in which he has, or can have, a personal interest conflicting, or which possibly may conflict, with the interests of those whom he is bound to protect.

" So strictly is this principle adhered to, that no question is allowed to be raised as to the fairness or unfairness of a contract so entered into.

. . .

" . . . Mr. Blaikie was not only a Director, but (if that was necessary) the Chairman of the Directors. In that character it was his bounden duty to make the best bargains he could for the benefit of the Company.

" While he filled that character, . . . he entered into a contract on behalf of the Company with his own firm, for the purchase of a large quantity of iron chairs at a certain stipulated price. His duty to the Company imposed on him the obligation of obtaining these chairs at the lowest possible price.

" His personal interest would lead him in an entirely opposite direction, would induce him to fix the price as high as possible. This is the very evil against which the rule in question is directed, and I here see nothing whatsoever to prevent its application. . . .

" . . . He put his interest in conflict with his duty, and whether he was the sole Director or only one of many, can make no difference in principle.

" The same observation applies to the fact that he was not the sole person contracting with the Company; he was one of the firm of Blaikie, Brothers, with whom the contract was made, and so interested in driving as hard a bargain with the Company as he could induce them to make.

" It cannot be contended that the rule to which I have referred is one confined to the English law, and that it does not apply to Scotland.

" It so happens that one of the leading authorities on the subject is a decision of this House on an appeal from Scotland. I refer to the case of *The York Buildings Company* v. *Mackenzie* ((1795) 3 Paton 378). . . .

" There the respondent, Mackenzie, while he filled the office of ' Common Agent ' in the sale of the estates of the appellants, who had become insolvent, purchased a portion of them at a judicial auction; and though he had remained in possession for above 11 years after the purchase, and had entirely freed himself from all imputation of fraud, yet this House held that filling as he did an office which made it his duty both to the insolvents and their creditors to obtain the highest price, he could not put himself in the position of purchaser, and so make it his interest that the price paid should be as low as possible."

NOTES

1. A director who holds shares is not, in his capacity as shareholder, in a fiduciary relationship towards the company.

Accordingly, in *McLintock* v. *Campbell*, 1916 S.C. 968, a director was held to have been entitled to transfer his shares, which were not fully paid, to a person of no means at a time when the financial position of the company was known to the director to be hopeless.

C., a director of the Cosmopolitan Insurance Corporation Ltd., held preferred and deferred shares of the company. In October 1914 he transferred his deferred shares, on which there was a total liability of £1,980, to Miss Berry, his housekeeper. He retained his preferred shares, all of which were fully paid.

In February 1915 a resolution was passed for the voluntary winding up of the company, and the liquidator presented a petition for rectification of the register by the restoration of C.'s name in place of Miss Berry's name.

Held that, since the transfer had been absolute and unqualified, C.'s name could not be restored to the register.

Lord President (Strathclyde) (at p. 972): " The shares held by a director of a company are his separate property, and he is in no sense a trustee of them for the company. Directors of a company are not trustees of their individual interests in the company. Like any other shareholder in the company they can transfer their shares to men of straw in order to avoid a call. . . . A transfer of his shares by a director of a company to a man of straw made for the sole purpose of avoiding a call will stand good, provided the divestiture is absolute and unqualified."

Lord Johnston (*diss.*) (at p. 973): "If Mr. Campbell, the respondent, is to escape, it can only be on grounds subversive of the common faith in the British practice of confiding the management of joint stock concerns to boards of directors.

"The question may be thus stated: Where a director must be aware that the ship is drifting on to the sands—still more where by his action he shows that he is aware—can he, down to the last moment, if the collective board make no move, by a transfer to a man of straw, save his own skin, regardless of the interests of the company; or has he individually, as well as the board collectively, a duty as director to protect the company against the consequences of such action on the part of himself as well as others, a breach of which duty will leave him liable in subsequent liquidation to have his name restored to the register of shareholders if it has been removed?

"I think that there is such a duty, and that in this case it has been breached with the consequences above indicated. . . .

". . . The director's functions are in one view those of an agent, and in another those of a trustee. But the former predominate over the latter. He does not act gratuitously, but for remuneration. It is true that the legal title of property of the company is not vested in him, and that his primary duty is not to conserve merely, as a trustee, the property committed to his charge, while making it with security return an income, but to apply it within definite lines at business risk. . . . I think that it may be correctly said that trust is involved in all agency, but a greater degree of trust in some kinds of agency than in others; and the fact that in a paid directorship the higher degree of trust is implied, as in the case of a managing partner, is made all the more pointed by the wide powers of management conferred on a board of directors and their independence of practical control from the shareholders. . . .

". . . Mr. Campbell cannot shelter himself behind the collective board. He was participant in their culpable negligence and inaction, and *individually he took advantage of it.* . . . He is bound to restore the Company in liquidation against the consequences of the advantage which he took of his own and his colleagues' laches."

Similarly, in *Harris* v. *A. Harris Ltd.* (Note 4 to *Rixon* v. *Edinburgh Northern Tramways Co.,* p. 254, above) directors were held entitled to use their voting power although the effect was to increase their own remuneration, and in *Baird* v. *J. Baird & Co. (Falkirk) Ltd.* (Note 5 to *Rixon* v. *Edinburgh Northern Tramways Co.,* p. 256, above) a director was held entitled to vote so as to prevent the passing of a resolution for the calling up of a loan which had been made to him by the company.

2. *A fortiori* directors owe no fiduciary duty to applicants for shares. This point occurs in the opinions in *Brown* v. *Stewart* (see chapter on Majority Rule and Minority Protection, at p. 251, above).

The Lord Ordinary (Stormonth-Darling) said (at 1 F. 319): " When, therefore, the directors, on April 23, allotted to him the number of shares for which he had applied, they accepted his offer precisely in its terms. It is said that . . . they ought not to have proceeded to allotment, but ought to have returned to the pursuer and the other applicants the money deposited on application. It seems to me that they were under no such obligation, because they had no trust duty to any applicant before he became a shareholder. Their duty was to the body corporate of which they were directors."

In the Inner House, Lord Kinnear said (at p. 323): " The material point is that in making the allotment the defenders were not acting as trustees for the pursuer. They were acting for the company already constituted, and making a bargain with the pursuer at arm's length. As the Lord Ordinary has pointed out, they had no duty to him till he became a shareholder."

The same point arose in *Wilson* v. *Dunlop, Bremner & Co. Ltd.*, 1921 1 S.L.T. 35 (O.H.) and 354.

W. raised an action against D. Ltd. and against its directors for payment of £941 4s. 3d. as damages on the ground of the defenders' failure to allot certain shares to him. In so far as the action was directed against the company, the legal basis of W.'s claim was breach of contract, and in so far as the individual directors were sued, the legal ground of action was breach of trust.

Held that in so far as the case was laid against the individual directors W.'s averments were irrelevant.

Lord Anderson (Ordinary) (at p. 38): " To an applicant for shares of the company directors are not responsible as trustees and liable as for breach of trust. In exceptional cases, such as *Brenes & Co.* (1914 S.C. 97), there may be fiduciary obligation on the part of directors to a third party, such as a creditor paying money to the director for company purposes, but there are in the present case no special circumstances to shew that the pursuer relied on the individual credit of the company's directors."

The Second Division adhered to the Lord Ordinary's interlocutor, holding that W. had not succeeded in setting out any relevant case of damages against any of the individual directors.

In the case of *Brenes & Co.* v. *Downie*, 1914 S.C. 97, referred to by the Lord Ordinary as being exceptional, the company consisted of two shareholders who were also its sole directors. These two individuals had received from the company's correspondents in Central America a sum of £1,000 to be applied in meeting bills of exchange drawn on the company and shortly to become due. The company did not meet the bills on their maturity.

The foreign correspondents brought an action against the two directors personally.

Held that the directors' actings amounted not merely to breach of contract but to breach of trust, for which they were personally and jointly and severally liable.

Lord Johnston (at p. 104): "What is complained of is that . . . Mr. Downie, the defenders' managing director, drew for his own purpose upon an account which he knew contained nothing but the proceeds of drafts which had been sent to his Company under a definite contract to be applied to a definite purpose, and which had not been so applied. I cannot hold that that was anything other than misappropriating property which he had no right to touch.

". . . This is technically a registered Company, but it is one of those private companies which it is now possible to create, consisting of two gentlemen who themselves are the directors, and themselves are the shareholders, and therefore themselves are the Company. . . . The directors of an ordinary limited public company cannot, of course, know the whole details of the company's banking accounts. I regard this case as one in which there is a company only in name; it consisted of two individuals knowing everything that was done in the company, and knowing, in particular, that the only sum that they had to draw upon was a sum placed in their hands for a definite purpose and under a definite obligation, and they actively and passively allowed it to be appropriated to the private purposes of one of them."

3. *Cook* v. *Barry, Henry & Cook Ltd.*, 1923 S.L.T. 692 (O.H.) illustrates the directors' fiduciary duty in relation to the allotment of shares.

C. had been the leading shareholder in B. Ltd. On his death his shares passed to his widow and two sons. The other two shareholders, who were the surviving directors of the company, so allotted unissued shares of the company as to deprive C.'s representatives of the voting control which C. had formerly held.

Held that the directors had acted in breach of their fiduciary duty.

Lord Morison (Ordinary) (at p. 693): "There was no dispute as to the law applicable to a question of this character. . . . Such a power as is conferred on the defenders . . . is a fiduciary power which must be exercised by them *bona fide* for the real interests of the company. . . .

". . . I hold on the evidence that they did not exercise the power *in bona fide* for the general advantage of the company, but in my opinion they made the issue solely in pursuance of their determination to establish the control of the company—a control which they . . . intended to use and did use for their own advantage and for the purpose of defeating the wishes of the pursuers, who were the majority of the shareholders of the company. In these circumstances it appears to me that the defenders acted in breach of their fiduciary duty and that the issue of the said shares . . . was illegal and *ultra vires*."

4. The decision in *John S. Boyle Ltd.* v. *Boyle's Trs.*, 1949 S.L.T. (Notes) 45 (O.H.) also turned on the fiduciary relationship between a company and a director.

B. had been the majority shareholder and governing director of B. Ltd. As governing director B. exercised very wide powers.

After B.'s death, questions arose between the company and B.'s trustees concerning the repayment of £3,000 which B. was alleged to have taken from the company's funds. The sum was proved to have been a loan made by the company to B. during her lifetime.

B.'s trustees contended that this loan could be proved only by the writ or oath of the debtor, while the company maintained that, as B. had stood in a special fiduciary relationship towards the company, the same formal proof as would have been required if the transaction had been between strangers was not necessary.

Held by Lord Sorn (Ordinary) that formal proof was not necessary. Decree *granted* for £3,000.

5. The fiduciary position of directors was commented on in the speeches in the House of Lords in *Hindle* v. *John Cotton Ltd.* (Note 1 to *Anderson* v. *James Sutherland (Peterhead) Ltd.,* p. 271, above).

Viscount Finlay (at 56 S.L.R. 630): " Where the question is one of abuse of powers, the state of mind of those who acted, and the motive on which they acted, are all important, and you may go into the question of what their intention was, collecting from the surrounding circumstances all the materials which genuinely throw light upon that question of the state of mind of the directors so as to show whether they were honestly acting in discharge of their powers in the interests of the company or were acting from some bye-motive, possibly of personal advantage, or for any other reason. . . . An inquiry . . . must take place. . . .

". . . I can see no grounds for reversing the decision of the Lord Ordinary that this matter should go to proof on the question of *bona fides.*"

Lord Shaw (at p. 631): " The substantial averment of the pursuer . . . is this, that the moving cause of the resolution to dismiss the pursuer was not the interests of the company, but was the aggrandisement of the directors themselves. Directors in view of the opportunity of such personal gain must of course be scrupulously careful in the wielding of the serious power committed to them to have regard to the true interests of the company itself."

6. In *Henderson* v. *The Huntington Copper and Sulphur Co. Ltd.* (see chapter on Promoters, p. 73, above) H. was held to have stood in a fiduciary relation to the company from the date when he agreed to become a director, and was therefore bound to pay to the company the £10,000 which he had received from the vendor of the mines purchased by the company.

Similarly, in *Scottish Pacific Coast Mining Co. Ltd.* v. *Falkner, Bell, & Co.* (see chapter on Promoters, p. 75, above) the firm in which W., a director of a new company, was a partner was held bound to pay to the company a profit of £7,000 which it had made as a result of the sale of mines to the company, since W. had, with the knowledge of his firm, occupied a fiduciary position towards the company.

7. In *Great North of Scotland Railway Co.* v. *Urquhart* (1884) 21 S.L.R. 377 the railway company alleged that there had been an agreement between the company and U., a director, that U. should, jointly with the company, purchase the estate of Milnfield and then convey a field adjoining Elgin railway station, part of the estate, to the company.

U. purchased the whole estate for himself.

The railway company failed to prove that there had been any such agreement as that alleged.

Held that U. was under no obligation to convey the field to the company.

Lord Young (at p. 382): " I assent of course to the proposition that a director of a company may not use his position to obtain a benefit for himself at the cost or to the prejudice of the company, and that if he does he will not be permitted to retain the benefit, but ordered to transfer it to the company. . . . But I find no facts here to sustain the conclusion that the defender used his position as chairman or director of the railway company to acquire the lands of Milnfield, or was in any way aided by that fact in doing so. He was as free as any other to purchase these lands at the sale, or at least was under no disability from the mere fact of his office, together with the knowledge that a part of them would be useful to the company."

8. In *Laughland* v. *Millar, Laughland, & Co.* (1904) 6 F. 413 a contract between the managers of a company and a director of it to the effect that, if the managers received a bonus of £700 from the company on the sale of its business, the director was to receive £200 from the managers, was held to be unenforceable, as being corrupt. The managers had received the bonus of £700 from the company but had refused to pay the £200 to the director. The action was brought by the director against the managers.

Lord McLaren (at p. 417): " This was a corrupt agreement by a director not to press the interests of the shareholders as against the interests of Millar & Laughland in consideration of his receiving £200."

Lord Kinnear (at p. 418): " Now, the matter of the destination of the balance of the price was a matter for the shareholders, because it was their money, and I do not see that the defenders and the pursuer had any right or duty to enter into a contract about it at all. The pursuer's business was to advise the shareholders. . . . According to the pursuer's own statement, it was his plain and obvious duty, in bringing the matter before the shareholders, to tell them that if they paid £700 to the defenders there was an agreement between them and him that he was to get £200, and I think he is chargeable with a grave breach of duty when he says that he got that for himself and did not disclose it to the shareholders. . . . The legal result . . . is perfectly clear, that a contract of this kind according to our law is ineffectual."

9. In *Liquidators of West Lothian Oil Co. Ltd.* v. *Mair* (1892) 20 R. 64 the question arose as to the validity of a contract between a

director and his company in a situation where the articles of association of the company provided that no contract entered into by the company with any director was to be voidable because of his directorship.

At the date of the liquidation of W. Ltd., 14,500 empty oil barrels were lying at the company's works, enclosed separately from other barrels by a locked fence, the key of which was held by M., a director.

In the course of the liquidation the barrels were sold, and both M. and the liquidator claimed the price. M. alleged that the barrels had been sold to him by the company.

Held that, because of the provision in the articles of association, the liquidator could not challenge the contract, and that the price therefore went to M.

10. The duty of a nominee director is primarily to the company of which he is a director in the event of there being a conflict between the company and the party who has nominated the director.

Lord Denning in *Meyer* v. *The Scottish Co-operative Wholesale Society Ltd.* (see chapter on Majority Rule and Minority Protection, at p. 257, above) (1958 S.C. (H.L.) 40 at p. 67): " It must be remembered that we are here concerned with the manner in which the affairs of the textile company were being conducted. That is, with the conduct of those in control of its affairs. . . . If those persons— the nominee directors or the shareholders behind them—conduct the affairs of the company in a manner oppressive to the other shareholders, the Court can intervene to bring an end to the oppression.

" What, then, is the position of the nominee directors here? . . . These three were . . . at one and the same time directors of the co-operative society . . . and also directors of the textile company. . . . As soon as the interests of the two companies were in conflict, the nominee directors were placed in an impossible position. . . . It is plain that in the circumstances, these three gentlemen could not do their duty by both companies, and they did not do so. They put their duty to the co-operative society above their duty to the textile company, in this sense, at least, that they did nothing to defend the interests of the textile company against the conduct of the co-operative society. They probably thought that ' as nominees ' of the co-operative society their first duty was to the co-operative society. In this they were wrong. By subordinating the interests of the textile company to those of the co-operative society, they conducted the affairs of the textile company in a manner oppressive to the other shareholders."

Director's duties of care

The Western Bank of Scotland v. Baird's Trustees
(1872) 11 M. 96

A joint stock banking company and its liquidators brought an action against B., who had been a director, for payment of

£299,736 7s. 6d. as "the amount of loss and damage due by the defender to the bank" as at the date when B. had ceased to be a director.

The pursuers alleged that B. had grossly neglected his duty in having allowed the manager, without control, to make large advances from the bank's funds in contravention of the provisions of the contract of copartnery.

Held that, with regard to the alleged loss by advances on accounts-current which were closed at the time when B. ceased to be a director, the pursuers had set forth a case sufficiently relevant to be admitted to probation.

LORD JUSTICE-CLERK (MONCREIFF) (at p. 109): "The present suit is laid entirely on the... allegation that these sums were lost either through the gross negligence of William Baird himself individually, or through the gross negligence of himself and of his other co-directors, in the discharge of the duties of the office....

"... The general question as to how far the director of a joint stock company—such as the Western Bank—is liable for mere omission to discharge his duty, or what amount or kind of omission will be held to be *crassa negligentia,* have never as yet been authoritatively determined.

"This record contains no allegation or suggestion of corrupt motive or fraudulent intent, neither is there any allegation of conspiracy, or concert, or joint action with the other members of the direction....

"It may be said, not without force, that the duty undertaken by the directors of joint stock companies, such as the Western Bank, is subject to some qualifications which may not be always incident to offices of agency or trust. Such officials are generally chosen from their commercial position, their habits of business, and the amount of credit which their name will command. They are generally persons who have their time occupied by avocations of their own. When the shareholders elected William Baird as a director of the Western Bank they could not have expected him to make himself conversant with all the details of the management, or the items of all the accounts kept at the head-office and the numerous branches of so vast a concern. The ordinary conduct of the bank was placed in the hands of a professional manager, to whose integrity, as well as to whose skill, the directors were entitled in great measure to trust.

"But, on the other hand, it is impossible for a Court of law to assume that such an appointment is a mere name. The duties which are prescribed by the contract must be performed by the directors. If these are not very specific, their scope and object at least are sufficiently intelligible, and if a director grossly neglects the discharge of them he must be liable in the consequences, as agents or trustees are who grossly neglect the interests of those for whose benefit they are appointed. Whatever the duties are, they must be discharged with fidelity and conscience, and with ordinary and reasonable care. It is not necessary that I should attempt to define where excusable remissness ends and gross negligence begins. That must depend to a large extent on the circumstances. It is enough to say that gross negligence in the performance of such a duty, the want of reasonable and ordinary fidelity and care, will infer liability for loss thereby occasioned. . . .

" . . . The general ground of complaint is that William Baird, along with his co-directors, grossly neglected to superintend and control the manager in granting credit on open accounts. That is the general charge brought against them, and, as far as it goes, it is a charge not of action, but of inaction. There are, besides, two allegations of knowledge on the part of William Baird and his associates which are material. . . .

" I cannot say that these allegations are in themselves irrelevant. If William Baird knew that the bank was in embarrassed circumstances, owing to improper advances by the manager, and knew also that the manager systematically gave advances without control by the directors, and if he failed to take any steps to put matters upon a more safe or proper footing, he did grossly neglect his duty."

NOTES

1. The extent to which directors may rely on statements made by officials of the company was examined in *Lees* v. *Tod, &c.* (see chapter on Prospectus, p. 93, above). In that case Lord Deas (at 9 R. 835) referred to Lord President McNeill's charge to the jury in *Addie* v. *Western Bank of Scotland* (1865) 3 M. 899 at p. 901: " In submitting to the shareholders a report on the affairs of the bank, and the results of its business for the past year, the directors have a duty to perform, and it is part of their duty not to put forth any statement as to the affairs or prosperity of the bank which they have not reasonable ground to believe to be true. There is implied in their report a representation to the effect that they have reasonable ground to believe in the truth of what they assert, and those to whom it is addressed or circulated are entitled so to understand it. This does not mean that it is incumbent on the directors personally to go through the books and test the accuracy of them, or of the results brought

out in them. It is not to be expected or supposed that the directors have done so, and their report is not to be taken as importing or implying that they have done so. They are entitled to rely on the information furnished to them by the officials to whom the details of the business are committed, and in whom confidence is placed. That affords reasonable ground for the directors believing in the truth of the results brought out, and of the inferences reasonably deducible from them."

The First Division held that the Lord President's charge to the jury had been rightly given. The decision was subsequently reversed by the House of Lords, but on different grounds (*The Western Bank of Scotland* v. *Addie* (1867) 5 M.(H.L.) 80).

2. *Liquidator of the Caledonian Heritable Security Co. Ltd.* v. *Curror's Trustee* (1882) 9 R. 1115 was an action by the liquidator of C. Ltd., which had been formed for the purpose of lending money on heritable security, against the sequestrated estate of a deceased director on the ground that the director was liable for losses alleged to have been caused by unsecured advances made during the director's tenure of office.

The Second Division, agreeing with the Lord Ordinary, held that the evidence (which included the signing of cheques by the director) was insufficient to support the director's liability.

Lord Young (at p. 1129): "The rule that each director of a company is liable for the money which he signs a cheque for, or authorises the expenditure of contrary to his duty, is that to which the pursuer appeals, and I am of opinion with the Lord Ordinary that the evidence which the liquidator has presented to us is insufficient to subject Mr. Curror to liability under it. Had I been satisfied that Mr. Curror knew of the account in question, and even tacitly sanctioned its existence and continuance, I should have been disposed to hold, although without any direct precedent so far as I know, that he was responsible for the loss on that account which he did not interpose to stop, while he might have done so to the effect of preventing that loss. ... The evidence is insufficient to support liability on that ground."

3. The director's duties of care depend to some extent on the nature of the company in which he holds office: see Lord Johnston in *Brenes & Co.* v. *Downie*, 1914 S.C. 97 at p. 104 (Note 2 to *Aberdeen Railway Co.* v. *Blaikie Bros.*, p. 276, above): "The directors of an ordinary limited public company cannot, of course, know the whole details of the company's banking accounts. I regard this case as one in which there is a company only in name; it consisted of two individuals knowing everything that was done in the company."

4. Liability for breach of the duty of care is joint and several. Therefore, in *Liquidators of the Western Bank of Scotland* v. *Douglas, &c.* (1860) 22 D. 447, the liquidators were held entitled to bring their action against any one or more of the directors, there being no ground for the plea that all parties interested in the action had not been called. The action was for losses alleged to have been

caused to the company by gross neglect of duty on the part of the directors, *i.e.* delict.

Lord Justice-Clerk (Inglis) (at p. 475): "The Court are of opinion, that this is . . . an action to enforce an obligation of reparation arising *ex delicto,* and not an action on contract, and that the defenders are in the position not of *correi debendi,* but of joint delinquents. . . .

". . . We hold it to be a settled principle in the law of Scotland, that the defenders are all conjunctly and severally liable . . . , and that it is in the option of the pursuer to call all who are so implicated, or any one or more of them. . . .

". . . It requires no express covenant to make the manager or directors of a company liable either for fraud or *crassa negligentia* in their management. And though it is natural in such a case to say, that the defenders have broken their contract-obligations as well as their common law obligations, the action is, nevertheless, laid truly on *delict,* and substantially on nothing else."

CHAPTER 16

THE SECRETARY

Position of secretary: *whether " clerk or servant "*
Liquidator, Scottish Poultry Journal Co.
(1896) 4 S.L.T. 167 (O.H.)

The question raised by this note was whether Gordon, formerly secretary and manager of the Scottish Poultry Journal and Financiers' Publishing Co., Glasgow, was entitled to a preference in the company's liquidation for four months' wages as a " clerk or servant " as defined by the Preferential Payments in Bankruptcy Act 1888.

The liquidator had allowed Gordon only an ordinary ranking, and against that decision Gordon appealed.

Held that Gordon was not entitled to a preferential ranking, since he was not a clerk or servant in the sense of the Act.

LORD STORMONTH DARLING (at p. 167): " The point which arose for decision was whether the words ' All wages or salary of any clerk or servant in respect of services rendered to the bankrupt or to the company during four months before the date of the receiving order, or, as the case may be, the commencement of the winding up, not exceeding £50,' covered the case of a gentleman describing himself as manager and secretary of the company. It was quite true that his salary did not seem to have been a large one. ... In one sense, no doubt, he was a servant of the company, just as the manager of a bank was a servant of the bank; but I am inclined to think that these words were used, not in the general sense, but as indicating the particular kind of servant who was entitled to this preference. One could not throw out the view that this whole rule of priority in bankruptcies in favour of a certain class was founded on considerations of humanity, and was really dictated by a desire to secure an alimentary allowance to a man dependent upon it for his daily bread. Construing the words clerk or servant, I come to the conclusion that this gentleman did not fall within either of them. He was certainly not a clerk, because that involved a position altogether subordinate to his. He was not a servant, because a servant under this Act meant a subordinate servant. Therefore I cannot disturb the finding of the liquidator."

NOTES

1. The same conclusion was reached by the same judge in *Liquidator—Clyde Football, &c., Co. Ltd.* (1900) 8 S.L.T. 328 (O.H.). The secretary claimed, under the same Act of 1888, to be paid certain arrears of salary in priority to other debts. He was a law agent, but counsel stated that his duties really were little more than those of a clerk.

Lord Stormonth Darling *refused* to allow a preference, saying (at p. 329): " I see no reason to go back on the view I expressed in the case of the *Scottish Poultry Journal Co.*; and so far as it goes, that view is supported by the judgment of Cozens-Hardy J. in the case of the *Newspapers Syndicate Co.* (L.R. 1900, 2 Ch.D. 349) this year; that being the case of a managing director, while this is the case of a secretary. I do not say that the mere name of a secretary will be sufficient to justify the denial of a preference, if he is merely a clerk. But I shall have great difficulty in saying that he is so if he does not devote his whole time to the work of the Company, but is, as this man is, a law agent, and has other employers or clients."

2. Two years later, Lord Stormonth Darling had before him another claim by a secretary for preferential ranking—*Laing* v. *Gowans* (*Liquidator of the Rutherford Tobacco and Cigarette Manufacturing Co. Ltd.*) (1902) 10 S.L.T. 461 (O.H.).

A petition for compulsory winding up of R. Ltd. had been presented on April 13, 1901. On May 14 the court pronounced the winding-up order and appointed the liquidator.

L., who had been appointed on December 29, 1900, as secretary of the company for one year at a salary of £120 *per annum*, lodged a claim for a preferential ranking of £35, being his salary for February, March, April and the first half of May 1901. The liquidator admitted L. to an ordinary ranking for £25, as salary for February, March and the first half of April, but disallowed his claim to the extent of £10 on the ground that all the company's contracts of employment had terminated on April 13.

L. appealed against this deliverance. He argued that if, in view of the three decisions above mentioned, he was not entitled to a preferential ranking for the £35 as a " clerk or servant " under the Act of 1888, he was at least entitled to a preferential ranking for the £10: the services which he had rendered from April 13 to May 14 had been indispensable to the company and the liquidator, and should be paid in full as expenses of liquidation. It was, he maintained, the order (and not the presentation of the petition) which operated as notice of discharge to servants. Otherwise, he argued, the business of a company would be paralysed immediately on the presentation of a winding-up petition, even though the petition might subsequently not be granted or its object be merely to prepare the way for reconstruction. If the secretary were not to be held entitled to a preferential ranking for his salary during the intervening period, he would have no motive to remain and assist in the preservation of the company's assets after the presentation of a winding-up petition, for the right to obtain a mere dividend on his salary for that period would be no sufficient inducement.

Lord Stormonth Darling *recalled* the liquidator's deliverance to the extent of allowing L. an ordinary ranking for the £10 claimed for the period between the presentation of the winding-up petition and the pronouncement of the winding-up order.

3. Since the time of these cases, the office of company secretary has developed into one which is in many instances held by a full-time professional person who often has legal, administrative, or accounting qualifications.

That such a person would be an employee of the company (and so qualify for preferential ranking in respect of salary) is supported by an *obiter dictum* of Lord Carmont in *Anderson* v. *James Sutherland (Peterhead) Ltd.* (see chapter on Directors, p. 269, above) at 1941 S.C. p. 214: " In the case before this Court the board has power to appoint its own directors to offices other than auditorship. One of the directors holds the position of secretary of the company, and it does not seem to me to be arguable that as such he is not in the employment of the company as one of its servants."

4. The limit of a clerk or servant's preferential ranking is now £800 (Companies Act 1948, s. 319, as amended by the Insolvency Act 1976, s. 1 and Sched. 1).

Duties of secretary

Niven v. Collins Patent Lever Gear Co. Ltd.
(1900) 7 S.L.T. 476 (O.H.)

N., secretary of C. Ltd., brought an action against C. Ltd. for payment of an account which included disbursements made by N. to a firm of which he was a partner.

C. Ltd. pleaded that N. had had no right or power to subject the company to liability for these expenses.

Held that N. was entitled to succeed, since he had acted under due authority.

LORD KINCAIRNEY (ORDINARY) (after reviewing the evidence (at p. 478): " [This action] is an action for repayment of an authorised outlay. . . . It is not said, at least it is not proved, that the pursuer wilfully misled the defenders. It is said that it was his duty to inform the defenders that they were not bound to pay the account. He says he could not have done that, because he thought they were bound; but I am not aware that it was his duty as secretary to instruct them as to their legal rights. He was not their agent, so I think it must be held, as there is no appointment of an agent in the minute book."

NOTES

1. *Edington* v. *Dumbar Steam Laundry Co.* (1903) 11 S.L.T. 117 (O.H.) shows that it was no part of the secretary's duty to lodge defences to an action against the company.

The company in general meeting had authorised their directors to negotiate and grant a lease of certain premises owned by the company. The secretary granted the lease. The holder of a bond over the premises then raised an action of reduction of the lease, and the secretary, without obtaining authority from the directors, instructed the company's law agent to lodge defences to the action. The law agent did so in the name of the company.

The directors then lodged a minute of disclaimer, and craved the court to sustain the minute and find the secretary liable to them in the expenses of the minute. No expenses were asked against the law agent, who had admittedly acted on the secretary's instructions and in good faith.

Lord Kyllachy (Ordinary) sustained the minute, and found the secretary liable to the minuters in expenses since he had been responsible for the unauthorised lodging of the defences and had appeared at the bar by counsel to defend that proceeding.

2. The duties of the secretary include the issuing of share certificates: in *Clavering, Son, & Co.* v. *Goodwins, Jardine, & Co. Ltd.* (1891) 18 R. 652 (see chapter on Shares, p. 196, above) Lord Justice-Clerk (J. H. A. Macdonald) said (at p. 660): " It appears that Mr. Jardine, who was one of the managing directors of the company, had induced the secretary of the company . . . to allow him to retain those shares, he taking from Mr. Jardine a cheque for the amount to be paid upon them, with the understanding that he was not to use the cheque till Mr. Jardine allowed him to do so. . . .

" The defence maintained upon the part of the company is that the secretary was not acting within his duty as their servant in doing what he did, and that as what was done was a fraud, they are not liable for his fraud. I cannot accept that. Their servant the secretary was authorised by them to conduct their business, and it was his duty to issue such certificates as were issued in this case, and he did issue the certificate, which is duly signed by two directors, as being a certificate for these shares, and on the transfer being intimated by Mr. Clavering to the company, he, as the officer of the company, wrote upon the margin the words which have been quoted in the course of the debate. Now, in doing these things, I hold that he was acting as the representative of the company whose duty it was to do such acts, and that the company must be responsible for the acts so done."

3. The Companies Act 1948, s. 32 (4) provides: " A deed to which a company is a party shall be held to be validly executed according to the law of Scotland on behalf of the company if it is executed in accordance with the provisions of this Act or is sealed with the common seal of the company and subscribed on behalf of the company by two of the directors or by a director and the secretary of the

company, and such subscription on behalf of the company shall be binding whether attested by witnesses or not."

Section 73 of the same Act provides: " The shares or other interest of any member in a company shall be personal estate, transferable in manner provided by the articles of the company, and shall not be of the nature of real estate."

Sections 29 (4) and 62 (1) of the Companies Act 1929 were in substantially the same terms, and in *Clydesdale Bank* (*Moore Place*) *Nominees Ltd.* v. *Snodgrass*, 1939 S.C. 805, on an interpretation of these statutory provisions, a transfer was held to have been validly executed although it had not been subscribed by the secretary. Neither the articles of the company whose shares were being transferred nor the articles of the company which was the transferor required the secretary to subscribe transfers.

Lord Jamieson (at p. 830): " I think . . . that the transfer is valid. It was executed in accordance with the articles of the Bank Nominees Company by being sealed with its common seal in presence of two directors who also signed, and their signatures attest that the seal was affixed in their presence."

Secretary has no lien over company's books

Gladstone v. McCallum
(1896) 23 R. 783

McC. had acted as secretary of the Australian Land and Exploration Syndicate Ltd. until G. was appointed liquidator in the voluntary winding up of the company.

A sum of £17 11s. remained due to McC. by the company for services rendered by McC. to the company as its secretary, and McC. maintained that he was entitled to retain the company's minute-book until this sum was paid to him.

G. presented a petition craving the court to ordain McC. to deliver the minute-book to G. as liquidator " without prejudice to any lien competent to him."

The court *granted* the prayer of the petition.

LORD PRESIDENT (J. P. B. ROBERTSON) (at p. 784): " Now, has any law been shewn in support of the proposition that the secretary of the company, who has been employed to write up the minutes, has a right of lien over the minute-books? There are well-known and well-recognised liens applicable to a different relationship of the parties and to a different possession of the articles in dispute from what we find here; and we could not give judgment for the respondent unless we were to affirm— what has not yet been decided—that every man who has been employed to write in the books in his master's office has a right of lien over the books until he has been paid for his services."

LORD MCLAREN (at p. 785): " I think there is no foundation in the facts as stated for any claim either of retention or of lien. Retention, as I understand it, is the right of an owner of property to withhold delivery of it under an unexecuted contract of sale or agreement of a similar nature, until the price due to him has been paid, or the counter obligation fulfilled. Lien, again, is the right of a person who is not the owner of property but is in possession of it on a lawful title, and whose right of lien, if it is not a general one—of which class of liens there are not many examples—is a right to retain the property until he has been compensated for something which he has done to it. In this case there is no right of retention, because the books belong to the company, and there is no right of lien, because they are not in the possession of the respondent but of the company. Accordingly this case is in a different category from that of a claim by a writer who is lawfully in possession of his client's papers under a contract of agency."

NOTES

1. Since the petition craved delivery of the minute-book " without prejudice to any lien competent to " the secretary, the statements as to the absence of lien were strictly *obiter* in this case, though they were sufficiently definite to leave no room for doubt as to what the law on the point was.

2. A distinct decision was given three years later in *The Barnton Hotel Co. Ltd.* v. *Cook* (1899) 1 F. 1190.

C., an Edinburgh accountant, had been secretary of B. Ltd. from its incorporation in 1896 until 1899, when he was discharged and an interim secretary appointed. C. refused to give the interim secretary possession of the company's books and papers. B. Ltd. had never acquired any premises for a registered office, and C.'s private office at 5 Queen Street had been registered as the company's registered office.

Held that C. was not entitled to retain the company's books and papers until the amount due to him for his services had been paid.

C. argued that he was in a totally different position from a salaried secretary employed in an office belonging to the company: such a secretary never had possession of the company's books except as the company's servant employed in its premises, whereas C., who was to be paid a *quantum meruit*, worked in his own office, and the books had been placed in his possession there to enable him to perform the duties for which he was employed. He attempted to distinguish *Gladstone's* case on the grounds that (1) the petition in that case had craved delivery only under reservation of any competent right of retention and (2) the opinions in that case assumed that the secretary was employed in an office belonging to the company.

Lord Kinnear (at p. 1193): " I think the ground of the decision is extremely well put in the note of the Sheriff, where he says that the books and other documents belonging to the pursuers came into the defender's hands as secretary (*i.e.*, as a servant of the company), and not under any special contract of employment relative to these documents, and therefore he holds that the possession of the defender was not such as to create a right of retention or lien. I entirely concur, and would only add that it is perfectly immaterial whether a person in the employment of another as clerk or servant carries on his work in one place or in another so long as the books and documents with which he is working are put into his hands in consequence and for the execution of that contract of service, and no other."

Sheriff (Rutherfurd) (at p. 1192): " In cases of this kind, the first point to be ascertained is the title on which the defender obtained possession of the articles which he claims right to retain until his debt is paid; for it is hardly necessary to observe that the mere circumstance of possession will not in every case confer the right of retention.

" On the other hand, papers, or other articles, forming the subject of a mutual contract, may be retained by one of the parties who has been employed to do work upon or in connection with them, until the other party fulfils his part of the agreement. *Meikle & Wilson* v. *Pollard* (1880) 8 R. 69, and *Robertson* v. *Ross* (1887) 15 R. 67, are examples of that. On the other hand, the right of retention must arise out of the contract on which the possession of the articles was obtained. Thus a servant is not entitled to retain his employer's property until he has received payment of his wages— . . . *Gladstone* v. *McCallum.* . . .

" In the present instance it appears that the register of shareholders, the books, and other documents belonging to the pursuers, came into the defender's hands as secretary (*i.e.*, as a servant of the company), and not under any special contract of employment relative to these documents. The defender was, properly speaking, merely the custodier of the books, &c., and his possession was for behoof of the company, whose registered office was, no doubt, in the premises occupied by him as an accountant. But it was not in his professional capacity of an accountant that he was employed by the pursuers, but as their secretary. If he had not been secretary to the company, the books, &c., would never have been in his possession or custody at all. In these circumstances the Sheriff is of opinion that the defender had not such possession as to create a right of retention or lien, and he concurs with the Sheriff-substitute in holding that there is no relevant defence to the action."

Chapter 17

PROTECTION OF OUTSIDERS

Loan ultra vires *of directors: lender entitled to assume that transaction had been duly sanctioned by company in general meeting*

Gillies v. The Craigton Garage Co. Ltd.
1935 S.C. 423

C. Ltd. had an issued share capital of £1,035. One of its articles of association provided that the amount borrowed by the directors for the purposes of the company should not at any time exceed the issued share capital without the sanction of the company in general meeting.

At a time when the company had on loan to it £500, Morgan, the company's managing director, persuaded G. to lend £750 to the company to enable it to purchase heritable property. In security of the loan the company disponed the property to G.

When G. attempted to enforce his security, C. Ltd. averred in defence that the loan transaction was void as being *ultra vires* of the directors.

G. maintained that, as the sanction required did not involve any alteration of the company's registered documents, he had been entitled to assume that the directors had obtained the necessary sanction.

C. Ltd. maintained that the circumstances of the transaction had been so unusual as to put G. on his inquiry as to whether the necessary sanction had been obtained.

Held that G. had been entitled to assume that the necessary sanction had been obtained.

Lord Blackburn (at p. 433): " There are two forms of resolution which a company may pass. It may be an ' ordinary ' resolution or it may be a ' special ' one. An ordinary resolution does not require to be advertised or to be made public in any form at all—it is a domestic matter for the company; a special resolution, on the other hand, requires to be recorded and so to be made available to any member of the public who wants to inquire into the affairs of the company. It is well settled—and the rule is known as *Turquand's* rule—that, where a contractor enters into a contract with a company he is bound to find out for himself everything that a company has done by ' special ' resolution, and, accordingly, if a special resolution had been required in connection with this loan and had been recorded and the lender had failed to satisfy himself about it, the fault for that would have rested upon his own shoulders. On the other hand, if an ordinary resolution was all that would have been required to authorise this loan, then the lender of the money would not have been bound to satisfy himself about that. He is entitled to assume that the internal affairs of the company have been managed properly and are in order.

" In this particular case . . . the resolution which ought to have been passed by the Company was an ordinary and not a special resolution, and was therefore entirely a domestic affair of the Company and was a matter which the lender was entitled to assume had been properly carried out. . . .

" It seems to me that, if ever there was a case to which *Turquand's* rule applied, this without any doubt whatever is one."

SHERIFF (MERCER) (at p. 428): " *Turquand's* case is directly in point. There the Company's constitution authorised the directors to borrow under certain circumstances, and one clause provided that they might borrow on bond such sums as should from time to time, by a resolution of the Company, be authorised to be borrowed. It was averred that there was no such resolution authorising the making of the bond; but it was held, affirming the judgment of the Queen's Bench, that the plaintiff was entitled to succeed, the obligee having, on the facts alleged, a right to presume that there had been a resolution at a general meeting authorising the borrowing of the money on bond. Jervis, C.J. (at p. 332) said, ' parties dealing with them [companies] are bound to read the statute and the deed of settlement. But they are not bound to do more. And the party here, on reading the deed of settlement, would find, not a prohibition from borrowing, but a permission to do so on certain conditions. Finding that the authority might be made complete by a resolution, he would have the right to infer the fact of a resolution authorising that which on the face of the document appeared to be legitimately done.' *Turquand* has been followed in many cases. . . . These authorities are, in my view, directly in point and are conclusive in the pursuer's favour."

NOTES

1. " *Turquand's* case " is *Royal British Bank* v. *Turquand* (1856) 6 El. & Bl. 327; (1855) 5 El. & Bl. 248.

2. An argument put forward for the defenders in *Gillies'* case was that *Turquand's* case had been applied in only one reported case in Scotland—*Heiton* v. *Waverley Hydropathic Co. Ltd.* (1877) 4 R. 830.

In that case Heiton sought a declarator that a field and orchard had been sold by the company to him, but the court held that there was no concluded contract of sale, the parties being still at the negotiating stage.

The original articles of association of the company gave the directors no power to sell heritage, but at a meeting in March 1874 the articles had been altered so as to confer such power on the directors with the consent of the shareholders at a general meeting. Heiton argued that, although there might have been informality in the notice calling the meeting of March 1874, that was not a matter into which third parties dealing with the directors were bound to inquire. He supported the argument by referring to *Turquand's* case.

In view of the decision reached, the observations on the application of *Turquand's* case, though definite, were *obiter*.

Lord Shand (at p. 841): " The objection taken amounts to this, that a party dealing with a joint stock company of this kind is bound not only to look at the constitution of the company, and at the resolution which the company may have come to, but to investigate all the details with reference to the calling of the meeting at which the resolution was arrived at, and to see whether the notices have been given, and circulars sent to the proper parties. I think that persons dealing with companies of this kind are entitled to assume that in matters of this description everything has been properly done. It would be a very serious thing if in regard to a company such as this the law were otherwise. I do not say it would lead to the disability of such companies to contract; but, if persons dealing with them were bound to examine into all these minute matters of detail before they could be satisfied that they had made a binding contract, it would be almost impossible to deal with such companies in safety; and it would be the worst result possible for such companies themselves, and a great injury to them, that the law should be declared in terms of the argument which we had at such great length from the respondents in this case."

3. The circumstances in *Paterson's Trustees* v. *The Caledonian Heritable Security Co. Ltd. and Liquidator* (1885) 13 R. 369 suggest that *Turquand's* case might have been referred to, but this is not indicated in the report.

C. Ltd. had power under its memorandum of association to lend money on heritable security and to do all things incidental or conducive to the attainment of that object. C. Ltd.'s manager, in order to prevent a sale at an unfavourable time of a property over which C. Ltd. had a second bond and which the first bondholder was about to sell, bought the property, paying the price with money lent by P.'s trustees, and taking the title to the property in his own name. The manager granted a bond over the property to the trustees as security.

C. Ltd. went into liquidation, and the liquidator repudiated both the purchase and the loan on security of the property on the ground (1) that neither transaction had been sanctioned by the directors and (2) that, even if they had been, they were *ultra vires* of the company and its directors.

Held that it had been within the scope of the manager's general powers to enter into the loan transaction on behalf of the company, and that, as the trustees had no concern with the application of the money, the company was liable for the loan.

Lord Justice-Clerk (Moncreiff) (at p. 378): " I do not go into the question whether the company authorised the [loan] transaction or not; there is the strongest possible reason for assuming that they did, and that in carrying it out they trusted, according to their ordinary practice, to the manager and agent, in whom they had perfect confidence. To those dealing with it the company's intervention is sufficiently proved by the impress of the company's seal on the bond.

" The question, then, to my mind is simply this, Had the company power to borrow? I have already answered that they had. They did borrow, and with the application of the money the lenders had no concern."

Lord Young (at p. 379): " Now, they [the company's officials] certainly had power to borrow money. Whether they had power to apply the money when borrowed in buying heritable property I do not inquire. They had power to borrow and if in borrowing they acted within their powers, though in applying the money borrowed they might be without their powers, the lenders had no need to concern themselves with the application.

". . . The memorandum of association . . . sets forth as one of the objects for which the company was established, the receiving ' money by way of loan, by cash-credit, debenture, deposit or otherwise.' . . . Is the lender, in lending to a company in such a position, bound to inquire what the company are going to do with the borrowed money? If so, to make themselves safe, they must not only know what the company is going to do with the money, but must insist upon being placed in the position of doing for the company what it proposes to do, and can legally do, for without that they could never be sure that the company will do what it proposes to do, and what the lenders have satisfied themselves the company can legally do. All this would be extremely inconvenient, and practically render the working of such a company impossible.

" That the company did borrow the money is quite clear. That they did borrow it for the purpose and apply it for the purpose of securing the complete property title is also quite clear. If that purpose and application were within the company's power, the pursuers are right on every point. But, even if the purpose and application were not within the company's power, the pursuers had no concern with that.

". . . The proper officers having recommended the loan, the company must make good the deficiency."

4. In *Allison* v. *Scotia Motor and Engineering Co. Ltd.* (1906) 14 S.L.T. 9 (O.H.) (Note 4 to *Anderson* v. *James Sutherland* (*Peterhead*)

Ltd., in the chapter on Directors, p. 272, above) a works manager was held to have been entitled to assume that a managing director had the necessary authority from the directors to appoint him as works manager.

Lord Mackenzie (at p. 10): " I think it is proved that the directors recognised Wark as, *de facto,* the managing director. . . . The pursuer dealt in *bona fide* with Wark, and was entitled to assume that he had the power to make the agreement."

Turquand's case is not referred to in the report of *Allison's* case.

5. Outsiders are not protected where the circumstances are such as to put them on inquiry: *Thompson* v. *J. Barke and Co. (Caterers) Ltd.,* 1975 S.L.T. 67 (O.H.) (Note 2 to *Life Association of Scotland* v. *Caledonian Heritable Security Co. Ltd. in Liquidation,* in the chapter on Memorandum of Association, at p. 54, above).

Lord Dunpark (at p. 72) quoted with approval the rule stated in Gower's *Modern Company Law* (3rd ed.), at p. 156: " ' [Hence] an outsider dealing with a company through an officer who is a . . . particular type of officer (*e.g.,* managing director) and who purports to exercise a power which that sort of officer would usually have, is entitled to hold the company liable for the officer's acts, even though the officer . . . is in fact exceeding his actual authority. But this is not so if the officer is in fact exceeding his actual authority and (*a*) the outsider knows that the officer . . . has no actual authority; (*b*) the circumstances are such as to put him on inquiry; or (*c*) the public documents make it clear that the officer has no actual authority.' "

Lord Dunpark considered that both exceptions (*b*) and (*c*) applied in the case before him.

CHAPTER 18

DIVIDENDS

Profits available for dividend: loss of circulating capital to be made good before revenue profits are ascertained: fixed and circulating capital distinguished

The City Property Investment Trust Corporation Ltd.
v. Thorburn
(1897) 25 R. 361

T., a holder of preferred shares, carrying a non-cumulative dividend of 5 per cent., in C. Ltd., objected to a loss of £4,940 14s. 7d. on the company's investments being debited against revenue with the result that a preference dividend of only 3 per cent. was to be paid.

A special case was presented to which C. Ltd. was the first party and T. was the second party.

Held that the investments were in the circumstances to be regarded as part of the circulating capital, and that C. Ltd. was therefore entitled to treat the loss as a loss of revenue.

LORD TRAYNER (at p. 367): "The directors purchased from time to time certain stocks or other securities which they sold when the market was favourable for doing so, and the profits made on such sales (that is, the excess in price received over the price originally paid) was treated as income and divided among the shareholders. Any loss arising from such sales was in like manner debited to income. . . .

"The second party objects . . . that the loss in question was a loss on fixed capital, and should therefore be charged against capital and not against revenue. If the second party was right in his facts, I should think his argument and contention sound. It would not be permissible to make up an estimated or actual loss by depreciation on fixed capital by charging it against or replacing it from the year's revenue. The shareholders are entitled to have their dividend out of the revenue for the year without that revenue being so reduced. But the argument fails if the fact fails, as I think it does. . . . Now, in what respect is it said that the stocks, &c., on which the loss occurred are fixed capital more than any other stock which the company held?

297

I have heard no reason assigned beyond this, that it had been held by the company for a longer period. ... But mere length of time in holding will not *per se* make fixed capital out of what would otherwise be floating or circulating capital. If the stocks in question had been held to meet some particular claim, or had been set aside by the company for some particular purpose, as, for example, as a permanent rent or income-producing subject, which involved the idea that the directors were not to part with or realise them, then they might be regarded as fixed capital. But if they were in the hands of the directors for realisation when opportunity occurred—for such realisation as would be advantageous to the company, without any restriction as to the time or price at which they might be sold—then they were like any other stocks held for realisation, the profit on which would go to enhance the revenue, or the loss to reduce it. It appears to me that this was the character of the investments on which the loss in question was sustained; they were part of the circulating capital of the company, and the loss actually sustained thereon in the year mentioned was a proper debit against the revenue for that year."

LORD MONCREIFF (at p. 368): " The question depends upon whether the investments upon which the loss has occurred are to be regarded as permanent investments or circulating capital. If the former, the loss sustained on them need not be replaced before paying dividends; if the latter, the loss must be made good out of revenue before dividends are paid.

" ... The objects of the company as disclosed in the memorandum of association ... do not necessarily suggest that the company are to carry on the business of trafficking in bonds, shares, stocks, and other securities. They are consistent with such securities being purchased and held as investments, and I do not see much difference between them and the objects as defined in the memorandum of association of the General and Commercial Investment Trust in the case of *Verner* v. *The General and Commercial Investment Trust* (L.R. [1894], 2 Ch. 239).

" At the same time those objects are not inconsistent with the company trafficking in securities, and I have been chiefly influenced by the consideration that it is established that in point of fact they did so traffic, and that it has been the practice of the company to credit to revenue profit made upon the sale of securities during those years in which a profit overhead was made upon the sales. ...

" The circumstances of the case of *Verner* v. *The General and Commercial Investment Trust* differed from those of the present case in this material respect, that in that case no trafficking with the assets took place. . . . The company seen to have purchased the securities as investments, and made the profit which they divided as revenue, not out of the sale of the securities, but out of the interest at a high rate which they received on the investments."

Profits available for dividend: loss on revenue account to be made good out of subsequent year's profits

Niddrie and Benhar Coal Co. Ltd. v. Hurll
(1891) 18 R. 805

N. Ltd.'s capital was divided into A or preference shares and B or ordinary shares, the former being entitled to a non-cumulative 10 per cent. preference dividend.

For several years there was a loss on the revenue account, resulting in a debit balance of £7,867 0s. 2d. at April 30, 1889.

During the year ending April 30, 1890, profits of £6,909 8s. 7d. were earned, and were applied in reducing the debit balance. No dividends were declared.

During the year ending April 30, 1891, the profits earned were sufficient to wipe out the remainder of the debit balance and to pay the 10 per cent. preference dividend for that year.

In a special case the question was whether the balance of the profits for the year ending April 30, 1891, should be applied in payment of a preference dividend on the A shares for the previous year or divided among the B shareholders as dividend for the year ending April 30, 1891.

Held that the A shareholders were not entitled to a dividend for the year ending April 30, 1890, since the profits of that year had been properly applied in reducing the debit balance on the revenue account.

LORD ADAM (at p. 808): " The answer to the first part of the question depends on this, whether there were any profits available for dividend for the year ending April 30, 1890. That leads one to consider, What are profits properly so called? and on that matter I quite agree with Mr. Buckley's definition, which is, that profits are the excess of the ordinary receipts over the expenses properly chargeable to revenue account. I also agree with him when he says that when a loss on the revenue account has been sustained, there is, of course, no profit until that loss has been made good either by set-off of previous undivided profits still in hand, or by profits subsequently earned. Now, that is the case we are dealing with here. We are dealing with a case of proper revenue account—with a proper revenue account shewing a debit balance of £957 11s. 7d. at the end of last year—and accordingly on a proper statement of accounts it is clear that there was no profit earned by the company last year at all—I mean profit available for dividend; and if that was so, then it is clear that the A shareholders were not entitled to dividend last year at all. Now, if that be so, they cannot be entitled to have a share of the current year's earnings applied to a dividend which never was earned. . . . According to the definition which I have read net profit only arises on the debit balance on the revenue account being made good. . . . Therefore . . . the only answer that can be given to the question is that the A shareholders are not entitled to have any part of the profits of the current year applied to payment of a dividend which was not earned last year. The clause in the memorandum says that the A shares shall rank prior to the B shares on the profits of each year. That is their whole right. And the fourth article distinctly says that no deficiency of dividend in any year shall be made good out of the profits of future years. I cannot see how, in the face of articles in these terms, it can be said that the dividend which amounted to nil in 1890 is to be made good out of the profits of the current year. . . .

. . .

" I am therefore of opinion that the proper disposal of the surplus which the company has earned is, first, to extinguish the debt of £957 11s. 7d.—although that question is not before us—and in the next place, that the A shareholders are entitled to 10 per cent., and after that that the B shareholders are entitled to have the balance applied in payment of dividend to them."

LORD MCLAREN (at p. 809): " I concur. It was contended by one of the parties that profit means merely the result of the operations of the financial year—the difference between the income and the expenditure of that year. I think that that is an incomplete definition, and is neither consistent with the law nor with sound commercial accounting. Profit and loss in my view represent the aggregate of all the commercial transactions of the company from the time when it commenced business, and the way in which it is reached is by bringing into the account of any year the balance of profit or loss resulting from the close of the previous year's transactions; and when that principle is applied it is plain enough in this case that the supposed profit has no real existence, because it is only obtained by leaving out of account the loss which falls to be extinguished, and which was at the debit at the commencement of the year's account."

NOTES

1. See also *The City Property Investment Trust Corporation Ltd.* v. *Thorburn* (p. 297, above), in which Lord Moncreiff said (at 25 R. 368) that, if the investments were to be regarded as circulating capital, "the loss must be made good out of revenue before dividends are paid."

2. English and Scottish authorities diverge on this point: the leading English case is *Ammonia Soda Co. Ltd.* v. *Chamberlain* [1918] 1 Ch. 266 (C.A.).

The recommendation of the Jenkins Committee favoured the establishment of the Scottish rule (Cmnd. 1749, para. 350 (1962)).

Profits available for dividend: payment out of reserve fund held to be dividend as between liferenter and fiar

Blyth's Trustees v. Milne
(1905) 7 F. 799

B.'s trust disposition and settlement directed his trustees to hold certain shares in the North British Rubber Co. Ltd. for his daughter Mrs. Milne in liferent and for her daughter, Olive Milne, in fee.

The directors of the company resolved to divide part of the reserve fund, which had been accumulated from undivided profits, among the shareholders, and simultaneously to issue preference shares equal in amount to the payment out of the reserve fund.

B.'s trustees took up their quota of the new shares, applying the bonus in payment of them.

Held that the operation was a payment of dividend and that Mrs. Milne, as liferenter, was entitled to have the bonus paid to her.

LORD PRESIDENT (DUNEDIN) (at p. 804): "I think it is quite clear, therefore, that while these directors were entitled to accumulate a reserve fund as they did out of undivided profits, they were not bound to keep it in that state, but they might, if they liked, divide it among the ordinary shareholders. . . . They then point out that the capital proposed to be issued in preference shares will exactly equal in amount the sum which they propose to distribute by way of bonus, and that accordingly as they intend to offer this capital to the shareholders before offering it to anyone else, each shareholder will find himself by the receipt of his bonus in the position of being able to take up this capital if he so pleases. . . .

" The option of this trust to acquire the preference shares was exercised by the trustees. . . . Now, there have been several such questions in cases like this, and . . . at this time of day I do not think there is any doubt as to the doctrine of law that is to be applied to such cases. . . . Now, when I look at what was done here, I am driven to the conclusion that what was done was the giving of a dividend, because in the circular letter of April 6 not only are you told that a warrant will be posted to you on May 13, but you are invited to apply for shares. . . . I have come clearly to be of opinion that this Company did as matter of fact pay a dividend in cash, as it was entitled to do."

LORD ADAM (at p. 806): " The case depends upon what view you take of the facts and of what the Company actually did and wished to do in the matter. . . . Having declared a bonus payable on May 13, 1904, they [the directors] sent the amount of the bonus due to each shareholder of the Company who was entitled to it. They sent to each of them and made actual payment of the bonus to each of the shareholders. It humbly appears to me that . . . that is a declaration of a dividend. . . . The shareholders were perfectly free to do as they liked in that matter; they had the matter in their own hands. They might have gone to the bank next day and got the money in exchange for the dividend warrant. There was no obligation upon them to take the shares. . . . Each case must turn upon its own facts, and looking to the actual facts in this case, and to what the directors did, I see no reason to suppose that this was not a valid declaration of dividend."

LORD KINNEAR (at p. 810): " I can gather nothing except that this £550 in dispute was paid as dividend, and therefore it belongs to the party having interest in the dividend accruing to the shareholders, and not to the party interested in the capital stock of the Company."

Profits available for dividend: *payment out of capital profits held
to be dividend as between liferenter and fiar*

Forgie's Trustees v. Forgie
1941 S.C. 188

F., by his trust disposition and settlement, directed his trustees
to hold his shares in William Baird & Co. Ltd. for certain parties
in liferent and for others in fee.

On the eve of liquidation the company made a payment out
of capital profits accumulated in past years from the realisation
of investments.

Held that the payment fell to be treated by the trustees as an
income payment.

LORD PRESIDENT (NORMAND) (at p. 191): "A testator, if he
foresees that a company in which he holds stock or shares may
after his death make a special payment, out of the ordinary
course of its annual dividends and of the nature of a bonus,
can by appropriate provisions in his will determine whether the
payment shall be dealt with as income or as capital of his
estate. But in fact the testator in this case made no provisions
of that nature. . . .

"It is therefore common ground that the question whether
the sum paid under the resolution is income or capital of the
trust must be decided by the nature of the payment as determined by the act of the company. . . .

". . . This case is not concerned with the allotment of bonus
shares to shareholders when the company applies undivided profits to paying up the new shares in full, and I do not propose
to enter upon the specialties proper to that kind of case.

"Now in the present case the company which made the
payment was not in fact in liquidation when the payment was
resolved upon, and it had taken no step in an authorised
reduction of capital. It was therefore not competent for it to
make any payment to stockholders out of funds available for
distribution to them except by way of dividing profits. On these
facts the payment must be treated by the trustees as an income
payment. It is irrelevant that the company intended an immediate liquidation, and that on the next day a special resolution
was passed to carry that intention into effect. . . . A company
is either in liquidation or it is not, and a company not in liquidation . . . cannot modify the character of the payments by an
intention to go into liquidation even if the resolution authorising
the payment is one of the preliminary steps towards immediate

liquidation. . . . The company chose to distribute among its share-holders its accumulated profits before liquidation and therefore necessarily in accordance with the law which controls limited companies as going concerns in their distribution of profits. . . .

" . . . Something was said about the substance of the trans-action as a whole being the real test of the character of the repayment. But the substance and the form are one, and there is no conflict between them. In substance and form there was payment before liquidation of profits not by way of reduction of capital but by way of division of profits."

Profits available for dividend: capital surplus arising from revaluation not distributable as dividend

Westburn Sugar Refineries Ltd. v. Inland Revenue
1960 S.L.T. 297

W. Ltd.'s premises had been extensively damaged by enemy action in 1941. After their reinstatement, the buildings, plant and machinery were revalued at a figure £155,910 in excess of their former balance-sheet value, and £155,910 appeared on the liabilities side of the balance sheet as " surplus on revaluation of fixed assets," constituting the main item in capital reserve.

The company then increased its capital and applied £152,250 from the capital reserve in paying up the new shares and allotting them to existing stockholders.

The Inland Revenue contended that in capitalising £152,250 from the capital reserve W. Ltd. had capitalised a " distributable sum " within the meaning of the Finance Act 1951.

Held that that sum was not a " distributable sum " since it represented merely an unrealised increment in the value of certain assets of the company.

LORD PRESIDENT (CLYDE) (at p. 304): " To attract profits tax the sum capitalised must be a distributable sum. . . . A distri-butable sum . . . is a sum which could be utilised in making a distribution. But in the present case what was capitalised was not a cash sum or even a trading receipt but an increment in the value of the fixed assets of the Company consequent upon the revaluation of the plant and buildings. . . .

" But if the nature of this item in the balance sheet is con-sidered, it seems to me clear that it could not have been utilised in making a distribution within the meaning of section 31 (5) of the Act, either by dividend or cash payment or in kind. For it represented an unrealised increment in the value of certain assets of the Company, and in no way resembled a realised sum of money. . . .

" But apart from these considerations there is a quite separate ground upon which in my opinion the contention of the Inland Revenue must fail. For, in my opinion, it would have been contrary to law for the Company to have distributed the sum in question. Palmer's *Company Law* (20th edn.), p. 645, in dealing with unrealised appreciation of fixed assets states: ' According to Bateman it is " accounting practice to show the net surplus as a capital reserve, *i.e.* as an amount not regarded as free for distribution." This is undoubtedly sound business practice which in most instances well-conducted companies will adhere to. A different question is whether the law compels a company to adopt this course or authorises a company to transfer the net surplus obtained by writing up fixed assets to a capital reserve or a profit and loss account on the liabilities side of the balance sheet. In the 19th edition of this work the view was expressed that on the principle of the cases admitting the distribution of *realised* capital assets. . . . " accretions to capital not realised but immediately realisable and proved to exist can apparently be brought in as profits, but this never seems to have been expressly authorised, and is subject to the risk of valuation, which is relied upon as proving the accretions to capital values, proving mistaken." The present editors submit that as a general proposition of law this statement is correct, but that in practice the transfer of the net surplus to the profit and loss account will be admissible only in extreme cases and that even then it is highly undesirable.'

" I am of opinion that these observations are sound, and that particularly in the case of an appreciation which is neither realised nor immediately realisable it would be illegal to distribute the surplus. This certainly accords with the uncontradicted evidence in this case of the practice among chartered accountants. It appears to me that were the Courts to hold otherwise it would involve opening the door to dangerously premature distributions of the funds of a company which a change in economic trading conditions might prove to be disastrous after the lapse of a few years. For nowadays particularly the values of fixed assets may fluctuate heavily.

" . . . It has never been held that unrealised accretions can be distributed, and in my view it would be wrong so to hold. The case which comes nearest the Inland Revenue's contention is the case of *Ammonia Soda Co.* v. *Chamberlain* [1918] 1 Ch.

266, but that case was highly special and in any event it was not dealing with a distribution among shareholders but the writing off of a loss in the profit and loss account, where obviously the considerations are quite different. On this whole matter it appears to me that sound accounting practice accords with what the law requires, and it would therefore have been illegal in the present case for the Company to have distributed by way of dividend among their shareholders what was in fact an unrealisable increment in the value of their fixed assets."

NOTES

1. Lord Sorn dissented, but on the main argument advanced by the Crown his opinion was in agreement with that of the Lord President. After reviewing English cases, including *Ammonia Soda Co.* v. *Chamberlain*, Lord Sorn said (at p. 307): " These were all the cases quoted to us, and the citation serves to confirm my understanding of the law, namely, that a capital appreciation may be divided once it is realised, but that it may not be used for the payment of dividends while it is only a paper appreciation. I think, moreover, that it is undesirable that the law should be otherwise."

2. In *Dimbula Valley (Ceylon) Tea Co. Ltd.* v. *Laurie* [1961] Ch. 373 Buckley J. declined to follow this case, concluding that a company could legitimately distribute by way of dividend a capital surplus resulting from revaluation of assets.

That case is now taken account of in Palmer's *Company Law* (22nd edn.) 72–16.

The Jenkins Committee favoured statutory recognition of the Scottish rule (Cmnd. 1749, para. 350 (1962)).

Profits available for dividend: effect of alleged payment of dividends out of capital

Liquidators of the City of Glasgow Bank v. Mackinnon
(1881) 9 R. 535

M. had been a director of an unlimited banking company from 1858 to 1870. The bank went into liquidation in 1878, and in 1880 the liquidators claimed from M. £311,666 16s. 9d. which had been paid to shareholders as dividends between 1858 and 1870, on the ground that that sum had not represented profits earned but had been paid out of capital.

The liquidators' claim failed because (1) since they had in hand sufficient assets to pay all the creditors in full, they represented only shareholders and had therefore no title to sue, the shareholders having already received the amount being claimed; (2) the claim was barred by lapse of time combined with the action of the directors between 1870 and 1878 and with certain steps taken by the liquidators themselves; and (3) the liquidators had not established that M. had been a party to any proceeding which could fairly be regarded as the paying of dividends out of capital.

LORD PRESIDENT (INGLIS) (at p. 577): " An allegation that dividends have been paid out of capital may be either a very simple act of misfeasance, easily proved as matter of fact, or it may be only an inference in fact from complicated and continuous transactions stretching over a long course of years, and capable of being construed and judged of only by the application of commercial and actuarial knowledge and skill. That the present case belongs to the latter, and not the former of these categories, may be presumed from the almost unprecedented bulk and variety of the evidence laid before the Court.

. . .

" . . . The first overt act of misfeasance charged against [the respondent] is, that he, as a director, signed the balance-sheet of 1859, to be submitted to the shareholders at the annual meeting of that year.

. . .

" . . . It seems to me . . . that in order to convict the directors of this company of paying a dividend out of capital in 1859, it is necessary to prove not merely (1) that they knew that the interest on the American railway investment, though due, was not paid, and (2) that it was brought to the credit of profit and loss, and so divided as clear profit; but also (3) that they had not reasonable ground for believing that the interest was well secured and would ultimately be recovered.

. . .

" . . . On a full consideration of the evidence, I am satisfied that in the present case the directors acted not only in good faith, but with fair and reasonable grounds for the judgment which they formed.

" . . . It is of course necessary to have regard to the whole conduct of the directors from that year down to 1870 (when the respondent resigned), to determine whether the considerations which seem to me to justify the recommendations of the dividend of 1859 are equally applicable to the varied condition of the American securities during the subsequent years.

. . .

" The directors had been constantly assured by their agents, during the twelve years in question, that their investments were sound, and in the end would certainly prove good both for principal and interest.

. . .

" The evidence as to the real value of these securities in 1870 is voluminous and multifarious, and an examination of it has left on my mind a decided impression, that, after many years of anxious and careful treatment of the investment of this portion of the bank's funds, the directors had got into comparatively smooth water, and were possessed of a property or investment of a sound description.

" Certainly this impression is very strongly confirmed by the undoubted fact, that in 1870 the investment began to pay interest, and continued to do so down to the stoppage of the bank in 1878. . . .

" Now, it must be remembered that the investment of £905,000, which was thus yielding interest . . . , was composed not only of the money advanced by the bank, but of all the unpaid interest . . . which had accrued due since 1856; and thus this £905,000, which formed in 1870 an important part of the capital of the bank well secured, included, as one of its component parts, that £311,000 of the bank's capital which the respondent is charged with having misapplied by paying it away in dividends . . . ; the result being that in 1870 the amount of the bank's capital stood undiminished by the operations complained of.

. . .

" . . . It is necessary to keep in view that, when the note was presented, Mr. Mackinnon had been for 10 years entirely unconnected with the management of the bank. . . .

" In the interval of more than 10 years many important events had taken place. . . .

" . . . The securities, in dealing with which the breach of trust is said to have been committed, have been realised by the liquidators at a great sacrifice.

" The respondent says that, if he had had notice, he would have been prepared to relieve the liquidators of the securities, by paying them a price largely in excess of what they obtained; and he complains that he was not afforded an opportunity of doing so.

" . . . He has occasion to say, that that sacrifice ought not to have been made behind his back, especially as the whole responsibility for what was done with these securities prior to 1870 is proposed to be laid on him alone. . . .

" In these very peculiar circumstances, I am of opinion that the present claim, even if it were on its merits well founded (which I think it is not), is barred by what has occurred between July 1870 and November 1880.

" There is only one other question on which I think it right to offer an opinion before concluding—I mean the question, whether the liquidators have a title to maintain this claim against the respondent.

" The liquidation has now advanced so far as to shew that the creditors of the company will be paid in full, and that a surplus will be left for division among the partners. The liquidators therefore are suing, not in the interest of creditors, but of shareholders. . . .

. . .

" The inquiry at once presents itself, what are the liquidators to do with the £311,000 demanded from the respondent when they get it into their hands? Are they simply to distribute it among the remaining solvent shareholders, according to the amount of their shares? The result would be that those shareholders who got their full share of the capital of the company improperly paid away in dividends would receive payment of these dividends a second time in whole or in part. . . .

. . .

" But there is a still more serious, and I think, a fatal objection to the title of the liquidators to insist in this demand. Every shareholder of the company for the time received his share of each of the dividends said to have been unlawfully paid, and so each share of the company's stock received just as much of these dividends as every other share. . . . If the shareholder who received payment of a dividend out of capital is to have the improperly divided capital replaced, in order that, in the liquidation, he and his co-partners may have the replaced capital divided among them rateably, then he must repay the dividend improperly paid and received; and his assignee or successor . . . must fulfil the obligation to repay the dividend. His claim, therefore, is barred on the principle, ' *Frustra petis quod mox es restituturus.* '

. . .

" I am for refusing the prayer of the note, for these three reasons: 1. That the liquidators have, at this stage of the liquidation, no title or legitimate interest to maintain the claim they make. 2. That the claim is barred by lapse of time, combined with the action of the managers and directors of the bank between 1870 and 1878, and the conduct of the liquidators in disposing of the railway securities, without any communication with the respondent, or notice to him. 3. That there is an entire failure to establish that the respondent was a party to any proceeding which can properly or fairly be described as paying dividends out of capital."

Payment of dividends: articles may require whole profits to be divided

Paterson v. R. Paterson & Sons Ltd.
1917 S.C. (H.L.) 13; 1916 S.C. 452

Article 12 of the articles of association of P. Ltd. provided that " after allowing for all charges, including the payment of directors' salaries, the profits of the company shall be applied " in payment of dividends.

A motion was carried at a general meeting approving of a proposal by the directors to transfer £3,000 from profits to reserve before paying dividends.

P., a dissentient shareholder, brought an action for reduction of the minute of that resolution, and for declarator that the profits fell to be divided among the shareholders in terms of article 12.

Held that P. was entitled to the reduction and declarator sought.

EARL LOREBURN (at p. 13): " The question really lies in a nutshell. The Company has placed to reserve the sum of £3,000 out of the profits of the year. Can it do so lawfully? That will depend upon the articles of association. . . . I find here that there is a direction in article 12 that the profits of the Company shall be paid to particular participants and in particular proportions. . . . I think the appeal ought to be dismissed."

LORD KINNEAR (at p. 15): " I think it is . . . a question of contract.

" The parties, who are members of this trading Company, have agreed by clause 12 of the articles of association, which has the effect of a contract *inter se,* that the profits of the Company shall be applied in a certain specified way which is set forth in detail. So far as the directors are concerned, this is a peremptory mandate which they are bound to obey. . . . But then it is said that there is brought in a discretion by the 99th article in Table A, which allows the directors to set aside a proportion of the profits to reserve if they so think fit. Nobody disputes that that is a most reasonable discretion for directors to have, and that it may be an extremely useful one. But, then is it consistent with an express direction in the form of a peremptory mandate that they shall distribute the profits in one particular way and no other? Table A is applicable to this Company only in so far as its provisions are not altered, modified, or excluded by the Company's own articles of association, and I am of opinion that article 99 is effectually excluded by clause 12. . . . The question is one of construction of a contract, and I think the Court has answered it in the right way."

LORD SHAW OF DUNFERMLINE (at p. 16): " A substantial part of the argument before your Lordships had of course reference to the possibility of reconciling the provisions of article 99 of Table A of the Companies Act with the provisions of section 12 of these articles of association. In my judgment they cannot be reconciled.

" . . . The direction in article 12 is a mandatory direction, and is comprehensively mandatory in the sense of compelling the total distribution of the year's profits. I think that cannot be reconciled (a mandatory and comprehensive direction for total distribution of the profits) with an optional reserve out of the profits resulting in only a partial distribution."

NOTES
1. In the Companies Act 1948, regulation 117 of Table A in the First Schedule corresponds to the article 99 referred to in this case.
2. In *Wemyss Collieries Trust Ltd.* v. *Melville* (1905) 8 F. 143, a special case between W. Ltd. and certain of its own preference shareholders, directors were held to have acted *intra vires* in carrying a sum to a reserve fund even although the effect of that was to deprive the preference shareholders of an additional one per cent. dividend to which they would otherwise have been entitled.

Payment of dividends: apportionment according to amount paid up on shares

Hoggan, &c. v. The Tharsis Sulphur and Copper Co. Ltd.
(1882) 9 R. 1191

The capital of T. Ltd. was divided into shares of £10 each. Some of the shares were fully paid up, while others were paid up only to the extent of £7 per share.

The only provision made by T. Ltd.'s articles of association for the payment of dividends was that the directors might from time to time " declare and divide an interim dividend out of the profits of the company, and pay the same to the members in proportion to the capital held by each." The articles gave the directors power to receive advances from members of sums beyond what had been called up on their shares and to pay interest " in lieu of dividends " thereon.

Dividends had always been paid in proportion to the amount paid up on the shares.

In 1882 certain holders of the shares on which only £7 had been paid up claimed that dividends fell to be paid upon the nominal amount of their shares and not merely upon the amount paid up.

Held that, in the absence of any provision to the contrary in the articles of association, dividends fell to be apportioned according to the amount paid up on the shares.

LORD PRESIDENT (INGLIS) (at p. 1206): " It is contended by pursuers that they are entitled to be paid dividends upon the full amount of their nominal capital in the company, and not upon their paid-up capital, . . . and in support of this contention they refer to the case of the *Oakbank Oil Company,* which was lately decided in this Division of the Court. Now, it appears to me that the present case is essentially different from that of the *Oakbank Oil Company.* In that case there was an article . . . which expressly directed in what way, and upon what capital, dividends were to be paid. It was the 71st article of the articles of association of that company, and it corresponded very much in its language with the 72nd head of table A of the Companies Act of 1862. But that rule or regulation did not stand alone as the foundation of the judgment of this Court in the case of the *Oakbank Oil Company.* It was a combination of that article with a certain interpretation clause that left the Court, as they thought, no choice but to construe the 71st article of association as directing that dividends were to be paid, not upon the paid-up capital, but upon the nominal capital of the company, and in proportion to the share that each member of the company had in the nominal capital. The interpretation clause fixed the precise meaning of the words which were used in the 71st article; and, in particular, it fixed the meaning of the word ' capital,' as there used, to be nominal capital, and the shares which were spoken of, to be shares of nominal capital; and thus it came about that the Court found they had no choice but to hold that, in the articles of that particular company, there was an express provision that the dividends should be paid, not according to the paid-up capital held by each shareholder, but according to the nominal capital. There was in that case also another clause ... providing that it should be competent for the directors to take payment of unpaid capital in advance, and pay interest thereon; and, at first sight, there is repugnance between that provision and the 71st article upon which our judgment was founded. But the repugnance was not so strong as to overcome the effect of the language used in the 71st article, as that language was defined by the interpretation clause. . . .

" In the present case the matter stands very differently indeed. There is not in the articles of association of this company any article corresponding to the 71st article of the Oakbank Company. There is not in this case any article which provides in what manner, or upon what capital, the dividends are to be paid. It is thus left, I think, to the common law principle, regulating the division of profits according to the ordinary law of partnership; and that, undoubtedly, would lead to the conclusion that the proper division is according to the amount of paid-up capital held by each shareholder. It is a rule founded upon the plainest equity, and it is a rule against which, I apprehend, there is no authority whatever; while among the text writers, Lord Justice Lindley has laid down as a rule certainly applicable in all companies where there is no provision to the contrary. Therefore, I think that, not having a special rule as to the capital upon which dividend is to be paid, we must follow the common law rule, which affirms that the dividend shall be proportioned to the amount of paid-up capital held by each shareholder.

" I am well aware that there is one of the articles of association here which deals with the matter of dividends somewhat indirectly. . . . [After quoting the article relating to interim dividends] Now, of course, it is not suggested by anybody that the final dividend for the year is to be paid according to one principle, and interim dividends according to another. . . . The argument presented to us by the pursuers here is, that this article . . ... assumes that the dividends are to be paid according to the nominal capital held by each shareholder, and not according to the paid-up capital; and they infer that from the use of the words ' in proportion to the capital held by each.' But capital is a term which may mean either nominal capital or paid-up capital; and there is certainly nothing in this 75th article to determine in which of the two senses the word is used here; nor is there, as there was in the case of the *Oakbank Company,* any interpretation of that word for the purpose of giving a construction to this 75th article. . . . I think we are bound to proceed, in the construction of this article, upon the assumption that the general rule applicable to the dividends of this company is the common law rule, that dividends shall be proportioned to the capital paid up, and not to the nominal capital held by each shareholder.

" Then we have here, as we had in the *Oakbank* case, the article . . . which authorises the directors to take advances upon unpaid capital from the shareholders, and to pay interest upon them; . . . it is in this case not repugnant to the other provisions of the articles, but in strict harmony with them. And further it is expressed in a way much more emphatic than it was in the case of the *Oakbank Company*, because the company are to pay interest on these advances ' at such rate as the member paying such sum in advance and the directors may agree upon, which interest shall be in lieu of dividend in respect of such advance.' . . .

" . . . I come to the conclusion, without any hesitation, that this is an entirely different case from the *Oakbank* case, and that the pursuers have entirely failed to make out that they have, in the memorandum and articles of association, any right to be paid dividends corresponding to the nominal or unpaid capital."

NOTE

The *Oakbank* case referred to later went to the House of Lords: *Oakbank Oil Co. Ltd.* v. *Crum* (1882) 10 R.(H.L.) 11, where the judgment of the First Division of the Court of Session ((1881) 9 R. 198) was affirmed.

The articles of association in that case provided that " the directors may . . . declare a dividend to be paid to the members in proportion to their shares," and that " capital " should mean " the capital for the time being of the company," and " shares " " the shares into which the capital is divided."

The capital of the company consisted of 60,000 shares of £1 each. Of these, 40,000 were fully paid up, while the remainder were paid up only to the extent of 5s. per share. A resolution of the company declaring a dividend bore that it should be paid " upon the paid-up capital of the company."

The question submitted in a special case between the company and C., the holder of shares on which only 5s. had been paid up, was whether C. was entitled to claim that all dividends declared should be declared in proportion to the number of shares held, without regard to the amount paid up on the shares, or whether it was within the power of the company to sanction a dividend payable to each shareholder in proportion to the amount paid up upon the shares.

Lord Chancellor (Selborne) (at p. 12): " The question depends, I think, entirely upon the true construction of the contract contained in the memorandum and articles of association of this company."

Lord Watson (at p. 17): " I am of opinion with your Lordships that the question here turns upon the meaning of the word ' shares ' as occurring in the 71st of the articles of association of this company, and I have come to the same conclusion as your Lordships, to the effect that the word ' shares ' in that article is used to signify the amount of subscribed capital which the member has either contributed already or has undertaken to contribute, and that it bears no reference whatever to the different amounts which may have been paid up under call upon different classes of shares."

Payment of dividends: payment in cash

Beaumont, &c. v. The Great North of Scotland Railway Co., &c.
(1868) 6 M. 1027

A railway company purported to authorise its directors to pay dividends by allotments of capital stock of the company instead of in cash.

Held that the resolution was *ultra vires.*

LORD DEAS (at p. 1034): " The only other point is as to the giving off the Formartine and Buchan stock, and on that point I entirely concur with the Lord Ordinary. Apart altogether from the authority of decisions, it comes to this, that the dividends would be paid with the capital, and not with the profits of the company. If the company were first to sell the shares, and then give the price to the shareholders, that would be giving the capital; and what has been done comes to precisely the same result. Each shareholder who received an allotment of that stock would receive a portion of the capital of the company which ought to be left to yield dividend."

LORD KINLOCH (at p. 1035): " On the second point, I think the case of *Hoole* is sound in principle, and ought to be adhered to."

LORD ORDINARY (BARCAPLE) (at p. 1032): " The last point in the case is as to the alleged illegality of a resolution, passed at a meeting of October 3, 1867, authorising the directors, in lieu of cash payments, to pay the dividends then declared on the two classes of preference stocks above mentioned by allotments of capital stock then unissued in the hands of the company. Reference on this point was made to the case of *Hoole* v. *Great Western Railway* (1867) L.R. 3 Ch.App. 262. The cases are different in so far as there was there a statutory provision that dividends should not be paid out of monies received for the shares. But on general principles, which were given effect to in that case, the Lord Ordinary is of opinion that the resolution was *ultra vires* of the company. It appears from the minute of the meeting, and the report of the directors on which it acted, that there were not funds presently available for payment of the dividend, although profits may have been actually made. The Lord Ordinary thinks that, in these circumstances, the company could not make use of their unissued shares to pay the dividend. They could not of course compel any shareholder to take stock, and the result of any of them refusing to do so would be to give to some of the shareholders their dividends in stock, as an equivalent for payment, and to others only the prospect of payment when funds can be set free for that purpose."

Creation of reserve before declaration of dividend

Cadell v. Scottish Investment Trust Co. Ltd.
(1901) 9 S.L.T. 299; (1901) 8 S.L.T. 480 (O.H.)

The accounts of S. Ltd. for the year to November 1, 1899, showed a balance on the revenue account of £23,978 12s. 9d. The directors paid 5 per cent. dividend on the preferred stock, and 2 per cent. dividend on the deferred stock, and carried forward £7,061 19s. 5d.

C., who held £1,000 of the deferred stock, brought an action against S. Ltd. for declarator that the company was bound to apply this balance in payment of such dividend on the deferred stock as it should suffice to pay.

By the articles of association the directors had power, before recommending any dividend, to " set apart " sums which in their judgment might be necessary to meet any claims or contingent liabilities against the company.

Held that on a sound construction of the articles S. Ltd. was entitled to be assoilzied.

Lord McLaren (at p. 299): " The pursuer objects to the manner in which the profits of the year are treated, because a balance of £7,000 odds has been carried forward, instead of being divided amongst the shareholders in addition to the dividend declared. . . . The general practice of companies certainly is not to divide the total profits but to carry forward a part to make provision for meeting current liabilities. In the case of an ordinary manufacturing company, this is very necessary, for otherwise, in such a case, the works would be brought to a standstill, or money for wages and material would have to be got by borrowing. It is not so necessary in the case of this company whose business is to buy and sell shares; but then the balance carried forward is proportionately small. Now, is there anything in the articles of association to prevent the company doing as it has done? Article 105 is very significant on that point. The company in general meeting declares the dividend of the year, but then the article proceeds: ' No larger dividend shall be declared than is recommended by the trustees. The declaration of the trustees as to the amount of the profits shall be conclusive.' That means that in case any shareholder would like a larger amount to be divided, this law stands in his way, because the directors have a discretion. What is it? Is it a discretion to declare a dividend larger than the earnings of the year, or smaller? It must be the latter. . . .

" . . . The company is said to have suffered considerably from the depreciation of its investment. That must often happen to a company of this kind which has to face the rise and fall of the market, and its directors must make provision for such a contingency if it is in their discretion. Under article 105 they have that discretion."

LORD ORDINARY (STORMONTH DARLING) (at p. 481): " ' Setting apart ' and ' carrying forward ' are really convertible terms. When you carry forward a balance, you set it apart, and *vice versa.* . . .

" I have no doubt of the legality of the course which was followed in 1899."

NOTES

1. Compare *Wemyss Collieries Trust Ltd.* v. *Melville* (1902) 8 F. 143 (Note 2 to *Paterson* v. *R. Paterson & Sons Ltd.,* p. 311, above); contrast *Paterson* v. *R. Paterson & Sons Ltd.* (p. 310, above).

2. Payment out of a reserve fund may be dividend: *Blyth's Trustees* v. *Milne* (p. 301, above).

CHAPTER 19

DEBENTURES

Company with power to borrow held to have implied power to grant heritable security

Paterson's Trustees v.
The Caledonian Heritable Security Co. Ltd. and Liquidator
(1885) 13 R. 369

C. Ltd. had power under its memorandum of association to lend money on heritable security, and to borrow on deposit or debenture, and to do all things incidental or conducive to the attainment of these objects.

C. Ltd. lent money on a second bond over a property, and to prevent an unfavourable sale by the prior bondholder the manager bought in the property, using money borrowed from a body of trustees to pay the price. The manager granted a bond over the property to the trustees as security.

In the liquidation of C. Ltd., the liquidator repudiated both the purchase of the property and the loan on security of it on the ground that both transactions were *ultra vires* of the company and its directors.

The lenders sued the company in liquidation for the amount of the loan.

Held that (1) as the company had power to borrow money the manager had acted within his power in the loan transaction and (2) the lenders had no concern with the application of the money and therefore the company was liable for the loan.

Opinions that in the circumstances the company had power to buy in the property.

LORD JUSTICE-CLERK (MONCREIFF) (at p. 377): " It is, I think, a simple case of lender and borrower, and the company who were the borrowers were entirely within their powers in entering into that contract. There is no suggestion that an ordinary loan by bond is not within the powers of the company, and none that the giving heritable security for such loan would alter its position. . . . But it is sought to bring the lender into contact with the prior transaction, whereby the borrowing company acquired the property. . . . The officebearers of the company came to be of opinion that it would be a good thing for the

318

company to buy in the property . . . rather than allow the money which they had advanced on it to be irretrievably sacrificed.
. . .

" . . . Mr. Bell advanced to the company the money of those marriage trustees to take up the prior bonds. . . .

" The question, then, to my mind is simply this, had the company power to borrow? I have already answered that they had. They did borrow, and with the application of the money the lenders had no concern. . . .

" I do not therefore think that it is necessary to go further into the question as to the company's power to buy the property. At the same time I may say that if they had power to lend on heritable security, which undoubtedly they had, I should, if necessary, be of opinion that they had power to do what they did by way of protecting their security from sacrifice, and that what they did do was a reasonable act in the interest of the shareholders."

NOTES

1. On the protection afforded to outsiders where a loan is *ultra vires* of the directors but not of the company, see *Gillies* v. *The Craigton Garage Co. Ltd.*, in the chapter on Protection of Outsiders (p. 292, above). Further quotations from the case of *Paterson's Trustees* are included in Note 3 to *Gillies'* case (p. 294).

2. On the invalidity of a security over the guarantee fund in a company limited by guarantee, see *Robertson* v. *British Linen Co.*, in the introductory chapter on Companies, p. 45, above. Security may be validly created over a guarantee fund which is independent of the statutory guarantee fund: *Lloyds Bank Ltd.* v. *Morrison & Son* (Note to *Robertson* v. *British Linen Co.*, p. 45, above).

Assignation of uncalled capital in security

Liquidator of the Union Club Ltd. v. Edinburgh Life Assurance Co.
(1906) 8 F. 1143

A club which was a registered company leased certain premises in Hanover Street, Edinburgh, from an assurance company at a yearly rent. By a minute of agreement between the club and the assurance company, the club, in security of the obligations undertaken by it in the lease, assigned to the assurance company its uncalled capital of 5s. per share on its issued shares of £1 each which were 15s. paid up and also of 5s. per share on shares which might afterwards be issued.

At the first general meeting of the club the secretary read a report by the committee of management. The report included the statement: " In security of these obligations the Committee has assigned to the Edinburgh Life Assurance Company the uncalled capital of 5s. per share."

The club resolved to wind up voluntarily.

The liquidator maintained that the assurance company was not entitled to any preference over the general body of creditors because the assignation had never been intimated to the shareholders. The assurance company argued that the assignation had been sufficiently intimated by the reading out of the report at the first general meeting.

Held that the assignation had not been validly intimated to the shareholders, and that therefore the assurance company had no preference in the winding up.

Lord President (Dunedin) (at p. 1145): " It is trite law in Scotland that an assignation, in order to make it a perfected security, must not only be an assignation but must be an assignation intimated.

" There was a somewhat heroic attempt . . . to shew that there had been intimation here. . . . There had been a general meeting at which some gentleman read out a manuscript report in which he said this thing had been done. There might or might not be a question as to how far that would be a proper intimation to a gentleman who was there and heard it, but to put it, as it was necessary to put it for the purposes of this case, as an intimation to the whole of the shareholders of the Club, many of whom were not there, is, I think, a sheer impossibility, and, therefore, . . . there has been no good security constituted, and consequently the landlord by this assignation of the uncalled capital has obtained no preference over the general body of creditors."

Lord McLaren (at p. 1145): " In the question of the validity of the assignment of the Company's uncalled capital, it is perhaps unfortunate that our decision may introduce a difference of practice into the law of England and Scotland, but then that difference is the necessary and unavoidable result of the common law of the two countries. Under our law intimation is not only necessary to put the debtor in good faith to pay to the assignee, and in bad faith if he pays to the original creditor, but it is necessary to transfer the right in a question of legal competition. Now, I agree with your Lordship that is impossible to say that there was in this case anything which we can recognise as equivalent to intimation. The law does recognise equivalents to the more formal intimation—which I think has almost disappeared in practice—I mean intimation by a notary and witnesses, but it must amount to substantial intimation, so that every one of the debtors, or his agent having authority to act for him, shall be notified that the creditor has assigned his right to another person."

NOTES

1. In *Liquidator of the Ballachulish Slate Quarries Co. Ltd.* v. *Malcolm and Others* (1908) 15 S.L.T. 963 (O.H.) an assignation in security of uncalled capital was held to have been validly intimated, with the result that M. and others were held entitled to have the sums realised from uncalled capital set aside and retained for security of their obligations.

Lord Johnston (Ordinary) (at p. 965): " I conclude therefore that a charge on the uncalled capital of the Company is just as competent in Scotland as in England. But then, in order that it may be effectual, it is necessary that it should be effected according to the law of Scotland—that is, that the law of Scotland, which requires intimation of an assignation, should be attended to. . . . But this has been done in the present case, as the bond of relief and assignation in security was intimated to each shareholder of the Company at the time it was granted, and I am not informed that there has been any change on the register of shareholders."

2. Section 1 (1) of the Companies (Floating Charges and Receivers) (Scotland) Act 1972 expressly provides that the property over which a floating charge may be created includes uncalled capital.

Issue of debentures: action of damages by debenture holder against promoter

Dunnett v. Mitchell
(1885) 12 R. 400

D., a Scotsman who had been resident for some years in Norway, came to Glasgow in 1877 to promote the formation of a small limited company to purchase the estate of Vaagsoeter in Norway.

M. was induced by D.'s representations as to the extent and the forests and minerals of the estate to advance certain sums on debenture-bonds of the new company.

The management of the company's affairs in Norway was at first in the hands of D. After D.'s dismissal in 1882 M. learned that D.'s representations had been false, and he brought an action of damages against D. on the ground that by false and fraudulent representations of D. he had been induced to advance money to the company and that there were no assets of the company to meet the debenture debt.

Held that M. had a good title to sue.

LORD YOUNG (at p. 402): " The respondent, when the company finally proved a failure, brought an action against the complainer for damages, rested on the ground that upon false representations by the complainer, fraudulently made, the company had been formed and the respondent and his friends had taken shares and advanced certain moneys on debenture, and in consequence had incurred certain losses through the complainer. In that action the respondent obtained decree in absence on December 8, 1883.

" The complainer brings a suspension of this decree. . . .

" The Lord Ordinary has set aside the decree in absence, on the ground that the only damage condescended on is damage arising from the purchase of the property in Norway, induced by the statements of the complainer, and that if there is a remedy against him for having so induced the purchase, that remedy lies with the company, which, if successful, will obtain the means of indemnifying the shareholders. And there may be a great deal to be said for that view. But in respect of the debenture debt that view is not applicable, for the company could have no action against the complainer on the ground that certain persons were, through his representations, induced to lend it money on its debenture bonds. In that case, if the action is otherwise relevant, then the debenture-holders are the only parties at whose instance it can proceed, and therefore, so far, dealing merely with the debenture debt by way of illustration, I think we must consider whether there are relevant grounds of action stated by the respondent.

" So doing, I think that the representations . . . being averred to be false, to the knowledge of and made fraudulently by the complainer, do afford relevant ground of action, and that if the respondent can prove that they were made, and were false to the knowledge of the complainer, and were made for the fraudulent purpose and with the effect . . . set forth, the respondent is entitled to reparation."

Redeemable debentures

The United Collieries Ltd. v. Lord Advocate
1950 S.C. 458

U. Ltd. made a large issue of debentures which were to mature in 1936. Provision was made for redemption by drawings before maturity.

By 1923 all the debentures had been drawn for repayment, but in some cases repayment had not actually been made because the company had been unable to trace the holders. In that year, in connection with a scheme of arrangement and reduction of capital sanctioned by the court, U. Ltd. deposited the amount of the unpaid debentures and the interest due on them in a bank. In 1924 the deposited money was withdrawn from the bank and invested.

In later years a few of the holders were traced and received payment of their debentures, without interest for the period since 1923 until payment.

In 1949 questions arose as to the disposal of the balance of the deposited fund and of the interest which had accrued on it. U. Ltd. claimed that the fund had been provided as a security for the unpaid holders, and that since the rights of these holders had now been cut off by the negative prescription, the company was entitled to the fund. The Lord Advocate, as representing the Crown as *ultimus haeres,* contended that only the unpaid holders had the beneficial interest in the fund, and that as the holders had not appeared to claim their rights, the fund should pass to the Crown as *bona vacantia.* There was also a claim by representatives of a holder whose debentures had been repaid in 1933 for interest for the period from 1923 to 1933 and for interest on that interest from 1933 until payment.

Held that (1) U. Ltd. had no beneficial interest in the fund after 1923, (2) from 1923 the fund and all accruing interest were held in trust for the unpaid debenture holders alone, (3) the rights of the holders to claim payment out of the fund had therefore not been cut off by the negative prescription, and (4) the representatives of the holder whose debentures had been repaid in 1933 were entitled to the interest which they claimed.

Held further that the fund should not be paid over to the Crown but be consigned in the hands of the Accountant of Court and dealt with in accordance with the Court of Session Consignations (Scotland) Act 1895.

LORD PRESIDENT (COOPER) (at p. 471): " The central problem is to place the correct interpretation upon a transaction effected by the company in 1923 as an integral part of the financial reconstruction which was then carried out with the approval of the Court. . . .

. . .

"... The weight of the company's effort was thrown into an endeavour to suggest that all that happened in 1923 was that the company provided the debenture trustees with substitute ' security ' to take the place of the lands, mineral leases, &c., by which the debenture issues had been secured, and which under the scheme of reconstruction were to be released. This suggestion impresses me as quite unacceptable, and as involving a misuse of the term ' security ' and a violent misinterpretation of what was in fact done. When a debtor, who admits liability for a debt of known amount but cannot find his creditor, and who for some reason desires to clear his feet of the liability, deposits the full amount of that debt in neutral custody for behoof of the absent creditor, it is impossible to assert that the debtor is giving ' security ' for the payment of his debt, unless the term is used in some loose and popular sense unknown to Scots law. A transaction of the type figured was known to Roman law in the *actio sequestraria*, and it and its incidents have been familiar in Scots law from the earliest times. ... Its correct designation is ' consignation,' and it is a species of the genus ' improper deposit.' In modern times, of course, consignation is usually ' judicial,' made under the orders of a Court by methods and with consequences prescribed by procedural statutes. But common law consignations still survive, and it is that description which the transaction of 1923 most nearly fits. It is the description which the company themselves chose to explain what they had done. In their petition to the Court for sanction of the 1923 scheme of arrangement and confirmation of the reduction of capital, the company formally stated that ' the company has *consigned* the said sum of £5,865 together with interest due thereon in the joint names of the company and the Collieries Trustee Company, Limited, as the trustee for the First Debenture holders, *for behoof of the holders of such unpaid debentures* pending the settlement thereof.' ... I have no doubt that it was only in reliance upon the plain meaning of this statement that the Court approved of the company's proposals. ... By using the words ' consign ... for behoof of the holders of such unpaid debentures ' the company represented to the Court that they had irrevocably impressed the money in the hands of the joint holders with a trust for the benefit of the absent creditors ... and I do not consider that they can now be heard to assert that they did anything else or anything less. In particular, if it had been stated to the Court in 1923—as it has now been argued to us— that the company reserved to themselves the right eventually to appropriate the money of the absent debenture holders who had lent it to the company, I am certain that the Court would have accepted no such proposal.

. . .

" . . . The disposal of the fund requires more consideration. The Lord Ordinary appears to have proceeded on the footing that the fund should now be made over absolutely to the Crown as *bona vacantia.* Before us that extreme view was not maintained, the attitude . . . being that, if and when the absent creditors appeared to claim, the Crown in accordance with Scottish practice would entertain the claims on their merits as claims by beneficiaries against a trust fund and as such not liable to prescribe. I think that it would be preferable in this case to achieve substantially the same result with statutory efficacy by appointing the pursuers and real raisers to consign the amount of the fund as finally adjusted in the hands of the Accountant of Court, in which event it will fall to be treated under the Court of Session Consignations (Scotland) Act 1895, and, if unclaimed, will eventually pass to the King's and Lord Treasurer's Remembrancer subject to the obligation imposed by section 16 of the Act.

" It remains to deal with the small claim for Mrs. Salvesen and others who received payment of their debt in 1933 without the interest which accrued upon it in the hands of the pursuers and real raisers between 1923 and 1933. The Lord Ordinary has rightly found them entitled to that interest. But before us they have been emboldened to ask by an amendment for a little more, *viz.,* interest from 1933 to date at 5 per cent. on the withheld interest upon the view that it was wrongfully withheld. . . . I see no answer to the claim that these parties should receive interest on the withheld interest at the rate actually earned, but not at 5 per cent."

LORD KEITH (at p. 475): " The fund *in medio* has since its creation been impressed with the qualities of a trust fund. The contention that it was never more than a security . . . is, I think, unsound. . . .

" It was contended for the company that, if this was a trust, there had emerged a resulting trust in favour of the company. I can see no room for any such result. The debentures had been issued for value and had become the property of the holders and their representatives. A trust for these persons could never result in a trust for the company."

Charges securing debentures: creation of floating charge ineffectual at common law

Carse v. Coppen
1951 S.C. 233

Shop Fronts (Great Britain) Ltd., whose registered office was in Glasgow, borrowed large sums from Coppen and granted in his favour two debentures which purported to create a floating charge over the company's whole undertaking, property and assets. The company had assets both in Scotland and in England.

In the liquidation of the company the liquidator presented a petition under section 307 of the Companies Act 1948 to have it determined by the court whether the debentures had created a valid and effectual floating charge over the company's assets in England. It was conceded that no valid and effectual floating charge had been created over the Scottish assets.

Held that the debentures had not created a valid and effectual floating charge over the assets in England either.

LORD PRESIDENT (COOPER) (at p. 239): " It is clear in principle and amply supported by authority that a floating charge is utterly repugnant to the principles of Scots law and is not recognised by us as creating a security at all. In Scotland the term ' equitable security ' is meaningless. Putting aside the rare and exceptional cases of hypothec, we require for the constitution of a security which will confer upon the holder rights over and above those which he enjoys in common with the general body of unsecured creditors of a debtor, (*a*) the transfer to the creditor of a real right in specific subjects by the method appropriate for the constitution of such rights in the particular classes of property in question, or (*b*) the creation of a nexus over specific property by the due use of the appropriate form of diligence. A floating charge, even after appointment of a receiver, satisfies none of these requirements.

" But, however plain it is that Scottish companies (or individuals) cannot create floating charges which the Scottish Courts will recognise. it does not *necessarily* follow, the respondents argue, that Scottish companies cannot create floating charges as regards English assets. In this petition we are compelled for the first time to face this issue, and its implications.

. . .

" . . . The law which determines the nature and extent of the powers of any corporation is the law of the country in which it is incorporated—in this case Scots law, which for present purposes means our common law of the transfer of property rights, read along with the Companies Act 1948. The answer given by that law is plain. 'The whole method of *creating* a floating charge . . . is absolutely foreign to our law' (*The Balla-chulish Slate Quarries Co.* v. *Bruce and Others* (1908) 16 S.L.T. 48, Lord President Dunedin at p. 51). 'This is a case of bungled conveyancing which has not successfully *created* any right of security in any part of the property, either in the uncalled capital or in *anything else*' (16 S.L.T. 48, Lord Kinnear at pp. 51 and 52).

"I am accordingly prepared to affirm that, when the Scottish Courts are asked by the liquidator of a Scottish company to state what effect he is to give to a universal assignment of the company's undertaking, property and assets by way of floating charge, the answer is 'None.' The law of Scotland does not empower Scottish corporations to create securities by such methods, which in the words of Lord Dunedin, are to us 'absolutely unmeaning' (*ibid.,* at p. 51)."

LORD CARMONT (at p. 243): "The law of Scotland does not recognise and can attach no meaning to a floating charge. The powers of a Scottish company in the matter of its general obligations are different from those of companies registered in other countries. Those differences are fixed by the law of Scotland as the domicile of the company. . . .

"... However restricted are the differences between companies registered in Scotland as compared with those in England, each recognises the other's domicile. A company's domicile is created by registration; it is, so to say, born in Scotland, and however widespread its activities and contacts with other legal systems in the days of its vigour, to Scotland it must come to be laid to rest when its days are done, and according to Scots law should its affairs be wound up."

NOTES

1. Lord Keith dissented: in his opinion the question fell to be decided by the law of England where the assets were situated. He continued (at p. 245): "I know of no principle on which it can be asserted that, because Scots law does not recognise a floating charge, a deed which attempts to constitute a floating charge over assets outside Scotland is essentially invalid. It is true that the debentures here purport to create a floating charge over the whole of the company's assets wherever situated; but that does not, in my opinion, make the floating charge fundamentally null. It leaves the creditor

with the right to enforce the charge wherever it can be made effective. . . .

. . .

" In the result, then, the floating charges in this case, whether regarded as securities or as diligences, in my opinion, fall to receive effect so far as assets in England are concerned according to the law of England."

2. In *The Ballachulish Slate Quarries Co. Ltd. and Another* v *Bruce and Others* (1908) 16 S.L.T. 48 referred to by the Lord President, the question was whether B. Ltd., which held a debenture from the Easdale Slate Quarries Co. Ltd., had a valid security over that company's uncalled capital.

Held that no valid security had been created in favour of B. Ltd.

Lord President (Dunedin) (at p. 51): " The person who has written these deeds has slavishly copied English forms, and has thus tried to introduce into Scotland forms which are here absolutely unmeaning; and we are asked to try and find out what is the effect in Scots law of a set of phrases which are not appropriate to the Scottish system at all. . . . Owing to the doctrines of our system as to creating securities over moveables, which I need not detail, it follows that practically the only way in which a security can be created over uncalled capital is to assign that uncalled capital to a named person and intimate the assignation personally to every shareholder. That will put the shareholder in the position of being *in mala fide* in paying the debt to the Company, and direct him, on the contrary, to make payment to the person in favour of whom the assignation is made. Nothing of that sort was done here. What was done was that there was an English form taken, and a very familiar one, namely, a document under which what is called a ' floating charge ' is created. . . . It is common knowledge that it is possible to create a floating charge over moveable estate in England; and if there is a proper authorisation to that effect under the articles and memorandum of association, you can make a floating charge include uncalled capital. But the whole method of creating a floating charge . . . is absolutely foreign to our law, and consequently the form which was here used was perfectly inappropriate to create a valid security over uncalled capital according to the forms of the law of Scotland."

Lord McLaren (at p. 51): " In order that there may be a good security over uncalled capital, it would be necessary that there should be an effective intimation to every individual shareholder, either by sending it by an officer or by getting an acknowledgment from each shareholder. . . . At the date of the assignment the so-called assignee was not put in the place of the cedent, and therefore I think the assignation was worthless, because it was not such an assignation of a right as the law of Scotland will recognise. The result is that these bondholders who claim a preference are in no better position than if they were ordinary creditors."

Lord Kinnear (at p. 51): " This is a case of bungled conveyancing which has not successfully created any right of security in any part of the property, either in the uncalled capital or in anything else."

3. Similarly, in *Clark, &c.* v. *The West Calder Oil Co., &c.* (1882) 9 R. 1017, where there had been a purported assignation of leases, moveables and plant to trustees for debenture holders, with intimation to the landlords but with no entry into possession by the assignees, the court held that in the company's liquidation the trustees had no preference over the company's ordinary trade creditors.

Lord President (Inglis) (at p. 1024): "This is a question which falls to be determined according to the principles of the common law. These trust-conveyances were not made under any Act of Parliament, or with the authority of any Act of Parliament, but they were simply trust-conveyances made in terms of agreements between the company and its debenture-holders, and taking this as a question of common law it does not seem to me to be attended with any difficulty whatever. The assignation of the leases, with no possession following upon it, creates no right whatever in the assignee except a mere personal claim against the granter of the assignation. . . . Till possession is actually obtained there is no real right, and no security created in favour of the assignee whatever. . . . For the last half century it has been settled by the well-known case of *Cabbell and Brock*, May 13, 1828, 3 W. and S. 75, and a series of cases connected with it, that an assignation of a lease without possession is quite unavailing as a real security. While this is clear as to the subjects let in lease, it is still more clear as regards the moveables on the ground. A mere assignation of corporeal moveables *retenta possessione* is nothing whatever but a personal obligation, and creates no preference of any kind, and therefore the result is that there is not at common law any valid security created in favour of the debenture-holders."

Lord Shand (at p. 1033): "There is no principle more deeply rooted in the law than this, that in order to create a good security over subjects delivery must be given. If possession be retained no effectual security can be granted. . . .

". . . It appears to me that legislation such as we have in the Companies Clauses Act would be necessary in order to give directors of joint stock companies in this part of the kingdom power to grant effectual debentures over property while the possession is retained. It may well be questioned whether the granting of such powers to all joint stock companies would be for the benefit of the public or of these companies generally. If such powers were given, the general creditors of a company dealing in the ordinary course of business would have no security at all either against the shareholders or the property of the company in cases where the shares had been fully paid up and the assets of the company fully charged with debentures. For my part I do not think that would be desirable."

4. Floating charges were introduced to Scotland by the Companies (Floating Charges) (Scotland) Act 1961. See now Companies (Floating Charges and Receivers) (Scotland) Act 1972.

Charges securing debentures: statutory floating charges: security for interest becoming due between attachment and payment

National Commercial Bank of Scotland Ltd. v. Liquidators of Telford Grier Mackay & Co. Ltd.
1969 S.C. 181

T. Ltd. granted to a bank a bond of cash credit secured by a floating charge under the Companies (Floating Charges) (Scotland) Act 1961.

On the liquidation of T. Ltd., the bank lodged a claim for the principal sum due under the bond and interest to the date of liquidation, and the liquidator paid this claim. The bank lodged no claim for interest from the date of liquidation until repayment, and the liquidators refused to pay such interest, maintaining that it was not secured by the floating charge and that in any event they were not entitled to pay in the absence of a claim.

Held that (1) the bank had security for the interest down to the date of repayment and (2) the bank was entitled to payment without lodging a claim.

LORD PRESIDENT (CLYDE) (at p. 191): "The concept of a floating charge has never been part of the common law of Scotland. But the employment of a floating charge has such obvious practical advantages in modern times that it was introduced into the law of Scotland by the Companies (Floating Charges) (Scotland) Act 1961. The ambit and effect of its introduction into our law must therefore be determined, in the first instance at least, by a consideration of what that statute, and primarily what section 1 of that statute, has enacted.
. . .
"Subsection (2) . . . provides: 'and, subject as aforesaid, the provisions of the Act of 1948 relating to winding up . . . shall have effect as if the charge were a fixed security over the property to which it has attached in respect of the principal of the debt to which it relates and any interest due there on . . .'
. . .
" . . . Under the charge in the present case the principal sum is the balance incurred or to be incurred under the bond, and the interest due thereon must be interest at the agreed rate until that balance is paid off. It is significant that the word used is 'any' interest, which clearly does not confine the liability to any date short of extinction of the cash credit bond. On the

plain wording of the subsection, therefore, the contention for the bank is in my opinion sound. . . .

" The liquidators, however, maintained that ' any interest due thereon ' means any interest due at the date of liquidation, and excludes interest due thereafter on the unpaid principal. It appears to me, however, in the first place that Parliament has not so provided. The interest secured is not restricted to the interest due at the date of liquidation. On the contrary, much more general language is employed—' any interest due thereon '—a phrase which in my view takes one back to the terms of the bargain between debtor and creditor. Under that bargain interest continues to run till the principal is paid in full.

" But, in the second place, there is no justification in the language of the subsection for regarding this provision as confined to the moment of liquidation. On the contrary, this third part of the subsection has a forward-looking content. It relates to a period when the security ' has ' attached. . . . It seems to me necessarily to follow that the attachment must operate *quoad* any interest due thereon until interest ceases to be due. . . . In my opinion, ' any interest due thereon ' means just what it says, and is not confined to pre-liquidation interest. . . .

" . . . If Parliament has equated the position of a holder of a floating charge to the position in Scotland of a creditor with a real right in the security subjects, then this would constitute a powerful reinforcement of the construction which I have put on the provisions of section 1 (2). For a creditor with a real right in the security subjects is entitled to interest up to the date of payment of the debt.

" That this is what Parliament has provided appears to me to follow from a consideration of the statutory provisions."

Lord Cameron (at p. 209): " A secured creditor with a real right in a security subject . . . is independent of the liquidator and entitled to work out satisfaction of his whole debt to the full extent of his security. There is nothing in the Bankruptcy (Scotland) Act 1913 which requires such a creditor to lodge a claim in the sequestration of his debtor."

NOTES

1. The first point decided in this case was followed in *Royal Bank of Scotland Ltd.* v. *Williamson,* 1972 S.L.T.(Sh.Ct.) 45, a case in which the bank had lodged a claim in the liquidation of Loch Garage (Lanark) Ltd. for £23,910 4s. 9d. (a sum made up partly of principal and partly of interest) with interest thereon from the date of liquidation until payment.

Held that the bank was entitled to interest on the principal sum from the date of liquidation until settlement, but was not entitled to interest on interest for that period of time.

2. The point was placed beyond doubt by the revised wording adopted in the Companies (Floating Charges and Receivers) (Scotland) Act 1972, s. 1 (2): "any interest due or to become due thereon."

Charges securing debentures: statutory floating charges: assignation: payments made to company's creditors

Libertas-Kommerz GmbH, Appellants
1978 S.L.T. 222 (O.H.)

J. Bobbins Ltd., a company registered in Scotland, granted a bond and floating charge to Doctor Graf in July 1971. Doctor Graf advanced sums of money to the company, and also made payments direct to creditors of the company.

In December 1971 Doctor Graf made an assignation of the bond and floating charge to a German company, "Elbenia," and in September 1971 Elbenia assigned the same rights to a Swiss company, "Libertas."

J. Bobbins Ltd. passed a resolution for creditors' voluntary winding up in Febuary 1972.

The liquidator rejected the claim lodged by Libertas in the liquidation, and Libertas appealed to the court against the liquidator's deliverance.

The liquidator supported his rejection of the claim on the grounds that (1) the rights of the security of the floating charge conferred on Doctor Graf were not assignable, (2) neither assignation had been validly intimated to the company or to the liquidator, and (3) since the floating charge had been created within 12 months of the commencement of the winding up and since Libertas did not assert that the company was solvent immediately after the creation of the charge, it was by section 322 (1) of the Companies Act 1948 invalid as regards the payments made direct to the company's creditors since these were not "cash paid to the company" for the purposes of that provision.

Held that (1) the rights were assignable, (2) the assignations had been sufficiently intimated, and (3) the payments made direct to the company's creditors did not fall into the category of "cash paid to the company" for the purposes of section 322 (1) of the Companies Act 1948.

LORD KINCRAIG (at p. 224): " I shall deal first with the contention that the floating charge was incapable of being voluntarily assigned. This is founded on the submission that because there was no provision made in the Companies (Floating Charges) (Scotland) Act 1961, which introduced floating charges into Scots law, for the registration in the Register of Floating Charges of the name of a holder other than the original holder, it must be implied that Parliament intended a floating charge to be incapable of being transferred by the original holder to another. . . . It was pointed out that the omission in the 1961 Act to provide for alteration of the register has been remedied by the Companies (Floating Charges and Receivers) (Scotland) Act 1972 (see s. 7), and it was submitted that the absence of such provisions in the 1961 Act showed that Parliament did not intend that floating charges could be competently assigned prior to the 1972 Act. . . .

" I reject this submission. The law of Scotland allows incorporeal rights to be assigned except those of a personal nature as, for example, an alimentary liferent. The 1961 Act does not expressly declare a floating charge to be unassignable by the holder. . . . Under section 106I of the 1948 Act the company itself was obliged to keep at its registered office a register of charges and to enter therein all floating charges over the property of the company, giving the relevant particulars, including the names of the persons entitled to the floating charge. . . . Recourse to the register kept by the company would reveal the names of any assignee of the floating charge since its initial registration, and it therefore cannot be said that a member of the public who wished to be informed of the identity of the holder of a floating charge over the property of the company, the initial creation of which was recorded in the register kept by the Registrar of Companies, could not so discover. Moreover, section 2 of the 1961 Act provides that a floating charge may be created only by the execution of an instrument of charge as nearly as practicable in the form set forth in the First Schedule to the Act. That form includes the phrase ' and their successors and assignees,' after the name of the person in whose favour the floating charge is granted. The inclusion of these words in the statutory form gives, in my judgment, statutory authority for the assignability of a floating charge. A grant to successors and assignees necessarily implies the right in the grantee to assign.

" . . . For the above reasons I find that the floating charge in favour of Doctor Graf was capable of being assigned to Elbenia and by that company to Libertas.

" The next point to consider is whether the assignations were validly intimated. . . . Counsel for Libertas contended that valid intimation of the assignations was made by Doctor Graf's letter . . . together with the acknowledgement by the liquidator. . . .

" . . . Counsel for Libertas submitted that intimation of the assignations is sufficient if on a reasonable interpretation of the letters . . . the liquidator was made aware of an assignation, and that it was being acted on in the sense of being put forward as the authority of the assignee to seek payment of the debt. . . .

" Counsel for the liquidator submitted that the writing relied on as intimation of the purported assignations must disclose in terms the kind of detail required by the statutory mode of intimation provided for in the 1862 Act, *i.e.* a reference to the assignation, its date and that the assignee was relying on it. . . . Such details were absent from the letters relied on. . . . I do not think it necessary to refer to the details of the assignation, if otherwise the intention is clear. . . .

" The next point to consider relates to the payments made . . . to three of the company's creditors. . . . Libertas submit that the payments . . . are the equivalent of cash paid to the company and therefore the floating charge is not invalid *quoad* these payments. The submission for the liquidator is that these were not cash payments to the company. . . .

" . . . The exception in section 322 is applicable in terms only to cash payments to the company, and I do not think that the court would be justified in construing that phrase as including cash payments made to any other person albeit on behalf of the company."

NOTE

There is no statutory form of instrument of charge in the Companies (Floating Charges and Receivers) (Scotland) Act 1972.

Charges securing debentures: registration of charges: charge on land situated in England

Amalgamated Securities Ltd., Petitioners
1967 S.C. 56

A. Ltd., a company registered in Scotland, owned land in both Scotland and England. It created charges on both sets of property in favour of certain trustees. The charges on the Scottish property were registered with the Registrar of Companies in Scotland. The charges on the English property were registered with the Registrar of Companies in England but not with the Registrar of Companies in Scotland.

Held that, by section 106A of the Companies Act 1948 (added to that Act by the Companies (Floating Charges) (Scotland) Act 1961), A. Ltd. was required to register the charges on the English property with the Registrar of Companies in Scotland, and extension of time for registration *granted*.

LORD PRESIDENT (CLYDE) (at p. 56): " This is an application to the Court of Session for an extension of time to register a charge. . . .

. . .

" . . . Section 106A provides in subsection (1) that every charge to which this section applies, which is created by a company incorporated in Scotland, requires to be registered with the Registrar of Companies. Subsection (2) of section 106A provides that this section shall apply to the following charges: (*a*) a charge on land wherever situated. The effect of these provisions, in my opinion, is that, in the case of a company incorporated in Scotland, it is necessary to register with the Registrar of Companies in Scotland a charge which is created either over Scottish or over English heritage. It seems to me that the use of the words ' wherever situated ' in subsection (2) of section 106A necessitates this conclusion.

. . .

" The only remaining question in the case . . . is whether this is an instance in which we should exercise our powers under section 106G of the Act. In my opinion it clearly is. This is a case which merits the application of that provision very much more than many other applications which have come before us."

Charges securing debentures: registration of charges: charge on shares in other companies

The Scottish Homes Investment Co. Ltd., Petitioners
1968 S.C. 244

S. Ltd., a company registered in Scotland, assigned to trustees for debenture stockholders, as security, certain shares which it held in other companies. The trust deed and the prescribed particulars were registered under section 106A of the Companies Act 1948.

Later S. Ltd. entered into a supplementary trust deed, and particulars of this trust deed were not timeously registered.

Held that registration of particulars relating to the supplementary trust deed was unnecessary; and particulars relating to the original trust deed *ordered* to be deleted.

LORD PRESIDENT (CLYDE) (at p. 248): "The charges which require to be registered in terms of the 1961 Act are defined in the Second Schedule to that Act in section 106A (2). If the charges involved in the present case do not fall within the charges detailed in that definition, no registration is necessary. The security involved in the present case is not heritage, but incorporeal moveable property. But the only property of that kind which comes within the definition is property falling within any of the six categories of incorporeal moveable property specified in section 106A (2) (c). The security under these two trust deeds clearly does not fall within any of these six categories. It follows, therefore, that no registration under section 106A of the Act is required.

"We are confirmed in this conclusion by the fact that in the corresponding English provision defining charges (to be found in section 95 (2) of the Companies Act 1948) a charge 'for the purpose of securing any issue of debentures' is expressly included among the charges which require to be registered. But for some inscrutable reason no corresponding provision has been made in regard to Scotland."

NOTE

Section 106A of the Companies Act 1948 is now as set out in the Schedule to the Companies (Floating Charges and Receivers) (Scotland) Act 1972.

Charges securing debentures: registration of charges: creation of further charge

Archibald Campbell, Hope & King Ltd., Petitioners
1967 S.C. 21

C. Ltd., a company registered in Scotland, entered into a trust deed by which it undertook to convey to trustees certain heritable property as security for an issue of debenture stock and for any further stock they might issue. *Ex facie* absolute dispositions of the properties were granted in favour of the trustees, were recorded in the General Register of Sasines and were registered with the Registrar of Companies in July 1964.

In December 1965 C. Ltd. issued further debenture stock and a supplemental trust deed provided that the properties disponed in 1964 should be security for the new as well as for the original stock. The dispositions were presented to the Registrar of Companies for re-registration.

The Registrar declined to accept them on the ground that, even if re-registration were competent, they had not been presented within 21 days of being recorded as required by section 106A of the Companies Act 1948.

C. Ltd. presented a petition under section 106G, for an extension of time for registration and for a direction to the Registrar to rectify the entries in the register by narrating that the dispositions secured the new as well as the original stock.

Held that (1) the prayer for an extension of time was inept, since the dispositions had already been registered and there was no statutory provision for re-registration, and (2) there was no ground for ordering rectification, since there had been no " omission or mis-statement of any particular " at the time of the registration as provided for in section 106G. Petition *refused.*

LORD PRESIDENT (CLYDE) (at p. 27): " The plain fact of the matter is that the statutory provisions are incomplete and provide no machinery for re-registering a charge such as an *ex facie* absolute disposition, which can be used as security for future as well as existing advances or loans. . . .

" We were referred to section 106G of the statute, which gives the Court certain dispensing powers. But this provision is not wide enough to enable the Court to legislate. It does enable the Court to remedy certain omissions or mis-statements by petitioners. But there was no such omission in the present case. . . . The present case discloses a clear deficiency in the statutory provisions, which can only be remedied by an amendment of the Act."

LORD GUTHRIE (at p. 29): " The Registrar was clearly right in his refusal to re-register the charges. . . . Registration can only take place within 21 days after the date of creation of the charge, and in the case of an *ex facie* absolute disposition, the date of creation is the date on which the right of the person entitled to the benefit of the charge was constituted as a real right. . . . The effect of the Act is that the charges created by these dispositions could only be registered within 21 days after the dates of the recording of the deeds. There is no provision in the Act authorising the Registrar to re-register a charge so created."

LORD CAMERON (at p. 33): "If there is a gap in the legislation, as I think there is, then it is for the Legislature, if it thinks proper, but not for the Court, to fill it."

NOTES

1. The provisions of the Act of 1961 were also shown to be unsuitable for the situation which arose in *Scottish & Newcastle Breweries Ltd.* v. *Liquidator of the Rathburne Hotel Co. Ltd.*, 1970 S.C. 215 (O.H.).

R. Ltd., a hotel company registered in Scotland, disponed heritable property to a brewery company by an *ex facie* absolute disposition. A minute of agreement between the companies declared that the property was held in security of advances of £1,800. Particulars of the charge were duly registered with the Registrar of Companies.

A supplementary minute of agreement was later executed, increasing the sum secured to £2,800. Particulars of this minute were registered with the Registrar of Companies.

R. Ltd. went into liquidation. The brewery company claimed a secured ranking for £2,800, but the liquidator admitted it to a secured ranking of only £1,800 on the ground that the supplementary minute was void against him under section 106A of the Companies Act 1948.

Held that the original charge created a security limited to £1,800 and that any alteration, including any increase in the amount secured, could be effected only by a fresh charge, which would require a disposition as well as a back letter or minute, and that, in any event, the requirements of registration could not be satisfied by the registration of the particulars of the supplementary minute, since these were not registered within 21 days of the creation of the charge. Accordingly the Lord Ordinary (Fraser) *sustained* the liquidator's deliverance.

Lord Fraser (at p. 222): "The supplementary minutes, having been unaccompanied by fresh dispositions, are void against the respondent and any creditors of the company and do not increase the amount for which the appellants hold security. . . .

"An alternative argument was also presented for the appellants, . . . to the effect that the requirements for registration were satisfied by the registration of the second supplementary minute. . . . In my opinion that contention is quite untenable, because in terms of section 106A (1), a charge is void against the liquidator and any other creditor, unless the prescribed particulars of the charge are delivered to the Registrar 'within 21 days after the date of its creation.' The date of creation of the charge, in accordance with subsection (10) (*b*), is the date on which a real right was constituted, namely, the date of recording of the *ex facie* absolute disposition. . . . The supplementary minute was not, and could not have been, registered within

21 days of that date, and therefore registration of the minute (or, more accurately, of particulars from the minute) at a later date cannot, in my opinion, give any security over the company's property in a question with the liquidator or creditors."

2. Section 106A (9) of the Companies Act 1948, as set out in the Schedule to the Companies (Floating Charges and Receivers) (Scotland) Act 1972, provides that where the amount secured by a charge created by an *ex facie* absolute disposition qualified by a back letter or other agreement (or created by a standard security qualified by an agreement) is purported to be increased by a further back letter or agreement, a further charge shall be held to have been created by the disposition (or standard security), as qualified by the further back letter or agreement, and the registration provisions apply to that further charge.

3. The standard security is now the only mode in which a new right in security over heritable property may be created (Conveyancing and Feudal Reform (Scotland) Act 1970).

Charges securing debentures: registration of charges: extension of time

M. Milne Ltd., Petitioners
(1963) 79 Sh.Ct.Rep. 105

M. Ltd., a company registered in Scotland, assigned the leasehold property known as Crown Inn, Dreghorn, to Scottish and Newcastle Breweries Ltd. in security of sums due or to become due by M. Ltd. to the brewery company. The charge ought to have been registered under section 106A (1) of the Companies Act 1948 within 21 days of its creation, but neither M. Ltd. nor the brewery company registered it owing to a misunderstanding between the parties acting for the two companies as to which was to effect the registration.

M. Ltd. applied to the sheriff court of Lanarkshire for an extension of time for registration on the ground that the omission to register was, for the purposes of section 106G of the Act of 1948, due to inadvertence and not of a nature to prejudice the position of the creditors or shareholders of the company, and generally that it was just and equitable that the relief provided by that section should be granted.

The petition was not opposed.

Authority *granted* to register the charge within 21 days of the order.

NOTE

An extension of time was also granted in *Amalgamated Securities*

Ltd., Petitioners (see p. 334, above), but was held not to be appropriate in *Archibald Campbell, Hope & King Ltd., Petitioners* (see p. 336, above).

Section 106G of the Act of 1948 is now to be found in the Schedule to the Companies (Floating Charges and Receivers) (Scotland) Act 1972.

Judicial factor

Fraser, Petitioner
1971 S.L.T. 146 (O.H.)

F., a former director of Neill & Co. Ltd., presented a petition in the Outer House of the Court of Session for the appointment of a judicial factor *ad interim* on the company's affairs. F. averred that he and certain of his family trusts held 51 per cent. of the shares, although it appeared that his name had been removed from the register of shareholders. He further averred that the question was of some urgency, and counsel for F. informed the Lord Ordinary that there was some doubt whether the wages due that week could be paid by the company if a judicial factor were not appointed in the course of the week.

Held that the petition was competent, and judicial factor *ad interim appointed.*

LORD FRASER (at p. 146): " Counsel for the petitioner submitted that the appointment of a judicial factor on the estate of a company incorporated under the Companies Acts was competent and was no different in principle from the appointment of a judicial factor on any other property or estate. In support of that proposition he was unable to refer me to any contested action where the matter had been decided, but he did refer to the case of *Paterson* v. *Best* (1900) 2 F. 1088, 8 S.L.T. 98, where it appears from the narrative and from the opinions, particularly of Lord Trayner and Lord Moncreiff, that a judicial factor had been appointed upon the estate of a railway company. Counsel for the respondents drew attention to the fact that the company was a railway company, for which certain statutory provisions authorise the appointment of a judicial factor in certain circumstances. It appears that the appointment which had been made in *Paterson's (supra)* case cannot have been made under the statutory powers and, accordingly, the case is an example of a judicial factor being appointed at common law upon the affairs of a limited company.

" Counsel for the petitioner submitted, in the second place, that it was competent for such an appointment to be made by a Lord Ordinary in the Outer House and that it was not necessary for the petition to be presented under the *nobile officium* to the Inner House. For that proposition he referred me to the case of *Petition Gaff* (1893) 20 R. 825, which was a petition for an appointment of a judicial factor on the estate of a building society and where it was expressly decided in the Inner House that the petition should have been presented to the Outer House. . . .

" . . . So far as the competency of the petition is concerned, I have reached the opinion that there is nothing incompetent about the appointment of a judicial factor on the estate of a limited company, and I rely particularly on the case of *Paterson* v. *Best*.

" So far as the competency of the petition in the Outer House is concerned, I think a much more difficult question arises. . . . But I think that the fact that the classes of petitions dealt with in the Outer House have, apparently, become wider with the passage of time, lends support to counsel for the petitioner's submission that this petition would fall within the powers of the Outer House. Having regard, particularly, to the case of *Gaff (supra)* that seems to me to be the present position. Accordingly I hold that the petition has been properly presented in the Outer House and that it is within my power to grant the petition if satisfied that it should be granted on the facts. So far as the facts are concerned, the petition seems to disclose a position of chaos requiring urgently to be dealt with and no submission to the contrary upon the facts was made by counsel for the respondents."

NOTES

1. *Paterson* v. *Best* was a petition presented by P. for the appointment of a judicial factor on the undertaking of the Dundee Suburban Railway Company. P. stated that he held a decree against the company for £300, on which a charge had expired without payment. The appointment was sought under section 4 of the Railway Companies (Scotland) Act 1867 or alternatively *ex nobili officio*. The works authorised by the company's special Act had never been begun.

Held that (1) section 4 of the Act of 1867 did not apply because the company had not an " undertaking " in the sense of that section, and (2) no case had been stated for an appointment *ex nobili officio*.

Lord Justice-Clerk (J. H. A. Macdonald) (at p. 1092): " Now, section 4, upon the face of it, has a distinct and clear object in my opinion. It was obviously not for the public advantage that creditors of a railway company should be allowed to do what creditors could do under ordinary circumstances when they have got a judgment, *viz.*, seize the property of their debtor. This would be an injury to the public, for railways are constituted for the public convenience. . . . Authority is given by Parliament for the appointment of a factor who shall take possession of the earnings of the company, and who, after making provision for the expenses of the railway company, and the other outgoings of the company, shall apply and distribute the balance in his hands to meet the claims of its just creditors. . . . My reading of clause 4 is that it applies to a company in the position of having an undertaking, with appliances and vehicles for the purpose of running, and engaged in running trains, the purpose of the Act being to provide for the continuance of the running of the road, while at the same time safeguarding the interests of the creditors. Therefore in my opinion that clause of the Act of Parliament has no application in this case. So far as we know . . . this company never had a single yard of road, or any plant, or vehicles of any kind. But then it is said that the *nobile officium* of the Court is properly invoked here. Under what circumstances? The creditor here says he is unable to ascertain how to go against his debtor. . . . That is just the position of a great many creditors who get judgments of the Court entitling them to attach their debtors' property directly by diligence in order to recover the debts which are due them. It is not to be said that creditors who have difficulty in finding out where funds are, or where property is, belonging to their debtors, are to come to the Court and ask the Court, in the exercise of its *nobile officium*, to appoint a judicial factor for the purpose of helping them to work out their claims."

Lords Trayner and Moncreiff expressed agreement with the Lord Justice-Clerk as to section 4 of the Act of 1867 and as to the *nobile officium*, but both referred to a judicial factor as having been already appointed.

Lord Trayner (at p. 1093): " The first difficulty in the way of granting this application arises from the fact (stated by the petitioner) that the estate in question has already been sequestrated and a judicial factor appointed thereon. The Court cannot grant a second sequestration, or appoint to an office that is already filled."

Lord Moncreiff (at p. 1093): " I am inclined to concur with Lord Trayner in the first place that we must hold that Mr. Chiene is still in the saddle. His appointment was until a board of directors should be duly constituted."

2. In *Gaff and Others, Petitioners* (1893) 20 R. 825, G. and other members of a building society presented a petition to the Inner House for the appointment of a judicial factor on the estate of the building society on the ground that the circumstances made it impossible to wind up the society under the Building Societies Act 1874.

Held that the petition ought to have been presented to the Outer House.

Receivers: directors not entitled to deal with property comprised in receivership

Imperial Hotel (Aberdeen) Ltd. v. Vaux Breweries Ltd.
1978 S.L.T. 113 (O.H.)

In connection with a modernisation programme, I. Ltd. granted a floating charge for £350,000 and a standard security over its hotel in favour of V. Ltd., a brewery company. I. Ltd. also granted a floating charge in favour of a bank.

In July 1974 the bank appointed a receiver of I. Ltd.'s whole assets.

In January 1975 V. Ltd. called up the standard security, and, when I. Ltd. failed to comply with the calling-up notice, V. Ltd. sold the hotel to Ushers Brewery Ltd.

I. Ltd. sought to reduce the missives of sale on the ground that V. Ltd. had not taken " all reasonable steps " to ensure that the price was the best that could be " reasonably obtained," as required by the Conveyancing and Feudal Reform (Scotland) Act 1970, s. 25.

Held that (1) a receiver having been appointed of the whole assets, the directors were not entitled to deal in any way with property comprised in the receivership, and (2) since Ushers Brewery Ltd. was *in bona fide*, I. Ltd. would not be entitled to reduction but only to damages. Action *dismissed*.

LORD GRIEVE (at p. 114): " Counsel for the first and second defenders [Vaux Breweries Ltd. and Ushers Brewery Ltd. respectively] submitted that the action was incompetent for two reasons. The first of these reasons was that no court action at the instance of a company in receivership was competent when, as here, the floating charge, by virtue of which the receiver had been appointed, was over the whole assets of the company. Court action was only competent at the instance of the receiver himself. Counsel submitted that the purpose behind the creation of receivers in Scotland as creatures of statute, under and in terms of the provisions of the Companies (Floating Charges and Receivers) (Scotland) Act 1972 . . . , was to give better protection to the floating charge holder and to obviate the winding up of the company concerned. In support of this general submission counsel referred me to certain sections of the Act in question.

" . . . Whether the appointment is made by the holder of the charge or by the court the effect of it is, as set out in sections 13 (7) and 14 (7), that the floating charge attaches to the property which is the subject of it as if the charge were a fixed security over the property to which it has attached. In this case the appointment of the receiver had the effect of attaching the floating charge to the whole assets of the pursuers' company. . . . One of the powers given to the receiver and contained in section 15 (1) (*f*) is the: ' power to bring or defend any action or other legal proceedings in the name and on behalf of the company.' Section 17 of the Act provides that a receiver is to be the agent of the company in relation to such property of the company as is attached by the floating charge. . . . Counsel submitted that where, as here, the receiver's appointment related to all the assets of the company, the company took a back seat during the currency of the receivership. This was evident from the fact that on the receiver's appointment the floating charge attached to the property which was the subject of it, and from the wide powers of management given to the receiver by section 15 of the Act of 1972. . . . Counsel submitted that, while the receiver was in office by virtue of a floating charge which covered all the assets of the company, no residual powers of management could be retained by the directors of the company. In particular they could not raise actions which related to property attached to the floating charge. . . . There could be no security at all to the floating charge holder if the directors of the company could exercise some or all of the powers given to the receiver. . . . In order to preserve the security of the floating charge holder it was necessary that the directors' powers of management of the company's assets, so far as attached to the receiver, remained in abeyance until the receiver had completed his function. . . . In England the directors' powers are in abeyance during the receivership. . . . *Prima facie* it would seem sensible that the powers of receivers in Scotland and England over the assets attached by their office should not differ to any material extent particularly having regard to the fact that many companies incorporated in Scotland possess assets in England and vice versa, and the only Scottish authority to which I was referred suggests that the provisions of the Act of 1972 achieve that purpose. In *Macleod* v. *Alexander Sutherland Ltd.,* the Lord Ordinary expressed the opinion that a company in receivership could not obtemper a decree *ad factum praestandum* because, during receivership, it could only act through the agency of the receiver, whose actings they had no power to control. This view seems to support the proposition that during receivership the directors' powers are in abeyance in Scotland as well as in England.

" In answer to this primary submission on competency by counsel for the first and second defenders, counsel for the pursuers submitted that it was dangerous to look at the position in relation to receivers in England. In Scotland the receiver was a creature of statute born of the Act of 1972 and, in order to discover what the extent of his powers were, and the effect, if any, which they had on the directors of the company concerned, one must look at the provisions of the Act of 1972 and only at these provisions. The answer to the question of competency turned on the provisions of section 15 of the Act of 1972 which was an enabling section. During the course of a receivership the company whose assets had attached to the receiver did not cease to exist and the directors of the company continued to hold office as such even where as here, all the company's assets had crystallised in the receiver. There was no express provision in the Act which precluded the directors from exercising their ordinary powers after the appointment of a receiver. . . . Counsel suggested that the powers given to the receiver under section 15 contained what might be described as a ' destination over ' to the directors of the company in the event of the receiver not exercising some of them. The position of a receiver could not be compared with that of a liquidator under the Companies Acts despite the similarity between the provisions of section 245 of the Companies Act 1948 and section 15 of the Act of 1972. Once the liquidator was in the saddle only he could act on the company's behalf and if he refused to do so there was no one left who could act. But if a receiver refused to act the directors were still in a position to do so. . . . The raising of this action for the pursuers was not inconsistent with the existence of a receivership over the whole assets of the pursuers, and therefore the action was competent.

" In my opinion, to give effect to the pursuers' submission would be contrary to the purpose behind the Act of 1972 which introduced receivers into the law of Scotland and would render nugatory the powers conferred on them by section 15 of that Act. . . . The receiver may only require to exercise some of his statutory powers of management. It is a matter for his discretion as to which powers he will exercise, and when he will exercise them. The powers given are wide, and no doubt deliberately so in order that the receiver's activities may not be unnecessarily circumscribed. It would be quite contrary to the object of the Act if a company, all of whose assets were attached to the receiver because all were covered by a floating charge or floating charges, could interfere, through its directors, with the exercise by the receiver of his discretion by, for instance, raising actions which the receiver did not consider should be raised.

" In my opinion it is quite apparent from the terms of the Act of 1972 and the nature of the duties which a receiver appointed under it is empowered to perform, that the receiver's primary duty is to the security holder, and that, in order to perform it properly, his discretion is not to be subject to interference by the directors of the company concerned. The company accepts that this must be the intention by virtue of the conditions under which they receive the loan, security for which is provided by the floating charge. . . .

" In this case it was the holder of a standard security who initiated and carried out the sale governed by the missives which the pursuers now seek to reduce, but, as the property in question was covered by a floating charge which gave rise to the receiver's appointment only he is empowered to question its validity.

" . . . In my judgment this action is incompetent. That is sufficient for disposal of the case but, in case I am wrong in the view I have expressed, I must go on to consider the defenders' second argument in support of their first plea-in-law. That argument was to the effect that where a party alleges that the defender in an action has failed in a duty which is owed to him the proper remedy is an action of damages and not an action of reduction. An action of reduction inevitably affects a third party who is not concerned with the breach of duty in question. . . .

" On this branch of the argument counsel for the pursuers accepted that an action of reduction, which could have the effect of reducing the sale of heritable subjects to a *bona fide* third party would be incompetent, but he maintained that where a third party was not *in bona fide* no such protection was given to him. Counsel submitted that his averments relating to the circumstances which preceded the sale to the second defenders were such as to disclose a state of knowledge on their part which required them, before concluding missives of sale, to satisfy themselves that the first defenders had carried out the duty which they owed to the pursuers by virtue of the terms of section 25 of the Conveyancing and Feudal Reform (Scotland) Act 1970. . . . The authority on which counsel for the pursuers based his general submission . . . was the case of *Rodger (Builders) Ltd.* v. *Fawdry* (1950 S.C. 483). . . . This is a case where, unlike *Rodger (Builders) Ltd.* v. *Fawdry*, a duty was owed by the seller to a third party who held a reversionary interest in the property, which interest was no concern of the purchasers, and whose right to maintain it remained unaffected by the purchasers entering into missives with the seller. Accordingly by entering into missives the purchaser did not put himself *in mala fide*. These facts in my view demonstrate that the remedy for any failure by the first defenders to perform the duty which they owed to the pursuers should be an action of damages at the pursuers' instance and not an action of reduction. . . .

" . . . On that ground also the action is incompetent."

NOTE

The Scottish authority referred to by Lord Grieve was *Macleod* v. *Alexander Sutherland Ltd.*, 1977 S.L.T. (Notes) 44 (O.H.).

In 1972 M. sold to S. Ltd. an area of ground at Inverness. The missives provided that S. Ltd. was to carry out certain construction work in relation to the ground. S. Ltd. failed to do so.

In 1974 a receiver was appointed by creditors who held a floating charge secured over the whole assets of S. Ltd.

M. raised an action seeking decree of implement and, failing implement, damages of £10,000. S. Ltd. admitted that it was in breach of contract and was liable to pay damages, but maintained that, since it was no longer carrying on business and had no means of performing the contract, M. was not entitled to decree of specific implement.

Lord Stott refused decree of implement and granted decree for payment of damages. His opinion refers to provisions in section 17 of the Companies (Floating Charges and Receivers) (Scotland) Act 1972 —a receiver is to be deemed to be the agent of the company in relation to the property attached (s. 17 (1)), subject to subsection (1), a receiver is to be personally liable on any contract entered into by him except in so far as the contract otherwise provides (s. 17 (2)), and a receiver who is personally liable under subsection (2) is to be entitled to be indemnified out of the property for which he was appointed (s. 17 (3)).

Lord Stott (at p. 45): " It is plain that the defenders are not in a position to obtemper decree of specific implement through their directors as would normally be the position if the company were not in receivership. Counsel for the pursuer, however, submitted that the position was fundamentally the same, inasmuch as they would be able to act through the receiver. But the receiver is not in the position of a director. No doubt he is deemed to be the agent of the company in relation to its property, but his acts are not the acts of the company. They are his own acts, and by s. 17 (2) of the Act he incurs personal liability on a contract entered into by him in the performance of his functions. It is true that, as counsel pointed out, he has a right to be indemnified out of the company's property, but whether that right is of practical value may be a question of circumstances, and in any event the fact remains that the primary liability rests on the receiver himself. Since *ex hypothesi* the responsibility for whatever is done in implement of the contract must in fact be done by the receiver it seems to me to be out of the question to pronounce a decree ostensibly against the company, which would in effect result in the receiver either incurring personal liability or in his bearing the responsibility for a contempt of court (whether his own or the company's). That consideration applies with all the greater force when I am asked to pronounce such a decree in an action to which the receiver is not a party."

Receivers: powers postponed to effectually executed diligence: arrestment not followed by furthcoming held not effectually executed diligence

Lord Advocate v. Royal Bank of Scotland Ltd. and Others
1978 S.L.T. 38, affirming 1976 S.L.T. 130 (O.H.)

The Inland Revenue obtained a decree for payment of about £4,900 against the Imperial Hotel (Aberdeen) Ltd., and on May 23, 1974, arrested £593·68 in the hands of a bank.

On July 17, 1974, a receiver was appointed by the holders of two separate floating charges over the company's whole property.

The Inland Revenue sued the bank and the receiver, claiming payment of the sum arrested.

The Revenue maintained that their arrestment was an " effectually executed diligence " within the meaning of section 15 (2) of the Companies (Floating Charges and Receivers) (Scotland) Act 1972 with the result that the receiver's powers were postponed to their own right to the sum arrested.

In defence the receiver contended that arrestment not followed by furthcoming was not an " effectually executed diligence."

Held that the arrestment was not an " effectually executed diligence," and action *dismissed*.

LORD PRESIDENT (EMSLIE) (at p. 42): " Arrestment has, no doubt, been called a diligence in certain contexts in which it would be tolerable to do so. The accurate description of an arrestment, however, is that it is merely an ' inchoate ' diligence (Stair III.1.42) a ' step ' of diligence or an ' inchoated or begun ' diligence (Erskine III.vi.2 and 15). . . . It is . . . part but not the essential part of a diligence consisting of arrestment and furthcoming.

" What an arrestment does, and all it does, is to render the arrested subjects litigious. It is in this sense and in this sense only that an arrestment is said to ' attach,' or create a nexus over, the property in the arrestee's hands. By rendering the subject matter litigious it constitutes or transfers no right in the subject matter arrested. . . .

" . . . By the operation of the provisions of the Act of 1972, Parliament made it possible for a creditor of an incorporated company to obtain without liquidating the company the high right of a fixed security, and created machinery by which that right could be exercised. . . .

" I now turn to the language of section 15 (2), which introduced for the first time to the law of Scotland the expression ' effectually executed diligence on . . . the property ' of a company without seeing fit to define it. . . . The registration of a floating charge . . . gives warning to a creditor who subsequently arrests, that if he does not proceed speedily to a completion of his ' begun ' diligence he is at risk of being faced with the appointment of a receiver. . . . I now ask myself whether effectually executed diligence on the property of the company within the meaning of section 15 (2) (a) includes a mere arrestment, bearing in mind that section 15 (2) (a) is designed to regulate a receiver's powers in exercising the right of a holder of a fixed security. In my opinion, when the subsection is properly construed, it cannot be so understood. Under reference to my analysis of the nature and effects of arrestment, it is at best a step in diligence *in personam*, and cannot properly be regarded as a diligence effectually executed on the subjects arrested or as a diligence with effects comparable to those of a fixed security."

LORD CAMERON (at p. 43): " The language and structure of this statute are of considerable obscurity. . . . It was said of the Treaty of Versailles of 1919 that it ' contained all the seeds of a just and enduring war.' It could readily be said of this statute that its provisions are well designed to provide a rich variety of issues for decision in delicate and prolonged litigation. . . .

    . . .

" . . . Arrestment is no more than an inchoate diligence, which must be followed by a furthcoming to secure satisfaction of the debt in respect of which it was laid on. . . . I find it difficult to see how it can be maintained that when all that has happened is the laying on of an arrestment, this can be held to be an effectual execution of diligence on the property of the debtor."

NOTE

Lord Johnston dissented. He said (at p. 48): " ' Diligence ' meaning ' arrestment ' has been in use for 200 years, and . . . arrestment is commonly referred to as diligence in the institutional and other writers and in the statutes. . . .

. . .

". . . It may be a misuse of language to talk of ' diligence on ' when what is meant is ' arrestment of ' but . . . there are numerous and authoritative examples of this use. In my opinion greater weight should be attached to the meaning given to the words by usage than that derived from a strict analysis. In my opinion the words ' diligence on ' are apt to include ' arrestment of.' "

Receivers: English company: powers of receiver in relation to property in Scotland

Gordon Anderson (Plant) Ltd. v.
Campsie Construction Ltd. and Anglo Scottish Plant Ltd.
1977 S.L.T. 7

A. S. Ltd., a company registered in England, created a floating charge over its property in favour of a bank. A receiver was appointed by the bank.

Subsequently a creditor of A. S. Ltd., having obtained a decree against A. S. Ltd., arrested property in the hands of C. Ltd. in Scotland.

The creditor raised an action of furthcoming against (1) the arrestee (C. Ltd.) and (2) the common debtor (A. S. Ltd.).

The second defender pleaded that the appointment of the receiver had created a completed security over the property in Scotland by virtue of section 15 (4) of the Companies (Floating Charges and Receivers) (Scotland) Act 1972, which provided: " A receiver or manager of the property and undertaking of a company incorporated in England which has or acquires property in Scotland shall have, in relation to such part of that property as is attached by the floating charge by virtue of which he was appointed, the same powers as he has in relation to that part of the property attached by the floating charge which is situated in England, so far as those powers are not inconsistent with the law of Scotland."

The pursuer contended that, as section 15 (4) did not declare that the property in Scotland was to be treated as " attached," the receiver did not have a completed security over that property and that decree of furthcoming should therefore be pronounced.

Held that on a proper construction of section 15 (4) the floating charge had on the appointment of the receiver attached to the property both in England and in Scotland, and that, as the pursuer had not effectually executed diligence on the Scottish property before the receiver's appointment, the defender should be assoilzied.

LORD PRESIDENT (EMSLIE) (at p. 13): "I turn to the language of section 15 (4). . . . What it in terms provides is that he is to have in relation to that part of the company's property 'as is attached' by the floating charge, the same powers as he has in relation to that part of the property 'attached' by the floating charge which is situated in England. Bearing in mind the effect of the appointment of a receiver of the property of a company incorporated in Scotland it is in my opinion not difficult to find in the language used in section 15 (4) the plain implication that the appointment of the receiver with which the subsection is concerned is to be understood in the law of Scotland to have had precisely the same effect. To appoint a receiver with powers necessarily presupposes that there is property over which he may exercise his powers and since that property must it seems to me be property to which the relevant floating charge has attached as a completed security it is reasonable to read section 15 (4) as proceeding upon this presupposition and indeed, clumsily though it may do so, giving expression to its validity by the use of the words 'as is attached' and 'attached.' Any other reading of section 15 (4) including the reading contended for by the pursuers would in my opinion deprive it of all operative content."

LORD THOMSON (at p. 17): "Broadly speaking I think a floating charge in Scots law is a statutory innovation upon the common law designed in the interests of commercial business to give to a creditor of a company the right to secure, by control to the exclusion of others over the assets of the company, repayment of monies due to him by the company but that only in the event of such repayment appearing otherwise precarious: *cf.* section 1 (1) of the Act. So, in the event of liquidation, the floating charge ceases to float and becomes fixed or completed and the creditor has a preferential right to payment over other non-secured creditors of the company. So, I would think, in the same way, if circumstances arise which entitle the creditor to appoint or have appointed a receiver, the company's assets which are subject to the floating charge become 'secured' for the payment of the sums due to the creditor under the charge. . . .

" . . . There is throughout the Act a distinction drawn between property 'subject to a floating charge' and property 'attached by' a floating charge, *e.g.*, sections 1 (2), 5 (2), 13 (7) and 14 (7). In my opinion 'attached to' in relation to the charge is to be read as the opposite or antithesis of 'subject to' in the sense that property is subject to a charge that 'floats' but the charge when it ceases to float is attached to the property and when that happens the charge instead of 'floating' becomes 'fixed,' *i.e.* completed in relation to the property formerly subject to the charge."

NOTES

1. Lord Avonside dissented. He said (at p. 15): "Part II of the 1972 Act for the first time in Scotland deals with legislation with the appointment of a receiver as a result of the existence of a floating charge and the results flowing from such an appointment. It is essential to note that the provisions are confined to Scottish companies only and are not as in the first part of general application to all incorporated companies. . . .

. . .

". . . A receiver appointed under a floating charge never had any security over property in Scotland until 1972. In that year the common law was altered but only so far as Scottish companies were concerned. The powers of an English receiver to ingather and deal with company property in Scotland attached by a floating charge were recognised so far as not inconsistent with the law of Scotland. But it is nowhere said that the appointment of a receiver to an English company has the effect of altering the common law of Scotland so as to create a security over Scottish property. As Lord President Cooper said in the *Carse* case, a floating charge even after the appointment of a receiver did not create any security over Scottish property. The Legislature has impinged on this principle so far as concerns the powers of and rights of a receiver appointed by the holder of a floating charge over the property of a Scottish company but is silent so far as concerns the appointment of a receiver to an English company by the holder of a floating charge over Scottish property belonging to that English company."

For the case of *Carse* referred to by Lord Avonside, see *Carse* v. *Coppen* (p. 326, above).

2. The Administration of Justice Act 1977, s. 7 (1) provides: " A receiver appointed under the law of any part of the United Kingdom in respect of the whole or part of any property or undertaking of a company having created a charge which, as created, was a floating charge may exercise his powers in any other part of the United Kingdom so far as their exercise is not inconsistent with the law applicable there."

By section 7 (2) " receiver " in section 7 (1) includes a manager and a person who is appointed both receiver and manager.

The section implemented a proposal put forward by the Scottish Law Commission (*Report on the Companies (Floating Charges) (Scotland) Act* 1961, (1970) Cmnd. 4336, Chap. 3, para. 60). It came into force on August 29, 1977.

Section 15 (4) of the Act of 1972 was repealed as no longer required (Administration of Justice Act 1977, s. 32 (4) and Sched. 5, Pt. VI).

GLOSSARY OF LATIN WORDS AND PHRASES USED IN THIS BOOK

a fortiori: all the more so; more emphatically (pp. 169, 276).

ab initio: from the beginning (p. 128).

actio sequestraria: a form of Roman legal process corresponding to consignation (p. 324).

ad factum praestandum: for the performance of an act; for specific implement (p. 344).

ad fundandam jurisdictionem: for the purpose of founding jurisdiction (pp. 129, 210, 217).

ad interim: in the meantime; temporary (p. 340).

animus: mind (p. 7).

ante: before; above (p. 128).

bona fide: good faith; honest; honestly (Latin ablative case of "*bona fides*," the ablative case being used in Latin after the preposition "*in*") (pp. 18, 69, 181, 198, 199, 200, 201, 214, 272, 277, 296, 346).

bona fides: good faith (pp. 101, 278).

bona vacantia: property which is without an owner (pp. 323, 325).

cit.: referred to (abbreviation of "*citatus*") (p. 163).

correi debendi: joint debtors, each liable only for his proportionate share of the debt (p. 284).

crassa negligentia: gross negligence (pp. 281, 284).

cum nota: along with a note; with some comment or reservation (p. 182).

curator bonis: guardian for property, the term used of the guardian appointed to look after the property of an insane person (pp. 28, 125, 126, 127).

de facto: in fact; as a matter of fact, whatever the legal position may be (pp. 147, 296).

dicta: statements; remarks (usually short for "*obiter dicta*") (pp. 43, 269).

dies inceptus pro completo habetur: a day which has begun is considered to be complete (pp. 233, 238).

eo instanti: at that moment (p. 73).

et separatim: and separately; and as a separate ground (p. 37).

ex contractu: literally, out of contract; under the law of contract (p. 198).

ex delicto: literally, out of delict; under the law of delict (pp. 246, 284).

355

ex facie: on the face; apparently (pp. 44, 98, 145, 220, 242, 337, 338, 339).

ex hypothesi: according to the hypothesis; according to the supposition which has been made (pp. 45, 348).

ex nobili officio: literally, out of the equitable power; on the ground of the " *nobile officium* " (equitable power of the Inner House of the Court of Session) (p. 341).

ex post facto: after the event; retrospectively (p. 172).

frustra petis quod mox es restituturus: it is in vain that you sue for what you will immediately be required to restore (p. 309).

habili modo: in the proper way; by competent evidence (p. 8).

ibid.: short for " *ibidem* "; at the same place (p. 327).

in bona fide: in good faith (pp. 93, 146, 204, 277, 343, 346).

in gremio: within it; as one of its terms (p. 68).

in mala fide: in bad faith (pp. 328, 347).

in medio: in the middle; in dispute (pp. 210, 325).

in modum probationis: by way of proof (p. 9).

in personam: against a person; giving rise to a personal, as opposed to a real, right (p. 349).

in solidum: for the whole; for the full amount (pp. 41, 142).

indicia: signs; indications (p. 271).

inter alia: amongst other things (pp. 12, 24, 47, 61, 63, 238).

inter se: amongst themselves (pp. 178, 201, 269, 310).

inter socios: amongst the members (p. 205).

intra quadriennium utile: literally, within the useful four-year period; within the four years immediately after the attainment of majority (p. 118).

intra vires: within the powers (pp. 54, 178, 185, 250, 255, 270, 311).

jurisdictionis fundandae causa: for the sake of founding jurisdiction (p. 218).

jus quaesitum: right acquired by a third party, *i.e.* by a person who is not one of the two contracting parties (p. 125).

jus tertii: literally, right of a third party, *i.e.* of someone other than the person who is claiming it; the phrase implies a negative—if it is said of a person, X, that a right is " *jus tertii*," this means that X is not entitled to the right, because it is a right which arises out of a contract between A and B, with the result that A or B is entitled to the right (p. 68).

media: methods; means (p. 241).

minor pubes: young person who is older than a pupil but has not yet attained majority; person between the ages of 12 and 18 (if female) or 14 and 18 (if male) (p. 118).

nobile officium: equitable power (of the Inner House of the Court of Session) (pp. 171, 172, 268, 341, 342).

obiter: by the way; not essential for the decision of the case; not forming part of the *ratio decidendi* of the case (the essential reasoning on which the decision is based) (pp. 130, 290, 294).

obiter dictum: thing said by the way; remark not essential for the decision of the case; statement which is not part of the *ratio decidendi* of the case (the essential reasoning on which the decision is based) (p. 287).

onus: burden (pp. 95, 203, 204).

ope exceptionis: by way of defence (p. 221).

pari passu: equally; rateably; equal; rateable (pp. 45, 165, 167).

per: (said) by; in the words of; according to the opinion of (pp. 43, 44, 87, 119, 214, 254).

per annum: yearly (p. 286).

per se: of itself; alone (pp. 14, 79, 154, 298).

persona: personality (pp. 4, 6, 7, 218).

persona standi: personality in law; title (p. 6).

personae: persons (p. 236).

prima facie: at first sight; until the contrary is proved (opposite of " conclusive ") (pp. 3, 115, 134, 158, 161, 164, 165, 166, 167, 177, 181, 182, 183, 197, 198, 199, 203, 243, 250, 271, 344).

pro rata: for a proportionate share; in proportion (the word " *parte* " is to be understood as following " *rata* ") (pp. 7, 136, 142, 143, 261).

prout de iure (or *jure*): by evidence of any kind (*i.e.* not necessarily written evidence) (p. 19).

punctum temporis: point of time (p. 20).

qua: as; in his capacity of (pp. 261, 270).

quadriennium utile: literally, useful four-year period; the four years immediately after the attainment of majority (p. 118).

quantum meruit: as much as he earned; sum based on services rendered (p. 290).

quasi: a sort of (a *quasi*-trustee is a person who stands in a position similar to, but who is not, a trustee (p. 212).

quid juris?: literally, what of the law?; what is the legal position? (p. 198).

quid pro quo: literally, something for something; consideration; return (p. 255).

quoad: to the extent of; as regards (pp. 331, 334).

res incepta pro finita habetur: a matter begun is considered as finished (p. 205).

restitutio in integrum: restoration to the original (position) (p. 92).

retenta possessione: possession having been retained (p. 329).

separatim: separately; as a separate ground (pp. 83, 134).
singuli in solidum: each one for the full amount (p. 142).
societas: the word used in Roman law for a partnership (p. 6).
socio nomine: in the firm name (pp. 6, 7).
subsidiarie: subsidiarily; in the second place (p. 7).
suo onere: along with its burden; accompanied by its debts (p. 16).
supra: above; earlier in the same book (pp. 123, 124, 340, 341).

ultimus haeres: ultimate heir; person who succeeds to estate when
     there is no other successor (p. 323).
ultra valorem: beyond the value (p. 91).
ultra vires: beyond the powers (pp. 45, 52, 53, 54, 55, 64, 70, 80, 98,
     100, 113, 114, 127, 128, 129, 132, 143, 172, 176, 178, 179, 224,
     247, 250, 252, 253, 254, 255, 257, 266, 277, 292, 295, 315, 316,
     318).
unico contextu: in one and the same context; in precisely the same
     context; at once (p. 105).
universitas: the word used in Roman law for a corporation (p. 6).

vice versa: the order being reversed; conversely (p. 317).